# Other Books and Series by Jeff Bowen

*Applications for Enrollment of Chickasaw Newborn Act of 1905*
*Volumes I thru VII*

*Cherokee Intermarried White 1906 Volume I & II*

Visit our website at **www.nativestudy.com** to learn more about these and other books and series by Jeff Bowen

# CHEROKEE INTERMARRIED WHITE 1906 VOLUME III

TRANSCRIBED BY
JEFF BOWEN

NATIVE STUDY
Gallipolis, Ohio
USA

# Other Books and Series by Jeff Bowen

*1901-1907 Native American Census Seneca, Eastern Shawnee, Miami, Modoc, Ottawa, Peoria, Quapaw, and Wyandotte Indians (Under Seneca School, Indian Territory)*

*1932 Census of The Standing Rock Sioux Reservation with Births And Deaths 1924-1932*

*Census of The Blackfeet, Montana, 1897-1901 Expanded Edition*

*Eastern Cherokee by Blood, 1906-1910, Volumes I thru XIII*

*Choctaw of Mississippi Indian Census 1929-1932 with Births and Deaths 1924-1931 Volume I*
*Choctaw of Mississippi Indian Census 1933, 1934 & 1937, Supplemental Rolls to 1934 & 1935 with Births and Deaths 1932-1938, and Marriages 1936-1938 Volume II*

*Eastern Cherokee Census Cherokee, North Carolina 1930-1939 Census 1930-1931 with Births And Deaths 1924-1931 Taken By Agent L. W. Page Volume I*
*Eastern Cherokee Census Cherokee, North Carolina 1930-1939 Census 1932-1933 with Births And Deaths 1930-1932 Taken By Agent R. L. Spalsbury Volume II*
*Eastern Cherokee Census Cherokee, North Carolina 1930-1939 Census 1934-1937 with Births and Deaths 1925-1938 and Marriages 1936 & 1938 Taken by Agents R. L. Spalsbury And Harold W. Foght Volume III*

*Seminole of Florida Indian Census, 1930-1940 with Birth and Death Records, 1930-1938*

*Texas Cherokees 1820-1839 A Document For Litigation 1921*

*Choctaw By Blood Enrollment Cards 1898-1914 Volumes I thru XVII*

*Starr Roll 1894 (Cherokee Payment Rolls) Districts: Canadian, Cooweescoowee, and Delaware Volume One*
*Starr Roll 1894 (Cherokee Payment Rolls) Districts: Flint, Going Snake, and Illinois Volume Two*
*Starr Roll 1894 (Cherokee Payment Rolls) Districts: Saline, Sequoyah, and Tahlequah; Including Orphan Roll Volume Three*

*Cherokee Intruder Cases Dockets of Hearings 1901-1909 Volumes I & II*

*Indian Wills, 1911-1921 Records of the Bureau of Indian Affairs Books One thru Seven;*
 *Native American Wills & Probate Records 1911-1921*

## Other Books and Series by Jeff Bowen

*Turtle Mountain Reservation Chippewa Indians 1932 Census with Births & Deaths, 1924-1932*

*Chickasaw By Blood Enrollment Cards 1898-1914 Volume I thru V*

*Cherokee Descendants East An Index to the Guion Miller Applications Volume I*
*Cherokee Descendants West An Index to the Guion Miller Applications Volume II (A-M)*
*Cherokee Descendants West An Index to the Guion Miller Applications Volume III (N-Z)*

*Applications for Enrollment of Seminole Newborn Freedmen, Act of 1905*

*Eastern Cherokee Census, Cherokee, North Carolina, 1915-1922, Taken by Agent James E. Henderson*
    *Volume I (1915-1916)*
    *Volume II (1917-1918)*
    *Volume III (1919-1920)*
    *Volume IV (1921-1922)*

*Complete Delaware Roll of 1898*

*Eastern Cherokee Census, Cherokee, North Carolina, 1923-1929, Taken by Agent James E. Henderson*
    *Volume I (1923-1924)*
    *Volume II (1925-1926)*
    *Volume III (1927-1929)*

*Applications for Enrollment of Seminole Newborn Act of 1905 Volumes I & II*

*North Carolina Eastern Cherokee Indian Census 1898-1899, 1904, 1906, 1909-1912, 1914 Revised and Expanded Edition*

*1932 Hopi and Navajo Native American Census with Birth & Death Rolls (1925-1931) Volume 1 - Hopi*
*1932 Hopi and Navajo Native American Census with Birth & Death Rolls (1930-1932) Volume 2 - Navajo*

*Western Navajo Reservation Navajo, Hopi and Paiute 1933 Census with Birth & Death Rolls 1925-1933*

*Cherokee Citizenship Commission Dockets 1880-1884 and 1887-1889 Volumes I thru V*

Copyright © 2014
by Jeff Bowen

ALL RIGHTS RESERVED
No part of this publication may be reproduced
or used in any form or manner whatsoever
without previous written permission from the
copyright holder or publisher.

Originally published:
Baltimore, Maryland
2014

Reprinted by:

Native Study LLC
Gallipolis, OH
*www.nativestudy.com*
2020

Library of Congress Control Number: 2020917307

ISBN: 978-1-64968-072-3

*Made in the United States of America.*

This series is dedicated to
Jerry Bowen
the Brave and the Strong.

## DEPARTMENT OF THE INTERIOR

### Commissioner to the Five Civilized Tribes

Muskogee, Indian Territory, March 9, 1907.

NOTICE IS HEREBY GIVEN that the undersigned, the Commissioner to the Five Civilized Tribes, has been designated by the Secretary of the Interior, as the official to make and approve appraisals of the value of improvements upon land in the Cherokee Nation which were made prior to November 5, 1906, by white persons who intermarried with Cherokee citizens prior to December 16, 1895, and who have the right under the Act of Congress approved March 2, 1907 (Public 180), to sell improvements.

NOTICE IS FURTHER GIVEN that former claimants to citizenship by intermarriage who have made permanent and valuable improvements on lands of the Cherokee Nation and who claim the right to sell the same under and by virtue of said Act of Congress of March 2, 1907 (Public 180), must appear before the Commissioner to the Five Civilized Tribes prior to April 1, 1907, and designate the land upon which are located the improvements which they claim the right to sell by virtue of said Act; and if any such intermarried citizen shall fail to appear before the Commissioner to the Five Civilized Tribes prior to April 1, 1907, it will be considered that he makes no claim to the benefits conferred by said Act. Such appearance and designation of improvements must be made before the Commissioner at his office in Muskogee, Indian Territory, at any time between Monday, March 11th, 1907, and Saturday, March 30th, 1907, inclusive, or at any of the following named places between the dates named at which places the Commissioner will have a representative to receive said designations and hear testimony relative thereto:

Bartlesville, Ind. Ter., Monday March 18th, 1907, to Saturday March 23rd, 1907, inclusive.
Tulsa, Ind. Ter., Monday March 25th, 1907, to Saturday March 30th, 1907, inclusive.
Claremore, Ind. Ter., Monday March 18th, 1907, to Saturday March 23rd, 1907, inclusive.
Nowata, Ind. Ter., Monday March 25th, 1907, to Saturday March 30th, 1907, inclusive.
Vinita, Ind. Ter., Monday March 18th, 1907, to Saturday March 23rd, 1907, inclusive.
Pryor Creek, Ind. Ter., Monday March 25th, 1907, to Saturday March 30th, 1907, inclusive.
Tahlequah, Ind. Ter., Monday March 18, 1907, to Saturday March 23rd, 1907, inclusive.
Sallisaw, Ind. Ter., Monday March 25th, 1907, to Saturday March 30th, 1907, inclusive.

Designations must be made in person by the intermarried white claimant, or in case proper proof is made that he is physically unable to appear, by some adult member of his immediate family, or in case proper proof is made of the fact that the intermarried white claimant is physically unable to appear and has no adult member of his immediate family, by a person holding a properly executed power of attorney; provided, that in every case the designation must be made by a party familiar with the character, ownership, location and value of the improvements to be designated. At the time of said designation the testimony of any competent person will be taken by the Commissioner as to the location, character and value of said improvements.

No former intermarried white claimant will be permitted to designate improvements upon more land than he would have been entitled to take in allotment for himself had he been admitted to citizenship. If any intermarried white claimant has made a tentative selection of a full allotment he will not be allowed to designate improvements upon other land.

NOTICE IS FURTHER GIVEN that if any citizen of the Cherokee Nation entitled to select an allotment shall claim that the improvements on land tentatively selected by a former intermarried white claimant, or held by him, do not belong to said intermarried white claimant, or makes any adverse claim to said improvements, or to the right of the intermarried white claimant to sell said improvements under the Act approved March 2, 1907 (Public 180), said citizen must appear before the Commissioner to the Five Civilized Tribes either at Muskogee, Indian Territory, prior to April 1, 1907, or at one of the places above designated and within the dates above designated and make formal complaint before the Commissioner to the Five Civilized Tribes of his contention. At Muskogee, Indian Territory, between March 11th and March 30th, 1907, inclusive, and at the other places herein named during the hearings at said places as herein fixed, plats will be open for inspection showing the location of tentative allotments made by former claimants to citizenship by intermarriage and all other land on which such claimants claim improvements, so far as indicated by the records of this office.

All persons interested should take careful note of the limitation of time herein provided for, within which designations and complaints may be made, and that they must be made by appearance before the Commissioner.

**TAMS BIXBY,**
Commissioner.

This particular notice concerns the appraisals of improvements on properties held by Cherokee intermarried whites. You would have found notices like this throughout the Nation to bring in people to finalize the allotment question, of who belonged and who did not.

E.C.M.                                                     Cherokee 58.

## DEPARTMENT OF THE INTERIOR,
### COMMISSIONER TO THE FIVE CIVILIZED TRIBES.

In the matter of the application for the enrollment of
ALBERTIN HAMPTON as a citizen by intermarriage of the Cherokee
Nation.

## D E C I S I O N

THE RECORDS OF THIS OFFICE SHOW: That at Fairland, Indian
Territory, July 9, 1900, Albertin Hampton appeared before the Commission to the Five Civilized Tribes, and made application for the
enrollment of himself as a citizen by intermarriage, and for the
enrollment of his wife, Jane E. Hampton, et al. as citizens by
blood of the Cherokee Nation. The application for the enrollment of
the said Jane E. Hampton et al. as citizens by blood of the Cherokee
Nation has been heretofore disposed of, and their rights to enrollment will not be considered in this decision. Further proceedings
in the matter of said application were had at Muskogee, Indian
Territory, September 3, 1902, October 14, 1902, and January 2, 1907.

THE EVIDENCE IN THIS CASE SHOWS: That the applicant herein,
Albertin Hampton, a white man, was married, in accordance with
Cherokee law, January 20, 1874, to his wife, Jane E. Hampton, nee
Thomas, who was at the time of said marriage a recognized citizen
by blood of the Cherokee Nation, and whose name appears on the approved partial roll of citizens by blood of the Cherokee Nation,
opposite No. 195; that since said marriage the said Albertin Hampton
and Jane E. Hampton have resided together as husband and wife, and
have continuously lived in the Cherokee Nation. Said Albertin
Hampton is identified on the Cherokee authenticated tribal roll of
1880, and the Cherokee census roll of 1896, as "Bert Hampton", an
intermarried citizen of the Cherokee Nation.

IT IS, THEREFORE, ORDERED AND ADJUDGED: That in accordance with
the decision of the Supreme Court of the United States, dated November
5, 1906, in the case of Daniel Red Bird et al. vs. the United States,

E.C.M.　　　　　　　　　　- 2 -　　　　　　　　　　Cherokee 58.

under the provisions of Section twenty-one, of the Act of Congress approved June 28, 1898 (30 Stat., 495), Albertin Hampton is entitled to enrollment as a citizen by intermarriage of the Cherokee Nation, and his application for enrollment as such is accordingly granted.

　　　　　　　　　　　　　　　　　　　　　　Commissioner.

Dated at Muskogee, Indian Territory, this JAN 18 1907

The above is an accepted decision of the Commissioner to the Five Civilized Tribes. The Attorney for the Cherokee Nation had fifteen days after the date of Commissioner's decision in which to protest.

Cherokee
58.

W. W. HASTINGS.
ATTORNEY

H. R. VANCE,
SECRETARY

OFFICE OF
Attorney for the Cherokee Nation,
MUSKOGEE, I. T.     January 18, 1907.

The Commissioner to the Five Civilized Tribes,

Muskogee, Indian Territory.

Sir:

Receipt is acknowledged of the testimony and of your decision enrolling Albertin Hampton, as a citizen by intermarriage of the Cherokee Nation. Time for protesting said decision is waived and I consent that said person may be placed upon the schedule immediately.

Yours very truly,

W. W. Hastings

Attorney for Cherokee Nation.

The above is a notice of the Attorney waiving the time for protesting the Commissioner's decision (on the two previous pages) concerning Albertin Hampton's application and consenting to place the applicant upon schedule immediately.

## INTRODUCTION

The *Cherokee Intermarried White*, National Archive film M-1301, Rolls 305-307, are found under the heading of Applications for Enrollment of the Commission to the Five Civilized Tribes. The genealogical value of this series concerning the relationships between many Cherokee tribesman and their marriages among another race is very important and virtually a treasure trove of information long sought after. While on the other hand what these cases are really about are the efforts of many to attain Cherokee land allotments. Referenced from the Supreme Court Decision, Cherokee Intermarriage Cases – 203 U.S. 76 (1906).

This collection of Intermarried claims involves two hundred and eighty-eight separate cases with a variety of scenarios from the divorced to the widowed to the deserving to the deceptive. During these times there were many that wanted what was rightfully only the Cherokees. You will see each case will be headed by the title from the first folder as an example: *Intermarried White I, Trans from Cher. 34*, the transfer number is the Dawes Commission number from the claimants spouse.

These cases are fascinating because of the generational bloodlines that can be verified by documentation rather than just word of mouth. From Kent Carter's book, *The Dawes Commission*, "The tribe also, continued to oppose the enrollment of whites who had married into the Cherokee tribe. That controversy dragged through the U.S. Court of Claims and then the Supreme Court, which finally ruled in favor of the tribe on November 05, 1906. The court upheld the Cherokee citizenship laws that denied rights to any white who had married into the tribe after November 1, 1877. It also upheld an 1839 law which stated that anyone who moved out of the nation lost their citizenship unless they were readmitted. The applications of 3,341 persons were rejected as a result of this ruling, and the allotment clerks were forced to undo a great deal of their work. With the issue finally settled by the courts, the commission was able to send the first schedule of Cherokees by intermarriage, containing fifty-five names, to the secretary of interior on June 10, 1907. Eventually only 286 people were enrolled as intermarried whites----far fewer than the number put on the rolls of the Choctaw and Chickasaw tribes, which had much more liberal laws on rights based on marriage." [1]

---

[1] The Dawes Commission and the Allotment of the Five Civilized Tribes, 1893-1914 by Kent Carter, pg. 121

In Cohen's Handbook of Federal Indian Law he states, "In the *Cherokee Intermarriage Cases,* the Supreme Court considered the claims of certain white persons, intermarried with Cherokee Indians, who wanted to participate in the common property of the Cherokee Nation. Such persons were permitted by tribal law to be tribal citizens with limited rights in tribal property. The tribe had also provided for the revocation of citizenship rights of a white person who intermarried with a Cherokee if the Cherokee spouse were abandoned or if a widower or widow married a non-Cherokee. The Court found that the Cherokee Nation had authority to qualify the rights of citizenship which it offered to its "naturalized citizens. Such tribal action defeated the claims of the plaintiffs:

The laws and usages of the Cherokees, their earliest history, the fundamental principles of their national policy, their constitution and statutes, all show that citizenship rested on blood or marriage; that the man who would assert citizenship must establish marriage; that when marriage ceased (with a special reservation in favor of widows or widowers) citizenship ceased; that when an intermarried white married a person having no rights of Cherokee citizenship by blood it was conclusive evidence that the tie which bound him to the Cherokee people was severed and the very basis of his citizenship obliterated."[2]

An important footnote that Cohen published within his pages for the above paragraph also needs to be studied. He noted, "Under Cherokee law white persons intermarrying with Cherokees before 1875 were tribal citizens for most purposes, including allotment of tribal land, but had no interest in tribal funds except those funds derived from tribal lands. A Cherokee law that became effective in 1875 provided that whites marrying Cherokees had no rights to tribal property but could obtain full citizenship by the payment of $500 to the tribe. In 1877 the tribe provided that no intermarried citizen could obtain any rights to tribal land or funds."[3]

During many years of study this author has found cases that should have been been accepted, especially with the particular documentation presented. All in all the outcome of the decision made should have rendered a different result. Also there have been many that numb the mind as to how they their cases were even considered. The years have given many the hopes that their ancestors were one of those that had a decent claim and an honest consideration. Like any time in history there are political struggles

---

[2] Felix S. Cohen's Handbook of FEDERAL INDIAN LAW 1982 ED. pgs 20-21.
[3] Felix S. Cohen's Handbook of FEDERAL INDIAN LAW 1982 ED. pg 21 footnote16.

and the human factor that points out man is not perfect. These pages were transcribed with the wish that another person somewhere along the line will find their relation from the past and give them the answers long hoped for.

Jeff Bowen
Gallipolis, Ohio
*NativeStudy.com*

# Cherokee Intermarried White 1906
# Volume III

**Cher IW 69**
**Trans from Cher 2512 3-15-07**

### DEPARTMENT OF THE INTERIOR.

### COMMISSION TO THE FIVE CIVILIZED TRIBES

Pryor Creek, I.T. September 11th 1900.

IN THE MATTER OF THE APPLICATION FO[sic] JOSEPH L. WARD FOR HIMSELF, HIS WIFE AND TWO CHILDREN, FOR ENROLLMENT AS CITIZENS OF THE CHEROKEE NATION; SAID JOSEPH L. WARD, BEING DULY SWORN by COMMISSIONER R.C[sic]. BRECKENRIDGE[sic], TESTIFIED AS FOLLOW[sic]:

Q How old are you Mr. Ward? A Fifty five years old.
Q What is your full name? A Joseph L. Ward.
Q What is your post office? A Mayesville[sic], Ark.
Q In what district do you live? A Delaware.
Q Who is it you want to have put on the roll? A Myself, my wife and two children.
Q Do you apply for yourself as a Cherokee by blood? A Yes, sir.
Q Do you apply for your wife as a Cherokee by blood or by adoption? A By adoption.
Q How long have you lived in the Cherokee Nation? A Fifty-five years.
Q All your life? A Yes, sir.
Q How long have you lived in the Delaware District? A I never lived anywhere else.
Q You are on the roll of 1880 from that District, are you? A Yes, sir.
Q And also for 1896? A Yes, sir.
Q Give me the name of your father. A James Ward.
Q Cherokee or white man? A Cherokee.
Q Is he living or dead? A He is dead.
Q How long has he been dead? A He died July 20th 1868.
Q Give me the name of your mother? A Louisa M.
Q Was she a Cherokee or white woman? A Cherokee.
Q Is she living or dead? A Dead.
Q How long has she been dead? A About four years I think, as well as I remember.
Q Give me your wife's name. A Alice N
Q How old is she? A She is 45 years old.
Q What was her name when you married her? A Scott.
Q Was that her maiden name? A Yes, sir.
Q When did you marry her? A Twenty-six years ago.
Q She is on the 1880 roll? A Yes, sir.
Q And also the roll of 1896? A Yes, sir.
Q She is living with you at this time? A Yes, sir.
Q Give me the name of her father. A William J. Scott.
Q White man? A Yes, sir from Kentucky. Logan County Kentuckey[sic].
Q Dead or alive? A Dead.

1

# Cherokee Intermarried White 1906
## Volume III

Q Give me the name of your wife's mother. A Martha.
Q White woman? A Yes, sir.
Q Dead or alive? A Dead
Q Now give me the name of the two children you apply for. A W. Mae Ward.
Q How old is that child? A Twenty years old.
Q And the next child? A Martha L. Ward.
Q And how old is she? A Fourteen.
Q These children are both living with you are they? A Yes, sir.
Q And they have lived with you in the Cherokee Nation all their lives? A Yes, sir.

(Joseph L. Ward identified on 1880 Roll, page 342, No. 3062, Delaware District, As Joseph L. Ward.)
(Alice N. Ward identified 1880 roll, page 342. No. 3063, Alice N. Ward, Delaware District)
(Child of applicant W. Mae Ward identified on 1880 roll, page 342, No. 3066, Willie MA. Ward.)

(Applicant identified on 1896 roll, page 559, No. 3620, Joseph L. Ward, Delaware District.)
(Wife of applicant identified on 1896 roll, page 593, No. #575 (577), Alice N. Ward Delaware District.)
(Child of applicant, identified on 1896 roll, page 559, No. 3622 Willie Mae Ward, Delaware District.)
(Child of applicant, Martha L. Ward identified on 1896 roll, page 559, No. 3623, Martha L. Ward, Delaware District.)

Applicant applied for the enrollment of himself and his wife and two children. He is identified on the rolls of 1880 and also 1896 as a native Cherokee. He has lived in the Cherokee Nation all of his life and he will be listed now for enrollment as a Cherokee by blood. His wife is identified with him on the rolls of 1880 and 1896. They have lived together continuously to the present time in the Cherokee Nation, and she will be listed now for enrollment as a Cherokee by adoption. Their two children, W. Mae and Martha L. are both identified with their parents on the roll of 1896, and the former is also identified with her parents on the roll of 1880. They are both living at this time, and they will be listed for enrollment as Cherokee's by blood.

The undersigned being duly sworn states that as stenographer to the Commission to the Five Civilized Tribes he correctly recorded the testimony and proceedings in this case, and that the foregoing is a true and complete transcript of his stenographic notes thereof.

William S Meeshean

Subscribed and sworn to before me this 12th day of September A.D. 1900.

TB Needles
Commissioner

# Cherokee Intermarried White 1906
## Volume III

◇◇◇◇◇

Cherokee 2512.

Department of the Interior,
Commission to the Five Civilized Tribes,
Muskogee, I. T., September 20, 1902.

In the matter of the application of Alice N. Ward for enrollment as a citizen by intermarriage of the Cherokee Nation.

W. W. Hastings, being sworn and examined by the Commission, testified as follows:
Q State your name, age and postoffice address? A My name is W.W. Hastings, age 35, postoffice Tahlequah.
Q Are you acquainted with Alice N. Ward, the applicant in this case? A Yes sir.
Q How long have you known her? A More than twenty years.
Q Is she a white woman? A Yes sir.
Q What is her husband's name? A Joe L. Ward.
Q Is he a Cherokee? A Yes sir.
Q Have they lived together continuously since their marriage? A Yes sir.
Q Are they living together at this time? A Yes sir.
Q Have they always lived in the Cherokee Nation since you have known them? A Yes sir.
Q Living there at this time? A Yes sir.

The undersigned, being duly sworn, states that as stenographer to the Commission to the Five Civilized Tribes he correctly recorded the testimony and proceedings in this case, and that the foregoing is a true and complete transcript of his stenographic notes thereof.

E.G. Rothenberger

Subscribed and sworn to before me this 23rd day of September, 1902.

BC Jones
Notary Public.

◇◇◇◇◇

## Cherokee Intermarried White 1906
## Volume III

DEPARTMENT OF THE INTERIOR.
Commission to the Five Civilized Tribes.
Muskogee, Indian Territory, October 14th, 1902.

---

In the matter of the application of Joseph L. Ward for the enrollment of himself as a citizen by blood; his wife, Alice N. Ward, as a citizen by intermarriage, and his children, W. Mae and Martha L. Ward, as citizens by blood of the Cherokee Nation.

---

Supplemental to #2512.

---

JOSEPH L. WARD, being duly sworn, testified as follows:
Examination by the Commission.
Q. What is your name? A. J. L. Ward.
Q. Joseph L. Ward, is it? A. Yes, sir.
Q. How old are you? A. 58 in July.
Q. What is your post office? A. Maysville.
Q. Arkansas? A. Yes, sir.
Q. Are you a Cherokee by blood? A. Yes, sir.
Q. How long have you lived in the Cherokee Nation? A. Nearly 58 years.
Q. Constinuously[sic]? A. Yes, sir.
Q. What is your wife's name? A. Alice N. Ward.
Q. She is a white woman? A. Yes, sir.
Q. She was married to you before 1880? A. Yes, sir; married in 1875.
Q. She is on the eighty roll with you? A. Yes, sir.
Q. Have you and your wife been living together all the time since 1880? A. Yes, sir.
Q. Never been separated? A. No, sir.
Q. Living together now? A. Yes, sir.
Q. How many children have you? A. I had four; there is one dead.
Q. How many living with you? A. One.
Q. What is its name? A. Martha.
Q. W. Mae; is that one of your children? A. Yes, sir; she is married now.

++++++++++++++++++++++++++++++++++++++++++++

Jesse O. Carr, being first duly sworn, states that as stenographer to the Commission to the Five Civilized Tribes he reported the above entitled case and that the foregoing is a true and complete transcript of his stenographic notes thereof.

Jesse O. Carr

# Cherokee Intermarried White 1906
# Volume III

Subscribed and sworn to before me this 3rd day of January, 1903.

John O Rosson<br>
Notary Public.

◇◇◇◇◇

Cherokee 2512.

## DEPARTMENT OF THE INTERIOR,
## COMMISSIONER TO THE FIVE CIVILIZED TRIBES.
## MUSKOGEE?[sic] I. T., DECEMBER 27, 1906.

In the matter of the application for the enrollment of ALICE N. WARD, as a citizen by intermarriage of the Cherokee Nation.

APPEARANCES:
  For Applicant- Her husband
  For Cherokee Nation, W. W. Hastings.

JOSEPH L. WARD, being first duly sworn by B. P. Rasmus, a Notary Public, testified as follows:

ON BEHALF OF THE COMMISSIONER:

Q What is your name? A Joseph L. Ward.
Q How old are you? A 52.
Q What is your postoffice? A Maysville, Arkansas.
Q Are you a Cherokee by blood? A Yes sir, so recogniced[sic].
Q Have you whildren[sic] W. Mae and Martha L.? A Yes sir.
Q They are also enrolled, are they? A Yes sir.
Q Have you a wife? A Yes sir.
Q What is her name? A Alice N.
Q Is she an applicant for enrollment as a citizen by intermarriage of the Cherokee Nation? A Yes sir.

> The witness is identified as a duly enrolled Cherokee citizen by blood, his name appearing upon an approved partial roll opposite No. 6380.

Q You say your wife is a white woman? A Yes sir
Q Is she living now? A Yes sir.
Q You and she living together? A Yes sir
Q Wjat[sic] is the reason she is not present today? A Why I guess ehe[sic] thought I could attend to the matter for her.
Q When were you and she married? A January 17, 1875.
Q Who married you? A Parson Redferry.
Q Did he give you a certificate? A No sir.

## Cherokee Intermarried White 1906
## Volume III

Q You had no license? A No sir, not required under the law to obtain a license.
Q Do you know whether a record was made of your marriage? A I think there was; I think I recorded it myself, being Deputy Clerk in Delaware District sometime after that.
Q You were present when we examined the records today were you? A Yes sir.
Q And we could find no record? A No sir; but it don't seem to me like those are one of the books.
Q Have you and your wife lived together continuously since your marriage? A Yes sir.
Q Was the man that married you a Minister of the Gospel? A Yes sir, but he is dead now
Q Was your wife ever married before she married you? A No sir.
Q Were you ever married before you married her? A No sir.
Q Were you a recognized citizen of the Cherokee Nation when you married your wife? A Yes sir, I was born and raised here.
Q Have you and she lived in the Cherokee Nation continuously since your marriage? A Yes sir.

    The witness and his wife are identified on the 1880 Authenticated Roll of citizens of the Cherokee Nation, opposite Nos. 3062 and 3063, in Delaware District.

(Witness excused).

    W. W. HASTINGS, being first duly sworn by B. P. Rasmus, a Notary Public, testified as follows on behalf of applicant

(Statement by Mr. Hastings).

    My name is W. W. Hastings; I am nearly 40 years of age, I was born the last day of 1866, and was quite a small boy in 1875 when the witness, Joseph L. Ward was married to his wife, Alice, I don't now recollect whether or not I attended the wedding or not but I knew of it; I do remember of attending the infair[sic] dinner given the next day after the marriage at the home of the mother of Joseph L. Ward. My home was some two and a half or three miles from them where I continued to live until I got grown, and I know that these people have continued to live together as husband and wife in the Cherokee Nation up to and including this time. I also remember that this was in the early part of 1875 but I don't recollect the exact day, but I know that it was either in January or February of that year.

(Witness excused).

    JACOB HISER, being first duly sworn by B. P. Rasmus, a Notary Public, testified as follows on behalf of applicant.

ON BEHALF OF THE COMMISSIONER:

# Cherokee Intermarried White 1906
## Volume III

Q What is your name? A Jacob Hiser.
Q How old are you? A 60.
Q What is your postoffice? A Maysville, Arkansas.
Q Are you an intermarried Cherokee? A Yes sir
Q Do you know this gentleman, Joseph L. Ward? A Yes sir
Q How long have you known him? A About as soon as I can remember I guess.
Q Do you know his wife? A Yes sir.
Q Is her name Alice N. Ward? A Yes sir/[sic]
Q Do you know whether or not they were married? A I didn't see them married but was right in sight of the place and seen other people that said the ceremony was performed they said, and seen them afterwards around as man and wife, and knowed[sic] they lived together as such.
Q Do you know who is supposed to have married them? A A man named Redferry.
Q Do you know whether they have lived together since then? A Yes sir
Q Do you live neighbor to them? A Yes sir/[sic]
Q Do you know that they have never been separated? A If they have I never heard of it
Q Was he a recognized Cherokee by blood when they married? A That is the way I understood it/[sic]

BY MR. HASTINGS:

Q Do you mean to say that you were near the place where they were said to have been married and could see the crowd where they were? A I was on the farm there not over 150 yards from the house and I saw the crowd gathering and leaving and it was said that they were married that day.
Q You so understood afterward they were married? A Yes sir, my wife was there and lot of other people, but I didn't go.
Q You say your wife went? A Yes sir, and sister-in-law.
Q Other members of your wife's family? A Yes sir
Q Do you know the date of their marriage? A I think it was in January, 1875, I guess.
Q Are you positive that they married prior to November 1, 1875? A Yes sir.

(Witness excused).

    Geo. H. Lessley, being first duly sworn, states that as stenographer to the Commissioner to the Five Civilized Tribes he reported the proceedings had in the above entitled cause, and that the above and foregoing is a true and corect[sic] transcript of his stenographic notes thereof.

Geo H. Lessley

Subscribed and sworn to before me this 10th day of January, 1907.

John E. Tidwell<br/>Notary Public.

## Cherokee Intermarried White 1906
## Volume III

C.E.W.                                                                  Cherokee 2512.

DEPARTMENT OF THE INTERIOR,

COMMISSIONER TO THE FIVE CIVILIZED TRIBES.

In the matter of the application for the enrollment of Alice N. Ward, as a citizen by intermarriage of the Cherokee Nation.

### D E C I S I O N

THE RECORDS OF THIS OFFICE SHOW: That at Pryor Creek, Indian Territory, September 11, 1900, application was received by the Commission to the Five Civilized Tribes for the enrollment of Alice N. Ward, as a citizen by intermarriage of the Cherokee Nation. Further proceedings in the matter of said application were had at Muskogee, Indian Territory, September 20, 1902, October 14, 1902, and December 27, 1906.

THE EVIDENCE IN THIS CASE SHOWS: That the applicant herein, Alice N. Ward, a white woman, was married in accordance with Cherokee law January 17, 1875 to her husband, Joseph L. Ward, who was at the time of said marriage a recognized citizen by blood of the Cherokee Nation, who is identified on the Cherokee authenticated tribal roll of 1880, Delaware District, page 342, number 3062 as a native Cherokee, and whose name appears upon the approved partial roll of citizens by blood of the Cherokee Nation, opposite number 6380; that since said marriage the said Joseph L. Ward and Alice N. Ward have resided together as husband and wife and have continuously lived in the Cherokee Nation. Said applicant is identified on the Cherokee authenticated tribal roll of 1880, and the Cherokee census roll of 1896 as an intermarried citizen of the Cherokee Nation.

IT IS, THEREFORE, ORDERED AND ADJUDGED: That in accordance with the decision of the Supreme Court of the United States, dated November 5, 1906, in the cases of Daniel Red Bird et al., vs. the United States, Nos. 125, 126, 127 and 128, the said applicant Alice N. Ward is entitled, under the provision of Section 21 of the Act of Congress approved June 28, 1898 (30 Stats., 495), to enrollment as a citizen by intermarriage of the Cherokee Nation, and her application for enrollment as such is accordingly granted.

                                             Tams Bixby
                                                                              Commissioner.

Dated at Muskogee, Indian Territory,
this          JAN 23 1907

# Cherokee Intermarried White 1906
## Volume III

Cherokee
2512

Muskogee, Indian Territory, December 24, 1906.

Alice N. Ward,
      Maysville, Arkansas.

Dear Madam:

    November 6, 1906, the United States Supreme Court held that white persons who intermarried with Cherokee citizens according to Cherokee law prior to November 1, 1875, are entitled to enrollment and allotments of land as citizens of the Cherokee Nation.

    You are advised that to properly determine your right to enrollment as a citizen by intermarriage of the Cherokee Nation, it will be necessary for you to appear before the Commissioner for the purpose of giving testimony as to the date of your marriage and whether or not your husband, by reason of your marriage to whom you claim the right to enrollment as a citizen by intermarriage of the Cherokee Nation, was a recognized Cherokee citizen at the time of your marriage to him.

    You are, therefore, directed to appear before the Commissioner at Muskogee, Indian Territory, at 9 o'clock A. M., on Thursday, January 3, 1907, and give testimony as above indicated.

                      Respectfully,

JMH                                     Acting Commissioner.

⋄⋄⋄⋄⋄

Cherokee
2512

Muskogee, Indian Territory, January 23, 1907.

W. W. Hastings,
      Attorney for the Cherokee Nation,
           Muskogee, Indian Territory.

Dear Sir:

    There is enclosed herewith a copy of the decision of the Commissioner to the Five Civilized Tribes, dated January 23, 1907, granting the application for the enrollment of Alice N. Ward as a citizen by intermarriage of the Cherokee Nation.

# Cherokee Intermarried White 1906
## Volume III

Respectfully,

Encl. H-60  
JMH

Commissioner.

◇◇◇◇◇

Cherokee 2512    W.W. HASTINGS.    OFFICE OF    H.M. VANCE.  
ATTORNEY.                                       SECRETARY.

### Attorney for the Cherokee Nation,
MUSKOGEE, I. T.

January 23, 1907.

The Commissioner to the Five Civilized Tribes,  
        Muskogee, Indian Territory.

Sir:

    Receipt is acknowledged of the testimony and of your decision enrolling Alice N. Ward as a citizen by intermarriage of the Cherokee Nation. Time for protesting said decision is waived and I consent that said person may be placed upon the schedule immediately.

                Respectfully,  
                W. W. Hastings  
                Attorney for Cherokee Nation.

◇◇◇◇◇

Cherokee 2512

                Muskogee, Indian Territory, January 23, 1907.

Alice N. Ward,  
    Maysville, Arkansas.

Dear Madam:

    There is enclosed herewith a copy of the decision of the Commissioner to the Five Civilized Tribes, dated January 23, 1907, granting your application for enrollment as a citizen by intermarriage of the Cherokee Nation.

    You will be advised when your name has been placed upon a schedule of citizens of the Cherokee Nation and approved by the Secretary of the Interior.

                Respectfully,

Encl. H-79  
JMH

Commissioner.

# Cherokee Intermarried White 1906
## Volume III

**Cher IW 70**
**Trans from Cher 2744  3-15-07**

◇◇◇◇◇

E.C.M.

## DEPARTMENT OF THE INTERIOR,

## COMMISSIONER TO THE FIVE CIVILIZED TRIBES.

In the matter of the application for the enrollment of

### JOHN C. HOGAN

as a citizen by intermarriage of the Cherokee Nation.

### CHEROKEE NO. 2744.

◇◇◇◇◇

### DEPARTMENT OF THE INTERIOR,
### COMMISSION TO THE FIVE CIVILIZED TRIBES,
### PRYOR CREEK, I. T., SEPTEMBER 14, 1900.

In the matter of the application of John C. Hogan for the enrollment of himself, wife and children as citizens of the Cherokee Nation; said Hogan being sworn by Commissioner T. B. Needles, testified as follows:

Q What is your name? A John C. Hogan.
Q Your age? A 53.
Q What is your post office address? A Pryor Creek.
Q What district do you live in? A Cooweescoowee.
Q Are you a recognized citizen of the Cherokee Nation? A Yes, sir.
Q By blood or inter-marriage? A Inter-marriage.
Q What is the name of your wife? A Margaret M. Hogan.
Q What was he name before you married her? A Adair.
Q When did you marry her? A In 1870/[sic]sic]
Q Is she living? A Yes, sir.
Q Her father and mother living? A Her mother is living; her father is dead.
Q Name of her mother? A Ann Adair.
Q Have you any children? A Yes, sir.
Q What is the name of the oldes[sic] under 21 years of age? A Graham.
Q How old is he? A 14.
Q The name of the next one? A Mayble[sic]; ten years old.

## Cherokee Intermarried White 1906
## Volume III

Q These children alive and living with you? A Yes, sir.

1880 enrollment; page 117, #1413, John Hogan, Cooweescoowee.
1880 enrollment; page 117, #1414, Margaret Hogan,      "
1896 enrollment; page 307, #446, John C. Hogan,        "
1896 enrollment; page 173, #2123, Margrette N. Hogan,  "
1896 enrollment; page 173, #2124, Graham Hogan,        "
1896 enrollment; page 173, #2125, Mable Hogan,         "

Com'r Needles:

The name of John C. Hogan and his wife, Margaret, appears upon the authenticated roll of 1880, he as John Hogan and she as Margaret. His name also appears upon the census roll of 1896. The name of his children, Graham and Mable, appears upon the census roll of 1896. They all being fully identified, and having made satisfactory proof as to his residence, the said John C. Hogan will be listed as a Cherokee citizen by inter-marriage, his wife, Margaret and his two children Graham and Mable as Cherokees by blood.

---oooOOOooo---

The undersigned, being first duly sworn states that as stenographer to the Commission to the Five Civilized Tribes, he correctly recorded the testimony and proceedings in this case, and that the foregoing is a true and complete transcript of his stenographic notes thereof.

J.O. Rosson

Subscribed and sworn to before me this 18th day of September, 1900.

CR Breckinridge

Commissioner.

DEPARTMENT OF THE INTERIOR.
Commission to the Five Civilized Tribes.
Muskogee, Indian Territory, September 30th, 1902.

In the matter of the application of John C. Hogan for the enrollment of himself as a citizen by intermarriage of the Cherokee Nation and for the enrollment of his wife, Margaret M. Hogan, and his children, Graham and Mabel Hogan, as citizens by blood of the Cherokee Nation.

Supplemental to #2744.

# Cherokee Intermarried White 1906
## Volume III

Appearances:

      S. H. Mayes for Applicant.
      J. C. Starr for Cherokee Nation.

S. H. MAYES, being duly sworn, testified as follows:--
Examination by the Commission.

Q. Your name, age and post office. A. S. H. Mayes, Prior[sic] Creek, age 57.
Q. Are you acquainted with John C. Hogan, who is an applicant before this Commission for enrollment as an intermarried citizen of the Cherokee Nation? A. Yes, sir.
Q. Do you know his wife Margaret M. Hogan? A. Yes, sir.
Q. Is she a citizen by blood of the Cherokee Nation? A. Yes, sir.
Q. Do you know when John C. Hogan and Margaret M. were married?
A. No, sir; I don't know when they were married.
Q. How you know about how long? A. Well, they have been married---I have known John Hogan and his wife for 20 years. Lived right there.
Q. They have lived together as husband and wife continusouly[sic] since 1880, have they? A. Yes, sir.
Q. Never been separated? A. No, sir.
Q. Living together on the first of September, 1902? A. Yes, sir.
[sic] Are Graham and Mabel living at this time? A. Yes, sir. They have a girl there that they are guardian for. I don't know whether it is on that roll or not.

    Jesse O. Carr, being first duly sworn, states that as stenographer to the Commission to the Five Civilized Tribes he reported the above entitled case and that the foregoing is a true and complete transcript of his stenographic notes thereof.

                                              Jesse O. Carr

Subscribed and sworn to before me this 13th day of October, 1902.

                                              BC Jones
                                              Notary Public.

# Cherokee Intermarried White 1906
## Volume III

Cherokee 2744.

DEPARTMENT OF THE INTERIOR,
COMMISSION TO THE FIVE CIVILIZED TRIBES.
Muskogee, I. T., October 16, 1902.

In the matter of the application of John C. Hogan for the enrollment of himself as a citizen by intermarriage of the Cherokee Nation, and for the enrollment of his wife, Margaret M. Hogan, and his two minor children, Graham and Mabel Hogan, as citizens by blood of the Cherokee Nation.

SUPPLEMENTAL PROCEEDINGS.

JOHN C. HOGAN, being sworn, testified as follows:

By the Commission,

Q What is your name? A John C. Hogan.
Q How old are you? A I am fifty-five years old.
Q What is your postoffice? A Prior[sic] Creek.
Q You're a white man, are you? A Yes, sir.
Q Are you on the roll of 1880 as a recognized citizen? A Yes, sir.
Q What is your wife's name? Margaret M. Adair.
Q Is she the wife through whom you claim your citizenship? A Yes, sir.
Q Was she your wife in '80? A Yes, sir.
Q Have you and your wife been living together since '80? A Yes, sir.
Q Have you ever been separated? A No, sir.
Q Living together now? A Yes, sir.
Q Have you been living in the Cherokee Nation all that time? A All the time ever since '70.
Q How many children have you by your wife, Margaret? A Two.
Q What are their names? A Graham and Mabel.

Retta Chick, being first duly sworn, states that, as stenographer to the Commission to the Five Civilized Tribes, she recorded the testimony and proceedings in the matter of the foregoing application, and that the above is a true and complete transcript of her stenographic notes thereof.

Retta Chick

Subscribed and sworn to before me this 10th day of November, 1902.

BC Jones
Notary Public.

## Cherokee Intermarried White 1906
## Volume III

F.R.                                                                          Cherokee 2744.

### DEPARTMENT OF THE INTERIOR,
### COMMISSIONER TO THE FIVE CIVILIZED TRIBES.
### Muskogee, I. T., January 15, 1907.

In the matter of the application for the enrollment of John C. Hogan as a citizen by intermarriage of the Cherokee Nation.
Applicant appears in person.
Cherokee Nation represented by W. W. Hastings.

John C. Hogan, being first duly sworn by B. P. Rasmus, a Notary Public for the Western District, Indian Territory, testified as follows:

By the Commissioner:
Q What is your name? A John C. Hogan.
Q Youa[sic] age? A Sixty years.
Q What is your postoffice address? A Pryor Creek I. T.
Q You claim the right to be enrolled as a citizen of the Cherokee nation[sic] by intermarriage? A Yes sir.
Q Through whom do you claim the right to such enrollment?
A Margaret Martha Adair.
Q When were you married to Margaret M. Adair?
A Married the 6th day of March, 1870.
Q Were you married pruor[sic] to the time you were married to Margaret M. Adair?
A No sir.
Q Was you her first husband? A Yes sir.
Q Was that marriage to Margaret M. Adair in 1870 under a license of the Cherokee nation? A Yes sir.
Q Have you copy of that license? A No, I have misplaced it somewhere.
Q Where was the license issued? A Going Snake District.
Q Who performed the marriage ceremony? A Uncle John Thompson Adair, Supreme Judge.
Q Do you know whether or not the license was filed? A Yes, a fellow by the name of Roberts went with me, when I got them filed
Q It has always been the understanding has it, that you were married to a Cherokee by blood in accordance with the Cherokee law? A Yes sir.
Q Have you lived in the Cherokee nation[sic] continuously since that time? A Yes sir.
Q Is there anyone here that was present at your marriage that can testify to its being under a Cherokee license? A Yes, there are two men, John Rufus Allison and W. P. Adair.

----------------

John R Allison, being first duly sworn by B. P. Rasmus a Notary Public for the Western District of Indian Territory, testified as follows:

## Cherokee Intermarried White 1906
## Volume III

By the Commissioner:
Q What is your name? A John R. Allison.
Q Your age? A Sisty[sic]-six years.
Q What is your postoffice address? A Adair, I. T.
Q You appear here for the purpose of giving testimony relative to the right to enrollment of John C. Hogan as a citizen by intermarriage of the Cherokee Nation? A Yes sir.
Q How long have you known John C. Hogan? A Ever since he was about ten years old.
Q Did you ever know Margaret M. Adair? A Yes sir.
Q Is she the wife of John C. Hogan? A She is.
Q Do you know when they were married? A They were married sometime in March, 1870.
Q Were you present at the marriage ceremony? A I was.
Q Do you know whether or not they were married under a license of the Cherokee nation? A I went with him to the Going Snake clerk and he got out his license there.
Q Do you know who performed the ceremony? A John T. Adair.
Q You saw the license did you? A Yes sir.
Q It is your understanding that they were married under that license? A Yes sir.
Q It has always been the understanding in that community that they were married in accordance with the Cherokee law under that license? A Yes sir.
Q They have resided together as husband and wife and lived continuously in the Cherokee Nation from the time of that marriage until the present time? A Yes sir.
Q You are a white man are you, Mr. Allison? A Yes sir.
Q You don't know who the signers to Mr. Hogan's petition were, do you? A No, I don't know; I have forgotten now.
Witness excused.

W. P. Adair, being first duly sworn by B. P. Rasmus, a Notary Public for the Western District of Indian Territory, testified as follows:
By the Commissioner:
Q What is your name? A W. P. Adair.
Q How old are you? A Forty-seven.
Q What is your postoffice address? A Adair, I. T.
Q You appears[sic] for the purpose of giving testimony relative to the right of John C. Hogan to enrollment as a citizen by intermarriage of the Cherokee Nation? A Yes sir.
Q How long have you known John C. Hogan? A Ever since I can remember.
Q Do you know Margaret M. Adair? A Yes sir.
Q What relation are you to her? A Brother.
Q Do you know whether Margaret M. Adair was married to John C. Hogan, and when?
A Yes, they were married March 6, 1870.
Q Were you present at the marriage ceremony? A Yes sir.
Q Do you know of your own personal knowledge that such marriage was under a license of the Cherokee Nation? A Yes sir.
Q You saw that license did you? A I don't remember much about that. I recollect about his having the papers.
Q It was the understanding generally that they were married in accordance with such Cherokee law? A Yes sir.

## Cherokee Intermarried White 1906
## Volume III

Q They have resided together as husband and wife, and lived continuously in the Cherokee Nation from the date of their marriage until the present time? A Yes sir.
Q You don't know of your own personal knowledge whether or not the license was returned and filed for record, or what disposition was made of it? A No, not exactly.
Q Margaret M. Adair had not been married prior to the time she married John C. Hogan? A No sir.
Q Mr. Hogan had not been married before he married her? A No sir.
Q You are a citizen by blood of the Cherokee Nation? A Yes sir
Q Margaret M. Adair was recognized as a citizen by blood of the Cherokee Nation such nation at the time of her marriage to John C. Hogan? A Yes sir.

The applicant, John C. Hogan, is identified on the 1880 roll, Cooweescoowee District opposite No. 1413.

The name of his wife, Margaret M. Hogan (nee Adair) also appears upon said roll Cooweescoowee District, opposite No. 1414. Her name is also included in the approved partial roll of the citizens of the Cherokee Nation opposite No. 23544.

The applicant and his wife are also included in the 1896 roll opposite Nos. 446 and 2123, respectively.

------------

Frances R. Lane upon oath states that as stenographer to the Commissioner to the Five Civilized Tribes she reported the testimony in the above entitled cause and that the foregoing is an accurate transcript of her stenographic notes thereof.

Frances R. Lane

Subscribed and sworn to before me this January 16, 1907.

Edward Merrick
Notary Public.

◇◇◇◇◇

E C M                                                                                                         Cherokee 2744.

### DEPARTMENT OF THE INTERIOR,

### COMMISSIONER TO THE FIVE CIVILIZED TRIBES.

In the matter of the application for the enrollment of JOHN C. HOGAN as a citizen by intermarriage of the Cherokee Nation.

## Cherokee Intermarried White 1906
## Volume III

### _D E C I S I O N_

THE RECORDS OF THIS OFFICE SHOW: That on September 14th, 1900 application was received by the Commission to the Five Civilized Tribes for the enrollment of John C. Hogan as a citizen by intermarriage of the Cherokee Nation. Further proceedings in the matter of said application were had at Muskogee, Indian Territory September 30th, 1902, October 16th, 1902 and January 15th, 1907.

THE EVIDENCE IN THIS CASE SHOWS: That the applicant herein, John C. Hogan, a white man, was married in accordance with Cherokee law March 6th, 1870 to this wife, Margaret M. Hogan, nee Adair, who was at the time of said marriage a recognized citizen by blood of the Cherokee Nation, who is identified on the Cherokee authenticated tribal roll of 1880, Cooweescoowee District No. 1414 as a native Cherokee, and whose name is included in the approved partial roll of citizens by blood of the Cherokee Nation, opposite No. 23544. It is further shown that from the time of said marriage the said John D. Hogan and Margaret M. Hogan resided together as husband and wife and continuously lived in the Cherokee Nation up to and including September 1st, 1902. Said applicant is identified on the Cherokee authenticated tribal roll of 1880 and the Cherokee census roll of 1896 as an intermarried citizen of the Cherokee Nation.

IT IS, THEREFORE, ORDERED AND ADJUDGED: That in accordance with the decision of the Supreme Court of the United States dated November 5, 1906 in the cases of Daniel Red Bird et al. vs. the United States, Nos. 125, 126, 127 and 128, the said applicant, John C. Hogan is entitled, under the provision of Section Twenty-one of the Act of Congress approved June 28, 1898 (30 Stats. 495), to enrollment as a citizen by intermarriage of the Cherokee Nation, and his application for enrollment as such is accordingly granted.

Tams Bixby<br>Commissioner.

Dated at Muskogee, Indian Territory,
this    JAN 23 1907

◇◇◇◇◇

Cherokee
2744

Muskogee, Indian Territory, December 24, 1906.

John C. Hogan,
    Pryor Creek, Indian Territory.

Dear Sir:

November 6, 1906, the United States Supreme Court held that white persons who intermarried with Cherokee citizens according to Cherokee law prior to November

## Cherokee Intermarried White 1906
## Volume III

1, 1875, are entitled to enrollment and allotments of land as citizens of the Cherokee Nation.

You are advised that to properly determine your right to enrollment as a citizen by intermarriage of the Cherokee Nation, it will be necessary for you to appear before the Commissioner for the purpose of giving testimony as to the date of your marriage and whether or not your wife, by reason of your marriage to whom you claim the right to enrollment as a citizen of the Cherokee Nation, was a recognized citizen of the Cherokee Nation at the time of your marriage to her, and whether or not you were married to her in accordance with Cherokee laws.

You are, therefore, directed to appear before the Commissioner at Muskogee, Indian Territory, at 9 o'clock A. M., on Thursday, January 3, 1907, and give testimony as above indicated.

Respectfully,

JMH  Acting Commissioner.

◇◇◇◇◇

Cherokee 2744

Muskogee, Indian Territory, January 23, 1907.

W. W. Hastings,
    Attorney for the Cherokee Nation,
        Muskogee, Indian Territory.

Dear Sir:

There is enclosed herewith copy of the decision of the Commissioner to the Five Civilized Tribes, dated January 23, 1907, granting the application for the enrollment of John C. Hogan as a citizen by intermarriage of the Cherokee Nation.

Respectfully,

Enc I-67  Commissioner.

RPI

◇◇◇◇◇

## Cherokee Intermarried White 1906
## Volume III

Cherokee 2744  W.W. HASTINGS, ATTORNEY.    OFFICE OF    H.M. VANCE, SECRETARY.

### Attorney for the Cherokee Nation,
MUSKOGEE, I. T. January 23, 1907.

The Commissioner to the Five Civilized Tribes,
Muskogee, Indian Territory.

Sir:

Receipt is acknowledged of the testimony and of your decision enrolling John C. Hogan as a citizen by intermarriage of the Cherokee Nation. Time for protesting said decision is waived and I consent that said person may be placed upon the schedule immediately.

Respectfully,
W. W. Hastings
Attorney for the Cherokee Nation.

<><><><><>

Cherokee 2744

Muskogee, Indian Territory, January 23, 1907.

John C. Hogan,
Pryor Creek, Indian Territory.

Dear Sir:

There is enclosed herewith copy of the decision of the Commissioner to the Five Civilized Tribes, dated January 23, 1907, granting your application for enrollment as a citizen by intermarriage of the Cherokee Nation.

You will be advised when your name has been placed upon a schedule of citizens of the Cherokee Nation and approved by the Secretary of the Interior.

Respectfully,

Enc I-86                                    Commissioner.

RPI

## Cherokee Intermarried White 1906
## Volume III

**Cher IW 71**
**Trans from Cher 2846  3-15-07**

DEPARTMENT OF THE INTERIOR.
COMMISSION TO THE FIVE CIVILIZED TRIBES.
VINITA, I. T., SEPTEMBER 17th, 1900.

IN THE MATTER OF THE APPLICATION OF Nancy Ann Glenn and husband for enrollment as citizens of the Cherokee Nation, and she being sworn by Commissioner, T. B. Needles, testified as follows:

Q  What is your name?  A  Nancy Ann Glenn.
Q  What is your age?  A  Forty-one.
Q  What is your Postoffice?  A  Grove.
Q  What district do you live in?  A  Delaware.
Q  Are you a recognized citizen of the Cherokee Nation?  A  Yes sir
Q  By blood or intermarriage?  A  By blood.
Q  What degree of blood do you claim?  A  About one fourth.
Q  How long have you lived in the Cherokee Nation?
A  Twenty five years: All my life.
Q  For whom do you apply?  A  Myself and husband.
Q  Any children?  A  No sir; my children are married.
Q  Is your husband present?  A  No sir.
Q  What is your father's name?  A  John Sutton.
Q  Was Sutton your maiden name?  A  Yes sir.
Q  Is your father living?  A  No sie/[sic]
Q  What is your mother's name?  A  Mary A. Sutton.
Q  Is she living?  A  No sir.
Q  When were you married? What is your husband's name?  A  S. C. Glenn.
Q  What is his first name?  A  Samuel.
Q  How old is he?  A  Fifty three.
Q  When were you married to him?  A  In 1875,
Q  Is he living?  A  Yes sir.
Q  Is he a white man?  A  Yes sir.
Q  What are the name of your children under twenty one years of age, at home, and unmarried?  A  I havn't[sic] any.
Q  Just apply for yourself and husband?  A  Yes sir.

   (1880 Roll, Page 260, #1114, Samuel Glenn, Delaware District)
   (1880 Roll, Page 260, #1115, Ann Glenn, Delaware District)
   (1896 Roll, page 574, #196, Samuel Glenn, Delaware District)
   (1896 Roll, Page 475, #1277, Annie Glenn, Delaware District)

The name of Nancy Ann Glenn and her husband, Samuel C. Glenn appear upon the authenticated roll of 1880; hers as Ann Glenn, and her husband as Samuel Glenn. Their

## Cherokee Intermarried White 1906
## Volume III

names also appear upon the Census roll of 1896. They being identified and having made satisfactory proof of their residence, he said Nancy Ann Glenn will be duly listed for enrollment by this Commission as a Cherokee citizen by blood, and her husband, Samuel C. Glenn as a citizen by intermarriage.

----------------------------------

The undersigned, being sworn, states that as stenographer to the Commission to the Five Civilized Tribes, he correctly recorded the testimony and proceedings in this case, and that the foregoing is a true and complete transcript of his stenographic notes thereof.

R R Cravens

Subscribed and sworn to before me this 17th day of September, 1900.

TB Needles
COMMISSIONER.

Statement of Applicant Taken Under Oath.

**CHEROKEE BY BLOOD AND ADOPTION.**

(53) Date SEP 17 1900    1900.
1 Name    Samuel C. Glenn    Grove I.T.
District    DELAWARE.    Year 1880    Page 260    No. 1114
Citizen by blood _____ Mother's citizenship _____
Intermarried citizen    Yes
Married under what law _____ Date of marriage _____
2 License (41)    Certificate _____
Wife's name    Nancy A Glenn nee Sutton
District    DELAWARE.    Year 1880    Page 260    No. 1115
Citizen by blood    Yes 1/4    Mother's citizenship _____
Intermarried citizen _____
Married under what law _____ Date of marriage _____
License _____ Certificate _____

Names of Children:

| | Dist. | Year | Page | No. | Age |
|---|---|---|---|---|---|
| | Dist. | Year | Page | No. | Age |
| | Dist. | Year | Page | No. | Age |
| | Dist. | Year | Page | No. | Age |
| | Dist. | Year | Page | No. | Age |

1 on 1880 roll as Samuel Glenn
2 "    "    "    "    Ann    "

# Cherokee Intermarried White 1906
# Volume III

JOR.
Cher. 2846.

Department of the Interior.
Commission to the Five Civilized Tribes
Tahlequah, I. T., October 20, 1902.

SUPPLEMENTAL TESTIMONY in the matter of the application for the enrollment of SAMUEL C. GLENN as a citizen by intermarriage of the Cherokee Nation.

SAMUEL C. GLENN, being first duly sworn, and being examined, testified as follows:

BY COMMISSION: What is your name? A Samuel C. Glenn.
Q How old are you? A Fifty-four.
Q What is your post office address? A Grove, I. T.
Q Are you a white man? A Yes sir.
Q Have you heretofore made application to this Commission for enrollment as a citizen by intermarriage of the Cherokee Nation? A Yes sir.
Q What is the name of your wife? A Nancy Ann.
Q Is she living? A Yes sir.
Q Is she a Cherokee by blood? A Yes sir.
Q Do you claim your right to enrollment by reason of your marriage to her? A Yes sir.
Q When were you and she married? A In 1875.
Q Were you married at that time according to Cherokee law? A Yes sir.
Q Does your name appear upon the roll of 1880? A Yes sir.
Q Were you ever married before you married her? A No sir.
Q Was she ever married before she married you? A No sir.
Q You are her first husband and she is your first wife? A Yes sir.
Q Have you and she lived together continuously since you were married? A Yes sir.
Q Were you living together on the 1st day of September, 1902? A Yes sir.
Q Have you ever been seprated[sic]? A No sir.
Q Have you resided in the Cherokee Nation continuously since you and she married? A Yes sir.
Q Has she also? A Yes sir.
Q Have you any minor children for whom you made application?
A Two, they were of age.
Q Are both your children living? A Yes sir.

This testimony will be filed with and made a part of the record in the matter of the application for the enrollment of Samuel C. Glenn as a citizen by intermarriage of the Cherokee Nation, Cherokee straight card field No. 2846.

------------------

# Cherokee Intermarried White 1906
## Volume III

Wm. Hutchinson, being first duly sworn, states that as stenographer to the Commission to the Five Civilized Tribes he correctly recorded the testimony and proceedings in this case, and that the foregoing is a true and complete transcript of his stenographic notes thereof.

Wm Hutchinson

Subscribed and sworn to before me this 30th day of October, 1902.

John O Rosson<br>Notary Public.

◇◇◇◇◇

Cherokee Field<br>No. 2846.

DEPARTMENT OF THE INTERIOR,

COMMISSIONER TO THE FIVE CIVILIZED TRIBES.

MUSKOGEE, INDIAN TERRITORY, JANUARY 3, 1907.

IN THE MATTER of the application for the enrollment of Samuel C. Glenn, as a citizen by intermarriage of the Cherokee Nation.

SAMUEL C. GLENN, Being first duly sworn by Walter W. Chappell, Notary Public, testified as follows:

EXAMINATION

ON BEHALF OF THE COMMISSIONER:

Q What is your name? A Samuel C. Glenn.
Q What is your age? A Fifty-eight.
Q What is your postoffice address? A Grove, I. T.
Q Are you a white man? A Yes, sir.
Q You are an intermarried citizen of the Cherokee Nation? A Yes, sir.
Q What is the name of the Cherokee wife that you claim your right to enrollment through? A Nancy Ann Sutton.
Q When were you married to Nancy Ann Sutton? A In 1875, October 19th. That is the date we have always kept and celebrated.
Q Was that marriage under a Cherokee license? A Yes.
Q Where were you married? A In Delaware District.
Q Have you any documentary evidence of your marriage? A Yes, sir:[sic]
Q You will please present the same? (Hands examiner papers).

## Cherokee Intermarried White 1906
## Volume III

ON BEHALF OF THE
COMMISSIONER:
Witness presented affidavit of James E. Harlin, purporting to show that said James E. Harlin was clerk of the Delaware District, Cherokee Nation, Indian Territory, during the years 1874 and 1875, and that on or about October 16th, 1875, he issued a marriage licence[sic] to Samuel C. Glenn and Nancy A. Sutton. Examiner declined to receive said paper and same was returned to witness.

Q Have you and your wife lived together continuously since your marriage? A Yes, sir.
Q You have both lived together continuously since your marriage in the Cherokee Nation? A Yes, sir.
Q Was she a recognized citizen of the Cherokee Nation at the time of your marriage to her? A Yes sir.
Q Were you ever married prior to your marriage to Nancy A. Glenn? A No sir.
Q Had she ever been married before? A No sir.
Q You say that a license was issued for your marriage? A Yes.
Q By whom? A James Harlin.
Q What became of that license? A Burned up when my house was burned.
Q What year? A In 1876.
Q Why didn't you procure a certified copy of your license?
A Never has been required of me. I didn't know what to do when I come here. My wife enrolled me at the Dawes Commission, and they never asked me for a certificate of the license, and the date given you here is the date that we celebrate for our wedding day.
Q Is your wife here today? A Yes sir.

(Witness dismissed).

ON BEHALF OF THE COMMISSIONER:

The witness and his wife Nancy A. Glenn, are listed for enrollment on Cherokee card, field No. 2846. They are identified on the 1880 authenticated roll of citizens of the Cherokee Nation, opposite Nos. 1114 and 1115, respectively, Delaware District. Nancy A. Glenn is included on the partial roll of citizens by blood of the Cherokee Nation, opposite No. 7150.

NANCY A. GLENN, being first duly sworn by Walter W. Chappell, Notary Public, testified as follows:

### EXAMINATION

ON BEHALF OF THE COMMISSIONER:

Q What is your name? A Nancy Ann Glenn.
Q What is your age? A I will be 48 years old the 5th day of February.

# Cherokee Intermarried White 1906
## Volume III

Q  Where abouts[sic] do you live?  A.  At Grove, Indian Territory.
Q  Are you a citizen by blood of the Cherokee Nation?  A  Yes.
Q  What is your husband's name?  A  Samuel C. Glenn.
Q  When were you married to him?  A  Married in 1875.
Q  What date?  A  October 19th I think, as well as I remember.
Q  Where were you married?
A  Married in the Cherok *(paper folded, remainder illegible)*
Q  What District?  A  Delaware District.
Q  By whom were you married?  A  Jeff McGee, - Judge McGee.
Q  Were you married under a Cherokee license?  A  Yes sir.
Q  Have you or your husband a copy of that license?  A  No sir, our house was burned in 1877, after we was married, and burned that up and we never got another one.
Q  Have you lived continuously with Samuel C. Glenn since your marriage to him?  A  Yes sir.
Q  Have you resided continuously in the Cherokee Nation?  A  Yes sir.
Q  Were you ever married prior to your marriage with Samuel C. Glenn?  A  No sir.

(Witness dismissed).

I, S. T. Wright, stenographer to the Commissioner to the Five Civilized Tribes, on oath, state that I recorded the testimony and proceedings had in the above entitled cause on January 3, 1907, and that the above and foregoing is a true and correct transcript of my stenographic notes thereof, taken on said date.

S.T. Wright

Subscribed and sworn to before me this January 4, 1907.

B.P. Rasmus
NOTARY PUBLIC.

◇◇◇◇◇

C.F.B.                                                                                      Cherokee 2846.

### DEPARTMENT OF THE INTERIOR,

### COMMISSIONER TO THE FIVE CIVILIZED TRIBES.
### MUSKOGEE, I. T., JANUARY 4, 1907.

In the matter of the application for the enrollment of Samuel C. Glenn as a citizen by intermarriage of the Cherokee Nation.

APPEARANCES: Applicant appears in person.

SAMUEL C. GLENN, being first duly sworn by B. P. Rasmus, Notary Public, testified as follows:

# Cherokee Intermarried White 1906
# Volume III

ON BEHALF OF THE COMMISSIONER:

Q What is your name? A Samuel C. Glenn.
Q What is your age? A I am about 58 years old.
Q What is your post office address? A Grove, Indian Territory.
Q You are a claimant for enrollment as a citizen by intermarriage of the Cherokee Nation, are you? A Yes sir.
Q You are unable to present a marriage license and certificate showing your marriage to your Cherokee wife? A Yes sir, it was burned.
Q In what district was it issued? A Delaware District.
Q It was issued by the Clerk of that district, was it? A Yes sir.
Q In what year? A Year of 75.
Q Did you secure witnesses to sign the license? A Yes sir.
Q Are any of the witnesses who signed it living? A Yes sir, there is one of them.

DAVID A. MCGHEE, being first duly sworn by B. P. Rasmus, Notary Public, testified as follows:

ON BEHALF OF THE COMMISSIONER:

Q What is your name? A David A. McGhee.
Q What is your age? A I am about 57 or 58 years old.
Q Are you a citizen by blood of the Cherokee Nation? A Yes sir.
Q Do you know a person in the Cherokee Nation by the name of Samuel C. Glenn?
A I know Samuel Glenn, the gentleman there.
Q He is an intermarried citizen of the Cherokee Nation, is he?
A Yes sir.
Q Do you remember when he married his Cherokee wife? A No, I dont[sic] remember the date, but I think it was along in the fall of '75, if I am not mistaken.
Q You remember the event? A Yes sir. Mr. Harlan was Clerk at the time, and he went out of office the 3rd of November, 1875.
Q Did he marry his wife in accordance with the laws of the Cherokee Nation?
A That was my understanding; I signed his petition recommending him. That was the law.
Q You were one of the signers to a petition for a license for him to marry this Cherokee by blood, were you? A Yes sir.
Q And it is your understanding that he secured the necessary signers, that the license was issued, and that he was married to his Cherokee wife in accordance with the laws of the Cherokee Nation? A That was my understanding, but I didn't see it.
Q You were not a witness to the marriage? A No sir.
Q You did not see the license? A No sir.
Q You are testifying as to the general report, the way it was understood to be, are you?
A Yes sir.
Q Has Samuel C. Glenn always been recognized by the tribal authorities as a citizen by intermarriage of the Cherokee Nation? A Yes sir.

## Cherokee Intermarried White 1906
## Volume III

Q And he has lived in the Cherokee Nation continuously since his marriage, has he? A Yes sir.
Q He and his wife have, since their marriage, continuously resided together as husband and wife, have they? A Yes sir, while they lived in my neighborhood; they moved away 10 or 12 years ago but up to that time they lived together, I know.

----------------------

The undersigned, being first duly sworn, states that as stenographer to the Commissioner to the Five Civilized Tribes, she correctly recorded the above and foregoing testimony, and that the same is a full, true and correct transcript of her stenographic notes thereof.

Sarah Waters

Subscribed and sworn to before me this 5th day of January, 1907.

John E. Tidwell
Notary Public.

◇◇◇◇◇

Cherokee 2846.

DEPARTMENT OF THE INTERIOR,
COMMISSIONER TO THE FIVE CIVILIZED TRIBES.
MUSKOGEE, I. T., JANUARY 7, 1907.

------------------------------

SUPPLEMENTAL TESTIMONY in the matter of the application for the enrollment of SAMUEL C. GLENN as a citizen by intermarriage of the Cherokee Nation.

APPEARANCES:   Applicant appears in person.
Thomas J. McGhee appears on behalf of applicant.

THOMAS J. MCGHEE, being first duly sworn by John E. Tidwell, Notary Public, testified as follows:

ON BEHALF OF THE COMMISSIONER:

Q What is your name? A Thomas J. McGhee.
Q What is your age? A 52.
Q What is your post office address? A Afton.
Q Are you acquainted with a person in the Cherokee Nation by the name of Samuel C. Glenn? A Yes sir.
Q Is he a citizen by intermarriage of the Cherokee Nation?
A Yes sir, so recognized.

## Cherokee Intermarried White 1906
## Volume III

Q  You appear here today for the purpose of giving testimony relative to his right to enrollment as a citizen by intermarriage of the Cherokee Nation, do you?  A  Yes sir.
Q  What is his wife's name?  A  Her maiden name was Annie Sutton.
Q  Is she living?  A  Yes sir.
Q  When did he marry her.[sic]  A  It was in the year '75, as well as I remember.
Q  Was she a recognized citizen of the Cherokee Nation at the time he married her?  A  Yes sir.
Q  Residing in the Cherokee Country, was she?  A  Yes sir, at a place known as Boudinot Tobacco Factory.
Q  Then she was residing in the Cherokee Country at the time of her marriage?  A  Yes sir.
Q  In what District were they married?  A  Delaware.
Q  Do you know whether or not Samuel C. Glenn secured a license and married his wife according to the laws of the Cherokee Nation?  A  Yes sir, for I performed the marriage ceremony myself; I was at that time Judge of the Cherokee Court.
Q  What time in the year of 1875 was it?  A  Why, my time expired in November; it was prior to November.
Q  At what time did your term of office expire, on what day of November?  A  It was either the first or second Monday in November.
Q  You are positive that you performed this marriage ceremony prior to the first day of November?  A  O[sic], yes.
Q  Did he secure a license?  A  Yes sir.
Q  By whom was it issued?  A  James E. Harlan; he was my Clerk.
Q  He was acting as your Clerk, was he?  A  Yes sir.
Q  He issued the license?  A  Yes sir.
Q  The license was issued, then, in accordance with the law, and this man was married in accordance with the law of the Cherokee Nation?  A  Yes sir.
Q  Since his marriage, have he and his wife continuously resided together as husband and wife.  A  Yes sir, they have lived right there in the Delaware District. I have known them ever since.
Q  They have lived in the Cherokee Country all the time, have they?  A  Yes sir.

---------------------------

The undersigned, being first duly sworn, states that as stenographer to the Commissioner to the Five Civilized Tribes, she correctly recorded the above and foregoing testimony, and that the same is a full, true and correct transcript of her stenographic notes thereof.

Sarah Waters

Subscribed and sworn to before me this 7th day of January, 1907.

John E. Tidwell<br>Notary Public.

◇◇◇◇◇

## Cherokee Intermarried White 1906
## Volume III

( COPY )

2d Recording Dist. )
)
Indian Territory. )
)

Grove, December 29th, 1906.

Affidavit of James E. Harlin.

Personally appeared before me on this 29th day of December A.D. 1906 James E. Harlin to me well known, who first being duly sworn on Oath, deposes and says: I am 74 years old and was Clerk of Delaware District in the Cherokee Nation - Indian Territory - in the years 1874 and 75. And on or about October the 16th 1875 I issued a Marriage License to Samuel C. Glenn a white man and Nancy A Sutton, a Cherokee woman by blood, the said Samuel C. Glenn having fully complied with all the laws, rules and regulations in force, and governing marriages of Cherokees and non Citizens at that time - and further affiant saith not.

(Signed) James E. Harlin.

The within affidavit Subscribed and sworn to before me this to this 29th day of December A. D. 1906.

(Signed) T. S. Remsen,
Notary Public.

SEAL
My Com. Expires May 2d, 1908.

The undersigned being first duly sworn states that as stenographer to the Commissioner to the Five Civilized Tribes, she made the above copy and that the same is a true and correct copy of the original affidavit.

Lola M. Champlin

Subscribed and sworn to before me this 19, day of January, 1907.

Chas E Webster
Notary Public.

◇◇◇◇◇

## Cherokee Intermarried White 1906
## Volume III

*(Below was originally handwritten as given on the microfilm. The transcribed copy immediately followed and is given below and typed as given.)*

COPY

Grove, I. T.
Dec. 31st 1906.

This is to certify that Nancy A. Harlin who is about 66 years of age a resident of Grove, I. T. is very feeble & infirm. Not able to do anything.

J. C. Holland
M. D.

I have been a practicing physician for about 13 years. The within affidavit subscribed and sworn to this 8th day of January, A. D. 1907.

T. S. Remsen
(SEAL) Notary public
My Comm. Expries May 2, 1908.

The undersigned being sirst duly sworn states that as stenographer to the Commissioner to the Five Civilized Tribes, she made the above copy and that the same is a true and complete copy of the original affidavit now on file in this office.

Lola M. Champlin

Subscribed and sworn to before me this 18, day of January 1907.

Chas E Webster
notary public

◇◇◇◇◇

*(The Affidavit of James E. Harlin, December 29th, 1906, above, given again)*

◇◇◇◇◇

## Cherokee Intermarried White 1906
## Volume III

*(Below Affidavit was originally handwritten as given on the microfilm. The transcribed copy immediately followed and is given below and typed as given.)*

COPY

2d Recording Dist.
Indian Territory.

Grove January 8th 1907.

Personally appeared before me a notary public in and for said Dist. and Territory, Nancy A. Harlin to me well known and entitled to credit who after being duly sworn declares as follows-- I am 66 years of age, my post office if Grove my residence is Grove, Ind. Ter. I am personally acquanted with Samuel C. Glenn I was married to James E. Harlin in 1872 in 1875 he was Clerk of Delaware District, Cherokee Nation and in October of 1875 he issued a marriage license to said Samuel C. Glenn to marry Anna Sutton a Cherokee woman by blood I saw my husband write the license out, and Mr. Glenn who was a Shoemaker made me a pair of shoes to help pay for the license. I know this was in the year 1875 as it was the year after the drouth, and 1875 was the year we drew bread money. I am now quite feeble- not able to get around much or go anywhere.

Nancy A. Harlin

The within affidavit subscribed and sworn to this 8th day of January A. D. 1907.

(SEAL)

T. S. Remsen
Notary Public.

My Coms. expires May 2d 1908.

The undersigned being first duly sworn states that as stenographer to the Commissioner to the Five Civilized Tribes, she made the above and foregoing copy and that the same is a true and correct copy of the original affidavit now on file in this office.

Lola M Champlin

# Cherokee Intermarried White 1906
# Volume III

Subscribed and sworn to before me this 19, day of January 1907.

Chas E Webster
Notary Public.

C.E.W.

Cherokee 2846.

DEPARTMENT OF THE INTERIOR,

COMMISSIONER TO THE FIVE CIVILIZED TRIBES.

-------------------------------------

In the matter of the application for the enrollment of Samuel C. Glenn, as a citizen by intermarriage of the Cherokee Nation.

D E C I S I O N

THE RECORDS OF THIS OFFICE SHOW: That at Vinita, Indian Territory, September 17, 1900, application was received by the Commission to the Five Civilized Tribes for the enrollment of Samuel C. Glenn, as a citizen by intermarriage of the Cherokee Nation. Further proceedings in the matter of said application were had at Tahlequah, Indian Territory, October 20, 1902, and at Muskogee, Indian Territory, January 3, 4 and 7, 1907.

THE EVIDENCE IN THIS CASE SHOWS: That the applicant herein, Samuel C. Glenn, a white man, was married in accordance with Cherokee law October 19, 1875, to his wife, Nancy A. Glenn, nee Sutton, who was at the time of said marriage a recognized citizen by blood of the Cherokee Nation, who is identified on the Cherokee authenticated tribal roll of 1880, Delaware District, page 260 number 1115, as a native Cherokee, and whose name is included in the approved partial roll of citizens by blood of the Cherokee Nation, opposite number 7150. It is further shown that from the time of said marriage the said Samuel C. Glenn and Nancy A. Glenn resided together as husband and wife and continuously lived in the Cherokee Nation. Said applicant is identified on the Cherokee authenticated tribal roll of 1880, and the Cherokee census roll of 1896 as an intermarried citizen of the Cherokee Nation.

IT IS, THEREFORE, ORDERED AND ADJUDGED: That in accordance with the decision of the Supreme Court of the United States, dated November 5, 1906, in the cases of Daniel Red Bird et al., vs. the United States, Nos. 125, 126, 127 and 128, the said applicant Samuel C. Glenn is entitled, under the provision of Section 21 of the Act of Congress approved June 28, 1898 (30 Stats., 495), to enrollment, as a citizen by

# Cherokee Intermarried White 1906
## Volume III

intermarriage of the Cherokee Nation, and his application for enrollment as such is accordingly granted.

Tams Bixby<br>Commissioner.

Dated at Muskogee, Indian Territory, this    JAN 23 1907

Cherokee
2846

Muskogee, Indian Territory, December 24, 1906.

Samuel C. Glenn,
    Grove, Indian Territory.

Dear Sir:

November 6, 1906, the United States Supreme Court held that white persons who intermarried with Cherokee citizens according to Cherokee law prior to November 1, 1875, are entitled to enrollment and allotments of land as citizens of the Cherokee Nation.

You are advised that to properly determine your right to enrollment as a citizen by intermarriage of the Cherokee Nation, it will be necessary for you to appear before the Commissioner for the purpose of giving testimony as to the date of your marriage and whether or not your wife, by reason of your marriage to whom you claim the right to enrollment as a citizen of the Cherokee Nation, was a recognized citizen of the Cherokee Nation at the time of your marriage to her, and whether or not you were married to her in accordance with Cherokee laws.

You are, therefore, directed to appear before the Commissioner at Muskogee, Indian Territory, at 9 o'clock A. M., on Thursday, January 3, 1907, and give testimony as above indicated.

Respectfully,

JMH                                                             Acting Commissioner.

## Cherokee Intermarried White 1906
## Volume III

In reply please refer
to the following:

**DEPARTMENT OF THE INTERIOR,**

UNITED STATES INDIAN SERVICE,

CC-      UNION AGENCY.

MUSKOGEE, IND T.,   Jan 4 1907

Mr. Samuel C. Glenn,
        Grove, I. T.

Sir:

    In reply to your verbal request that your marriage certificate issued to you in the Delaware district in 1875, and supposed to have been filed at this office, be returned to you, I beg to advise you that this office has no record of such marriage certificate.

    On February 23, 1899, all of the records of this Agency were destroyed by fire, and if your certificate was filed with the Agent, it was undoubtedly destroyed at that time.

    Very respectfully,

*(Name Illegible)*
United States Indian Agent.

BM(E)

*(Handwritten at bottom of letter)*

Appt knows he never filed his "cert" with agent - He said so - Agency had nothing to do with it NR

◇◇◇◇◇

Cherokee 2846

Muskogee, Indian Territory, January 23, 1907.

W. W. Hastings,
    Attorney for the Cherokee Nation,
        Muskogee, Indian Territory.

Dear Sir:

    There is enclosed herewith copy of the decision of the Commissioner to the Five Civilized Tribes, dated January 23, 1907, granting the application for the enrollment of Samuel C. Glenn as a citizen by intermarriage of the Cherokee Nation.

## Cherokee Intermarried White 1906
## Volume III

Respectfully,

Enc I-74  
RPI

Commissioner.

◇◇◇◇◇

Cherokee 2846   W.W. HASTINGS, ATTORNEY.   OFFICE OF   H.M. VANCE, SECRETARY.

### Attorney for the Cherokee Nation,
MUSKOGEE, I. T.

January 23, 1907.

The Commissioner to the Five Civilized Tribes,
    Muskogee, Indian Territory.

Sir:

    Receipt is acknowledged of the testimony and of your decision enrolling Samuel C. Glenn as a citizen by intermarriage of the Cherokee Nation. Time for protesting said decision is waived and I consent that said person may be placed upon the schedule immediately.

Respectfully,  
W. W. Hastings  
Attorney for the Cherokee Nation.

◇◇◇◇◇

Cherokee 2846

Muskogee, Indian Territory, January 23, 1907.

Samuel C. Glenn,  
    Grove, Indian Territory.

Dear Sir:

    There is enclosed herewith copy of the decision of the Commissioner to the Five Civilized Tribes, dated January 23, 1907, granting the application for your enrollment as a citizen by intermarriage of the Cherokee Nation.

    You will be advised when your name has been placed upon a schedule of citizens of the Cherokee Nation and approved by the Secretary of the Interior.

Respectfully,

Enc I-91  
RPI

Commissioner.

# Cherokee Intermarried White 1906
# Volume III

**Cher IW 72**
**Trans from Cher 2853 3-15-07**

DEPARTMENT OF THE INTERIOR,

COMMISSIONER TO THE FIVE CIVILIZED TRIBES.

In the matter of the application for the enrollment of

MATILDA STURDIVANT

as a citizen by intermarriage of the Cherokee Nation.

---

CHEROKEE 2853

DEPARTMENT OF THE INTERIOR.
COMMISSION TO THE FIVE CIVILIZED TRIBES.
VINITA, I. T., SEPTEMBER 17th, 1900.

IN THE MATTER OF THE APPLICATION OF Martin Butler Sturdevant[sic], wife and child for enrollment as citizens of the Cherokee Nation, and he being sworn by Commissioner, T. B. Needles, testified as follows:

Q What is your name? A Martin Butler Sturdevant.
Q What is your age? A Going on fifty seven.
Q What is your Postoffice? A Grove.
Q What district do you live in? A Delaware.
Q Are you a recognized citizen of the Cherokee Nation? A Yes sir.
Q By blood or intermarriage? A By blood.
Q What degree of blood do you claim? A About one fourth I reckon.
Q How long have you lived in the Cherokee Nation continuously?
A I have lived here all my life.
Q For whom do you apply for enrollment? A For myself and my children.
Q Your father and mother are not living? A No sir.
Q Is your wife living? A Yes sir.
Q Do you apply for her? A Yes sir.
Q You apply for yourself, wife and child then? A Yes sir.
Q What is the name of your wife? A Matilda Sturdevant.
Q Is she a Cherokee citizen by blood? A No sir.
Q When did you marry her? A I[sic] has been about thirty seven years.

## Cherokee Intermarried White 1906
## Volume III

Q Her father and mother are not living? A No sir.
Q What are the names of your children? [sic] Richard Sturdevant.
Q How old is Richard? A He is nineteen.
Q Is he living and living with you? A Yes sir.

    (1880 Roll, Page 476, #1644, Buck Studefan, Going Snake Dis't)
    (1880 Roll, Page 476, #1645, Malinda Stedefan[sic], Going Snake " )
    (1896 Roll, Page 532, #2839, Richard Sturdevant, Delaware Dis't)
    (1896 Roll, Page 588, #497, Tilda Sturdevant, Delaware Dis't   )
    (1896 Roll, Page 532, #2834, Buck Sturdevant, Delaware Dis't)

    The name of Martin Butler Sturdevant appears upon the authenticated roll of 1880, as Buck Studefan, and upon the census roll of 1896, as Buck Sturdevant. The name of his wife, Matilda Sturdevant appears upon the authenticated roll of 1880, as Malinda Studefan, and upon the census roll of 1896 as Tilda Sturdevant. The name of his son, Richard Sturdevant appears upon the census roll of 1896, they all being duly identified according to the page and number of the rolls, as indicated in the testimony: And having made satisfactory proof as to their residence, the said Martin Butler Sturdevant and his son, Richard Sturdevant, will be duly listed for enrollment by this Commission as Cherokee citizens by blood, and his wife, Matilda Sturdevant, as a Cherokee citizen by intermarriage.

---

    The undersigned, being sworn, states that as stenographer to the Commission to the Five Civilized Tribes, he correctly recorded the testimony and proceedings in this case, and that the foregoing is a true and complete transcript of his stenographic notes thereof.

                                                                 R R Cravens

Subscribed and sworn to before me
this 17th day of September, 1900.

                                                                 TB Needles
                                                                 C O M M I S S I O N E R .

◇◇◇◇◇

# Cherokee Intermarried White 1906
# Volume III

JOR.
Cher. 2853.

Department of the Interior.
Commission to the Five Civilized Tribes.
Tahlequah, I. T., October 20, 1902.

SUPPLEMENTAL TESTIMONY in the matter of the application for the enrollment of MATILDA STURDIVANT as a citizen by intermarriage of the Cherokee Nation.

MATILDA STURDIVANT, being first duly sworn, and being examined, testified as follows:

BY COMMISSION: What is your name? A Matilda Sturdivant.
Q How old are you? A I will be fifty-seven years old the 14th day of next June.
Q What is your post office address? A Grove.
Q You are a white woman, are you? A Yes sir.
Q Has application been made to this Commission for your enrollment as a citizen by intermarriage of the Cherokee Nation? A Yes sir.
Q What is the name of your husband? A Martin Butler Sturdivant.
Q Is he living? A Yes sir.
Q Is he a Cherokee by blood? A Yes sir.
Q Do you claim your right to enrollment by reason of your marriage to him? A Yes sir.
Q When were you and he married? A We were married in 1836, it was the year after peace, the 4th day of February.
Q It was 1866, the year after peace? A Yes sir, 1866, that is the year, it was on the 4th day of February.
Q Have you and he lived together continuously since that time? A Yes sir.
Q Does your name appear on the roll of 1880? A Yes sir.
Q Were you and he living together on the 1st day of September, 1902[sic]
A Yes sir.
Q Have you ever been separated at all? A No sir.
Q Were you ever married before you married him? A No sir.
Q Was he ever married before he married you? A No sir, not that I know of.
Q Did you ever hear of his being married before her married you? A No sir.
Q Have you any reason whatever to believe that he was ever married before?
A No sir, I have known him ever since he was a boy.
Q You know then that he was never married? A Yes sir.
Q Have you resided in the Cherokee Nation continuously since you and he marred[sic]?
A Yes sir.
Q Has he resided here continuously since that time? A Yes sir.
Q You have how many minor children that application was made for? A Seven.
Q You have one Richard living with you? A Yes sir.
Q They are all living? A Yes sir.

39

## Cherokee Intermarried White 1906
## Volume III

This testimony will be filed with and made a part of the record in the matter of the application for the enrollment of Matilda Sturdivant as a citizen by intermarriage of the Cherokee Nation, Cherokee straight card field No. 2853.

------------------

Wm. Hutchinson, being first duly sworn, states that as stenographer to the Commission to the Five Civilized Tribes he correctly recorded the testimony and proceedings in this case, and that the foregoing is a true and complete transcript of his stenographic notes thereof.

Wm Hutchinson

Subscribed and sworn to before me this 30th day of October, 1902.

John O Rosson<br>NP

◇◇◇◇◇

Cherokee Field Card<br>No. 2853.

### DEPARTMENT OF THE INTERIOR

### COMMISSIONER TO THE FIVE CIVILIZED TRIBES,

### MUSKOGEE, INDIAN TERRITORY, JANUARY 3, 1907.

IN THE MATTER OF THE APPLICATION for the enrollment of Matilda Sturdivant, as a citizen by intermarriage of the Cherokee Nation.

MATILDA STURDIVANT, being first duly sworn by Walter W. Chappell, Notary Public, testified as follows:

### EXAMINATION

ON BEHALF OF THE COMMISSIONER:

Q What is your name? A Matilda Sturdivant.
Q What is your age? A I will be 61 in June.
Q What is your postoffice address? A Grove.
Q You claim citizenship by intermarriage to a citizen of the Cherokee Nation?
  A Yes sir.
Q Through whom do you make this claim? A Martin B. Sturdivant.
Q What was his citizenship? A Cherokee by blood.
Q When were you married to him? A In 1866, 4th day of February.
Q Where were you married? A At my mother's here, 12 miles west of Siloam Springs in the Cherokee Nation.
Q In what District was that? A Delaware.

## Cherokee Intermarried White 1906
## Volume III

Q Were you married under a Cherokee license? A No sir, it wasn't required then.
Q Who performed the marriage ceremony? A Doctor Powell, he was a doctor.
Q Is there any one here to-day who was present at your marriage? A No sir, I don't know whether there is any one living or not, I haven't heard of any one for sometime; and I can't say whether they are living now or not.
Q Were you ever married prior to your marriage to Martin B. Sturdivant? A No sir.
Q Had he been married before that time? A No sir.
Q Is your husband living at this time? A Yes sir.
Q Have you lived together continuously since your marriage? A Yes sir.
Q In the Cherokee Nation? A Yes sir.
Q Is there any one here who knows that you have lived together ever since you marriage? A My son-in-law knows we have lived together. I don't know how long it was. Mr. Duckworth is here and he knows we have lived together ever since we was first married.

ON BEHALF OF THE COMMISSIONER: The applicant with her husband, Martin B. Sturdivant, is listed for enrollment on Cherokee card, field No. 2853. They are identified on the 1880 authenticated roll of citizens of the Cherokee Nation, opposite Nos. 1645 and 1644, respectively, Going Snake District.

The applicant's husband is upon approved partial roll of citizens of the Cherokee Nation opposite No. 70167.

(Witness dismissed).

JOHN D. SMITH, being first duly sworn by Walter W. Chappell, Notary Public, testified as follows:

### EXAMINATION
ON BEHALF OF THE COMMISSIONER:

Q What is your name? A John D. Smith.
Q What is your age? A Seventy-two.
Q What is your postoffice address? A Grove.
Q Do you know Matilda Sturdivant? A Yes sir.
Q Are you related to her in any way? A No sir.
Q How long have you known her? A Been about twenty years, I have known her.
Q Do you know her husband? A Yes sir.
Q Where did they reside during the time you knew them?
A On Flint Creek, in that neighborhood there.
Q Did you say you had only known them twenty years? A Yes, about twenty years.
Q Then, of course, you don't know anything with reference to their marriage? A No sir.
Q During all the time you knew them, were they regarded in their community as man and wife, legally married? A Yes.

(Witness dismissed).

## Cherokee Intermarried White 1906
## Volume III

I, S. T. Wright, stenographer to the Commissioner to the Five Civilized Tribes, on oath, state that I recorded the testimony and proceedings had in the above cause on January 3, 197, and that the above and foregoing is a true and correct transcript of my stenographic notes thereof, taken on said date.

S.T. Wright

Subscribed and sworn to before me this January 4th, 1907.

B.P. Rasmus<br>NOTARY PUBLIC

◇◇◇◇◇

Cherokee-2853.

## DEPARTMENT OF THE INTERIOR,
## COMMISSIONER TO THE FIVE CIVILIZED TRIBES.
### Muskogee, Indian Territory, January 3, 1907.

---

Supplemental testimony in the matter of making proof of the marriage of Matilda Sturdivant to her Cherokee husband, prior to November 1, 1875.

---

Lewis L. Duckworth, being sworn by W. W. Chappell, a Notary Public, testified as follows:

COMMISSIONER:

Q. What is your name? A. Lewis L. Duckworth.
Q. Your age? A. 64.
Q. Your post office address? A. Siloam Springs, Arkansas.
Q. You claim to be a citizen by intermarriage of the Cherokee Nation? A. Yes sir.
Q. Do you know Matilda Sturdivant? A. Yes sir.
Q. How long have you known her? A. I don't know just exactly but from some time in the latter part of '66.
Q. Was she married when you first knew her? A. Yes sir.
Q. To whom? A. Sturdivant -- we called him Buck. I don't know what his name was.
Q. You don't know, of your own knowledge, anything regarding the marriage -- the ceremony of this marriage? A. No sir.
Q. During your acquaintance with these people did they live together as husband and wife? A. Yes sir, they have been living together ever since I got acquainted with them. I reckon I knew them before that time, but to be certain, I will say about the latter part of 1866.
Q. Do you know who married these people? A. No sir, I don't.

# Cherokee Intermarried White 1906
## Volume III

Witness excused.

Anna Eliza Chandler, being sworn by W. W. Chappell, a Notary Public, testified as follows:

COMMISSIONER:

Q. What is your name? A. Anna Eliza Chandler.
Q. What is your age? A. 59.
Q. What is your post office address? A. Vinita.
Q. Do you know Matilda Sturdivant, and if so, how long have you known her?
A. I have known her ever since we were girls.
Q. Did you know her prior to the time of her marriage with Martin B. Sturdivant?
A. Yes sir, I knew her before she was married
Q. Do you know when she was married? A. No sir, I think she must have been married sometime in '66.
Q. Do you know the man she married? A. I have seen him, and knowed[sic] him all along when I would see him.
Q. You were not present at the marriage? A. No sir.
Q. Are you related to Matilda Sturdivant in any way? A. No sir.
Q. You do not know anything, of your own personal knowledge, as to that marriage?
A. No sir, only I heard that she -- that they were married, and then I seen them afterwards, but I couldn't say for I wasn't there -- I wouldn't say.
Q. They lived together as man and wife, and held themselves out as such in that community from 1866? A. Yes sir, to just as long as I knowed[sic] them.

Witness excused.

-------------------------------------------------------

Eula Jeanes Branson, being sworn, states that she correctly reported the proceedings had in the above and foregoing on the 3rd. day of January, 1907.

Eula Jeanes Branson

Subscribed and sworn to before me this the 3rd. day of January, 1907.

Edward Merrick
Notary Public.

# Cherokee Intermarried White 1906
# Volume III

F.R.                                                                                     Cherokee 2853.

## DEPARTMENT OF THE INTERIOR,
## COMMISSIONER TO THE FIVE CIVILIZED TRIBES.
Muskogee, I. T., January 11, 1907.

In the matter of the application for the enrollment of Matilda Sturdevant[sic] as a citizen by intermarriage of the Cherokee Nation.

Jesse Barnett, being first duly sworn by Walter W. Chappell, a Notary Public for the Western District, Indian Territory, testified as follows:

### SUPPLEMENTAL TESTIMONY.

By the Commissioner:
Q What is your name? A Jesse Barnett.
Q How old are you? A Going on 54 years.
Q What is your postoffice address? A Leach, I. T.
Q You appear here for the purpose of giving testimony relative to the right to enrollment of Matilda Sturdevant as a citizen by intermarriage of the Cherokee nation, do you? A Yes sir.
Q How long have you known Matilda Sturdevant? A Ever since I can remember.
Q About how many years? A Ever since I can remember; ever since I was a child.
Q Do you know to whom Matilda Sturdevant was married? A Yes, Martin B. Sturdevant.
Q When was she married to him? A They must have been married along in 1870, as well as I remember.
Q Was you present at the ceremony? A Yes sir.
Q Were they married in accordance with Cherokee laws? A I think so; the best I understand Cherokee law they was
Q Was it under a license of the Cherokee nation? A No, I think not.
Q Mr. Sturdevant, being a citizen, was not required to have a license? A No sir.
Q Do you know where they were married? A Yes sir, up close to the line of Going Snake and Delaware Districts:
Q Who married them? A I have forgotten.
Q It has always been the understanding, has it, that Martin B. Sturdevant and Matilda Sturdevant were married in accordance with the Cherokee laws? A Yes, it was my understanding.
Q Do you know whether or not Martin B. Sturdevant was married prior to the time he married Matilda Sturdevant? A The only marriage I ever heard of either one of them.
Q Is Matilda Sturdevant living at this time? A I think so I have not seen her for sometime.
Q About how long since you have seen her? A It has been 10 or 12 years since I saw her.

## Cherokee Intermarried White 1906
## Volume III

Q From the time of their marriage up until the last time you saw Matilda Sturdevant, did Matilda Sturdevant and Martin B. Sturdevant live together continuously as husband and wife in the Cherokee Nation? A Yes sir.
Witness excused.

----------

Martin B. Sturdevant, being first duly sworn by Walter W. Chappelle[sic], a Notary Public for the Western District of Indian Territory, testified as follows:

By the Commissioner:
Q What is your name? A Martin B. Sturdevant.
Q What is your age? A Sixty-two.
Q What is your postoffice address? A Grove, I. T.
Q You appear here for the purpose of giving testimony relative to the right to enrollment of Matilda Sturdevant as a citizen by intermarriage of the Cherokee nation? A Yes sir.
Q She is your wife? A Yes sir.
Q When were you married to her? A I think it was 1866.
Q You are a citizen of the Cherokee nation by blood? A Yes sir.
Q And you were recognized as such citizen at the time you married Matilda Sturdevant? A Yes sir.
Q The marriage ceremony was in accordance with the laws of the Cherokee nation? A Yes sir.
Q Is Matilda Sturdevant living at this time? A Yes sir.
Q Have you and Matilda Sturdevant lived together as husband and wife continuously in the Cherokee Nation since the time of your marriage to her until the present time? A Yes sir.
Q At the time of your marriage did you secure a certificate from the person performing the ceremony, or any papers or records of the license? A No, he said he would have it recorded at Bentonville, Arkansas.
Q By whom were you married? A Married by a man by the name of Dr. Powell.
Q Was he a preacher? A Yes sir.
Q Did I understand you to say that the marriage was performed in the Cherokee nation? A Yes sir.
Q Why would it be filed for record at Bentonville, Ark.? A I don't know why.
Q After it was filed for record was it ever returned to you? A No sir.
Q Did you ever endeavor to secure a copy of that record? A No sir.

Witness excused.

George Still being first duly sworn by Walter W. Chappelle, a Notary Public for the Western District of Indian Territory, testified as follows;

By the Commissioner:
Q What is your name? A George Still.
Q What is your age? A Sixty-one.

## Cherokee Intermarried White 1906
## Volume III

Q What is your postoffice address? A Leach, I. T.
Q You appear here for the purpose of giving testimony relative to the right to enrollment of Matilda Sturdevant as a citizen by intermarriage of the Cherokee Nation? A Yes sir.
Q How long have you known Matilda Sturdevant? A I can't tell just how long it has been.
Q About how long to the best of your recollection? A It was before the war. I have known her ever since.
Q Did you know her at the time she was married to Martin B. Sturdevant? A Yes sir.
Q Were you present at that marriage? A No I was not there when they was married; but they said they was married, and they have been living together ever since.
Q Then it has always been the understanding that Martin B. Sturdevant and Matilda Sturdevant were married in accordance with the laws of the Cherokee nation? A Yes sir.
Q And they have lived together continuously as man and wife in the Cherokee nation ever since their marriage? A Yes sir.
Q Not having been present at the marriage you don't know of your own knowledge who performed the ceremony, do you? A No, I was not there. I aint[sic] got any education or anything of the kind.
Witness excused.

J. H. Gibson being first duly sworn by Walter W. Chappell, a Noatry[sic] Public for the Western District of Indian Territory, testified as follows:

By the Commissioner:
Q What is your name? A J. H. Gibson.
Q Your age? A Forty-five.
Q Your postoffice address? A Grove, I. T.
Q You appear here for the purpose of giving testimony relative to the rirght[sic] to enrollment of Matilsa[sic] Sturdevant as a citizen by intermarriage of the Cherokee nation? A Yes.
Q How long have you known Matilda Sturdevant? A About twenty years.
Q Where has she resided during all the time you have known her? A For 7 or 8 years, nine miles west of Siloam Springs in the Cherokee Nation, Indian Territory, and the remaining time, for the past 12 years--something like 12 years, she has lived on cow skin prairie near Grove.
Q Do you know her husband, Martin B. Sturdevant? A Yes.
Q How long have you known him? A Over twenty years.
Q During the 20 years you say you have been acquainted with Matilda Sturdevant and her husband Martin B. Sturdevant have they lived together within the Cherokee nation as man and wife? A Yes sir.
Q They have been held out as such in the community, and so regarded by their neighbors? A Yes sir.

-----------

Frances R. Lane upon oath, states that as stenographer to the Commissioner to the Five Civilized Tribes she reported the testimony in the above entitled cause and that the foregoing is an accurate transcript of her stenographic notes thereof.

## Cherokee Intermarried White 1906
## Volume III

Frances R. Lane

Subscribed and sworn to before me this January 11, 1907.

Edward Merrick
Notary Public.

◇◇◇◇◇

C.E.W.

Cherokee 2853.

DEPARTMENT OF THE INTERIOR,

COMMISSIONER TO THE FIVE CIVILIZED TRIBES.

---

In the matter of the application for the enrollment of as a citizen by intermarriage of the Cherokee Nation.

D E C I S I O N

THE RECORDS OF THIS OFFICE SHOW: That at Vinita, Indian Territory, September 17, 1900, application was received by the Commission to the Five Civilized Tribes for the enrollment of Matilda Sturdivant, as a citizen by intermarriage of the Cherokee Nation. Further proceedings in the matter of said application were had at Tahlequah, Indian Territory, October 20, 1902, an at Muskogee, Indian Territory, January 3 and 11, 1907.

THE EVIDENCE IN THIS CASE SHOWS: That the applicant herein, Matilda Sturdivant, a white woman, was married in accordance with Cherokee law about the year 1866 you her husband, Martin B. Sturdivant, who was at the time of said marriage a recognized citizen by blood of the Cherokee Nation, who is identified on the Cherokee authenticated tribal roll of 1880, Going Snake District, page 476, number 1644, as a native Cherokee, and whose name appears upon the approved partial roll of citizens by blood of the Cherokee Nation, opposite number 7167; that since said marriage the said Martin B. Sturdivant and Matilda Sturdivant have resided together as husband and wife and have continuously lived in the Cherokee Nation. Said applicant is identified on the Cherokee authenticated tribal roll of 1880, and the Cherokee census roll of 1896 as an intermarried citizen of the Cherokee Nation.

IT IS, THEREFORE, ORDERED AND ADJUDGED: That in accordance with the decision of the Supreme Court of the United States, dated November 5, 1906, in the cases of Daniel Red Bird et al., vs. the United States, Nos. 125, 126, 127 and 128, the said Matilda Sturdivant is entitled, under the provisions of Section 21 of the Act of Congress approved June 28, 1898 (30 Stat., 495), to enrollment, as a citizen by intermarriage of the Cherokee Nation, and her application for enrollment as such is accordingly granted.

## Cherokee Intermarried White 1906
## Volume III

Tams Bixby<br>Commissioner.

Dated at Muskogee, Indian Territory,
this    JAN 21 1907

◇◇◇◇◇

Cherokee
2853

Muskogee, Indian Territory, December 24, 1906.

Matilda Sturdivant,
    Grove, Indian Territory.

Dear Madam:

    November 6, 1906, the United States Supreme Court held that white persons who intermarried with Cherokee citizens according to Cherokee law prior to November 1, 1875, are entitled to enrollment and allotments of land as citizens of the Cherokee Nation.

    You are advised that to properly determine your right to enrollment as a citizen by intermarriage of the Cherokee Nation, it will be necessary for you to appear before the Commissioner for the purpose of giving testimony as to the date of your marriage and whether or not your husband, by reason of your marriage to whom you claim the right to enrollment as a citizen by intermarriage of the Cherokee Nation, was a recognized Cherokee citizen at the time of your marriage to him.

    You are, therefore, directed to appear before the Commissioner at Muskogee, Indian Territory, at 9 o'clock A. M., on Thursday, January 3, 1907, and give testimony as above indicated.

Respectfully,

JMH Acting Commissioner.

◇◇◇◇◇

## Cherokee Intermarried White 1906
## Volume III

Cherokee 2853

Muskogee, Indian Territory, January 21, 1907.

W. W. Hastings,
    Attorney for the Cherokee Nation,
        Muskogee, Indian Territory.

Dear Sir:

    There is enclosed herewith copy of the decision of the Commissioner to the Five Civilized Tribes, dated January 21, 1907, granting the application for the enrollment of Matilda Sturdivant as a citizen by intermarriage of the Cherokee Nation.

        Respectfully,

Enc I-41
RPI
        Commissioner.

◇◇◇◇◇

Cherokee 2853    W.W. HASTINGS.    OFFICE OF    H.M. VANCE.
        ATTORNEY.                                SECRETARY.

### Attorney for the Cherokee Nation,
MUSKOGEE, I. T.    January 21, 1907.

The Commissioner to the Five Civilized Tribes,
    Muskogee, Indian Territory.

Sir:

    Receipt is acknowledged of the testimony and of your decision enrolling Matilda Sturdivant as a citizen by intermarriage of the Cherokee Nation. Time for protesting said decision is waived and I consent that said person may be placed upon the schedule immediately.

        Respectfully,
        W. W. Hastings
        Attorney for the Cherokee Nation.

◇◇◇◇◇

## Cherokee Intermarried White 1906
## Volume III

Cherokee 2853

Muskogee, Indian Territory, January 24, 1907.

Matilda Sturdivant,
Grove, Indian Territory.

Dear Madam:

There is enclosed herewith copy of the decision of the Commissioner to the Five Civilized Tribes, dated January 17, 1907, granting the application for your enrollment as a citizen by intermarriage of the Cherokee Nation.

You will be advised when your name has been placed upon a schedule of citizens of the Cherokee Nation and approved by the Secretary of the Interior.

Respectfully,

Enc I-105
RPI

Commissioner.

---

**Cher IW 73**
**Trans from Cher 2963  3-15-07**

◇◇◇◇◇

E.C.M.

DEPARTMENT OF THE INTERIOR,

COMMISSIONER TO THE FIVE CIVILIZED TRIBES.

---

In the matter of the application for the enrollment of

NANCY E. ROGERS

As a citizen by intermarriage of the Cherokee Nation.

---

CHEROKEE NO. 2963.

◇◇◇◇◇

## Cherokee Intermarried White 1906
## Volume III

DEPARTMENT OF THE INTERIOR.
COMMISSION TO THE FIVE CIVILIZED TRIBES.
VINITA, I. T., SEPTEMBER 18th, 1900.

IN THE MATTER OF THE APPLICATION OF Thomas T. Rogers, wife and children for enrollment as citizens of the Cherokee Nation, and he being sworn by Commissioner, T. B. Needles, testified as follows:

Q What is your name? A Thomas T. Rogers.
Q What is your age? A Fifty three.
Q What is your Postoffice? A South West City, Missouri.
Q What district do you live in? A Delaware.
Q Are you a recognized citizen of the Cherokee Nation? A Yes sir.
Q By blood? A Yes sir.
Q What degree of blood do you claim? A One eighth?[sic]
Q For whom do you apply for enrollment? A Myself, wife and five children.
Q What is the name of your father? A Robert R. Rogers.
Q Is he living? A Dead.
Q Was he a Cherokee citizen by blood? A Yes sir.
Q What is the name of your mother? A Batise
Q Her first name A Mary A.
Q Is she living? A She is dead.
Q Was she a Cherokee citizen by blood? A No sir.
Q What is the name of your wife? A Elizabeth; Nancy Elizabeth.
Q How old is she? A Forty four years old.
Q Is she a Cherokee citizen by blood? A No sir.
Q She was a white person? A Yes sir.
Q Have you a certificate of marriage? A No sir; we married in 1874.
Q Have you been living with your wife ever since 1874? A Yes sir.
Q What is the name of your wifes[sic] father? A William E. Brink.
Q Is he a non citizen? A Yes sir.
Q Is her mother a non citizen? A Yes sir.
Q Have you any children at home, under twenty one years of age?
A Rolie[sic] E. Rogers.
Q How old is he? A Twenty.
Q What is the name of the next one? A Zilpha.
Q How old is Zilpha? A Seventeen.
Q What is the name of the next one? A William E.
Q How old? A Eleven.
Q Are these children living with you at this time? A Yes sir.

    (1880 Roll, Page 304, #2149, Thomas Rogers, Delaware District)
    (1880 Roll, Page 304, #2150, Nancy Rogers, Delaware District)
    (1896 Roll, Page 523, #2582, Thomas T. Rogers, Delaware Dis't)
    (1896 Roll, Page 523, #458, Nancy E. Rogers, Delaware District)
    (1896 Roll, Page 523, #2585, Rollie E. Rogers, Delaware Dis't)

## Cherokee Intermarried White 1906
## Volume III

(1896 Roll, Page 523, #2586, Zilpha E. Rogers, Delaware  " )
(1896 Roll, Page 523, #2587, William E. Rogers, Delaware  " )

The name of Thomas T. Rogers, and that of his wife, Nancy Elizabeth, appearing on the authenticated roll of 1880, he as Thomas Rogers, and she as Nancy Rogers; their names also appearing on the census roll of 1896 as Thomas T. and Nancy E. Rogers; and the names of their children, Rolie E., Zilpha E., and William E. Rogers, appearing upon the census roll of 1896; they all being fully identified, and having made satisfactory proof of their residence, the said Thomas T. Rogers, and his wife and children, as enumerated in the testimony will be duly listed for enrollment by this Commission as Cherokee citizens by blood.

The undersigned, being sworn, states that as stenographer to the Commission to the Five Civilized Tribes, he correctly recorded the testimony and proceedings in this case, and that the foregoing is a true and complete transcript of his stenographic notes thereof.

R R Cravens

Subscribed and sworn to before me
this 19th day of September, 1900.

TB Needles
C O M M I S S I O N E R .

◇◇◇◇◇

BCJ

Cherokee 2963

Department of the Interior,
Commission to the Five Civilized Tribes,
Cherokee Land Office,
Tahlequah, I.T., August 19, 1903.

In the matter of the application of Thomas T. Rogers for the enrollment of himself and his children, Rollie E., Zilpha E. and William E. Rogers, as citizens by blood, and for the enrollment of his wife, Nancy E. Rogers, as a citizen by intermarriage of the Cherokee Nation.

SUPPLEMENTAL TESTIMONY.

Principal applicant present in person;
Cherokee Nation not represented.

THOMAS T. ROGERS, being duly sworn and examined by the Commission, testified as follows:

## Cherokee Intermarried White 1906
## Volume III

Q What is your name? A Thomas T. Rogers.
Q How old are you? A About 57.
Q What is your postoffice address? A Dodge.
Q Do you claim to be a citizen by blood of the Cherokee Nation? A Yes sir.
Q Have you got a wife named Nancy E.? A Yes sir.
Q She claims to be a citizen by intermarriage? A Yes sir.
Q You have three children named Rollie E., Zilpha E. and William E.? A Yes sir.
Q These are under age, are they? A William E. is under age.
Q Give me the names of all of your children? A Laura A. Rogers.
Q What is the next one? A Thomas J. Rogers, Rollie E. Rogers, Zilpha E. Rogers and William E. Rogers.
Q You have 5 children? A Yes sir.
Q Your present wife is the mother of all these children? A Yes.
Q Your mother was a citizen of the Creek Nation was she? A Yes.
Q Have you ever applied to this Commission to be enrolled as a Creek? A No sir, not to this Commission.
Q Is your name on any Creek roll? A I reckon; I made application and they enrolled me on the Creek roll.
Q What roll? A I don't know just what roll; it was about the time the Commission come in here.
Q About '93? A I have a certificate, didn't bring it with me; didn't think it was necessary; I am so forgetful, can't remember dates.
Q A certificate of what? A Of citizenship in the Creek Nation.
Q Where did you get that certificate? A At Okmulgee.
Q From the Creek Council? A Yes sir.
Q Were you ever admitted to citizenship in the Creek Nation by the Creek Council? A They admitted me at that time; I was living in the Cherokee Nation; lived here the biggest portion of the time.
Q You state, however, that you have never applied to this Commission to be enrolled as a citizen of the Creek Nation? A No sir. Yes, I did too; I was rejected on the ground that I could not hold rights in both nations. They give me the preference to enroll in that nation and I wouldn't accept that then.
Q When did you make application, in what year? A 5 or 6 years ago I reckon, in the neighborhood.
Q You elected to be enrolled as a citizen of the Cherokee Nation, did you? A Yes sir.
Q It is still your desire to be enrolled as a citizen of the Cherokee Nation, is it? A Yes sir.

++++++++++++++++++++++++

Mabel F. Maxwell, being duly sworn, states that, as stenographer to the Commission to the Five Civilized Tribes, she correctly recorded the supplemental testimony taken in this case, and that the above and foregoing is a true and complete transcript of her stenographic notes thereof.

Mabel F. Maxwell

# Cherokee Intermarried White 1906
# Volume III

Subscribed and sworn to before me this 19th day of August, 1903.

> Samuel Foreman
> Notary Public.

◇◇◇◇◇

Cherokee 2963.

> Department of the Interior,
> Commission to the Five Civilized Tribes,
> Muskogee, I. T., October 14, 1902.

In the matter of the application of Thomas T. Rogers for the enrollment of himself and children, Rollie E., Zilpha E. and William E. Rogers, as citizens by blood, and for the enrollment of his wife, Nancy E. Rogers, as a citizen by intermarriage of the Cherokee Nation; he being sworn and examined by the Commission, testified as follows:

Q What is your name? A Thomas T. Rogers.
Q How old are you? A About fifty-seven I guess.
Q What is your postoffice? A Dodge, Indian Territory.
Q Are you a Cherokee by blood? A Yes sir.
Q How long have you lived in the Cherokee Nation? A All my life, or the greater portion of it.
Q Have you lived here since 1880? A Yes sir.
Q What is your wife's name? A Nancy E.
Q Was she your wife in 1880? A Yes sir.
Q Is she on the roll with you as an intermarried woman? A Yes sir.
Q Have you and your wife lived in the Cherokee Nation since 1880? A Yes sir.
Q Never been separated? A No sir.
Q You were living together on the first day of last September? A Yes sir.
Q How many children at home with you? A I have five altogether.
Q How many living at home? A Four at home.
Q The oldest one is over twenty-one? A Yes sir, and the second one is over twenty-one.
Q You made application for three children when you applied here two years ago? A Yes sir.
Q These three children are living? A Yes sir.

--------------------------------

The undersigned, being duly sworn, states that as stenographer to the Commission to the Five Civilized Tribes he correctly recorded the testimony and proceedings in this case, and that the foregoing is a true and correct transcript of his stenographic notes thereof.

> E.G. Rothenberger

## Cherokee Intermarried White 1906
## Volume III

Subscribed and sworn to before me this 7th day of November, 1902.

BC Jones
Notary Public.

◇◇◇◇◇

Cherokee 2963

DEPARTMENT OF THE INTERIOR,
COMMISSIONER TO THE FIVE CIVILIZED TRIBES.
MUSKOGEE, IND. TER. JANUARY 15, 1907.

In the matter of the application for the enrollment of NANCY E. ROGERS as a citizen by intermarriage of the Cherokee Nation.

NANCY E. ROGERS being sworn by B. P. Rasmus, a Notary Public, testified as follows:

Q. What is your name? A Before I was married?
Q. Now? A. Nancy E. Rogers
Q. What is your age? A. Fifty years old.
Q. What is your postoffice address? A. Dodge, Indian Territory.
Q. You are an applicant for enrollment as a citizen by intermarriage of the Cherokee Nation are you? A. Yes sir.
Q. You have no Cherokee blood? A. No sir.
Q. Your only claim to enrollment as a citizen of the Cherokee Nation is by virtue of your marriage to a citizen of the Cherokee Nation is it? A. Yes sir.
Q. What is the name of the citizen through whom you claim the right to enrollment?
A. Thomas T. Rogers
Q. Is he living? A. Yes sir.
Q. When were you married to Thomas T. Rogers
A. November 9, 1874.
Q. Was he living in the Cherokee Nation at that time? A. Yes sir.
Q. Was he a recognized citizen of the Cherokee Nation at that time? A. Yes sir.
Q. Was he your first husband? A. Yes sir.
Q. Were you his first wife? A. Yes sir.
Q. Since your marriage to Thomas T. Rogers have you and he continuously resided together as husband and wife? A. Yes sir.

The applicant, Nancy E. Rogers is identified on the Cherokee authenticated tribal roll of 1880, Delaware District, No. 2150, her husband, Thomas T. Rogers is identified on said roll at No. 2149, and his name appears on the approved partial roll of citizens by blood of the Cherokee Nation opposite No. 23695.

# Cherokee Intermarried White 1906
## Volume III

Q. You have no documentary evidence have you, showing your marriage to Thomas T. Rogers? A. No sir, it was not required at that time.
Q. By whom were you married? A. By Jeff McGhee.
Q. Was he a Minister of the Gospel? A. No sir; he was Clerk of the District where we were married.
Q. He was Clerk of Delaware District, Cherokee Nation, and married you during his term of office as Clerk of that District? A. Yes sir.

THOMAS T. ROGERS being first duly sworn by B. P. Rasmus, a Notary Public, testified as follows:

Q. What is your name? A. Thomas T. Rogers
Q. What is your afe[sic] A. Sixty last October.
Q. What is your postoffice address? A. Dodge, Indian Territory
Q. You are the husband of Nancy E. Rogers who has just testified? A. Yes sir.
Q. She is an applicant before this office for enrollment as a citizen by intermarriage of the Cherokee Nation is she? A. Yes sir.
Q. She claims the right to enrollment as a citizen by intermarriage of the Cherokee Nation by virtue of her marriage to you, does she? A. Yes sir.
Q. When were you and she married? A. The ninth day of November, 1874.
Q. Is she your first wife? A. Yes sir.
Q. Are you her first husband? A. Yes sir.
Q. Since your marriage to her have you and she continuously lived together as husband and wife? A. Yes sir.
Q. And resided continuously in the Cherokee Nation? A. Yes sir.

----------------------------------------------------------------------

The undersigned being first duly sworn states that as stenographer to the Commissioner to the Five Civilized Tribes she correctly recorded the testimony taken in this case, and that the above and foregoing is a full, true and correct transcript of her stenographic notes thereof.

Lucy M. Bowman

Subscribed and sworn to before me this 17th day of January, 1907.

B.P. Rasmus
Notary Public.

## Cherokee Intermarried White 1906
## Volume III

E C M

Cherokee 2963.

### DEPARTMENT OF THE INTERIOR,

### COMMISSIONER TO THE FIVE CIVILIZED TRIBES.

In the matter of the application for the enrollment of NANCY E. ROGERS as a citizen by intermarriage of the Cherokee Nation.

### D E C I S I O N

THE RECORDS OF THIS OFFICE SHOW: That on September 18th, 1900 application was received by the Commission to the Five Civilized Tribes for the enrollment of Nancy E. Rogers as a citizen by intermarriage of the Cherokee Nation. Further proceedings in the matter of said application were had at Tahlequah, Indian Territory, August 19th, 1903 and at Muskogee, Indian Territory, October 14th, 1902 and January 15th, 1907.

THE EVIDENCE IN THIS CASE SHOWS: That the applicant herein, Nancy E. Rogers, a white woman, married on November 9th, 1874 one Thomas T. Rogers, who was at the time of said marriage a recognized citizen by blood of the Cherokee Nation, who is identified on the Cherokee authenticated tribal roll of 1880, Delaware District No. 2149 as a native Cherokee, and whose name appears upon the approved partial roll of citizens by blood of the Cherokee Nation. It is further shown that from the time of said marriage the said Thomas T. Rogers and Nancy E. Rogers resided together as husband and wife and continuously lived in the Cherokee Nation up to and including September 1st, 1902. Said applicant is identified on the Cherokee authenticated tribal roll of 1880 and the Cherokee census roll of 1896 as an intermarried citizen of the Cherokee Nation.

IT IS, THEREFORE, ORDERED AND ADJUDGED: That in accordance with the decision of the Supreme Court of the United States, dated November 5, 1906, in the cases of Daniel Red Bird et al., vs. the United States, Nos. 125, 126, 127 and 128, the said applicant, Nancy E. Rogers is entitled, under the provisions of Section Twenty-one of the Act of Congress approved June 28, 1898 (30 Stats. 495), to enrollment as a citizen by intermarriage of the Cherokee Nation, and her application for enrollment as such is accordingly granted.

Tams Bixby
Commissioner.

Dated at Muskogee, Indian Territory,
this    JAN 23 1907

## Cherokee Intermarried White 1906
## Volume III

Cherokee
2963

Muskogee, Indian Territory, December 24, 1906.

Nancy E. Rogers,
    Southwest City, Missouri.

Dear Madam:

    November 6, 1906, the United States Supreme Court held that white persons who intermarried with Cherokee citizens according to Cherokee law prior to November 1, 1875, are entitled to enrollment and allotments of land as citizens of the Cherokee Nation.

    You are advised that to properly determine your right to enrollment as a citizen by intermarriage of the Cherokee Nation, it will be necessary for you to appear before the Commissioner for the purpose of giving testimony as to the date of your marriage and whether or not your husband, by reason of your marriage to whom you claim the right to enrollment as a citizen by intermarriage of the Cherokee Nation, was a recognized Cherokee citizen at the time of your marriage to him.

    You are, therefore, directed to appear before the Commissioner at Muskogee, Indian Territory, at 9 o'clock A. M., on Thursday, January 3, 1907, and give testimony as above indicated.

                                Respectfully,

JMH                                               Acting Commissioner.

◇◇◇◇◇

Cherokee 2963

                                    Muskogee, Indian Territory, January 23, 1907.

W. W. Hastings,
    Attorney for the Cherokee Nation,
        Muskogee, Indian Territory.

Dear Sir:

    There is enclosed herewith copy of the decision of the Commissioner to the Five Civilized Tribes, dated January 23, 1907, granting the application for the enrollment of Nancy E. Rogers, as a citizen by intermarriage of the Cherokee Nation.

# Cherokee Intermarried White 1906
## Volume III

Respectfully,

Commissioner.

Enc I-75

RPI

◇◇◇◇◇

Cherokee 2963    W.W. HASTINGS.    OFFICE OF    H.M. VANCE.
ATTORNEY.          SECRETARY.

**Attorney for the Cherokee Nation,**
MUSKOGEE, I. T.    January 23, 1907.

The Commissioner to the Five Civilized Tribes,
    Muskogee, Indian Territory.

Sir:

    Receipt is acknowledged of the testimony and of your decision enrolling Nancy E. Rogers as a citizen by intermarriage of the Cherokee Nation. Time for protesting said decision is waived and I consent that said person may be placed upon the schedule immediately.

Respectfully,
W. W. Hastings
Attorney for the Cherokee Nation.

◇◇◇◇◇

Cherokee 2963

Muskogee, Indian Territory, January 23, 1907.

Nancy E. Rogers,
    Dodge, Indian Territory.

Dear Madam:

    There is enclosed herewith copy of the decision of the Commissioner to the Five Civilized Tribes, dated January 23, 1907, granting the application for your enrollment as a citizen by intermarriage of the Cherokee Nation.

    You will be advised when your name has been placed upon a schedule of citizens of the Cherokee Nation and approved by the Secretary of the Interior.

Respectfully,

Commissioner.

Enc I-93
RPI

# Cherokee Intermarried White 1906
# Volume III

**Cher IW 74**
**Trans from Cher 3060 3-15-07**

E.C.M.

## DEPARTMENT OF THE INTERIOR,

## COMMISSIONER TO THE FIVE CIVILIZED TRIBES.

In the matter of the application for the enrollment of

ELIZA F. WARD

as a citizen by intermarriage of the Cherokee Nation.

CHEROKEE 3060.

## DEPARTMENT OF THE INTERIOR,
## COMMISSION TO THE FIVE CIVILIZED TRIBES,
## VINITA, I.T., SEPTEMBER 19, 1900.

In the matter of the application of George D. Ward for enrollment of himself, wife and one child, as citizens of the Cherokee Nation, said Ward being sworn by Commissioner Needles, testified as follows:

Q What is your name? A George D. Ward.
Q Your age? A 53.
Q Your postoffice? A Afton.
Q What district do you live in? A Delaware.
Q Are you a recognized citizen of the Cherokee Nation? A Yes.
Q By blood? A Yes.
Q What degree of blood do you claim? A 1/12.
Q For whom do [sic] apply for enrollment? A Myself, wife and one child.
Q Does you name appear upon the authenticated roll of '80? A Yes.
Q Are your father and mother living? A No sir.
Q What is the name of your wife? A Eliza.
Q When did you marry her? A 1870.
Q Her name appears upon the roll of '80? A Yes.
Q Is she a Cherokee citizen by blood? A No sir.
Q Were her father and mother non-citizens? A Yes.

## Cherokee Intermarried White 1906
## Volume III

Q What is the name of your child? A Etheylnne[sic], 13 years old.
    On '96 roll, page 55, number 3354, as Ethelyne.
Q Is this child alive and living with you? A yes.
Q Is your wife living? A Yes.
    Applicant on '80 roll, page 343, number 3067, as G.D. Ward.
    Applicant's wife on '80 roll, page 343, number 3068, as Eliza F. Ward.
    Applicant on '96 roll, page 551, number 3352.
    Applicant's wife on '96 roll, page 594, number 599.

    The names of George D. Ward and his wife, Eliza F., appears upon the authenticated roll of '80 as well as the census roll of '96, they being duly identified thereby and making satisfactory proof as to residence, will be duly listed for enrollment by this Commission, the said George D. Ward as a Cherokee by blood, and his wife as a Cherokee citizen by intermarriage; and the name of his child, Etheylnne, appears upon the census roll of '96, and being duly identified, will also be listed by this Commission as a Cherokee citizen by blood.

    The undersigned, being first duly sworn, states that as stenographer to the Commission to the Five Civilized Tribes, he correctly recorded the testimony and proceedings in this case, and that the foregoing is a true and complete transcript of his stenographic notes thereof.

                                        B McDonald

Subscribed and sworn to before me this 21st day of Sept., 1900.

                        CR Breckinridge
                                              Commissioner.

◇◇◇◇◇

Cherokee 3060.

                    Department of the Interior,
              Commission to the Five Civilized Tribes,
                Muskogee, I. T., October 17, 1902.

    In the matter of the application of George D. Ward for the enrollment of himself and child, Ethlynne Ward, as citizens by blood, and for the enrollment of his wife, Eliza F. Ward, as a citizen by intermarriage of the Cherokee Nation; he being sworn and examined by the Commission, testified as follows:

Q What is your name? A George D. Ward.
Q How old are you? A Fifty-five.
Q What is your postoffice? A Afton.
Q Are you a Cherokee by blood? A Yes sir.
Q How long have you been living in the Cherokee Nation? A Ever since I was born, only a little while during the war I was in the army.

## Cherokee Intermarried White 1906
## Volume III

Q What is your wife's name? A Eliza F. Ward.
Q Is she a white woman? A Yes sir.
Q Was she your wife in 1880? A Yes sir.
Q She is on the roll of 1880 with you as your wife? A Yes sir. We were married in 1870, the 26th of December.
Q Have you and your wife, Eliza F., been living together in the Cherokee Nation since 1880? A Yes sir.
Q Have you ever been separated? A No sir.
Q You are living together at this time are you? A Yes sir.
Q How many children have you by your wife, Eliza? A We had five, four living and one dead.
Q Three of them have enrolled themselves? A Yes sir, all married but one.
Q Which one is living at home with you? A Ethlynne.
Q That child is living? A Yes sir.
Q And has lived in the Cherokee Nation all her life has she? A Yes sir.

---------------------------------

The undersigned, being duly sworn, states that as stenographer to the Commission to the he correctly recorded the testimony and proceedings in this case, and that the foregoing is a true and complete transcript of his stenographic notes thereof.

E.G. Rothenberger

Subscribed and sworn to before me this 17th day of November, 1902.

BC Jones
Notary Public.

◇◇◇◇◇

Cherokee Field
Card No. 3060.

### DEPARTMENT OF THE INTERIOR,

### COMMISSIONER TO THE FIVE CIVILIZED TRIBES,

### MUSKOGEE, INDIAN TERRITORY, JANUARY 3, 1907.

IN THE MATTER of the application for the enrollment of Eliza F. Ward, as a citizen by intermarriage of the Cherokee Nation.

GEORGE D. WARD, being first duly sworn testified as follows;
Sworn by Walter W. Chappell, Notary Public.

### EXAMINATION

# Cherokee Intermarried White 1906
## Volume III

ON BEHALF OF THE COMMISSIONER:

Q What is your name? A George Deshields Ward.
Q What is your age? A I will be sixty, 4th day of June.
Q What is your postoffice address? A Afton.
Q Do you claim to be a citizen by intermarriage of the Cherokee Nation? A No sir, I claim to be a citizen by blood. My wife was a white woman.
Q In whose behalf do you appear here today? A In behalf of my wife Eliza F. Ward.
Q What is her name? A Eliza F. Ward.
Q Why did she not appear here today? A Because we couldn't both leave, and she couldn't come by herself, and we have a little grand-child sick.
Q Through whom does she claim her right to citizenship? A Through me, I guess.
Q What was the date of your marriage to Eliza F. Ward? A If I aint[sic] mistaken it was 1869, December 26th.
Q Where were you married? A Married on Bridge's Prairie, near Bill Hastings father's and mother's.
Q What District in the Cherokee Nation? A Delaware District.
Q Was that marriage according to the Cherokee license? A Never had no license, and didn't require any. Married by a Christian preacher, - he was a preacher.
Q Who performed the ceremony? A Reverend Farthing.
Q Have you any documentary evidence of your marriage? A No sir, never did have anything.
Q No certificate or papers? A No sir, never required anything.
Q Is the man who married you living at this time? A I can't tell you; he was preaching there in that country at that time.
Q When was the last time you heard of him? A I don't remember how long; he left there and I don't know where he went to. He was located there at that time.
Q Is there any one here who was present at that time? A If Bill Hastings is here he was there when that marriage was performed.
Q He was only three years old then? A I know. - - Mr. Moseley was there, I guess he would know.
Q There is no one present today who saw you married? A No sir, I guess not; I haven't looked around.
Q Have you and your wife lived together continuously since your marriage? A Yes sir.
Q Where were you living when you married? A Bridges Prairie.
Q Cherokee Nation? A Yes sir; her mother lived not far from Bentonville.
Q Were you a recognized citizen of the Cherokee Nation when you married your wife?
A Yes sir, I have never been anything only a citizen.
Q Were you ever married before you married your present wife? A No sir.
Q Had she ever married before she married you? A No sir.
Q Has she lived with you continuously in the Cherokee Nation since your marriage?
A Yes sir.

ON BEHALF OF THE COMMISSIONER:

## Cherokee Intermarried White 1906
## Volume III

The witness and his wife Eliza F. Ward are listed for enrollment on Cherokee card, field No. 3060. They are identified on the 1880 authenticated roll of citizens of the Cherokee Nation, opposite Nos. 3067 and 3068, respectively, Delaware District. Witness is identified on the approved partial roll of citizens of the Cherokee Nation by blood opposite No. 23787.

(Witness dismissed).

------

I, S. T. Wright, stenographer to the Commissioner to the Five Civilized Tribes, on oath, state that I recorded the testimony and proceedings had in the above entitled cause on January 3, 1907, and that the above and foregoing is a true and correct transcript of my stenographic notes thereof, taken on said date.

S.T. Wright

Subscribed and sworn to before me this January 4th, 1907.

B.P. Rasmus
NOTARY PUBLIC.

◇◇◇◇◇

C. F. B.                                                                    Cherokee 3060.

DEPARTMENT OF THE INTERIOR,
COMMISSION TO THE FIVE CIVILIZED TRIBES.
Muskogee, Indian Territory, January 7, 1907.

In the Matter of the Application for the Enrollment of Eliza F. Ward as a citizen by intermarriage of the Cherokee Nation.

APPEARANCES:  Katherine J. Ward and W. W. Ward for Applicant.
W. W. Hastings, Attorney.

Katherine J. Ward being first duly sworn by John E. Tidwell, Notary Public, testified as follows:

ON BEHALF OF COMMISSIONER.

Q What is your name?  A Katherine J. Ward.
Q What is your age?  A 62.
Q What is your post office address?
A Pryor Creek.
Q Are you a citizen of the Cherokee Nation?
A Yes; by intermarriage.

# Cherokee Intermarried White 1906
# Volume III

Q Do you know a person in the Cherokee Nation by the name of Eliza F. Ward?
A Yes sir.
Q Is she married?
A Yes sir.
Q What is her husband's name?
A George Ward.
Q Is she a Cherokee by blood?
A No sir.
Q Is her husband a Cherokee by blood?
A Yes sir.
Q She claims the right to enrollment as a citizen of the Cherokee Nation by virtue of her marriage to her husband, George Ward?
A Yes sir.
Q When was she married, do you know?
A In 1869; November I think it was.
Q Were you present at the ceremony?
A Yes sir.
Q Was her husband, George Ward, a recognized citizen of the Cherokee Nation at the time she married him?
A Yes sir; at the time and before, all his life.
Q Were they residing in the Cherokee Country at that time?
A Yes sir.
Q Since their marriage, have they continuously lived together as husband and wife?
A Yes sir.
Q Never has been a separation of any king?
A No sir.
Q And they have always lived in the Cherokee country?
A Yes sir.

W. W. Ward being first duly sworn by John E. Tidwell, Notary Public, testified as follows:

ON BEHALF OF COMMISSIONER.

Q What is your name?      A W. W. Ward.
Q What is your age?        A 52.
Q What is your post office address?
A Claremore, Indian Territory.
Q Are you a citizen by blood of the Cherokee Nation?
A Yes sir.
Q Do you know a person in the Cherokee Nation by the name of George Ward?
A Yes sir.
Q Is he a Cherokee by blood?
A Yes sir.
Q Is he married?
A Yes sir.

## Cherokee Intermarried White 1906
## Volume III

Q What is his wife's name?
A Eliza.
Q What is her full name?
A That's all I know of it.
Q How long have you known George Ward and his wife?
A I have known him all my life; 52 years.
Q He is a citizen by blood of the Nation?
A Yes sir.
Q His wife is not a citizen by blood?
A No sir; by adoption.
Q She claims the right to enrollment as a citizen of the Cherokee Nation by virtue of her marriage to him?
A Yes sir.
Q When were they married?
A I don't remember the date; between '60 and '70.
Q Do you remember when they were married?
A Yes sir.
Q Were you present at the marriage ceremony?
A No sir.
Q Were you living near where they were at the time they were married?
A Within about two miles of where they were married.
Q You know of the marriage at the time it was solemnized?
A Yes sir; they were married about two miles from home and then they came over and took dinner.
Q You know of your own personal knowledge that since that time George Ward and his wife Eliza F. Ward have continuously resided together as man and wife and have lived in the Cherokee Nation all that time?
A Yes sir.

---

The undersigned being first duly sworn states that as stenographer to the Commission to the Five Civilized Tribes, she correctly recorded the testimony taken in this case and that the foregoing is a full, true and correct transcript of her stenographic notes thereof.

Myrtle Hill

Subscribed and sworn to before me this the 8th day of January, 1907.

John E. Tidwell
Notary Public.

## Cherokee Intermarried White 1906
## Volume III

E.C.M.                                                                                              Cherokee 3060.

### DEPARTMENT OF THE INTERIOR,

### COMMISSIONER TO THE FIVE CIVILIZED TRIBES.

---

In the matter of the application for the enrollment of ELIZA F. WARD as a citizen by intermarriage of the Cherokee Nation.

### D E C I S I O N

THE RECORDS OF THIS OFFICE SHOW: That at Vinita, Indian Territory, September 19, 1900, application was received by the Commission to the Five Civilized Tribes for the enrollment of Eliza F. Ward as a citizen by intermarriage of the Cherokee Nation. Further proceedings in the matter of said application were had a Muskogee, Indian Territory, October 17, 1902, and January 3 and 7, 1907.

THE EVIDENCE IN THIS CASE SHOWS: That the applicant herein, Eliza F. Ward, a white woman, married December 26, 1869, or 1870, one George D. Ward, who was at the time of said marriage a recognized citizen by blood of the Cherokee Nation, and whose name appears on the approved partial roll of citizens by blood of the Cherokee Nation, opposite No. 23787, and who is identified on the Cherokee authenticated tribal roll of 1880, Delaware District, No. 3067, as a native Cherokee; that from the time of said marriage the said George D. Ward and Eliza F. Ward resided together as husband and wife, and continuously lived in the Cherokee Nation up to and including September 1, 1902. Said Eliza F. Ward is identified on the Cherokee authenticated tribal roll of 1880, and the Cherokee census roll of 1896, as an intermarried citizen of the Cherokee Nation.

IT IS, THEREFORE, ORDERED AND ADJUDGED: That in accordance with the decision of the Supreme Court of the United States, dated November 5, 1906, in the cases of Daniel Red Bird et al. vs. the United States, Nos. 125, 126, 127 and 128, the said applicant, Eliza F. Ward, is entitled, under the provisions of Section 21, of the Act of Congress approved June 28, 1898 (30 Stats., 495), to enrollment as a citizen by intermarriage of the Cherokee Nation, and her application for enrollment as such is accordingly granted.

                                                                Tams Bixby
                                                                            Commissioner.

Dated at Muskogee, Indian Territory,
this     JAN 21 1907

◇◇◇◇◇

## Cherokee Intermarried White 1906
## Volume III

Cherokee
3060

Muskogee, Indian Territory, December 24, 1906.

Eliza F. Ward,
    Afton, Indian Territory.

Dear Madam:

    November 6, 1906, the United States Supreme Court held that white persons who intermarried with Cherokee citizens according to Cherokee law prior to November 1, 1875, are entitled to enrollment and allotments of land as citizens of the Cherokee Nation.

    You are advised that to properly determine your right to enrollment as a citizen by intermarriage of the Cherokee Nation, it will be necessary for you to appear before the Commissioner for the purpose of giving testimony as to the date of your marriage and whether or not your husband, by reason of your marriage to whom you claim the right to enrollment as a citizen by intermarriage of the Cherokee Nation, was a recognized Cherokee citizen at the time of your marriage to him.

    You are, therefore, directed to appear before the Commissioner at Muskogee, Indian Territory, at 9 o'clock A. M., on Thursday, January 3, 1907, and give testimony as above indicated.

Respectfully,

JMH                                               Acting Commissioner.

◇◇◇◇◇

Cherokee 3060

Muskogee, Indian Territory, January 21, 1907.

W. W. Hastings,
    Attorney for the Cherokee Nation,
        Muskogee, Indian Territory.

Dear Sir:

    There is enclosed herewith copy of the decision of the Commissioner to the Five Civilized Tribes, dated January 21, 1907, granting the application for the enrollment of Eliza F. Ward as a citizen by intermarriage of the Cherokee Nation.

# Cherokee Intermarried White 1906
# Volume III

Respectfully,

Commissioner.

Enc I-30

RPI

◇◇◇◇◇

Cherokee 3060     W.W. HASTINGS.    OFFICE OF    H.M. VANCE.
                      ATTORNEY.                                    SECRETARY.

### Attorney for the Cherokee Nation,

MUSKOGEE, I. T.    January 21, 1907.

The Commissioner to the Five Civilized Tribes,
       Muskogee, Indian Territory.

Sir:

       Receipt is acknowledged of the testimony and of your decision enrolling Eliza F. Ward as a citizen by intermarriage of the Cherokee Nation. Time for protesting said decision is waived and I consent that said person may be placed upon the schedule immediately.

Respectfully,

W. W. Hastings
Attorney for the Cherokee Nation.

◇◇◇◇◇

Cherokee 3060

                  Muskogee, Indian Territory, January 24, 1907.

Eliza F. Ward,
       Afton, Indian Territory.

Dear Madam:

       There is enclosed herewith a copy of the decision of the Commissioner to the Five Civilized Tribes, dated January 21, 1907, granting the application for your enrollment as a citizen by intermarriage of the Cherokee Nation.

       You will be advised when your name has been placed upon a schedule of citizens of the Cherokee Nation and approved by the Secretary of the Interior.

Respectfully,

Commissioner.

Encl. H-7
   JMH

# Cherokee Intermarried White 1906
## Volume III

Cher IW 75
Trans from Cher 3072  3-15-07

C.E.W.

### DEPARTMENT OF THE INTERIOR,

### COMMISSIONER TO THE FIVE CIVILIZED TRIBES.

In the matter of the application for the enrollment of

ISAAC M. MODE

as a citizen by intermarriage of the Cherokee Nation.

CHEROKEE 3072

### DEPARTMENT OF THE INTERIOR,
### COMMISSION TO THE FIVE CIVILIZED TRIBES,
### VINITA, I.T., SEPTEMBER 20, 1900.

In the matter of the application of Isaac Mode for the enrollment of himself, wife and children as citizens of the Cherokee Nation said Mode being sworn by Commissioner C. R. Breckinridge, testified as follows:

Q Give me your full name, please?  A Isaac Mode.
Q How old are you?  A 64.
Q What is your post office?  A Vinita.
Q In what district do you live?  A Delaware.
Q Who is it you want to have put on the roll?  A Myself, wife and eight children.
Q Do you apply for yourself, as a Cherokee by blood?  A Adoption.
Q Your wife a Cherokee by blood?  A Yes, sir.
Q What proportion of Cherokee blood does she claim?  A I do not know.
Q Have you your marriage license and certificate?  A Yes, sir.
    Com'r Breckinridge:--The applicant presents a Cherokee license issued by the Clerk of Delaware district, December 4, 1872, authorizing his marriage to Sarah Nidiffer. The license contains an endorsement in Cherokee, which is said to be the certificate of marriage.
Q Your wife is still living?  A Yes, sir.
Q And you and she lived together ever since your marriage?  A Yes, sir.

## Cherokee Intermarried White 1906
## Volume III

Q  And lived all the time in the Cherokee Nation?  A  With the exception that I went out for my health once.
Q  In what district were you living in 1880?  A  Delaware.
Q  And in Delaware in 1896?  A  Yes, sir.
Q  How old is your wife?  A  45.
Q  Your wife's full name is Sarah Mode at this time?  A  Yes, sir
Q  Give me the name of your wife's father?  A  Isaac Nidiffer.
Q  Cherokee?  A  Yes, sir.
Q  Dead or alive?  A  Dead.
Q  How long has he been dead?  A  Ten years.
Q  Give me the given name of your wife's mother?  A  Lucy.
Q  Cherokee or white woman?  A  Cherokee.
Q  Dead or alive?  A  Dead.
Q  How long since she died?  A  I think it is 13 years.
Q  Now give me please the names of your children and their ages?
A  Francis M.; 19 years old.
Q  The next child?  A  Maud M.; 13 years old.
Q  The next child?  A  William E.; 9 years old.
Q  The next child?  A  Henry D.; 6 years old.
Q  The next child?  A  George M.; 4 years old.
Q  The next child?  A  Viola; four months old.
Q  These children are all living now are they?  A  Yes, sir.

    1880 enrollment  ;  page 287, #1734, Isaac Mode Delaware.
    1880 enrollment;  page 287, #1735, Sarah Mode, Delaware.
    1896 enrollment;  page 581, #333, Isaac Mode,          "
    1896 enrollment;  page 508, #2183, Sarah Mode,         "
    1896 enrollment;  page 508, #2185, Francis M. Mode, Delaware.
    1896 enrollment;  page 508, #2187, Maud M.         "          "
    1896 enrollment;  page 508, #2188, William E.      "          "
    1896 enrollment;  page 508, #2189, Henry D.        "          "
    1896 enrollment;  page 508, #2190, George F[sic].  "          "

Q  Your wife is a native Cherokee?  A  Yes, sir.
Q  Lived here all her life?  A  Yes, sir.

    Com'r Breckinridge:--The applicant applies for the enrollment of himself, his wife and six minor children:  His wife is identified on the rolls of 1880 and 1896 as a native Cherokee.  She has lived in the Cherokee Nation all her life, and she will be listed now for enrollment as a Cherokee by blood.  She was married before 1880.  The applicant is identified on the rolls of 1880 and 1896 as a Cherokee by adoption.  He has lived with his wife in the Cherokee Nation ever since their marriage in 1872, and he will be listed now for enrollment as a Cherokee by adoption.  Of their six children, the first five enumerated in the testimony, are identified with their parents on the roll of 1896.  They are all living at this time, and they will be listed now for enrollment a Cherokees by blood.  When the

# Cherokee Intermarried White 1906
# Volume III

Commission is supplied with a proper certificate of the birth of the youngest child, Viola Mode, this child also will be listed for enrollment as a Cherokee by blood.

---oooOOOooo---

J. O. Rosson, being first duly sworn, states that as stenographer to the Commission to the Five Civilized Tribes, he correctly recorded the testimony and proceedings in this case, and that the foregoing is a true and complete transcript of his stenographic notes thereof.

JO Rosson

Subscribed and sworn to before me this 22d day of September, 1900.

TB Needles<br>Commissioner.

R.

DEPARTMENT OF THE INTERIOR.<br>Commission to the Five Civilized Tribes.<br>Muskogee, Indian Territory, October 6th, 1902.

In the matter of the application of Isaac M. Mode for the enrollment of himself as a citizen by intermarriage of the Cherokee Nation and for the enrollment of his wife, Sarah Mode, and his children, Frances M., Maud M., William E., Henry D., Georgia[sic] and Viola Mode, as citizens by blood of the Cherokee Nation.

Supplemental to #3072.

Applicant appears in person.<br>Cherokee Nation by J. C. Starr.

ISAAC M. MODE, being duly sworn, testified as follows:
Examination by the Commission.
Q. What is your full name? A. Isaac M. Mode.
Q. You have a middle name? A. Yes, sir.
Q. Do you want to be enrolled as Isaac M. Mode? A. Yes, sir.
Q. How old are you? A. 66.
Q. What is your post office? A. Vinita.
Q. What is the name of your wife? A. Sarah Mode.
Q. When were you married to her? A. '72, as well as I recollect.

## Cherokee Intermarried White 1906
## Volume III

Q. Your wife is a Cherokee by blood? A. Yes, sir.
Q. Have you lived with her in the Cherokee Nation ever since you were married? A. Yes, sir; except went to Colorado springs for her health and was gone about-----
Q. When did you go? A. '78.
Q. Living continuously in the Cherokee Nation since 1880[sic]? A. Yes, sir.
Q. Was she your first wife? A. Yes, sir.
Q. You her first husband? A. Yes, sir.
Q. How many children have you? A. Nine.
Q. There is six under age? A. Yes, sir.
Q. How many living at home with you? A. Six.
Q. Frances M.; she living at home? A. She is living at Mr. Dickson's, my son-in-law.
Q. Where is that, in the Cherokee Nation? A. Yes, sir.
Q. Are Maud M., William E., Henry D., Georgia[sic] and Viola all living at home with you now? A. Yes, sir.

+++++++++++++++++++++++++++++++++++++++++++++++++

Jesse O. Carr, being first duly sworn, states that as stenographer to the Commission to the Five Civilized Tribes he reported the above entitled case and that the foregoing is a true and complete transcript of his stenographic notes thereof.

Jesse O. Carr

Subscribed and sworn to before me this 6th day of November, 1902.

BC Jones
Notary Public.

◇◇◇◇◇  7599
or
23794
Cherokee Field card
No. 3072.

DEPARTMENT OF THE INTERIOR

COMMISSIONER TO THE FIVE CIVILIZED TRIBES

MUSKOGEE, INDIAN TERRITORY, JANUARY 3, 1907.

IN THE MATTER of the application for the enrollment of Isaac M. Mode as a citizen by intermarriage of the Cherokee Nation.

ISAAC M. MODE, being first duly sworn by Walter W. Chappell, Notary Public, testified as follows:

EXAMINATION

# Cherokee Intermarried White 1906
# Volume III

ON BEHALF OF THE COMMISSIONER:

Q What is your name? A Isaac Mode.
Q What is your postoffice address? A Vinita, Indian Territory.
Q How old are you, Mr. Mode? A I am seventy-two years old.
Q Do you claim to be a citizen by intermarriage of the Cherokee Nation? A Yes sir.
Q Through whom do you claim this? A Sarah Elizabeth Mode.
Q Sarah Elizabeth Neidiffer was her maiden name.
Q Is she living at this time? A Yes sir.
Q When were you married to her? A 8th day of December, 1872.
Q Where were you married? A Delaware District, Cherokee Nation.
Q Were you married under a Cherokee license? A Yes sir.
Q Where did you procure that license? A Jeff McGee, clerk of the court. - No, I am wrong, Cunningham, Doctor Cunningham.
Q Where was his office? A About seven miles west of where I lived in Delaware District.
Q Have you a certified copy of that license? A No sir. I delivered it over to the Dawes Commission.
Q When did you deliver it to the Dawes Commission? A When I was allotting my land at Vinita; I have forgotten the date now.

ON BEHALF OF THE COMMISSIONER:

The record in the matter of the application of Isaac Mode for enrollment as a citizen of the Cherokee Nation, card field No. 3072, shows, that the applicant presented at Vinita, Indian Territory on September 20, 1900, a Cherokee license issued by the clerk of the Delaware District December 4, 1872, authorizing his marriage to Sarah Neidiffer, and that said license contained the endorsement in Cherokee, which it was stated was a certificate of marriage. Attention is invited to the record in this case.

Q Had you ever been married prior to your marriage to Elizabeth Mode? A No sir.
Q Where have you lived since your marriage? A Lived there in the Delaware District near Vinita.
Q Have you resided with her continuously since that time? A Yes sir.
Q Was your wife ever married prior to the time she married you? A No sir.

(Witness dismissed).

ON BEHALF OF THE COMMISSIONER:

The applicant Isaac Mode and his wife Sarah Mode are listed for enrollment on Cherokee card, field No. 3072. They are identified on the 1880 authenticated roll of citizen of the Cherokee Nation, Delaware District, opposite Nos. 1734 and 1735, respectively. Sarah Mode is included on the

## Cherokee Intermarried White 1906
## Volume III

approved partial roll of citizens by blood of the Cherokee Nation, opposite No. 7599.

I, S. T. Wright, stenographer to the Commissioner to the Five Civilized Tribes, on oath, state that I recorded the testimony and proceedings had in the above entitled cause on January 3, 1907, and that the above and foregoing is a true and correct transcript of my stenographic notes thereof, taken on said date.

ST Wright

Subscribed and sworn to before me this January 4th, 1907.

B.P. Rasmus
NOTARY PUBLIC.

◇◇◇◇◇

### COPY

This is to certify that Isaac Mode a white man was licenses to marry Sarah Nidiffer a female Cherokee on the 4th Dec 1872 and the license executed and returned 8th day December 1872. Being in accordance with an act of the National Council bearing date Oct 15th 1855 regulating intermarriage of white men with citizens of this Nation.

J. T. Cunningham

Clerk D. C. D. D.

The undersigned being first duly sworn states that as stenographer to the Commissioner to the Five Civilized Tribes, she made the above copy and that the same is a true and correct copy of the original marriage record now on file in this office.

Lola M Champlin

Subscribed and sworn to before me this 17 day of January 1907.

Chas E Webster
notary public.

◇◇◇◇◇

## Cherokee Intermarried White 1906
## Volume III

C.E.W.                                                                                                   Cherokee 3072.

### DEPARTMENT OF THE INTERIOR,

### COMMISSIONER TO THE FIVE CIVILIZED TRIBES.

---

In the matter of the application for the enrollment of Isaac M. Mode, as a citizen by intermarriage of the Cherokee Nation.

### D E C I S I O N

THE RECORDS OF THIS OFFICE SHOW: That at Vinita, Indian Territory, September 20, 1900, application was received by the Commission to the Five Civilized Tribes for the enrollment of Isaac M. Mode, as a citizen by intermarriage of the Cherokee Nation. Further proceedings in the matter of said application were had at Muskogee, Indian Territory, October 6, 1902, and January 3, 1907.

THE EVIDENCE IN THIS CASE SHOWS: That the applicant herein, Isaac M. Mode, a white man, was married in accordance with Cherokee law December 8, 1872 to his wife, Sarah Mode, who was at the time of said marriage a recognized citizen by blood of the Cherokee Nation, who is identified on the Cherokee authenticated tribal roll of 1880, Delaware District, page 287, number 1735, as a native Cherokee, and whose name appears upon the approved partial roll of citizens by blood of the Cherokee Nation, opposite number 7599; that since said marriage the said Isaac M. Mode and Sarah Mode have resided together as husband and wife and have continuously lived in the Cherokee Nation. Said Isaac M. Mode is identified on the Cherokee authenticated tribal roll of 1880, and the Cherokee census roll of 1896 as an intermarried citizen of the Cherokee Nation.

IT IS, THEREFORE, ORDERED AND ADJUDGED: That in accordance with the decision of the Supreme Court of the United States, dated November 5, 1906, in the cases of Daniel Red Bird et al., vs. the United States, Nos. 125, 126, 127 and 128, the said applicant Isaac M. Mode is entitled, under the provision of Section 21 of the Act of Congress approved June 28, 1898 (30 Stat., 495), to enrollment, as a citizen by intermarriage of the Cherokee Nation, and his application for enrollment as such is accordingly granted.

                                                     Tams Bixby
                                                                  Commissioner.

Dated at Muskogee, Indian Territory,
this      JAN 22 1907

## Cherokee Intermarried White 1906
## Volume III

*(The two letters below do not belong with the current applicant.)*

Muskogee, Indian Territory, June 8, 1906.

Thaddeus Mitchell,
    Gans, Indian Territory.

Dear Sir:

    Receipt is hereby acknowledged of application for the enrollment as a citizen of the Cherokee Nation of Nora Belle Mitchell, born March 20, 1905.

Respectfully,

Commissioner.

MMP

◇◇◇◇◇

Cherokee
N. B. 3072

Muskogee, Indian Territory, September 22, 1906

Thaddeus Mitchell,
    Gans, Indian Territory.

Dear Sir:

    In connection with the application for the enrollment of your child, Nora Belle Mitchell, as a citizen of the Cherokee Nation, you are directed to forward to this office, by return mail, either the original or a certified copy of the marriage license and certificate of yourself and said child's mother.

    You are requested to return this letter with your reply.

Respectfully,

Commissioner.

MMP

◇◇◇◇◇

## Cherokee Intermarried White 1906
## Volume III

Cherokee
3072

Muskogee, Indian Territory, December 24, 1906.

Isaac M. Mode,
    Vinita, Indian Territory.

Dear Sir:

    November 24[sic], 1906, the United States Supreme Court held that white persons who intermarried with Cherokee citizens according to Cherokee law prior to November 1, 1875, are entitled to enrollment and allotments of land as citizens of the Cherokee Nation.

    You are advised that to properly determine your right to enrollment as a citizen by intermarriage of the Cherokee Nation, it will be necessary for you to appear before the Commissioner for the purpose of giving testimony as to the date of your marriage and whether or not your wife, by reason of your marriage to whom you claim the right to enrollment as a citizen of the Cherokee Nation, was a recognized citizen of the Cherokee Nation at the time of your marriage to her, and whether or not you were married to her in accordance with Cherokee laws.

    You are, therefore, directed to appear before the Commissioner at Muskogee, Indian Territory, at 9 o'clock A. M., on Thursday, January 3, 1907, and give testimony as above indicated.

                    Respectfully,

JMH                                     Acting Commissioner.

◇◇◇◇◇

Cherokee
3072

Muskogee, Indian Territory, January 22, 1907.

W. W. Hastings,
    Attorney for the Cherokee Nation,
        Muskogee, Indian Territory.

Dear Sir:

    There is enclosed herewith a copy of the decision of the Commissioner to the Five Civilized Tribes, dated January 22, 1907, granting the application for the enrollment of Isaac M. Mode as a citizen by intermarriage of the Cherokee Nation.

## Cherokee Intermarried White 1906
## Volume III

Respectfully,

Commissioner.

Encl. H-27
JJH

◇◇◇◇◇

Cherokee 3072    W.W. HASTINGS, ATTORNEY.    OFFICE OF    H.M. VANCE, SECRETARY.

### Attorney for the Cherokee Nation,
MUSKOGEE, I. T.    January 23, 1907.

The Commissioner to the Five Civilized Tribes,
Muskogee, Indian Territory.
Sir:

    Receipt is acknowledged of the testimony and of your decision enrolling Isaac M. Mode as a citizen by intermarriage of the Cherokee Nation. Time for protesting said decision is waived and I consent that said person may be placed upon the schedule immediately.

W. W. Hastings
Yours very truly,

Attorney for Cherokee Nation.

◇◇◇◇◇

Cherokee 3072

Muskogee, Indian Territory, January 23, 1907.

Isaac M. Mode,
    Vinita, Indian Territory.

Dear Sir:

    There is enclosed herewith a copy of the decision of the Commissioner to the Five Civilized Tribes, dated January 22, 1907, granting the application for your enrollment as a citizen by intermarriage of the Cherokee Nation.

    You will be advised when your name has been placed upon a schedule of citizens of the Cherokee Nation and approved by the Secretary of the Interior.

Respectfully,

Commissioner.

Encl. H-101
JJH

# Cherokee Intermarried White 1906
## Volume III

**Cher IW 76**
**Trans from Cher 3094 3-15-07**

E.C.M.

## DEPARTMENT OF THE INTERIOR,

### COMMISSIONER TO THE FIVE CIVILIZED TRIBES.

---

In the matter of the application for the enrollment of

JINCY J. ENGLAND

as a citizen by intermarriage of the Cherokee Nation.

---

CHEROKEE 3094.

Department of the Interior,
Commission to the Five Civilized Tribes,
Vinita, I. T., September 20, 1900.

In the matter of the application of Benjamin Cornelius England for the enrollment of himself and child as Cherokees by blood and his wife as a Cherokee by intermarriage; being sworn and examined by Commissioner Needles, he testified as follows:

Q What is your name? A Benjamin Cornelius England.
Q What is your age? A 53.
Q What is your post office address? A Afton.
Q What district do you live in? A Delaware.
Q Are you a recognized citizen of the Cherokee Nation? A Yes, sir.
Q By blood? A Yes, sir.
Q What degree of blood do you claim? A About 1/8.
Q For whom do you apply? A Myself, wife and children.
Q What is the name of your father? A Joseph.
Q He living? A No, sir, he is dead.
Q What is the name of your mother? A Sabra.
Q She living? A No sir, she is dead.
Q What is the name of your wife? A Jincy J.
Q Is she a citizen by blood? A No, sir, an adopted citizen.
Q When did you marry her? A In 1869, in the spring.
Q Her father and mother non citizens? A Non citizens.

# Cherokee Intermarried White 1906
## Volume III

Q What is her age? A She is about 51.
Q What is the name of your child? A Benjamin, 14 years old
Q What is the name of the next one? A That is all.
Q He is alive and living with you? A Yes, sir.
Q How long have you lived in the Cherokee Nation? A All my life.
Q Your residence is her and always has been? A Yes, sir.
(On 1880 roll, page 253, No. 936, Bnej[sic]. England, Delaware district. Jincy J. England on 1880 roll, page 253, Jensey C[sic]. England, Delaware district. Benjamin Cornelius England on 1896 roll, page 466, No. 1024, Bnejamin[sic] Cornelius England, Delaware district. Jincy J. England on 1896 roll, page 570, No. 162, Jincy Jane England, Delaware district. Benjamin England on 1896 roll, page 466, No. 1027, Delaware district.)

  The name of Bnejamin[sic] C. England appears upon the authenticated roll of 1880 as Bnejamin[sic] England and on the census roll of 1896 as Bnejamin Cornelius, and the name of his wife appears upon the authenticated roll of 1880 as Jensey C. and upon the census roll of 1896 as Jincy Jane England. The name of his son, Benjamin, appears upon the census roll of 1896, and they all being duly identified according to the page and number of said roll, and having made satisfactory proof as to their residence, the said Bnejamin C. England and his son, Benjamin, will be duly listed for enrollment by this Commission as Cherokee citizens by blood, and his wife, Jincy J., as a Cherokee citizen by intermarriage.

-----0-----

  Bruce C. Jones, being duly sworn, says that as stenographer to the Commission to the Five Civilized Tribes her correctly recorded the proceedings and testimony in the above case, and the foregoing is a true and complete transcript of his stenographic notes thereof.

                        Bruce C. Jones
Sworn to and subscribed before me this the 20th of September, 1900.

             CR Breckinridge
                             Commissioner.

◇◇◇◇◇

R.

### DEPARTMENT OF THE INTERIOR.
### Commission to the Five Civilized Tribes.
### Muskogee, Indian Territory, October 1st, 1902.

---

  In the matter of the application of Benjamin C. England for the enrollment of himself as a citizen by blood of the Cherokee Nation; for the enrollment of his wife, Jincy J. England, as a citizen by intermarriage of the Cherokee Nation, and for the enrollment of his son, Benjamin England, as a citizen by blood of the Cherokee Nation.

---

## Cherokee Intermarried White 1906
## Volume III

Supplemental to #3094.

---

Appearance:

Applicant appears in person.
Cherokee Nation by J. C. Starr.

---

BENJAMIN C. ENGLAND, being duly sworn, testified as follows:
Examination by the Commission.
Q. What is your name? A. Benjamin C. England.
Q. What is your post office? A. Afton.
Q. What is your age at this time? A. 54 years old.
Q. Are you the same Benjamin C. England who made application to this Commission on September 20th, 1900, for enrollment as a citizen by blood and for the enrollment of your wife as a citizen by intermarriage? A. Yes, sir.
Q. What is your wife's name? A. Jincy Jane.
Q. How old is she at this time? A. She is 53 years old.
Q. When were you and she married? A. Spring of '69.
Q. Were you ever married prior to your marriage to this wife? A. No, sir.
Q. Was she ever married prior to her marriage to you? A. No, sir.
Q. You are her first husband, she is your first wife? A. Yes, sir.
Q. Have you and she lived together continuously from the time of your marriage until the present time as husband and wife? A. Yes, sir.
Q. And were on September 1st, 1902? A. Yes, sir.
Q. How long have you lived in the Cherokee Nation? A. All my life.
Q. How long has your wife lived here? A. About 55 years, I guess.
Q. Has she lived here all the time since 1880? A. Yes, sir.
Q. Never lived outside? A. No, sir.
Q. Is your son Benjamin living at this time? A. Yes, sir.
Q. Has he lived all his life in the Cherokee Nation? A. Yes, sir.
Q. Living with you at this time? A. Living with me now.

---

Jesse O. Carr, being first duly sworn, states that as stenographer to the Commission to the Five Civilized Tribes he reported the above entitled case and that the foregoing is a true and complete transcript of his stenographic notes thereof.

Jesse O. Carr

Subscribed and sworn to before me this 22nd day of October, 1902.

BC Jones
Notary Public.

# Cherokee Intermarried White 1906
## Volume III

CHEROKEE-3094.

DEPARTMENT OF THE INTERIOR,
COMMISSIONER TO THE FIVE CIVILIZED TRIBES.
Muskogee, Indian Territory, January 4, 1907.

----------------

In the matter of making proof of the marriage of Jincy J. England to her Cherokee husband, prior to November 1, 1875.

----------------------------

Benjamin C. England, being sworn by W. W. Chappell, a Notary Public, testified as follows:

COMMISSIONER:

Q. What is your name? A. Benjamin C. England.
Q. What is your age? A. 59.
Q. What is your post office address? A. Afton, I.T.
Q. You appear in whose behalf here today? A. My wife, Jincy J. England.
Q. You are a citizen by blood of the Cherokee Nation? A. Yes sir.
Q. Your wife, Jincy J. England, claims citizenship in the Cherokee Nation by intermarriage? A. Yes sir.
Q. Through you? A. Yes sir.
Q. When were you married to her? A. We were married in the spring of '69 -- in March.
Q. Where were you married? A. In Delaware District, Cherokee Nation.
Q. Were you married under a Cherokee license? A. No sir. There were no licenses issued to citizens that married white women then -- if there was I never heard of it.
Q. Who performed the ceremony? A. A.[sic] The judge of the District -- Eloway Butler.
Q. Have you any documentary evidence covering this marriage? A. No sir.
Q. Do you know what record was made of your marriage? A. I do not.
Q. Is the Judge, who performed the ceremony, living at this time? A. No sir, he is dead.
Q. Is there anyone here today who was present at your marriage? A. Yes sir. Dave McGee is here, and he was present.
Q. Were you ever married prior to your marriage to Jincy J. England[sic] A. No sir.
Q. Was she ever married prior to the time she married you? A. No sir.
Q. Is she living at this time? A. Yes sir.
Q. Have you lived together continuously as man and wife since your marriage? A. Yes sir.
Q. Where? A. In Delaware District, Cherokee Nation.

## Cherokee Intermarried White 1906
## Volume III

Q. Why didn't your wife appear here today? A. She wasn't hardly able, and another thing, she is a very large, fleshy woman, and couldn't get on and off the trains, etc. It was almost impossible for her to come without someone coming with her.
Q. Do you know anyone else who is living at the present time who was present at your marriage? A. Yes sir.
Q. What are their names? A. Cobb Welch's wife at Grove, I.T., and I think, if I am not mistaken, that Joe Fox's wife was present. They are the daughters of Judge Butler, and I think they were both present at that time. And also Bill Butler, the old man's son, and Joe Ward was present at that time.

Witness excused.

(The applicant, Jincy J. England, and her husband, Benjamin C. England, appear upon the authenticated roll of 1880, as citizens of the Cherokee Nation, opposite Nos. 937 and 936 respectively, Delaware District. Benjamin C. England is also included in the approved partial roll, opposite No. 76601.)

David A. McGee, being sworn by W. W. Chappell, a Notary Public, testified as follows:

COMMISSIONER:

Q. What is your name? A. David A. McGee.
Q. What is your age? A. 68.
Q. What is your post office address? A. Dodge, Indian Territory
Q. Are you related to Benjamin C. and Jincy J. England in any way? A. No sir.
Q. How long have you known these people? A. I have known Benjamin C. England since we were boys.
Q. Were you present at their marriage? A. O don't remember positively whether I was or not, but I think I was. We were young folks together.
Q. Do you know where they were married? A. At Judge Butler's I think.
Q. When? A. As well as I remember either in '69 or '70.
Q. Do you know whether or not they were married under a Cherokee license? A. There were no Cherokee licenses issued at that time for a Cherokee man to marry a white woman.
Q. Do you know who performed the ceremony? A. I am not positive but I think though -- if I ain't mistaken -- I wouldn't be positive, but I think Judge Butler, a full blood Methodist preacher I used to interpret for him.
Q. Do you remember whether or not this marriage of Benjamin C. and Jincy J. England was in accordance with the customs of the Cherokee Nation? A. Yes sir it was.
Q. Did Benjamin C. and Jincy J. England live together from that time on as man and wife? a Yes sir.
Q. Did they reside in the Cherokee Nation? A. Yes sir.
Q. How long have you lived in the Cherokee Nation? A. I was born and raised here.
Q. Are you a citizen by blood? A. Yes sir.

## Cherokee Intermarried White 1906
## Volume III

Witness excused.

---

Eula Jeanes Branson, being sworn, states that she correctly reported the proceedings had in the above and foregoing, on the 4th. day of January, 1907.

Eula Jeanes Branson

Subscribed and sworn to before me, this 4th. day of January, 1907.

Edward Merrick<br>Notary Public.

◇◇◇◇◇

E.C.M.                                                                                          Cherokee 3094.

### DEPARTMENT OF THE INTERIOR,

### COMMISSIONER TO THE FIVE CIVILIZED TRIBES.

---

In the matter of the application for the enrollment of JINCY J. ENGLAND as a citizen by intermarriage of the Cherokee Nation.

### D E C I S I O N

THE RECORDS OF THIS OFFICE SHOW: That at Vinita, Indian Territory, September 20, 1900, application was received by the Commission to the Five Civilized Tribes for the enrollment of Jincy Jane England as a citizen by intermarriage of the Cherokee Nation. Further proceedings in the matter of said application were had at Muskogee, Indian Territory, October 1, 1902, and January 4, 1907.

THE EVIDENCE IN THIS CASE SHOWS: That the applicant herein, Jincy J. England, a white woman, married in the year 1869 one Benjamin C. England, who was at the time of said marriage a recognized citizen by blood of the Cherokee Nation, whose name appears on the approved partial roll of citizens by blood of the Cherokee Nation, opposite No. 7660, and who is identified on the Cherokee authenticated tribal roll of 1880, Delaware District, No. 936, as a native Cherokee; and that from the time of said marriage the said Benjamin C. England and Jincy Jane England resided together as husband and wife, and continuously lived in the Cherokee Nation up to and including September 1, 1902. Said Jincy J. England is identified on the Cherokee authenticated tribal roll of 1880, and the Cherokee census roll of 1896, as an intermarried citizen of the Cherokee Nation.

IT IS, THEREFORE, ORDERED AND ADJUDGED: That in accordance with the decision of the Supreme Court of the United States, dated November 5, 1906, in the cases

## Cherokee Intermarried White 1906
## Volume III

of Daniel Red Bird et al. vs. the United States, Nos. 125, 126, 127 and 128, the said applicant, Jincy J. England, is entitled, under the provisions of Section 21, of the Act of Congress approved June 28, 1898 (30 Stats., 495), to enrollment as a citizen by intermarriage of the Cherokee Nation, and her application for enrollment as such is accordingly granted.

Tams Bixby
Commissioner.

Dated at Muskogee, Indian Territory,
this   JAN 21 1907

◇◇◇◇◇

Cherokee 3084[sic]

Muskogee, Indian Territory, January 21, 1907.

W. W. Hastings,
Attorney for the Cherokee Nation,
Muskogee, Indian Territory.

Dear Sir:

There is enclosed herewith copy of the decision of the Commissioner to the Five Civilized Tribes, dated January 21, 1907, granting the application for the enrollment of Jincy J. England as a citizen by intermarriage of the Cherokee Nation.

Respectfully,

Enc I-31                                                    Commissioner.

RPI

◇◇◇◇◇

Cherokee 3084    W.W.HASTINGS.    OFFICE OF    H.M. VANCE.
                 ATTORNEY.                     SECRETARY.

**Attorney for the Cherokee Nation,**
MUSKOGEE, I. T.   January 21, 1907.

The Commissioner to the Five Civilized Tribes,
Muskogee, Indian Territory.

Sir:

Receipt is acknowledged of the testimony and of your decision enrolling Jincy J. England as a citizen by intermarriage of the Cherokee Nation. Time for protesting said decision is waived and I consent that said person may be placed upon the schedule immediately.

## Cherokee Intermarried White 1906
## Volume III

> Respectfully,
> W. W. Hastings
> Attorney for the Cherokee Nation.

Cherokee 3084[sic]

> Muskogee, Indian Territory, January 24, 1907.

Jincy J. England,
    Afton, Indian Territory.

Dear Madam:

    There is enclosed herewith copy of the decision of the Commissioner to the Five Civilized Tribes, dated January 21, 1907, granting the application for your enrollment as a citizen by intermarriage of the Cherokee Nation.

    You will be advised when your name has been placed upon a schedule of citizens of the Cherokee Nation and approved by the Secretary of the Interior.

> Respectfully,

Enc I-104

                                                       Commissioner.

RPI

---

**Cher IW 77**
**Trans from Cher 3165 3-15-07**

## Cherokee Intermarried White 1906
## Volume III

E.C.M.

DEPARTMENT OF THE INTERIOR,

COMMISSIONER TO THE FIVE CIVILIZED TRIBES.

---

In the matter of the application for the enrollment of

JEMIMA McCRARY

As a citizen by intermarriage of the Cherokee Nation.

---

CHEROKEE NO. 3165.

◇◇◇◇◇

Department of the Interior,
Commission to the Five Civilized Tribes,
Vinita, I.T, September 21, 1900

In the matter of the application for the enrollment of Jamima[sic] McCrary; being sworn and examined by Commissioner Breckenridge[sic], she testified as follows:

Q What is your full name? A Jamima McCrary.
Q How old are you? A I am 63.
Q What is your post office? A Vinita.
Q In what district do you live? A Cooweescoowee.
Q Who is it you want to have put on the roll, yourself? A Myself and two children.
Q Are you a Cherokee by blood? A No, sir, by intermarriage.
Q When were you married? A Married in 1869
Q Is your husband living? A No, sir, he is dead.
Q What was his name? A N. B. McCrary.
Q When did he die? A He has been dead three months, he died in June.
Q He was a Cherokee was he? A Yes, sir.
Q You haven't married since his death? A No, sir, he has just been dead three months.
Q In what district did you live in 1880? A Lived in Cooweescoowee district.
Q Give me the name of your two children, please? A Elzemar, 20 years old.
Q What is the name of the next child? A Stirling[sic] P., 18 years old.
Q Both living now, are they? A Yes, sir, both living.
(Jamima McCrary on 1880 roll, page 138, No. 1842, Joannah McCrairy[sic], Cooweescoowee district; on 1896 roll, page 315, No. 685, Gemima McCrairy, Cooweescoowee district. Elzemar McCrary on 1896 roll, page 207, No. 3045, Alzema McCrary, Cooweescoowee district. Stirling P. McCrary on 1896 roll, page 207, No.

## Cherokee Intermarried White 1906
## Volume III

3046, Sterling McCrary, Cooweescoowee district. Elzemar McCrary on 1880 roll, page 138, No. 1847, Alzira McCrairy, Cooweescoowee district.)

    The applicant applies for the enrollment of herself and two children. She is identified on the rolls of 1880 and 1896 as an adopted white. She is identified with her deceased husband on both of said rolls. He died some three months ago, and she has not been remarried. She has lived in the Cherokee Nation ever since 1889, and she will be listed now for enrollment as a Cherokee by adoption. Her two children are identified with her on the roll of 1896, the oldest child being identified also upon the roll of 1880. Both are minors and both are living at this time, and they will be listed for enrollment as Cherokees by blood.

-----o-----

    Bruce C. Jones, being duly sworn, says that as stenographer to the Commission to the Five Civilized Tribes he correctly recorded the proceedings and testimony in the above case, and that the foregoing is a true and complete transcript of his stenographic notes thereof.

                                                               Bruce C Jones

Sworn to and subscribed before me this the 21st of September, 1900.

                              CR Breckinridge

                                                                             Commissioner.

                             ◇◇◇◇◇

Cher
Supp'l to # 3165

                              Department of the Interior,
                Commission to the Five Civilized Tribes,
                     Muskogee, I. T., October 10, 1902.

    In the matter of the application of JEMIMA McCRARY, for the enrollment of herself, as a citizen by intermarriage, and her children, ELZEMAR and STERLING P. McCRARY, and her grand-daughter, HATTIE ROBERTSON, as citizens by blood, of the Cherokee Nation:

    JEMIMA McCRARY, called as a witness, being duly sworn and examined by the Commission, testified as follows:

Q  Your full name is Jemima McCrary ?  A  Yes sir.
Q  How old are you ?  A  Sixty five.
Q  What is your post office address ?  A  Vinita.
Q  You are a white woman ?  A  Yes sir.
Q  Your name appears on the 1880 roll as an intermarried white ?  A  Yes sir.
Q  Was your husband living in 1880 ?  A  Yes sir.
Q  What is his name ?  A  N. B. McCrary.
Q  Is your husband dead ?  A  Yes sir.

# Cherokee Intermarried White 1906
## Volume III

Q When did he die ? A Two years ago this last June.
Q Had you and your husband lived together in the Cherokee Nation from 1880 up to the time he died two years ago ? A Yes sir.
Q Never were separated ? A No sir.
Q Of course you have not married again ? A Oh no sir.
Q How many children have you living with you ? A There aint[sic] but one living with me, Sterling is off at work.
Q Elzemar is married ? A Yes sir.
Q Hattie Robertson is her child ? A Yes sir.
Q Are they in the Cherokee Nation ? A Not at this time; they are in the Creek Nation.
Q They are in the Indian Territory ? A Yes sir. Their home is in the Cherokee Nation.
Q You have made your home in the Cherokee Nation ever since 1880 ? A Yes sir.
Q Nowhere else ? A No sir, I haven't been anywhere; I have been living twenty six or seven years at Vinita.

----------

E. C. Bagwell, on oath states that, as stenographer to the Commission to the Five Civilized Tribes, he correctly recorded the testimony and proceedings had in the above entitled cause, and that the foregoing is an accurate transcript of his stenographic notes thereof.

E.C.Bagwell

Subscribed and sworn to before me this October 25, 1902.

BC Jones
Notary Public.

◇◇◇◇◇

Cherokee No. 3165.

DEPARTMENT OF THE INTERIRO[sic].
COMMISSIONER TO THE FIVE CIVILIZED TRIBES.

Muskogee, Indian Territory, January 3, 1907.

-------------------------------------

In the matter of the application for the enrollment of Jemima McCrary as a citizen by intermarriage of the Cherokee Nation.

-------------------------------------

Jamima[sic] McCrary being first duly sworn and examined, testifies as follows:

BY THE COMMISSIONER:

## Cherokee Intermarried White 1906
## Volume III

Q What is your name? A Jamima McCrary.
Q How old are you? A I was born in 1837, I will soon be 70 years old.
Q What is your Post Office address? A Vinita.
Q You claim to be an intermarriage[sic] citizen of the Cherokee Nation.
Q Yes, sir.
Q Through whom do you claim your intermarriage rights?
A My husband, N. B. McCrary.
Q When were you married to N. B. McCrary? A We was married in '69.
Q Where were you married? A We were married in Arkansas.
Q Did you get a certificate? A No, sir, the Justice of the Peace married us.
Q Were you married before you married Mr. McCrary? A Yes, sir.
Q What was the name of your first husband? A McCulloch.
Q Was he living or dead at the time you married McCrary? A Dead.
Q Was McCrary married before he married you? A No, sir.
Q Did you live together continuously since your marriage up to the time of his death?
A Yes, sir.
Q Have you married again since his death in 1900? A No, sir.
Q Was your husband a citizen of the Cherokee Nation when you married him in '69?
A Yes, sir, lived there, it was his home.
Q A Recognized citizen was he? A Yes, sir.
Q Did you live with him in the Cherokee Nation? from the time of your marriage in 1869 up to his death in 1900? A Yes, sir, we lived a while in Arkansas and we moved here in 1872.
Q When was your husband admitted to citizenship, after you moved here in 1872.[sic]
A He was always a citizen, he didn't have to be admitted.
Q Did you have any property here in 1872 when you came here.[sic] A No, sir.
Q Did your husband? A Yes, sir. He had a farm over here when we came here in 1872. They all lived here - his father and sisters.
Q Did you live here continuously from 1872 up to the time your husband died in 1900?
A Yes, sir.

The applicant is identified in the 1880 roll opposite No. 1842.

Martha A. Miller being first duly sworn and examined, testifies as follows:

BY THE COMMISSIONER:

Q What is your name? A Martha A. Miller.
Q Where do you live? A Fairland.
Q How old are you? A 49.
Q Do you know Jamima McCrary? A Yes, sir.
Q Do you know N. B. McCrary? [sic] Yes, sir.
Q Are they husband and wife? A Yes, sir.
Q Do you know when they were married? A I don't recollect. I was quite a small girl then.
Q What relation are you to Jamima McCrary? A She is my mother.

## Cherokee Intermarried White 1906
## Volume III

Q  What relation are you to N. B. McCrary?  A  He is my step-father.
Q  Where were they married?  A  They was married in Arkansas.
Q  How long after they were married in Arkansas before they moved to the Cherokee Nation?  A  I don't know. It wasn't very long.
Q  Do you remember they removed to the Cherokee Nation?  A  No, sir, I don't remember what year it was.
Q  Is there any one here to-day that can establish the fact that N. B. McCrary was a citizen of the Cherokee Nation at the time your mother married him in 1869?  A  I don't know as there is, there might be.

WITNESS EXCUSED.

F. Elma Lane, upon oath, states that she reported the proceedings in the above entitled cause and that the foregoing was a true and correct transcript of her stenographic notes taken therein.

F. Elma Lane

Subscribed and sworn to before me this 3rd day of January, 1907.

Chas E Webster<br>Notary Public.

LGD                                                                                       Cherokee 3165.

DEPARTMENT OF THE INTERIOR,<br>COMMISSIONER TO THE FIVE CIVILIZED TRIBES.

Muskogee, Indian Territory, January 3, 1907.

Supplemental testimony in the matter of the application of JEMIMA McCRARY for enrollment as a citizen by intermarriage of the Cherokee Nation.

Alfred C. Raymond, being first duly sworn by B. P. Rasmus, a notary public, testified as follows:

Q  What is your name?  A  Alfred C. Raymond.
Q  What is your age?  A  79 years old.
Q  What is your postoffice address?  A  Vinita, I. T.
Q  Are you acquainted with Jemima McCrary?  A  I am.
Q  Are you any relation to her?  A  Yes, by marriage. Her husband is my wife's brother.
Q  Was he a citizen of the Cherokee Nation?  A  He was.
Q  When was he admitted to citizenship?  A  He was a citizen by birth.
Q  Was he born in the Cherokee Nation  A  I don't know.

## Cherokee Intermarried White 1906
## Volume III

Witness excused.

Mary R. Strange, being first duly sworn by B. P. Rasmus, a notary public, testified as follows:

Q What is your name? A Mary R. Strange.
Q What is your age A 36 years old.
Q What is your postoffice address? A Chelsea, I. T.
Q Are you acquainted with Jemima McCrary? A I am.
Q What relation is she to you? A She is my aunt.
Q Did you know her husband, N. B. McCrary? A Yes sir.
Q Was he a citizen of the Cherokee Nation? A He was.
Q Do you know when he was admitted to citizenship? A He was not admitted, he was a citizen by blood. He came here when he was a child.
Q When was the first time you knew N. B. McCrary? A In 1877 I believe it was.
Q Was he considered a citizen at the time? A He was.

Witness excused.

William Howell, being first duly sworn by B. P. Rasmus, a notary public, testified as follows:

Q What is your name? A William Howell.
Q What is your age? A 60 years old.
Q What is your postoffice address? A Oseuma, I. T.
Q Are you a citizen of the Cherokee Nation? A Yes.
Q Do you know Jemima McCrary? A I do.
Q Did you know N. B. McCrary, her husband, in his lifetime? A Yes.
Q How long did you know N. B. McCrary? A Since 1873, got acquainted in the war.
Q Where did you get acquainted during the war? A Here at Fort Gibson. He was a soldier.
Q Did he vote?[sic] and exercise the rights of a citizen of the Cherokee Nation at that time? A Yes.
Q When did N. B. McCrary die, do you know.[sic] A No sir, I dont[sic].
Q You know he was always recognized as a citizen of the Cherokee Nation during his lifetime? A Ever since I knew him.

Witness excused.

Demie T. Stubblefield, being first duly sworn, states on oath that, as stenographer to the Commissioner to the Five Civilized Tribes, she reported the above proceedings and that the same is a true and correct transcript of her stenographic notes thereof.

Demie T. Stubblefield

# Cherokee Intermarried White 1906
## Volume III

Subscribed and sowrn[sic] to before me this, January 4, 1907.

Edward Merrick<br>Notary Public.

◇◇◇◇◇

### MARRIAGE LICENSE.

STATE OF ARKANSAS.  COUNTY OF BENTON.

TO ANY PERSON AUTHORIZED BY LAW TO SOLEMNIZE MARRIAGE++GREETING :-

You are hereby commanded to solemnize the Rites and publish the Bans of Matrimony between Mr. B. F. Robertson, of Grove, I.T., aged 29 years, and Miss Mary E. McCrary of Bentonville, in the County of Benton and State of Arkansas, aged 22 years, according to law, and do you officially sign and return this License to the parties herein named.

WITNESS MY HAND AND OFFICIAL SEAL, this 8th. day of Sept. A.D. 1900.   (Signed.) Harry Harry[sic] Clerk.

_____D.C.

Seal.

xxxxxxxxxxxxxxxxxxxxxxxxxxxxxxxxxxxxxxxxxxxxxxxxxxxxxxxxxxxxxxxxxxxxxxxxxxxxxxxxx

### Certificate of Marriage.

State of Arkansas

County of Benton.   I, F.H. Foster do hereby certify that on the 8th. day of Sept. A.D. 1900, I did duly and according to law as commanded in the foregoing License, solemnize the Rites and publish the Bans of Matrimony between the parties therein named.

Witness my hand, this 8th. day of Sept. A.D. 1900.

(Signed)   F.H. Foster Co. Judge.

Ten Cents Revenue.

(Stamp.)

xxxxxxxxxxxxxxxxxxxxxxxxxxxxxxxxxxxxxxxxxxxxxxxxxxxxxxxxxxxxxxxxxxxxxxxxxxxxxxxxx

### Certificate of Record.

State of Arkansas   I, Harry Hurst, Clerk of the County Court

County of Benton.   of said County, certify that the above License for and Certificate of the Marriage of the parties therein named, were, on the 8th. day of

## Cherokee Intermarried White 1906
## Volume III

Sept. A.D. 1900, filed in my office and the same are now duly recorded on page 15, Book F., of Marriage Records.

Signed, Harry Hurst. Clerk.

Seal.

Endorsed on back: MARRIAGE LICENSE. Issued to B.F. Robertson and Mary e. McCrary on the 8th. day of Sept. 1900.

---

UNITED STATES OF AMERICA.
*Indian Territory,* } ss.
Northern ....... District.

I, Preston S. Davis, a Notary Public within and for the District and Territory aforesaid do hereby certify that the within and foregoing is a true and correct copy of the original Marriage license of the parties therein named taken from the said original by me this day and compared and found to be correct.

In testimony whereof I have hereunto set my hand and affixed my seal at Vinita, I.T. on this the 27th. day of March, A.D. 1902, and of the Independence of the United States the One Hundred and Twenty Sixth Year.

Preston S. Davis<br>Notary Public.<br>My Com. Ex. 2/18th. 1905.

◇◇◇◇◇

E C M                                                    Cherokee 3165.

DEPARTMENT OF THE INTERIOR,

COMMISSIONER TO THE FIVE CIVILIZED TRIBES.

---

In the matter of the application for the enrollment of JEMIMA McCRARY as a citizen by intermarriage of the Cherokee Nation.

_D_E_C_I_S_I_O_N_

THE RECORDS OF THIS OFFICE SHOW: That on September 21st, 1900 application was received by the Commission to the Five Civilized Tribes for the

## Cherokee Intermarried White 1906
## Volume III

enrollment of Jemima McCrary as a citizen by intermarriage of the Cherokee Nation. Further proceedings in the matter of said application were had at Muskogee, Indian Territory, October 10th, 1902 and January 3rd, 1907.

THE EVIDENCE IN THIS CASE SHOWS: That the applicant herein, Jemima McCrary, a white woman, married in 1869 one N. B. McCrary, since deceased, who was at the time of said marriage a recognized citizen by blood of the Cherokee Nation, who is identified on the Cherokee authenticated tribal roll of 1880, Cooweescoowee District, No. 1841 as a native Cherokee, marked "Dead"; and that at the time of said marriage the said Jemima McCrary was the widow of one McCulloch. It is further shown that from the time of said marriage until the death of N. B. McCrary, which occurred in June, 1900 the said N. B. McCrary and Jemima McCrary resided together as husband and wife and continuously lived in the Cherokee Nation; that since the death of said N. B. McCrary the said Jemima McCrary has remained unmarried and continuously lived in the Cherokee Nation. Said applicant is identified on the Cherokee authenticated tribal roll of 1880 and the Cherokee census roll of 1896 as an intermarried citizen of the Cherokee Nation.

IT IS, THEREFORE, ORDERED AND ADJUDGED: That in accordance with the decision of the Supreme Court of the United States dated November 5th, 1906, in the cases of Daniel Red Bird, et al. vs. the United States, Nos. 125, 126, 127 and 128, the said applicant, Jemima McCrary is entitled, under the provisions of Section Twenty-one of the Act of Congress approved June 28th, 1898 (30 Stats. 495), to enrollment as a citizen by intermarriage of the Cherokee Nation, and her application for enrollment as such is accordingly granted.

Tams Bixby
Commissioner.

Dated at Muskogee, Indian Territory,
this     JAN 23 1907

◇◇◇◇◇

Cherokee 3165

Muskogee, Indian Territory, January 23, 1907.

W. W. Hastings,
    Attorney for the Cherokee Nation,
        Muskogee, Indian Territory.

Dear Sir:

There is enclosed herewith copy of the decision of the Commissioner to the Five Civilized Tribes, dated January 23, 1907, granting the application for the enrollment of Jemima McCrary as a citizen by intermarriage of the Cherokee Nation.

# Cherokee Intermarried White 1906
## Volume III

>                Respectfully,
>
>                                            Commissioner.

Enc I-63

RPI

◇◇◇◇◇

Cherokee 3165    W.W. HASTINGS.    OFFICE OF    H.M. VANCE.
                          ATTORNEY.                     SECRETARY.

### Attorney for the Cherokee Nation,
MUSKOGEE, I. T.    January 23, 1907.

The Commissioner to the Five Civilized Tribes,
      Muskogee, Indian Territory.
Sir:

      Receipt is acknowledged of the testimony and of your decision enrolling Jemima McCrary as a citizen by intermarriage of the Cherokee Nation. Time for protesting said decision is waived and I consent that said person may be placed upon the schedule immediately.

>                Respectfully,
>                        W. W. Hastings
>                        Attorney for the Cherokee Nation.

◇◇◇◇◇

Cherokee 3165

>                Muskogee, Indian Territory, January 23, 1907

Jemima McCrary,
      Tulsa, Indian Territory.

Dear Madam:

      There is enclosed herewith copy of the decision of the Commissioner to the Five Civilized Tribes, dated January 23, 1907, granting your application for enrollment as a citizen by intermarriage of the Cherokee Nation.

      You will be advised when your name has been placed upon a schedule of citizens of the Cherokee Nation and approved by the Secretary of the Interior.

>                Respectfully,

Enc I-82                                                      Commissioner.
RPI

# Cherokee Intermarried White 1906
## Volume III

**Cher IW 78**
**Trans from Cher 3170  3-15-07**

C.F.B.

## DEPARTMENT OF THE INTERIOR,

### COMMISSIONER TO THE FIVE CIVILIZED TRIBES.

In the matter of the application for the enrollment of

### ROBERT R. TAYLOR

as a citizen by intermarriage of the Cherokee Nation.

### CHEROKEE 3170

Department of the Interior,
Commission to the Five Civilized Tribes,
Vinita, I.T., September 21, 1900.

In the matter of the application of Robert R. Taylor for the enrollment of himself, wife and children as Cherokee citizens; being sworn and examined by Commissioer[sic] Needles he testified as follows:

Q What is your name?  A  Robert R. Taylor.
Q What is your age?  A  I am sixty-seven years old.
Q What is your post-office address?  A  Vinita.
Q What district do you live in?  A  Cooweescoowee District.
Q Are you a recognized citizen of the Cherokee Nation?  A  Yes sir.
Q By blood or intermarriage?  A  Intermarriage.
Q For whom do you apply?  A  My wife and children and myself.
Q Your father and mother are non-citizens?  A  Yes sir.
Q What is the name of your wife?  A  Cynthia J.
Q When were you married to her?  A  In 1871.
Q Your wife's father and mother living?  A  No sir, mother is living; her father is not living.
Q What are the names of your children?  A  Robert Lee Taylor, nineteen years old; Bertie Taylor, seventeen years old; Gertie Taylor, seventeen years old. They are twins.
Q What is the name of the next one?  A  Surse Taylor.
Q How old is Surse?  A  Fifteen years old.

## Cherokee Intermarried White 1906
## Volume III

Q What is the name of the next one? A Hubert.
Q How old is Hubert? A Twelve.
Q What is the next one? A Ten.
Q What is the name? A Jemima W.
Q Next one? A That's all.
Q Are these children alive and living with you? A Yes sir there are two of them up at school at Columbia at this time; they went last week.
Q How long have you been living in the Cherokee Nation continuously? A Since 1871.
Q You and your wife together? A Yes sir.
1880 roll page 329 #2708 Robert R. Taylor, Delaware District;
1880 roll page 329 #2709 Cynthia J. Taylor, Delaware District;
1896 roll page 326 #984 Robert R. Taylor, Cooweescoowee District;
1896 roll page 268 #4791 Cynthia J. Taylor,     "
1896 roll page 268 #4794 Robert L. Taylor     "
1896 roll page 268 #4795 Bertie Taylor, Cooweescoowee     "
1896 roll page 268 #4796 Gertie Taylor     "
1896 roll page 268 #4797 as Circy Taylor     "
1896 roll page 268 #4798 as Herbert Taylor     "
1896 roll page 268 #4799 Jemima W. Taylor     "

Com'r Needles: The name of Robert R. Taylor appears upon the authenticated roll of 1880 as well as the census roll of 1896; the same of his wife, Cynthia J. also appears upon the authenticated roll of 1880 as well as the census roll of 1896; the names of his children, Robert L., Bertie, Gertie, Surse, Hubert and Jemima W. appear upon the census roll of 1896; and they all being fully identified according to page and number on said rolls as indicated in the testimony, and having made satisfactory proof as to their residence, said Robert R. Taylor will be dly[sic] listed for enrollment by this Commission as a Cherokee citizen by intermarriage; his wife Cynthia J. and their children as enumerated herein will be duly listed for enrollment as Cherokee citizens by blood.

M.D. Green, being first duly sworn, states that as stenographer to the Commission to the Five Civilized Tribes he correctly recorded the testimony and proceedings in this case and that the foregoing is a true and complete transcript of his stenographic notes thereof.

MD Green

Subscribed and sworn to before me this 24 day of September 1900.

CR Breckinridge

Commissioner.

## Cherokee Intermarried White 1906
## Volume III

Cherokee 3170.

DEPARTMENT OF THE INTERIOR,
COMMISSION TO THE FIVE CIVILIZED TRIBES,
Muskogee, I. T., October 22, 1902.

In the matter of the application of Robert R. Taylor for the enrollment of himself as a citizen by intermarriage, and for the enrollment of his wife, Cynthia Taylor, and his six minor children, Robert L., Bertie, Gertie, Surse, Hubert and Jemima W. Taylor, as citizens by blood, of the Cherokee Nation.
SUPPLEMENTAL PROCEEDINGS.

ROBERT R. TAYLOR, being sworn, testified as follows:

By the Commission,

Q Your name is Robert R. Taylor? A Yes, sir.
Q How old are you? A Sixty-seven.
Q What is your postoffice? A Vinita.
Q Are you a white man? A Yes, sir.
Q Is your name on the roll of 1880 as an adopted white citizen? A Yes, sir.
Q What is your wife's name? A Cynthia J. Taylor.
Q Is she a Cherokee by blood? A Yes, sir.
Q Was she your wife in 1880? A Yes, sir.
Q Is she the wife through whom you claim your right to citizenship? A Yes, sir.
Q You and your wife been living together since 1880? A Yes, sir.
Q Living together now? A Yes, sir.
Q Has the Cherokee Nation ben your home and have you resided there since 1880?
A Yes, sir.
Q Never lived anywhere else? A No, sir.
Q How many children have you? A Eleven.
Q Eleven? A Yes, sir.
Q How many are living at home with you? A Five.
Q Robert L. has married since you enrolled him, has he? A Yes, sir.
Q Have there been any deaths in your family in the past two years? A No, sir.
Q These children of yours have lived in the Cherokee Nation ever since they were born?
A Yes, sir, never lived nowhere else only when they were out in the States going to school.

Retta Chick, being first duly sworn, states that, as stenographer to the Commission to the Five Civilized Tribes, she recorded the testimony and proceedings in the matter of the foregoing application, and that the above is a true and complete transcript of her stenographic notes thereof.

Retta Chick

## Cherokee Intermarried White 1906
## Volume III

Subscribed and sworn to before me this 25th day of November, 1902.

PG Reuter<br>Notary Public.

◇◇◇◇◇

C.F.B.  Cherokee 3170

### DEPARTMENT OF THE INTERIOR,
### COMMISSIONER TO THE FIVE CIVILIZED TRIBES.
### MUSKOGEE, IND. TER., JANUARY 4, 1907.

In the matter of the application for the enrollment of ROBERT R. TAYLOR as a citizen by intermarriage of the Cherokee Nation.

APPEARANCES:  Applicant appears in person:
Cherokee Nation not represented:

ROBERT R. TAYLOR being first duly sworn by B. P. Rasmus, a Notary Public, testified as follows:

Q. What is your name? A. Robert R. Taylor.
Q. What is your age? A. I am seventy-one years old.
Q. What is your postoffice address? A. Vinita.
Q. You claim the right to enrollment as a citizen by intermarriage of the Cherokee Nation do you? A. Yes sir.
Q. You have no Cherokee blood? A. No sir.
Q. You claim that right solely by reason of your marriage to a citizen of the Cherokee Nation? A. Yes sir.
Q. What is the name of the citizen through whom you claim the right to enrollment as a citizen of the Cherokee Nation? A. Cynthia J. Horn.
Q. When were you married to her? A. Married in 1871.
Q. Was she a recognized citizen of the Cherokee Nation at the time you married her? A. Yes sir.
Q. Living in the Cherokee Nation was she? A. Yes sir.
Q. Were you ever married prior to your marriage to her? A. I married her in Texas, and came here, and in March, '71, I got out a license and married her here.
Q. You married your wife first, in Texas? A. Yes sir, and then came here. She was a Cherokee.
Q. Was she living in Texas at the time you married her? A. The first time she was; but the second time we were living here.
Q. She was making Texas her home at that time? A. The first time she was.
Q. And after your first marriage to your wife you removed to the Cherokee Nation? A. Yes sir.

## Cherokee Intermarried White 1906
## Volume III

Q. After coming to the Cherokee Nation was your wife recognized as a citizen of the Cherokee Nation or was it necessary for her to go before the authorities and be admitted?
A. She had to go before the Court and be admitted.
Q. What year was she admitted? A. In 1871, soon after we came here.
Q. Were you married to her in accordance to Cherokee law prior of subsequent to her admission to Cherokee citizenship? A. I was married to her, and Judge Elliott told me to marry her according to Cherokee law, and get up my papers and then I would be admitted to citizenship.
Q. Was your wife ever married prior to her marriage to you? A. No sir.
Q. You were never married except to her? A. No sir.
Q. Have you any evidence of a documentary character to show your marriage to your wife in the Cherokee Nation? A. Yes sir. ( Presents papers)

The applicant presents an original marriage license and certificate showing that on April 1, 1871, a license was issued by T. J. McGhee, Clerk of Delaware District, Cherokee Nation, in accordance with Cherokee law, authorizing the marriage of R. R. Taylor to Cynthia Horn, a Cherokee citizen; that said parties were united in marriage May 1, 1871, by James Ketchum.

This marriage license and certificate will be filed with and made a part of the record in this case.

The applicant, Robert R. Taylor, is identified on the Cherokee authenticated tribal roll of 1880, Delaware District, No. 2708. His wife Cynthia J. Taylor, is included in an approved partial roll of citizens by blood of the Cherokee Nation, opposite No. 7833.

---

The undersigned, being first duly sworn, states that as stenographer to the Commissioner to the Five Civilized Tribes she correctly recorded the testimony taken in this case, and that the above and foregoing is a full, true and correct transcript of her stenographic notes thereof:

Lucy M. Bowman

Subscribed and sworn to before me this 4th day of January, 1907.

John E. Tidwell
Notary Public.

# Cherokee Intermarried White 1906
## Volume III

*(The Marriage License and Certificate below typed as given.)*

|  |  |  |
|---|---|---|
| CHEROKEE NATION | ) | To any regular minister of the |
|  | ) |  |
| DELAWARE DISTRICT | ) | Gospel to execute and return greeting: |

    You are hereby command to solemnize the rights of matrimony of marriage between R. R. Taylor Synthia Horn a female citizen of the Cherokee Nation according to the ceremony usly observed in your respectfully churchis the said R. R. Taylor having complies with the Laws of this Nation Herein fail not given Under my Hand in office this 1st day April 1871

                                         (Signed) T. J. McGhee
                                            Clrk D C D D
                                                    C. N.

    The undersigned citizens of the Cherokee Nation hereby recommend that license be issued to R. R. Taylor a white man to be joined in the bonds of matrimony to miss Cynthia Horn a Cherokee citizen.

May 1st 1871
  David Landrum
John Landrum                                                           SEAL
Nicholas Thomas
Luise Roggers
A. G. Hawk.
George X Buffington.
    his mark
By Landrum.

    This is to sertify thate I have thise Day joinde R R Taylor Sinethey Horn in the Holey Bonds of Matrimoney this 7 of May 1871.

                                              James X Ketchum

                                                  his
                                         James X Ketchum
                                              mark

                                            This my marke.

    This is to certify the within an the original Licens on file in the Clerk office Del Dist C. N.

    This the 7th day Nov 1887 .

## Cherokee Intermarried White 1906
## Volume III

(Signed)T. J. McGhee
Clk Del Dist.

The undersigned, being first duly sworn, states that as stenographer to the Commissioner to the Five Civilized Tribes, she made the above and foregoing copy, and that the same is a full, true and correct copy of the original marriage certificate now on file in this office.

Mattie M Pace

Subscribed and sworn to before me this January 16, 1907.

Chas E Webster
Notary Public.

◇◇◇◇◇

C.F.B. Cherokee 3170.

### DEPARTMENT OF THE INTERIOR,

### COMMISSIONER TO THE FIVE CIVILIZED TRIBES.

In the matter of the application for the enrollment of ROBERT R. TAYLOR as a citizen by intermarriage of the Cherokee Nation.

### D E C I S I O N

THE RECORDS OF THIS OFFICE SHOW: That at Vinita, Indian Territory, September 21, 1900, application was received for the enrollment of Robert R. Taylor as a citizen by intermarriage of the Cherokee Nation. Further proceedings in the matter of said application were had at Muskogee, Indian Territory, October 22, 1902, and January 4, 1907.

THE EVIDENCE IN THIS CASE SHOWS: That the applicant herein, Robert R. Taylor, a white man, married on May 7, 1871, his wife, Cynthia J. Taylor, nee Horn, in accordance with Cherokee law, and who was at the time of said marriage a recognized citizen by blood of the Cherokee Nation, who is identified on the Cherokee authenticated tribal roll of 1880, Delaware District, No. 2709, as a native Cherokee, and whose name appears on the approved partial roll of citizens by blood of the Cherokee Nation, opposite No. 4833; that since said marriage the said Robert R. and Cynthia J. Taylor have resided together as husband and wife, and have continuously lived in the Cherokee Nation. Said applicant is duly identified on the Cherokee authenticated tribal roll of 1880, and the Cherokee census roll of 1896, as an adopted white citizen of the Cherokee Nation.

## Cherokee Intermarried White 1906
## Volume III

IT IS, THEREFORE, ORDERED AND ADJUDGED: That in accordance with the decision of the Supreme Court of the United States, dated November 5, 1906, in the cases of Daniel Red Bird et al. vs. the United States, Nos. 125, 126, 127 and 128, the said applicant, Robert R. Taylor, is entitled, under the provisions of Section 21 of the Act of Congress approved June 28, 1898 (30 Stats., 495), to enrollment as a citizen by intermarriage of the Cherokee Nation, and his application for enrollment as such is accordingly granted.

Tams Bixby<br>Commissioner.

Dated at Muskogee, Indian Territory,
this    JAN 23 1907

◇◇◇◇◇

Cherokee
3170

Muskogee, Indian Territory, January 23, 1907.

W. W. Hastings,
    Attorney for the Cherokee Nation,
        Muskogee, Indian Territory.

Dear Sir:

There is enclosed herewith a copy of the decision of the Commissioner to the Five Civilized Tribes, dated January 23, 1907, granting the application for the enrollment of Robert R. Taylor as a citizen by intermarriage of the Cherokee Nation.

Respectfully,

Encl. H-57                                             Commissioner.
JMH

◇◇◇◇◇

## Cherokee Intermarried White 1906
## Volume III

Cherokee 3170    W.W. HASTINGS. ATTORNEY.    OFFICE OF    H.M. VANCE. SECRETARY.

**Attorney for the Cherokee Nation,**

MUSKOGEE, I. T.    January 23, 1907.

The Commissioner to the Five Civilized Tribes,
    Muskogee, Indian Territory.

Sir:

    Receipt is acknowledged of the testimony and of your decision enrolling Robert R. Taylor as a citizen by intermarriage of the Cherokee Nation. Time for protesting said decision is waived and I consent that said person may be placed upon the schedule immediately.

        Respectfully,
        W. W. Hastings
        Attorney for Cherokee Nation.

◇◇◇◇◇

Cherokee
3170

        Muskogee, Indian Territory, January 23, 1907

Robert R. Taylor,
  Vinita, Indian Territory.

Dear Sir:

    There is enclosed herewith a copy of the decision of the Commissioner to the Five Civilized Tribes, dated January 23, 1907, granting your application for enrollment as a citizen by intermarriage of the Cherokee Nation.

    You will be advised when your name has been placed upon a schedule of citizens of the Cherokee Nation and approved by the Secretary of the Interior.

        Respectfully,

E.R.C.                                                               Commissioner.
Enc. E.C. 82.

◇◇◇◇◇

## Cherokee Intermarried White 1906
## Volume III

Cherokee I.W. 78

Muskogee, Indian Territory, April 8, 1907.

Robert R. Taylor,
    Vinita, Indian Territory.

Dear Sir:

    Your marriage license and certificate filed in the matter of your application for enrollment as a citizen by intermarriage of the Cherokee Nation, is returned to you herewith, copies of the same being retained in the files of this office.

    Respectfully,

Incl. P-4-23                                                       Acting Commissioner.
  MMP

---

**Cher IW 79**
**Trans from Cher 3274 3-15-07**

◇◇◇◇◇

E.C.M.

DEPARTMENT OF THE INTERIOR,

COMMISSIONER TO THE FIVE CIVILIZED TRIBES.

In the matter of the application for the enrollment of

DAVID W. HARRISON

as a citizen by intermarriage of the Cherokee Nation.

CHEROKEE 3274.

◇◇◇◇◇

# Cherokee Intermarried White 1906
## Volume III

Department of the Interior,
Commission to the Five Civilized Tribes,
Vinita, I.T., September 22, 1900

In the matter of the application of David Wilson Harrison for the enrollment of himself and wife as Cherokee citizens; being sworn and examined by Commissioner Needlesye[sic] testified as follows:

Q What is your name? A David Wilson Harrison.
Q How old are you? A Fifty-seven.
Q What is your post-office address? A Bluejacket.
Q In what district do you live? A Cooweescoowee.
Q Are you a recognized citizen of the Cherokee Nation? A Citizen by marriage.
Q For whom do you apply for enrollment? A Myself and wife.
Q What is the name of your wife? A Mary A.
Q What is her age? A 60.
Q She is a Cherokee citizen by blood? A Yes sir.
Q What degree of blood does she claim? A 1/16.
Q You and her always lived in the Cherokee Nation? A We were married about- awhile before we came here and we came here in 1870. And have been living here ever since.
Q Her father and mother are not living? A No sir

1880 roll page 268 #1285 D. W. Harrison, Delaware District;
1880 roll page 268 #1286 as Mary F. Harrison "
1896 roll page 178 #2267 as Mary A. Harrison Cooweescoowee
1896 roll page 309 #530 David W. Harrison "

Com'r Needles: The name of David W. Harrison appears upon the authenticated roll of 1880 as well as the census roll of 1896 as an intermarried white citizen; the name of his wife, Mary A., appears upon the authenticated roll of 1880 as Mary F. and upon the census roll of 1896 as Mary A., she being duly identified according to page and number of said rolls, and they having made satisfactory proof as to the residence, he the said David W. Harrison will be duly listed for enrollment by this Commission as a Cherokee citizen by intermarriage and his wife Mary A. will be listed for enrollment as a Cherokee citizen by blood.

M.D. Green, being first duly sworn states that as stenographer to the Commission to the Five Civilized Tribes he correctly recorded the testimony and proceedings in this case and that the foregoing is a true and complete transcript of his stenographic notes thereof.

MD Green

Subscribed and sworn to before me this 24 day of September 1900.

CR Breckinridge
Commissioner.

## Cherokee Intermarried White 1906
## Volume III

R.

DEPARTMENT OF THE INTERIOR.
Commission to the Five Civilized Tribes.
Muskogee, Indian Territory, October 7th, 1902.

---

In the matter of the application of David W. Harrison for the enrollment of himself as a citizen by intermarriage of the Cherokee Nation and for the enrollment of his wife, Mary A. Harrison, as a citizen by blood of the Cherokee Nation.

---

Supplemental to #3274.

---

Applicant appears in person.
Cherokee Nation by J. C. Starr.

---

DAVID W. HARRISON, being duly sworn, testified as follows:
Examination by the Commission.

Q. State your full name, Mr. Harrison? A. David W.
Q. How old are you? A. 58.
Q. What is your post office? A. It is Afton now.
Q. It was Bluejacket before, was it? A. Yes, sir.
Q. Are you the same David W. Harrison who made application to this Commission on September 22nd, 1900, to be enrolled as a citizen by intermarriage of the Cherokee Nation? A. Yes, sir.
Q. What is the name of your wife through whom you claim citizenship? A. M.A.
Q. Mary A.? A. Yes, sir.
Q. When did you marry Mary A.? Before 1880? A. Yes, sir.
Q. She is on the eighty roll? A. Yes, sir.
Q. You are on the eighty roll? A. Yes, sir.
Q. Have you lived in the Cherokee Nation since 1880? A. Yes, sir.
Q. Never been out of the Cherokee Nation? A. We stayed at Miami about two months.
Q. When was this time you stayed at Miami? A. I couldn't tell you exactly, I don't believe.
Q. How many years ago A. About two years ago.
Q. What did you go there for? A. I had some properly over there and she wasn't in very good health and we went up there to stay awhile to see if it would be better.
Q. You have a farm? A. Yes, sir.
Q. Did you move your effects? A. Didn't move everything. I left my stuff on the farm.

## Cherokee Intermarried White 1906
## Volume III

Jesse O. Carr, being first duly sworn, states that as stenographer to the Commission to the Five Civilized Tribes he reported the above entitled case and that the foregoing is a true and complete transcript of his stenographic notes thereof.

Jesse O. Carr

Subscribed and sworn to before me this 11<sup>th</sup> day of November, 1902.

BC Jones<br>Notary Public.

◇◇◇◇◇

Cherokee 3274.

DEPARTMENT OF THE INTERIOR,<br>COMMISSIONER TO THE FIVE CIVILIZED TRIBES.<br>DECEMBER 27, 1906, MUSKOGEE, I. T.

In the matter of the application for the enrollment of DAVID W. HARRISON as a citizen by intermarriage of the Cherokee Nation.

APPEARANCES;
   For Applicant, Present in person.
   For Cherokee Nation, W. W. Hastings.

DAVID W. HARRISON, being first, duly sworn by B. P. Rasmus, a Notary Public, testified as follows:

ON BEHALF OF THE COMMISSIONER:

Q What is your name?  A David W. Harrison.
Q Your age?  A 62 last September.
Q Your postoffice?  A I live at Afton now.
Q Are you an applicant for enrollment as a citizen by intermarriage of the Cherokee Nation?  A Yes sir.
Q What is the name of your wife?  A Mary A.
Q Is she living?  A Yes sir/[sic]
Q Is she a Cherokee by blood?  A Yes sir
Q When were you married?  A Married in 1870
Q What time?  A I don't recollect the date, I couldn't tell you that, in March though I think; spring of 1870.
Q Have you any documentary evidence of your marriage?  A No sir, I haven't.
Q Who married you?  A Watt Duncan
Q What was his initials?  A W. A. Duncan I think.
Q What was he?  A He was a Methodist Minister I think.
Q Did you have your license recorded?  A Yes sir, I had a copy but lost them.

# Cherokee Intermarried White 1906
## Volume III

Q In what District did you get your license? A In Flint District

The original marriage records of Flint District are in possession of this office and in Book "B" of said records, page 107 is a copy of the license and certificate of marriage of D. Wilson Harrison and Mary Ann McDonald. The license was issued March 15, 1870, and the certificate of marriage shows that the parties were united in matrimony by W. A. Duncan, a Minister of the Gospel, on March 17, 1870.

Q Are you the identical person mentioned in this marriage record which I have cited and which you heard as D. Wilson Harrison? A Yes sir.
Q Is your wife, your present wife, the identical person mentioned as Mary Ann McDonald? A Yes sir.
Q Have you and she lived together continuously since your marriage? A Yes sir.
Q Was she living in the Cherokee Nation when you married her? A Yes sir.
Q Has she lived in the Cherokee Nation since then? A Yes sir.
Q Was she a recognized Cherokee by blood when you married her? A Yes sir.
Q Were you ever married before you married her? A No sir.
Q Was she ever married before she married you? A No sir.

The applicant and his wife, Mary A. Harrison are listed for enrollment upon Cherokee Field Card No. 3274, Mary A. Harrison is identified upon an approved partial roll of citizens by blood of the Cherokee Nation, opposite No. 8059.

--------------------------oOo-------------------------

Geo. H. Lessley, being first duly sworn, states that as stenographer to the Commissioner to the Five Civilized Tribes, he reported the proceedings had in the above entitled cause, and that the above and foregoing is a true and correct transcript of his stenographic notes thereof.

Geo H Lessley

Subscribed and sworn to before me this 10th day of January, 1907.

Chas E Webster<br>Notary Public.

## Cherokee Intermarried White 1906
## Volume III

E.C.M.

Cherokee 3274.

### DEPARTMENT OF THE INTERIOR,

### COMMISSIONER TO THE FIVE CIVILIZED TRIBES.

---

In the matter of the application for the enrollment of DAVID W. HARRISON as a citizen by intermarriage of the Cherokee Nation.

### D E C I S I O N

THE RECORDS OF THIS OFFICE SHOW: That at Vinita, Indian Territory, September 22, 1900, application was received by the Commission to the Five Civilized Tribes for the enrollment of David W. Harrison as a citizen by intermarriage of the Cherokee Nation. Further proceedings in the matter of said application were had at Muskogee, Indian Territory, October 7, 1902, and December 27, 1906.

THE EVIDENCE IN THIS CASE SHOWS: That the applicant herein, David W. Harrison, was married in accordance with Cherokee law March 17, 1870, to his wife, Mary A. Harrison, nee McDonald, who was at the time of said marriage a recognized citizen by blood of the Cherokee Nation, who is identified on the Cherokee authenticated tribal roll of 1880, Delaware District, No. 1286, as a native Cherokee, and whose name appears opposite No. 8059 on the approved partial roll of citizens by blood of the Cherokee Nation. It is further shown that since said marriage the said David W. Harrison and Mary A. Harrison have resided together as husband and wife, and have continuously lived in the Cherokee Nation. Said applicant is identified on the Cherokee authenticated tribal roll of 1880, and the Cherokee census roll of 1896, as an intermarried citizen of the Cherokee Nation.

IT IS, THEREFORE, ORDERED AND ADJUDGED: That in accordance with the decision of the Supreme Court of the United States, dated November 5, 1906, in the cases of Daniel Red Bird et al. vs. the United States, Nos. 125, 126, 127 and 128, the said applicant, David W. Harrison, is entitled, under the provisions of Section 21, of the Act of Congress approved June 28, 1898 (30 Stats., 495), to enrollment as a citizen by intermarriage of the Cherokee Nation, and his application for enrollment as such is accordingly granted.

Tams Bixby
Commissioner.

Dated at Muskogee, Indian Territory,
this    JAN 21 1907

# Cherokee Intermarried White 1906
## Volume III

Cherokee
3274

Muskogee, Indian Territory, January 21, 1907.

W. W. Hastings,
    Attorney for the Cherokee Nation,
        Muskogee, Indian Territory.

Dear Sir:

    There is enclosed herewith a copy of the decision of the Commissioner to the Five Civilized Tribes, dated January 21, 1907, granting the application of David W. Harrison as a citizen by intermarriage of the Cherokee Nation.

        Respectfully,

Enc I-35
                                                    Commissioner.

RPI

◇◇◇◇◇

Cherokee 3274   W.W. HASTINGS,   OFFICE OF   H.M. VANCE,
                     ATTORNEY.                                  SECRETARY.

**Attorney for the Cherokee Nation,**
            MUSKOGEE, I. T.     January 24, 1907.

The Commissioner to the Five Civilized Tribes,
    Muskogee, Indian Territory.

Sir:

    Receipt is acknowledged of the testimony and of your decision enrolling David W. Harrison as a citizen by intermarriage of the Cherokee Nation. Time for protesting said decision is waived and I consent that said person may be placed upon the schedule immediately.

        Respectfully,
           W. W. Hastings
           Attorney for the Cherokee Nation.

◇◇◇◇◇

## Cherokee Intermarried White 1906
## Volume III

Cherokee
3274

Muskogee, Indian Territory, January 21, 1907.

David W. Harrison,
 Afton, Indian Territory.

Dear Sir:

There is enclosed herewith a copy of the decision of the Commissioner to the Five Civilized Tribes, dated January 21, 1907, granting your application for enrollment of as a citizen by intermarriage of the Cherokee Nation.

You will be advised when your name has been placed upon a schedule of citizens of the Cherokee Nation and approved by the Secretary of the Interior.

Respectfully,

E.R.C.                                                                Commissioner.
Enc. E.C. 66

---

**Cher IW 80**
**Trans from Cher 3337   3-15-07**

◇◇◇◇◇

E.C.M.

DEPARTMENT OF THE INTERIOR,

COMMISSIONER TO THE FIVE CIVILIZED TRIBES.

In the matter of the application for the enrollment of

BURGES G. CHANDLER

as a citizen by intermarriage of the Cherokee Nation.

CHEROKEE 3337.

◇◇◇◇◇

## Cherokee Intermarried White 1906
## Volume III

DEPARTMENT OF THE INTERIOR,
COMMISSION TO THE FIVE CIVILIZED TRIBES,
VINITA, I.T., SEPT., 24, 1900.

In the matter of the application of Burges G. Chandler for enrollment of himself, wife and three children as citizens of the Cherokee Nation, said Chandler being sworn by Commissioner Needles, testified as follows:

Q What is your name? A Burges G. Chandler.
Q What is your age? A 58.
Q What is your postoffice? A Vinita.
Q What district do you live in? A Coocooweescoowee[sic].
Q Are you a recognized citizen of the Cherokee Nation? A Yes.
Q For whom do you apply? A Myself, wife and three children.
Q Are you a citizen by blood? A No sir.
Q By intermarriage? A Yes.
Q Your father and mother are non-citizens and are not living? A Yes.
Q What is the name of your wife? A Ann E.
Q What is her age? A 52.
Q Her postoffice address? A Vinita.
Q When were you married to her? A '70.
Q What are the names of your children under 21? A Vann S., 17 years old.
    On '96 roll, page 133, number 1028, as Vann Stewart.
Q Next? A Nannie L., 14 years old.
    On '96 roll, page 133, number 1029.
Q Next? A David, 9 years old.
    On '96 roll, page 133, number 1030.
Q Are these children alive and living with you at this time? A Yes.
    Applicant on '80 roll, page 233, number 445, as B. G. Chandler.
    Applicant's wife on '80 roll, page 233, number 446, as Chanler[sic].
    Applicant on '96 roll, page 299, number 237.
    Applicant's wife on '96 roll, page 133, number 1026.
Q Have you lived continuously in the Cherokee Nation for the last 20 years? A Yes.

The name of Burges G. Chandler appears upon the authenticated roll of '80 as B. G. Chandler and the name of the applicant's wife appears upon the roll of '80 as Chanler. Their names also appear upon the census roll of '96 as well as the names of their children, Vann S., Nannie L., and David. They all being duly identified according to page and number of the rolls as indicated in the testimony, the said Burges G. Chandler will be duly listed for enrollment as a citizen of the Cherokee Nation by intermarriage and his wife and children as citizens by blood.

The undersigned, being first duly sworn, states that as stenographer to the Commission to the Five Civilized Tribes, he correctly recorded the testimony and proceedings in this case, and that the foregoing is a true and complete transcript of his stenographic notes thereof.

# Cherokee Intermarried White 1906
# Volume III

B McDonald

Subscribed and sworn to before me this 29th day of Sept., 1900.

CR Breckinridge

Commissioner.

Cherokee 3337.

Department of the Interior,
Commission to the Five Civilized Tribes,
Muskogee, I. T., October 3, 1902.

In the matter of the application of Burges G. Chandler for the enrollment of himself as a citizen by intermarriage, and for the enrollment of his wife, Ann E., and children, Vann S., Nannie L., and David Chandler, as citizens by blood of the Cherokee Nation; he being sworn and examined by the Commission, testified as follows:

Q What is your name? A Burges G. Chandler.
Q What is your age at this time? A Sixty years old.
Q What is your postoffice? A Vinita.
Q Are you the same Burges G. Chandler who made application to this Commission for enrollment as an intermarried citizen on September 24, 1900? A Yes sir.
Q What is your wife's name? A Ann E.
Q Is she a citizen by blood of the Cherokee Nation? A Yes sir.
Q When were you married to your wife, Ann E.? A In '71 I believe.
Q Married under a Cherokee license? A Yes sir.
Q Were you ever married prior to your marriage to this wife? A No sir.
Q Was she ever married before? A Yes sir.
Q How many times? A Once.
Q Was her first husband living or dead when you married her? A He was dead.
Q You are Ann E.'s second husband are you? A Yes sir.
Q And she is your first wife? A Yes sir.
Q Have you and she lived together continuously from the time of your marriage up until the present time? A Yes sir.
Q Never been separated? A No sir.
Q Never married any other woman since you married this woman? A No sir.
Q Living together as husband and wife on the first day of September, 1902? A Yes sir.
Q How long have you lived in the Cherokee Nation? A Have lived here ever since 1878.
Q Have you lived here continuously since 1880 in the Cherokee Nation? A Yes sir.
Q Has your wife lived in the Cherokee Nation since 1880 up until the present time? A Yes sir.
Q Are these children, Vann S., Nannie L. and David your children by your wife, Ann E.? A Yes sir.

# Cherokee Intermarried White 1906
## Volume III

Q Are they all living at this time? A Yes sir.
Q Have they lived in the Cherokee Nation all their lives? A Yes sir.

---

The undersigned, being duly sworn, states that as stenographer to the Commission to the Five Civilized Tribes he correctly recorded the testimony and proceedings in this case, and that the foregoing is a true and correct transcript of his stenographic notes thereof.

E.G. Rothenberger

Subscribed and sworn to before me this 21st day of October, 1902.

BC Jones<br>Notary Public.

◇◇◇◇◇

CHEROKEE-3337.

DEPARTMENT OF THE INTERIOR,
COMMISSIONER TO THE FIVE CIVILIZED TRIBES.
Muskogee, Indian Territory, January 4, 1907.

---

In the matter of making proof of the marriage of Burges G. Chandler to his Cherokee wife, prior to November 1, 1875.

---

Burges G. Chandler, being sworn by W. W. Chappell, a Notary Public, testified as follows:

COMMISSIONER:

Q. What is your name? A. Burges G. Chandler.
Q. What is your age? A. 65.
Q. What is your post office address? A. Vinita.
Q. Do you claim to be a citizen by intermarriage of the Cherokee Nation? A. I do, sir.
Q. Through whom do you claim your citizenship? A. Through my wife, sir.
Q. What is your wife's name? A. Anna Eliza Chandler. Her name was Gunter.
Q. Where were you married to her? A. In Going Snake District.
Q. When were you married to her? A. On August 20, 1870.
Q. Were you married under a Cherokee license? A. I were.

## Cherokee Intermarried White 1906
## Volume III

Q. Have you a copy of that license? A. No sir. I lost it since the Commission commenced. I had it in my pocket when I went to enroll my family and they didn't call on me for them, and I lost them someway.
Q. Who issued those license? A. I think the name of the man was Sharp.
Q. What was his official capacity? A. Clerk of the District. I believe it was him, or a man by the name of Thornton.
Q. Who performed the ceremony? A. A Moravian preacher, but I forget his name. He kept the Moravian mission out there. Me and my wife have been trying to study up his name, but we have forgot it. I have got witnesses here that know all about it.
Q. Was that marriage license filed for record? A. Yes sir.
Q. Where? A. In Going Snake District, at the Clerk's office.
Q. Can you get a certified copy of it at this time? A. No, not unless it is in that Going Snake record.
Q. Were you ever married prior to your marriage to Anna Eliza Chandler? A. No sir.
Q. Had she ever been married prior to her marriage to you? A. Yes sir, she was a widow.
Q. To whom had she been previously married? A. John Powell.
Q. Was he living at the time she married you? A. No sir, he was dead.
Q. What is the date of his death? A. I think he died the latter part of '68, or maybe the first of '69 and I don't know which. Maybe it was the spring of '69 that he died.
Q. Is Anna Eliza Chandler living at this time? A. Yes sir.
Q. Have you resided with her continuously from the time of your marriage up to the present time? A. Yes sir.
Q. In the Cherokee Nation? A. I was backwards and forwards in business, but we claimed this as our home.
Q. Is there anyone here today who was present at your marriage? A. Yes sir.
Q. What are their names? A. I know Lafayette Duckworth is here, and he was there. He is the man that got up my petition.
Q. You say that you secured a certified copy of that marriage license, and it was lost by you? A. I got the license back after it was recorded, and took that to the Dawes Commission when they were enrolling at Vinita. I put them in my pocket and took them and they never asked me for it, and some how or other I got it lost.

(Applicant is identified upon the 1880 Roll opposite No. 445, and upon the 1896 Census Roll opposite No. 237. The wife of said applicant is identified upon the 1880 Roll opposite No. 446, and upon the 1896 Census Roll opposite No. 133. Her name also appears upon the final roll of citizens by blood of the Cherokee Nation, opposite No. 8186.)

Q. Are there present today any of the signers of your petition? A. I don't know. This witness can tell you more about that than I can.

Witness excused.

## Cherokee Intermarried White 1906
## Volume III

Lewis L. Duckworth, being sworn by W. W. Chappell, a Notary Public, testified as follows:

Q. What is your name? A. Lewis L. Duckworth.
Q. What is your age? A. 64.
Q. What is your post office address? A. Siloam Springs, Ark.
Q. Do you know Burges G. Chandler and Anna Eliza Chandler? A. Yes sir.
Q. Are you related to them in any way? A. Only by marriage.
Q. How are you related? A. My wife is a sister to Mrs. Chandler
Q. Is Anna Eliza Chandler a citizen by blood of the Cherokee Nation[sic] A. Yes sir.
Q. Do you know when she was married to Burges G. Chandler? A. It was in '70 and I think in the month of August.
Q. Were you present at that marriage? A. Yes sir.
Q. Do you know who issued the license? A. No sir, I don't remember the name of the clerk.
Q. Do you remember by whom they were married? A. I don't remember his name. He was a Moravian preacher.
Q. Where were they married? A. In Going Snake District.
Q. Were you one of the signers to the petition for this witness? A. I think not. We got the license under the Cherokee law, and under that law all the signers had to be Cherokee by blood.
Q. You claim by intermarriage? A. Yes sir.
Q. You do not know any of the signers to the petition? A. I think I remember that Thompson Bean signed it -- they were all Indians by blood -- I am not positive about that, but I think that is right.
Q. Have Burges G. and Anna Eliza Chandler resided together continuously since they were married? A. Yes sir.
Q. As husband and wife? A. Yes sir.
Q. Been held out as such to the community? A. Yes sir.
Q. Did you ever see the license under which they were married? A. Yes sir -- I know he had a license. I got up his petition, and they were married at my house.
Q. Do you know what became of the license? A. No sir.

Witness excused.

Anna Eliza Chandler, being sworn by W. W. Chappell, a Notary Public, testified as follows:

COMMISSIONER:

Q. What is your name? A. Anna Eliza Chandler.
Q. What is your age? A. 59.
Q. What is your post office address? A. Vinita.
Q. You are a citizen of the Cherokee Nation by blood? A. Yes sir.
Q. You are the wife of Burges G. Chandler? A. Yes sir.
Q. When were you married to him? A. In '70.

## Cherokee Intermarried White 1906
## Volume III

Q. Where were you married? A. In Going Snake District.
Q. Was the marriage under a Cherokee license? A. Yes sir.
Q. Do you know who issued the license? A. The Clerk's name was Wright.
Q. Who performed the ceremony? A. I can't call the preacher's name. I have tried and tried.
Q. State what became of the license? A. I don't know what became of them after I gave them to Mr. Chandler.
Q. Was the license returned to be recorded? A. Yes sir, and then we got them back.
Q. Please state what followed from that time on with reference to the license? A. I put them in a little tin box down in an old trunk and they stayed there till the Dawes Commission come to Vinita, and Mr. Chandler said he thought they would want it, so I hunted it up and gave it to Mr. Chandler, and afterwards I asked him -- I said "Well, did you have to give your license to the Dawes Commission"? and he said "they never asked me for it." Then I said "what did you do with it", and he said "I put it in the bank in a box for safe-keeping", and when he went to age it, it wasn't there.
Q. Were you ever married prior to your marriage to Burges G. Chandler? A. Yes sir.
Q. To whom? A. John Powell.
Q. Was he living at the time of your marriage to Chandler? A. No sir.
Q. You have lived together continuously as man and wife since your marriage in '70?
A. Yes sir.

Witness excused.

---

Eula Jeanes Branson, being sworn, states that she correctly reported the proceedings had in the above and foregoing on the 4th. day of January, 1907.

Eula Jeanes Branson

Subscribed and sworn to before me, this 4th. day of January, 1907.

Edward Merrick
Notary Public.

## Cherokee Intermarried White 1906
## Volume III

Cherokee 3337.

DEPARTMENT OF THE INTERIOR,
COMMISSIONER TO THE FIVE CIVILIZED TRIBES.
Muskogee, Ind. Ter., January 7, 1907.

In the matter of the application for the enrollment of Burges G. Chandler as a citizen by intermarriage of the Cherokee Nation.

Burgess G. Chandler being first duly sworn by Edward Merrick, a Notary Public for the Western District of Indian Territory, testified as follows:

By the Commissioner:
Q What is your name? A Burges G. Chandler.
Q What is your age? A Sixty-five.
Q What is your postoffice address? A Vinita, I. T.
Q You claim citizen in the Cherokee nation[sic] by intermarriage[sic] A Yes sir.
Q Through whom do you claim such right? A My wife.
Q What is her name? A Annie E. Chandler, formerly Powell, formerly Gunther.
Q When were you married to Ann E. Powell? A I gave them the 20th of August the other day, but now I find that it is the 21st of August, 1870.
Q At what place were you married? A Going Snake District.
Q By whom were you married? A His name is right there; I can't recall it just now; he was a Moravian preacher.
Q Have you any documentary evidence of this marriage? A None but this.
> The applicant presents an instrument purporting to be the certificate of Wesley J. Spaugh, minister of the Moravian church, that on August 21, 1870, he married B. G. Chandler and Miss Anna E. Powell, Indian Territory formerly Gunther.
> An endorsement on said certificate shows that same was filed for record by W. H. Hunton, District Judge of Goning[sic] Snake District, Cherokee Nation.
> Said instrument is filed in this case and made a part hereof.

Q Were you eve married prior to your marriage to Anna E. Powell? A No sir.
Q Was Annie E. Powell ever married prior to her marriage to you? A Yes sir.
Q To whom? A John Powell.
Q Was John Powell living at the time of her marriage to you? A No sir.
Q Was Annie E. Chandler married prior to the time of her marriage to John Powell?
A Not as I know of. I never heard of it if she was.
Q Is Annie E. Chandler living at this time? A Yes sir.
Q Have you and she lived together continuously as husband and wife in the Cherokee nation[sic] since the date of your marriage in 1870 until the present time? A Yes, we was out part of the time?
Q When were you away? A We was out in '72 I think.
Q How long did you remain away at that time? A I don't know. We never moved all our household effects.

## Cherokee Intermarried White 1906
## Volume III

Q Duting[sic] the time of your absence from the Cherokee Nation did you still consider the Cherokee Nation your home? A I did. I have always considered it so ever since I was married.

       The applicant, Burges G. Chandler is identified on the Cherokee authenticated tribal roll of 1880, Delaware District, opposite No. 445. The name of his wife Annie E. Campbell[sic] is included in an approved partial roll of citizens by blood of the Cherokee Nation opposite No. 8186.
The name of the applicant and his wife also appear on the 1896 roll opposite Nos. 237 and 1026.

-------

       Frances R. Lane upon oath states that as stenographer to the Commissioner to the Five Civilized Tribes she reported the testimony in the above entitled cause and that the foregoing is an accurate transcript of her stenographic notes thereof.

                                                   Frances R Lane

Subscribed and sworn to before me this January 8, 1907.

                                                   Edward Merrick
                                                   Notary Public.

◇◇◇◇◇

```
                    )
Cherokee Nation     )
                    )
Going Snake Dist.   )
                    )
```

       To all whom it may concern be it know that authority is hereby granted to any of the judges of any of the courts in the Cherokee Nation and all ministers of all evangelical denominations having the care of souls are hereby authorized and empowered to solemnize the rites of matrimony according to the ceremonies usually observed and employed in such cases between Mr. B. G. Chandler an unmarried citizen of the United States and Miss Ann E. Powel[sic] formerly Miss Ann E. Gunter a Cherokee citizen he the said B. G. Chandler having complied with the law in such cases this given from under my hand in office this the 18th day of Aug. 1870.

                                            John Thornton clk of the
                                            G. Snake Dist Court, C.N.

# Cherokee Intermarried White 1906
# Volume III

CERTIFICATE ON BACK:

To all whom it may concern; this is to certify that I, W. J. Spaugh, a minister of the Moravian Church have this the 21 of Aug. 1870, joined together in the holy estate of matrimony Mr. B. G. Chandler & Mrs. Anna E. Powel, formerly Gunther.

Wesley J. Spaugh,

Mr. B G Chandler you Marriage is Recorded as Law requires.

W. G. Thornton<br>Dist Judge G. S. Dist C.N.

---

This certifies that the undersigned, being duly sworn, states that as stenographer to the Commissioner to the Five Civilized Tribes, she made the above and foregoing copy, and that the same is a full, true and correct copy of the original instrument now on file in this office.

Sarah Waters

Subscribed and Sworn to before me this 17th day of January, 1907.

John E. Tidwell<br>Notary Public.

◇◇◇◇◇

E.C.M.                                                                                                      Cherokee 3337.

DEPARTMENT OF THE INTERIOR,

COMMISSIONER TO THE FIVE CIVILIZED TRIBES.

In the matter of the application for the enrollment of BURGES G. CHANDLER as a citizen by intermarriage of the Cherokee Nation.

D E C I S I O N

THE RECORDS OF THIS OFFICE SHOW: That at Vinita, Indian Territory, September 24, 1900, application was received by the Commission to the Five Civilized Tribes for the enrollment of Burges G. Chandler as a citizen by intermarriage of the Cherokee Nation. Further proceedings in the matter of said application were had at Muskogee, Indian Territory, October 3, 1902, and January 4 and 7, 1907.

## Cherokee Intermarried White 1906
## Volume III

THE EVIDENCE IN THIS CASE SHOWS: That the applicant herein, Burges G. Chandler, a white man, was married in accordance with Cherokee law August 21, 1870, to his wife, Ann E. Chandler, who was at the time of said marriage a recognized citizen by blood of the Cherokee Nation, who is identified on the Cherokee authenticated tribal roll of 1880, Delaware District, No. 446, as a native Cherokee; and whose name appears opposite No. 8186 on the approved partial roll of citizens by blood of the Cherokee Nation. It is further shown that since said marriage the said Burges G. Chandler an Ann E. Chandler have e resided together as husband and wife, and have continuously lived in the Cherokee Nation. Said applicant is identified on the Cherokee authenticated tribal roll of 1880, and the Cherokee census roll of 1896, as an intermarried citizen of the Cherokee Nation.

IT IS, THEREFORE, ORDERED AND ADJUDGED: That in accordance with the decision of the Supreme Court of the United States, dated November 5, 1906, in the cases of Daniel Red Bird et al. vs. the United States, Nos. 125, 126, 127 and 128, the said applicant, Burges G. Chandler, is entitled, under the provisions of Section 21, of the Act of Congress approved June 28, 1898 (30 Stats., 495), to enrollment as a citizen by intermarriage of the Cherokee Nation, and his application for enrollment as such is accordingly granted.

Tams Bixby
Commissioner.

Dated at Muskogee, Indian Territory,
this    JAN 21 1907

◇◇◇◇◇

Cherokee 3337

Muskogee, Indian Territory, January 21, 1907.

W. W. Hastings,
  Attorney for the Cherokee Nation,
    Muskogee, Indian Territory.

Dear Sir:

  There is enclosed herewith copy of the decision of the Commissioner to the Five Civilized Tribes, dated January 21, 1907, granting the application for the enrollment of Burges G. Chandler as a citizen by intermarriage of the Cherokee Nation.

Respectfully,

Enc I-32               Commissioner.

RPI

◇◇◇◇◇

# Cherokee Intermarried White 1906
## Volume III

Cherokee 3337    W.W. HASTINGS. ATTORNEY.    OFFICE OF    H.M. VANCE. SECRETARY.

**Attorney for the Cherokee Nation,**

MUSKOGEE, I. T.    January 21, 1907.

The Commissioner to the Five Civilized Tribes,
     Muskogee, Indian Territory.

Sir:

     Receipt is acknowledged of the testimony and of your decision enrolling Burges G. Chandler as a citizen by intermarriage of the Cherokee Nation. Time for protesting said decision is waived and I consent that said person may be placed upon the schedule immediately.

                       Respectfully,

                       W. W. Hastings
                       Attorney for the Cherokee Nation.

◇◇◇◇◇

Cherokee 3337

                       Muskogee, Indian Territory, January 24, 1907.

Burges G. Chandler,
     Vinita, Indian Territory.

Dear Sir:

     There is enclosed herewith copy of the decision of the Commissioner to the Five Civilized Tribes, dated January 21, 1907, granting the application for your enrollment as a citizen by intermarriage of the Cherokee Nation.

     You will be advised when your name has been placed upon a schedule of citizens of the Cherokee Nation and approved by the Secretary of the Interior.

                       Respectfully,

Enc I-103                                    Commissioner.

RPI

◇◇◇◇◇

## Cherokee Intermarried White 1906
## Volume III

Cherokee I.W. 80

Muskogee, Indian Territory, April 8, 1907.

Burges G. Chandler,
    Vinita, Indian Territory.

Dear Sir:

    Your marriage license and certificate, filed in connection with your application for enrollment as a citizen by intermarriage of the Cherokee Nation, is returned to you herewith, copies of the same being retained in the files of this office.

Respectfully,

Incl. P-4-22
MMP

Acting Commissioner.

---

**Cher IW 81**
**Trans from Cher 3397 3-15-07**

◇◇◇◇◇

DEPARTMENT OF THE INTERIOR,
COMMISSION TO THE FIVE CIVILIZED TRIBES,
VINITA, I.T., SEPTEMBER 24, 1900.

    In the matter of the application of William H. Howell for the enrollment of himself and wife as citizens of the Cherokee Nation; said Howelll[sic] being sworn by Commissioner T.B. Needles, testified as follows:

Q What is your name? A William H. Howell.
Q What is your age, Mr. Howell? A 55.
Q What is your post office address? A Oceoma[sic].
Q What district do you live in? A Delaware.
Q Are you a recognized citizen of the Cherokee Nation? A Yes, sir.
Q By intermarriage? A Yes, sir.
Q For whom do you apply for enrollment? A My wife and myself.
Q What is the name of your wife? A Eliza.
Q When were you married to her? A '69.

    1880 enrollment; page 267, #1247, William Howell, Delaware.
    1880 enrollment; page 267, #1248, Eliza Howell, Delaware.
    1896 enrollment; page 574, #254, William Howell, Delaware.
    1896 enrollment; page 477, #1350, Eliza Howell, Delaware.

# Cherokee Intermarried White 1906
## Volume III

Q What is the age of your wife? A 55.
Q You have lived in the Cherokee Nation ever since you were married? A Yes, sir.

Com'r Needles:--The name of William H. Howell and his wife Eliza Howell appear upon the authenticated roll of 1880 as well as the census roll of 1896. They being dully[sic] identified and having made satisfactory proof as to his residence, the said William H. Howell will be duly listed by this Commission for enrollment as a Cherokee citizen by intermarriage, and his wife, Eliza, as a Cherokee by blood.

---oooOOOooo---

J. O. Rosson, being first duly sworn, states that as stenographer to the Commission to the Five Civilized Tribes, he correctly recorded the testimony and proceedings in this case, and that the foregoing is a true and complete transcript of his stenographic notes thereof.

JO Rosson

Subscribed and sworn to before me this 25th day of September, 1900.

TB Needles<br>Commissioner.

R.

## DEPARTMENT OF THE INTERIOR.
### Commission to the Five Civilized Tribes.
### Muskogee, Indian Territory, October 4th, 1902.

In the matter of the application of William H. Howell for the enrollment of himself as a citizen by intermarriage of the Cherokee Nation and for the enrollment of his wife, Eliza Howell, as a citizen by blood of the Cherokee Nation.

Supplemental to #3397.

Appearances:
Applicant appears in person.
Cherokee Nation by J. C. Starr.

WILLIAM H. HOWELL, being duly sworn, testified as follows:
Examination by the Commission:
Q. What is your name, please? A. William H. Howell.

# Cherokee Intermarried White 1906
## Volume III

Q. What is your age at this time? A. 57.
Q. What is your post office? A. Oseuma, Indian Territory.
Q. Are you the same William H. Howell for whom application was made to this Commission for enrollment as an intermarried citizen on September 24th 1900?
A. Yes, sir.
Q. What is your wife's name? A. Eliza.
Q. Has she got any middle name? A. No, sir.
Q. Is she a citizen by blood? A. Yes, sir.
Q. When were you and your wife Eliza Married? A. '69, in February.
Q. Were you ever married prior to your marriage to your wife Eliza? A. No, sir.
Q. Was she ever married prior to her marriage to you? A. No, sir.
Q. You are her first husband, she is your first wife? A. Yes, sir.
Q. Have you and she lived together as husband and wife from the time of your marriage up to the present time? A. Yes, sir.
Q. Never been separated? A. No sir.
Q. You have never been married to any other woman since your marriage to Eliza Howell A. No, sir.
Q. Living together as husband and wife on the first of September, 1902? A. Yes, sir.
Q. Have you and your wife Eliza lived in the Cherokee Nation all the time since 1880 up to the present time? A. Yes, sir.
Q. Never been out of the nation? A. She was at Southwest City. I sent her down there for her health.
Q. Did you go there with her.[sic] A. No, sir; I stayed most of the time on the ranch.
Q. What year was she in Southwest city? A. A.[sic] I guess that was about-----
Q. How many years ago? A. About 17 years aho[sic]; 16 or 17.
Q. She has lived in the Cherokee Nation all the time since then? A. Yes, since and before that.
Q. Did you keep house in Southwest City? A. Yes, sir; we kept house and I stayed over on the place.
Q. She has never lived out for the last 17 years? A. No, sir.
Q. Nor you haven't either? A. No, sir.

Jesse O. Carr, being first duly sworn, states that as stenographer to the Commission to the Five Civilized Tribes he reported the above entitled case and that the foregoing is a true and complete transcript of his stenographic notes thereof.

Jesse O. Carr

Subscribed and sworn to before me this 28th day of October, 1902.

BC Jones
Notary Public.

## Cherokee Intermarried White 1906
## Volume III

LGD

Cherokee 3397.

DEPARTMENT OF THE INTERIOR,
COMMISSIONER TO THE FIVE CIVILIZED TRIBES.

Muskogee, Indian Territory, January 3, 1907.

In the matter of the application of WILLIAM H. HOWELL for enrollment as a citizen by intermarriage of the Cherokee Nation.

William H. Howell, being first duly sworn by B. P. Rasmus, a notary public, testified as follows:

Q What is your name? A William H. Howell.
Q What is your age? A 60 years old.
Q What is your post office address? A Oseuma, I. T.
Q Do you claim to be a citizen by intermarriage of the Cherokee Nation.[sic] A Yes.
Q Through whom do you claim your rights? A Eliza Ballard, my wife.
Q When were you married to her? A In February, 1869.
Q Was she a citizen of the Cherokee Nation at the time you married her? A Yes.
Q Were you married according to the Cherokee law? A Yes.
Q Have you got your license? A Yes. (Presents a copy of license to be filed in his case).
Q Do you want to offer this in evidence? A Yes.

Applicant offers in evidence license issued to him on the 10th day of February, 1869, by T. J. McGehee[sic], Clerk of the Delaware District, to marry Miss Eliza Ballard, a citizen by blood of the Cherokee Nation, which shows that he was married on the 12th day of February, 1869.

Q Have you a certificate of marriage? A No sir.
Q Who married you? A Preacher Ketchum.
Q Were you married under this license? A Yes. It was returned to me.
Q Were you ever married before you married Eliza Ballard? A No.
Q Was she ever married before she married you? A No.
Q Have you lived together as husband and wife continuously in the Cherokee Nation from the time of your marriage up to the present time? A Yes.

The applicant is identified on the 1880 Cherokee roll, Delaware District, opposite No. 1247. His wife, through whom he claims citizenship, is identified on said roll in the said District opposite No. 1248. She is also identified upon the final roll of citizens by blood of the Cherokee Nation opposite No. 8304.

## Cherokee Intermarried White 1906
## Volume III

Witness excused.

Demie T. Stubblefield, being first duly sworn, on oath states that as stenographer to the Commissioner to the Five Civilized Tribes she reported the above proceedings, and that the above and foregoing is a true and correct transcript of her stenographic notes thereof.

Demie T. Stubblefield

Subscribed and sworn to before me this, January 4, 1907.

Edward Merrick<br>Notary Public.

◇◇◇◇◇

*(The Marriage License and Certificate below typed as given.)*

( C O P Y )

Clerk Office )
)
Delaware Dist )
)
Cherokee Nation )

        This is to Certify By Me that William H. Howel a Citizen of the United States Was License to Marry Eliza Ballard A Legal Citizen of the Cherokee Nation By Cherokee Blood License Issued on the 10th Day February 1869 and the Said License Executed and Returned on the 12th Day February 1869 The Said William H. Howel having fully Complied with the Law enacted By the National Council Baring date October the 15th 1855 Regulating Intermarriage of White men and forigners To Cherokee Women

(Signed)   T. J. McGhee<br>Clerk Delaware Dist C N

This is To Certify By me That The above is a true Copy from the Record on this the 1st Day October 1887

(Signed)   T. J. McGhee<br>Clerk Delaware Dist C N

This certifies that the undersigned, being duly sworn, states that, as stenographer for the Commissioner to the Five Civilized Tribes, she made the above and foregoing copy,

## Cherokee Intermarried White 1906
## Volume III

and that the same is a full, true and correct copy of the original instrument now on file in this office.

Georgia Coberly

Subscribed and sworn to before me this 17th day of January, 1907.

Chas E Webster<br>Notary Public.

◇◇◇◇◇

E.C.M.                                                                                                                                     Cherokee 3397.

DEPARTMENT OF THE INTERIOR,

COMMISSIONER TO THE FIVE CIVILIZED TRIBES.

In the matter of the application for the enrollment of WILLIAM H. HOWELL as a citizen by intermarriage of the Cherokee Nation.

D E C I S I O N

THE RECORDS OF THIS OFFICE SHOW: That on September 24, 1900, application was received by the Commission to the Five Civilized Tribes for the enrollment of William H. Howell as a citizen by intermarriage of the Cherokee Nation. Further proceedings in the matter of said application were had at Muskogee, Indian Territory, October 4, 1902, and January 3, 1907.

THE EVIDENCE IN THIS CASE SHOWS: That the applicant herein, William H. Howell, a white man, was married in accordance with the Cherokee law February 12, 1869, to his wife, Eliza Howell, nee Ballard, who was at the time of said marriage a recognized citizen by blood of the Cherokee Nation, who is identified on the Cherokee authenticated tribal roll of 1880, Delaware District, No. 1248, as a native Cherokee, and whose name is included in the approved partial roll of citizens by blood of the Cherokee Nation, opposite No. 8304. It is further shown that from the time of said marriage the said William H. Howell and Eliza Howell resided together as husband and wife, and continuously lived in the Cherokee Nation up to and including September 1, 1902. Said applicant is identified on the Cherokee authenticated tribal roll of 1880, and the Cherokee census roll of 1896, as an intermarried citizen of the Cherokee Nation.

IT IS, THEREFORE, ORDERED AND ADJUDGED: That in accordance with the decision of the Supreme Court of the United States, dated November 5, 1906, in the cases of Daniel Red Bird et al. vs. the United States, Nos. 125, 126, 127 and 128, the said applicant, William H. Howell, is entitled, under the provisions of Section 21, of the Act of Congress approved June 28, 1898 (30 Stats., 495), to enrollment as a citizen by

# Cherokee Intermarried White 1906
## Volume III

intermarriage of the Cherokee Nation, and his application for enrollment as such is accordingly granted.

            Tams Bixby
                 Commissioner.

Dated at Muskogee, Indian Territory,
this  JAN 2 1907

◇◇◇◇◇

Cherokee
3397.

          Muskogee, Indian Territory, December 27, 1906.

William H. Howell,
    Osema[sic], Indian Territory.

Dear Sir:

  November 6, 1906, the United States Supreme Court held that white persons who intermarried with Cherokee citizens according to Cherokee law prior to November 1, 1875, are entitled to enrollment and allotments of land as citizens of the Cherokee Nation.

  You are advised that to properly determine your right to enrollment as a citizen by intermarriage of the Cherokee Nation, it will be necessary for you to appear before the Commissioner for the purpose of giving testimony as to the date of your marriage and whether or not your wife, by reason of your marriage to whom you claim the right to enrollment as a citizen of the Cherokee Nation, was a recognized citizen of the Cherokee Nation at the time of your marriage to her, and whether or not you were married to her in accordance with Cherokee laws.

  You are therefore directed to appear before the Commissioner at Muskogee, Indian Territory, at 9 o'clock A. M., on Friday, January 4, 1907, and give testimony as above indicated.

            Respectfully,

H.J.C.                Acting Commissioner.

◇◇◇◇◇

# Cherokee Intermarried White 1906
# Volume III

Cherokee 3397

Muskogee, Indian Territory, January 21, 1907.

W. W. Hastings,
    Attorney for the Cherokee Nation,
        Muskogee, Indian Territory.

Dear Sir:

    There is enclosed herewith a copy of the decision of the Commissioner to the Five Civilized Tribes, dated January 21, 1907, granting the application for the enrollment of William H. Howell as a citizen by intermarriage of the Cherokee Nation.

        Respectfully,

Enc I-37                                               Commissioner.

RPI

◇◇◇◇◇

Cherokee 3397     W.W. HASTINGS, ATTORNEY.     OFFICE OF     H.M. VANCE, SECRETARY.

**Attorney for the Cherokee Nation,**
MUSKOGEE, I. T.     January 21, 1907.

The Commissioner to the Five Civilized Tribes,
    Muskogee, Indian Territory.

Sir:

    Receipt is acknowledged of the testimony and of your decision enrolling William H. Howell as a citizen by intermarriage of the Cherokee Nation. Time for protesting said decision is waived and I consent that said person may be placed upon the schedule immediately.

        Respectfully,
            W. W. Hastings
            Attorney for the Cherokee Nation.

◇◇◇◇◇

# Cherokee Intermarried White 1906
## Volume III

Cherokee 3397

Muskogee, Indian Territory, January 24, 1907.

William H. Howell,
    Osema[sic], Indian Territory.

Dear Sir:

    There is enclosed herewith a copy of the decision of the Commissioner to the Five Civilized Tribes, dated January 21, 1907, granting your application for enrollment as a citizen by intermarriage of the Cherokee Nation.

    You will be advised when your name has been placed upon a schedule of citizens of the Cherokee Nation and approved by the Secretary of the Interior.

                      Respectfully,

Encl. H-31                                       Commissioner.
JMH

◇◇◇◇◇

Cherokee I.W. 81

Muskogee, Indian Territory, April 8, 1907.

William H. Howell,
    Oseuma, Indian Territory.

Dear Sir:

    Your marriage license and certificate filed in the matter of your application for enrollment as a citizen by intermarriage of the Cherokee Nation, is returned to you herewith, copies of the same being retained in the files of this office.

                      Respectfully,

Incl. P-4-21                                 Acting Commissioner.
MMP

---

**Cher IW 82**
**Trans from Cher 3495  3-15-07**

◇◇◇◇◇

## Cherokee Intermarried White 1906
## Volume III

E.C.M.

### DEPARTMENT OF THE INTERIOR,

### COMMISSIONER TO THE FIVE CIVILIZED TRIBES.

---

In the matter of the application for the enrollment of

### JOHN T. SCOTT

as a citizen by intermarriage of the Cherokee Nation.

---

### CHEROKEE 3495

◇◇◇◇◇

Department of the Interior,
Commission to the Five Civilized Tribes,
Vinita, I.T., September 25, 1900.

In the matter of the application of John T. Scott for the enrollment of himself, wife and children as Cherokee citizens; being sworn and examined by Commissioner Breckinridge he testified as follows:

Q What is your full name? A John T. Scott.
Q How old are you? A 62.
Q What is your post-office? A Vinita.
Q What district do you live in? A Delaware.
Q Who is it you want to have put on the roll? A Myself wife and three children.
Q Are you a Cherokee by blood? A White man.
Q Your wife a Cherokee? A Yes sir.
Q What proportion of Cherokee blood? A Quarter.
Q Have you a marriage license and certificate? A I have a certificate.
Q What has become of your license? A The judge lost them, and give me a certificate.
Q You are on the roll of 1880? A No sir. I wasn't at home when they enrolled.
Q When were you married? A 15th of November 1869.
Q Who were you married to then? A Amanda Cherokee Duncan.
Q Is she a Cherokee or a white woman? A Cherokee.
Q Is she dead or alive? A She is living.
Q Have you lived with her ever since your marriage in 1869.[sic] A Yes sir.
Q What district were you living in in 1880? A Delaware.
Q In 1896, in Delaware? A Yes sir.
Q Give me the names of your children? A George Washington, 16 years old. James William, 13 years old; Charles Duncan, 7 years old.

135

## Cherokee Intermarried White 1906
## Volume III

Q That's all is it? A Yes sir.
Q All living now are they? A All living.
Q How old is your wife now? A 50 years old.
Q Give me her father's name? A Y. C. G. Duncan.
Q Dead or alive? A Dead.
Q Cherokee or a white man? A Cherokee.
Q How long has he been dead? A 18 years.
Q Her mother's name? A Siney Duncan.
Q Cherokee or a white woman? A Cherokee.
Q Dead or alive? A Dead.
Q How long has she been dead? A 21 years.
1880 roll page 314 #2341 John Scott, Delaware District.
1880 roll page 314 #2342 Cherokee Scott, Delaware, Native Cherokee
1896 roll page 588 (#429) John T. Scott, Delaware District; #479
1896 roll page 528 #2726 Amanda C. Scott, Delaware;
1896 roll page 528 #2728 George W. Scott        "
1896 roll page 528 #2729 James W. Scott, Delaware;
1896 roll page 528 #2730 Charles D. Scott Delaware Dist.
Q Is your wife named Amanda Cherokee? A Yes sir.
Q But you wat[sic] her name down Cherokee? A She always signed her name Cherokee; her full lawful name is Amanda Cherokee.
Q Has your wife lived in the Cherokee Nation all her life? A Yes sir.

Com'r Breckinridge: The applicant applies for the enrollment of himself, his wife and three children; his wife is identified on the rolls of 1880 and 1896 as a native Cherokee; she has lived in the Cherokee Nation all her life and she will be listed now for enrollment as a Cherokee by blood. The applicant is identified with his wife on the rolls of 1880 and 1896; he has lived with her in the Cherokee Natin[sic] ever since their married[sic] in 1867[sic], and he will be listed now for enrollment as a Cherokee by adoption. Their three children, whose names are given in the testimony, are identified with their parents on the roll of 1896; they are living at this time and they will be listed now for enrollment as Cherokees by blood.

M.D. Green, being first duly sworn, states that as stenographer to the Commission to the Five Civilized Tribes he correctly recorded the testimony and proceedings in this case and that the foregoing is a true and complete transcript of his stenographic notes thereof.

MD Green

Subscribed and sworn to before me this 26 day of September 1900.

CR Breckinridge

Commissioner.

◇◇◇◇◇

# Cherokee Intermarried White 1906
# Volume III

DEPARTMENT OF THE INTERIOR.
Commission to the Five Civilized Tribes.
Muskogee, Indian Territory, October 9th, 1902.

In the matter of the application of John T. Scott for the enrollment of himself as a citizen by intermarriage of the Cherokee Nation and for the enrollment of his wife, Amanda C. Scott, and his children, George W., James W. and Charles D. Scott, as citizens by blood of the Cherokee Nation.

Supplemental to #3495.

JOHN T. SCOTT, being duly sworn, testified as follows:--
Examination by the Commission.
Q. What is your name? A. John T. Scott.
Q. How old are you? A. 64.
Q. What is your post office? A. Vinita.
Q. You are a citizen of the Cherokee Nation by intermarriage? A. Yes, sir.
Q. On the eighty roll as an intermarried white man? A. Yes, sir.
Q. What was the name of your wife in 1880? A. We were married in '69. Her name was Cherokee Duncan.
Q. The same wife you have now? A. Yes, sir.
Q. Have you and your wife been living in the Cherokee Nation since 1880? A. Yes, sir; since '69.
Q. You have never made your home outside of the Cherokee Nation? A. No, sir.
Q. Never been separated? A. No, sir.
Q. How many children have you? A. Seven.
Q. How many at home now? A. Three.
Q. You and your wife were living together on the first of September, 1902? A. Yes, sir.

-:-:-:-:-:-:-:-:-:-:-:-:-:-:-:-:-:-:-

Jesse O. Carr, being first duly sworn, states that as stenographer to the Commission to the Five Civilized Tribes he reported the above entitled case and that the foregoing is a true and complete transcript of his stenographic notes thereof.

Jesse O. Carr

Subscribed and sworn to before me this 18th day of December, 1902.

PG Reuter
Notary Public.

## Cherokee Intermarried White 1906
## Volume III

C. F. B.  Cherokee 3495.

DEPARTMENT OF THE INTERIOR,
COMMISSION TO THE FIVE CIVILIZED TRIBES.
Muskogee, Indian Territory, January 7, 1907.

In the Matter of the Application for the Enrollment of John T. Scott as a citizen by intermarriage of the Cherokee Nation.

APPEARANCES:
Applicant appears in person.
Cherokee Nation represented by H. M. Vance, in behalf of W. W. Hastings, Attorney.

John T. Scott being first duly sworn by John E. Tidwell, Notary Public, testified as follows:

ON BEHALF OF COMMISSIONER.

Q What is your name?  A John T. Scott.
Q What is your age?  A In my 70th year.
Q What is your post office address?
A Vinita, Indian Territory.
Q Do you claim the right to enrollment as a citizen by intermarriage of the Cherokee Nation?
A Yes sir.
Q You have no Cherokee blood?
A No sir.
Q Your only claim to the right to enrollment as a citizen of the Cherokee Nation is by virtue of your marriage to a citizen by blood of the Nation?
A Yes sir.
Q What is the name of the Citizen through whom you claim that right?
A Amanda Cherokee Duncan.
Q When did you marry her?
A In '69.
Q Was she a recognized citizen of the Cherokee Nation at the time you married her?
A Yes sir.
Q Living in the Cherokee country?
A Right in the Cherokee country; never lived anywhere else.
Q Did you marry her in accordance with the laws of the Cherokee Nation?
A Yes sir.
Q Have you your license with you?
A I have a certificate from the Judge.

# Cherokee Intermarried White 1906
## Volume III

The applicant presents an original marriage certificate showing that on November 15, 1869, J. T. Scott was lawfully married to Cherokee Duncan. This certificate is signed by W. G. Thornton, Junior, Judge of Going Snake District.

Q Did you secure your license prior to the time this Judge married you?
A I had gone to the clerk and applied for license but he didn't have any writing material and he told me to pay him the money and he would leave the license with his father, who was the Judge.
Q You had secured the necessary signers to your petition?
A Yes sir; and presented them to the Clerk and then he said the Judge would also have to approve it. He misplaced the license and gave me this as evidence.
Q When did this Judge give you this certificate?
A Shortly after we were married.
Q Is this the date, September 8, 1870?
A Yes.
Q Is this person mention in this certificate as Cherokee Duncan identical with the person you mention as your wife, whose name you gave as Amanda C. Scott?
A Yes sir.
Q Since your marriage to your wife, Amanda C. Scott, November 15, 1869, have you and she continuously lived together as husband and wife?
A Yes sir.
Q You have always lived in the Cherokee Nation?
A Yes sir.

The witness, John T. Scott is identified on the Cherokee Authenticated Tribal Roll of 1880, Delaware District, No. 2341. His wife is also identified on said roll at No. 2342 and her name is included in the partial roll of citizens by blood of the Cherokee Nation, opposite No. 8507.

---

The undersigned being first duly sworn states that as stenographer to the Commission to the Five Civilized Tribes, she correctly recorded the testimony taken in this case and that the foregoing is a full, true and correct transcript of her stenographic notes thereof.

Myrtle Hill

Subscribed and sworn to before me this the 8th day of January, 1907.

John E. Tidwell
Notary Public.

## Cherokee Intermarried White 1906
## Volume III

*(The Marriage Certificate below typed as given.)*

Going Snake District Sept 8/70

This is to certify that J.T. Scott was lawfully married to Cherokee Duncan Nov 15-1869

W.G. Thornton

Is Judg of Going Sake D.S

The undersigned being duly sworn states, that as stenographer, she made the above copy, and that the same is a true and correct copy of the instrument now on file in this office.

Mary Tabor Mallory

Subscribed and sworn to before me this the 17th. day of January 1907.

Chas E Webster
Notary Public.

◇◇◇◇◇

E C M                                                                                          Cherokee 3495

DEPARTMENT OF THE INTERIOR,
COMMISSIONER TO THE FIVE CIVILIZED TRIBES.

In the matter of the application for the enrollment of John T. Scott as a citizen by intermarriage of the Cherokee Nation.

D E C I S I O N.

THE RECORDS OF THIS OFFICE SHOW: That at Vinita, Indian Territory, September 25, 1900, application was received by the Commission to the Five Civilized Tribes for the enrollment of John T. Scott as a citizen by intermarriage of the Cherokee Nation. Further proceedings in the matter of said application were had at Muskogee, Indian Territory, October 9, 1902 and January 7, 1907.

THE EVIDENCE IN THIS CASE SHOWS: That the applicant herein, John T. Scott was married in accordance with Cherokee law November 15, 1869 to his wife Amanda C. Scott, nee Duncan, who was at the time of said marriage a recognized citizen by blood of the Cherokee Nation, who is identified on the Cherokee Authenticated Tribal Roll of 1880, Delaware District, number 2342, as a native Cherokee, and whose name

## Cherokee Intermarried White 1906
## Volume III

appears on the approved partial roll of citizens by blood of the Cherokee Nation opposite number 8507. It is further shown that sine said marriage the said John T. Scott and Amanda C. Scott have resided together as husband and wife and have continuously lived in the Cherokee Nation. Said applicant is identified on the Cherokee Authenticated Tribal Roll of 1880 and the Cherokee Census Roll of 1896 as an intermarried citizen of the Cherokee Nation.

IT IS THEREFORE ORDERED AND ADJUDGED: That in accordance with the decision of the Supreme Court of the United States, dated November 5, 1906, in the case of Daniel Red Bird, et al. vs. the United States, numbers 125, 126, 127, 128, the said applicant John T. Scott is entitled, under the provisions of Section 21, of the Act of Congress approved June 28, 1898 (30th Stats. 495), to enrollment as a citizen by intermarriage of the Cherokee Nation, and his application for enrollment as such is accordingly granted.

Tams Bixby
Commissioner.

Dated at Muskogee, Indian Territory,
this    JAN 21 1907

◇◇◇◇◇

Cherokee
3495

Muskogee, Indian Territory, January 21, 1907.

W. W. Hastings,
    Attorney for the Cherokee Nation,
        Muskogee, Indian Territory.

Dear Sir:

There is enclosed herewith a copy of the decision of the Commissioner to the Five Civilized Tribes, dated January 21, 1907, granting the application for the enrollment of John T. Scott as a citizen by intermarriage of the Cherokee Nation.

Respectfully,

Enc I-36                                                                Commissioner.

RPI

◇◇◇◇◇

# Cherokee Intermarried White 1906
## Volume III

Cherokee 3495

W.W. HASTINGS.
ATTORNEY.

OFFICE OF

H.M. VANCE.
SECRETARY.

**Attorney for the Cherokee Nation,**

MUSKOGEE, I. T.   January 21, 1907.

The Commissioner to the Five Civilized Tribes,
Muskogee, Indian Territory.

Sir:

Receipt is acknowledged of the testimony and of your decision enrolling John T. Scott as a citizen by intermarriage of the Cherokee Nation. Time for protesting said decision is waived and I consent that said person may be placed upon the schedule immediately.

Respectfully,
W. W. Hastings
Attorney for the Cherokee Nation.

◇◇◇◇◇

Cherokee 3495

Muskogee, Indian Territory, January 24, 1907.

John T. Scott,
Vinita, Indian Territory.

Dear Sir:

There is enclosed herewith copy of the decision of the Commissioner to the Five Civilized Tribes, dated January 21, 1907, granting the application for your enrollment as a citizen by intermarriage of the Cherokee Nation.

You will be advised when your name has been placed upon a schedule of citizens of the Cherokee Nation and approved by the Secretary of the Interior.

Respectfully,

Commissioner.

Enc I-107

RPI

◇◇◇◇◇

# Cherokee Intermarried White 1906
## Volume III

Cherokee I.W. 82

Muskogee, Indian Territory, April 8, 1907.

John T. Scott,
    Vinita, Indian Territory.

Dear Sir:

   Your marriage license and certificate filed in the matter of your application for enrollment as a citizen by intermarriage of the Cherokee Nation, is returned to you herewith, copies of the same being retained in the files of this office.

                    Respectfully,

Incl. P-4-24                                     Acting Commissioner.
   MMP

---

**Cher IW 83**
**Trans from Cher 3666  3-15-07**

⋄⋄⋄⋄⋄

E.C.M.

### DEPARTMENT OF THE INTERIOR,

### COMMISSIONER TO THE FIVE CIVILIZED TRIBES.

In the matter of the application for the enrollment of

### THOMAS HOWIE

as a citizen by intermarriage of the Cherokee Nation.

### CHEROKEE 3666

⋄⋄⋄⋄⋄

# Cherokee Intermarried White 1906
# Volume III

DEPARTMENT OF THE INTERIOR,
COMMISSION TO THE FIVE CIVILIZED TRIBES,
VINITA, I.T., SEPTEMBER 28, 1900.

In the matter of the application of Thomas Howie for the enrollment of himself and wife as citizens of the Cherokee Nation; said Howie being sworn by Commissioner C. R. Breckinridge, testified as follows:

Q Give me your full name, please? A Thomas Howie.
Q How old are you? A Going on 73.
Q What is your post office? A Vinita.
Q In what district do you live? A Cooweescoowee.
Q Who is it you want to have put on the roll? A My wife and myself.
Q Do you apply as a Cherokee by blood? A I am [sic] adopted white man.
Q Your wife is a Cherokee, is she? A Yes, sir.
Q What proportion of Cherokee blood has your wife? A One-eighth.
Q You you[sic] your marriage license and certificate? A I have it--delapidated[sic] some.
Q When were you married? A I was married in 1871 or '72.
Q In what district were you in 1880? A Always lived in Cooweescoowee.
Q What is your wife's name? A Maiden name was Mary Trott Frazier.
Q How old is she? A 68 /[sic]
Q Did you marry her before 1880? A Yes, sir.
Q Is she with you on the roll of 1880? A Yes, sir.
Q You and she oived[sic] together ever since your marriage? A Yes, sir.

    1880 enrollment; page 113, #1334, Thomas Howey, Cooweescoowee.
    1880 enrollment; page 113, #1335, Mary Howey, Cooweescoowee.
    1896 enrollment; page 309, #533, Thomas Howeie[sic], Cooweescoowee.
    1896 enrollment; page 178, #2276, Mary Howie, Cooweescoowee.

Q Have you and your wife continued to lived[sic] in the Cherokee Nation ever since your marriage? A Yes, sir.

Com'r Breckinridge:--The applicant applies for the enrollment of himself and wife: They are both identified on the rols[sic] of 1880 and 1896, she as a native Cherokee, and he as a Chrokee[sic] by adoption. They have lived together and in the Cherokee Nation ever since the enrollment of 1880, adn[sic] they will be listed for enrollment now, his wife as a native Cherokee, and he as a Chrokee[sic] by intermarriage.

---oooOOOooo---

J. O. Rosson, being first duly sworn, states that as stenographer to the Commission to the Five Civilized Tribes, he correctly recorded the testimony and proceedings in this case, and that the foregoing is a true and complete transcript of his stenographic notes thereof.

## Cherokee Intermarried White 1906
## Volume III

J O Rosson

Subscribed and sworn to before me this 1st day of October, 1900.

TB Needles<br>Commissioner.

Cherokee 3666.

Department of the Interior,<br>Commission to the Five Civilized Tribes,<br>Muskogee, I. T., October 4, 1902.

In the matter of the application of Thomas Howie for the enrollment of himself as a citizen by intermarriage, and for the enrollment of his wife, Mary Howie, as a citizen by blood of the Cherokee Nation.

William Brown, being sworn and examined by the Commission, testified as follows:
Q What is your name? A William Brown.
Q What is your age? A Fifty-four years old.
Q What is your postoffice? A Vinita.
Q Are you acquainted with Thomas Howie who is an applicant before this Commission for enrollment as an intermarried citizen? A Yes sir.
Q What is his wife's name? A Mary.
Q Is she a citizen by blood of the Cherokee Nation? A Yes sir.
Q How long have you known Thomas Howie? A About twenty years.
Q How long have you known his wife? A About the same.
Q Have they lived together as husband and wife for the last twenty years? A Yes sir.
Q Never been separated during that time? A No, sir.
Q Were they living together on the first day of September, 1902? A Yes sir.
Q Thomas Howie has never been married to any other woman during the last twenty years? A No, sir.
Q How long has he lived in the Cherokee Nation? A The last twenty years to my knowledge.
Q And his wife has lived with him during that same time, has she, in the Cherokee Nation? A Yes sir.

---------------------------------

The undersigned, being duly sworn, states that as stenographer to the Commission to the Five Civilized Tribes he correctly recorded the testimony and proceedings in this case, and that the foregoing is a true and correct transcript of his stenographic notes thereof.

E.G. Rothenberger

# Cherokee Intermarried White 1906
# Volume III

Subscribed and sworn to before me this 22nd day of October, 1902.

BC Jones
Notary Public.

◇◇◇◇◇

Cherokee 3666.

Department of the Interior,
Commission to the Five Civilized Tribes,
Muskogee, I. T., October 9, 1902.

In the matter of the application of Thomas Howie for the enrollment of himself as a citizen by intermarriage, and for the enrollment of his wife, Mary Howie, as a citizen by blood of the Cherokee Nation; he being sworn and examined by the Commission, testified as follows:

Thomas
Q What is your name? A ~~James~~ Howie.
Q What is your postoffice? A Vinita.
Q Are you a white man? A Yes sir.
Q You are on the 1880 roll as an intermarried white man are you? A Yes sir.
Q What was the name of your wife in '80? A Mary Howie.
Q The same wife you have now? A Yes sir.
Q You have been living together in the Cherokee Nation ever since 1880 have you? A Ever since '71.
Q You and your wife have never been separated? A Never have. We are living together yet.
Q Have you any children at home with you? A No sir, my wife was a widow when I married her; she has two, one of them is dead.

---

The undersigned, being duly sworn, states that as stenographer to the Commission to the Five Civilized Tribes he correctly recorded the testimony and proceedings in this case, and that the foregoing is a true and correct transcript of his stenographic notes thereof.

E.G. Rothenberger

Subscribed and sworn to before me this 15th day of December, 1902.

BC Jones
Notary Public.

◇◇◇◇◇

## Cherokee Intermarried White 1906
## Volume III

Cherokee
No. 3666

DEPARTMENT OF THE INTERIOR
COMMISSIONER TO THE FIVE CIVILIZED TRIBES
Muskogee, Indian Territory

January 4, 1907

In the matter of the application for the enrollment of Thomas Howie as a citizen by intermarriage of the Cherokee Nation.

William L. Trott, representing the applicant, being first duly sworn, testified as follows:

Q What is your name? A William L. Trott
Q How old are you? A 62
Q What is your postoffice address? A Vinita, I.T.
Q Do you appear here today as the representative of Thomas Howie? A Yes sir
Q Is Thomas Howie living or dead at this time? A He is dead
Q How do you represent him? A As administrator of the estate of Thomas Howie.
Q When did Thomas Howie die? A He dies[sic] three years ago last April.
Q Was Thomas Howie an applicant for enrollment as a citizen by intermarriage of the Cherokee Nation during his lifetime? A Yes sir.
Q Through whom did he claim his right to enrollment as a citizen by intermarriage?
A From his wife, Mary Trott, or Mary Tiger when he married her.
Q Was his wife any relation of yours? A A Half-sister
Q Was she ever married before she married Thomas Howie? A Yes sir
Q Was Thomas Howie ever married before he married Mary Tiger? A That I don't know, not that I know of, never heard of it if he was
Q Where were they married? A In Cooweescoowee District
Q At what time? A In '71, 1871
Q What time of the year? A dont[sic] remember.

    Book A of Marriage Records of Cooweescoowee district on Page 7 contains the following entry:
    "April 1, 1871 Marriage License issued to Thos Howie a citizen of the U.S. to marry Mrs. Mary Tiger, citizen of the Cherokee N. Issued by J.B. Mayes, Clerk district court. Married by Rev. John A. Richards on 3rd of April, 1871 and also married by Hamilton Balentime[sic] minister of the gospel on November 10, 1872"

Q Why were they married twice, if you know? A I don't know thats[sic] the first I knew of it.
Q Was Mrs. Tiger a recognized citizen of the Cherokee Nation at the time she married Thomas Howie? A Yes sir

## Cherokee Intermarried White 1906
## Volume III

Q Was Thomas Howie always recognized as a citizen by adoption of the Cherokee Nation after his marriage to Mary Tiger? A Yes sir
Q Did he hold property in the Cherokee Nation as a citizen after that time? A Yes sir
Q Prior to November 1, 1875? A Yes from the time he was married up to his death he held property
Q Did he always vote in the Cherokee elections? A Yes sir
Q Have you any other witnesses that knew Thomas Howie in his lifetime?
A There are several men from the neighborhood I can get.

Witness excused

The applicant is identified on the 1880 Cherokee Roll opposite No. 1334. His wife through whom he claims his right to enrollment is identified on said roll opposite No. 1335. She is also identified on the final roll of citizens by blood of the Cherokee Nation, opposite No. 8917

Robert W. Tittle, being called as a witness for the applicant and being first duly sworn, testified as follows:

Q What is your name? A Robert W. Tittle
Q Did you know Thomas Howie in his life time? A Yes sir
Q Did you know his wife Mary Howie? A Yes sir
Q Do you know when they were married? A No sir
Q How long did you know them? A I knew them for--well say 8 or 10 years. He lived or farmed next to me, he was a near neighbor
Q Was he always recognized as a citizen by adoption of the Cherokee Nation during his life time? A Yes sir
Q Were they always recognized as husband and wife in the neighborhood? A Yes sir
Q Do you know whether he was ever married before he married Mary Tiger? A I do not sir.
Q Where was Thomas Howie born? A I couldn't tell you sir.

Witness excused.

Louisa J. Trott being called as a witness and being first duly sworn, testified as follows:

Q What is your name? A Louisa J. Trott
Q How old are you Mrs. Trott? A 56
Q What is your postoffice address? A Vinita
Q Do you know Thomas Howie and Mary Howie? A Yes sir
Q Is Thomas Howie living or dead at this time? A He's dead
Q When did he die? A He died three years ago last April.
Q How long have you known Thomas Howie and Mary Howie? A They were married in '71 I think, and I think I have known then[sic] ever since they were married.

## Cherokee Intermarried White 1906
## Volume III

Q  Were you present at their wedding? A  No sir, they were married at Prior Creek, or Choteau

Q  Did they live together as husband and wife from 1871 up to the time of the death of Thomas Howie? A  Yes sir.

Witness excused

Gertrude Hanna, being duly sworn, states that as stenographer to the Commissioner to the Five Civilized Tribes she report[sic] the above numbered case on Jan. 4, 1907 and that the above and foregoing is a true and correct transcript of her stenographic notes taken therein

Gertrude Hanna

Subscribed and sworn to before me this 5 day of January, 1907

Chas E Webster<br>Notary Public.

◇◇◇◇◇

E C M  Cherokee 3666

DEPARTMENT OF THE INTERIOR,<br>COMMISSIONER TO THE FIVE CIVILIZED TRIBES.

In the matter of the application for the enrollment of Thomas Howie as a citizen by intermarriage of the Cherokee Nation.

D E C I S I O N.

THE RECORDS OF THIS OFFICE SHOW: That at Vinita, Indian Territory, September 28, 1900, application was received by the Commission to the Five Civilized Tribes for the enrollment of Thomas Howie as a citizen by intermarriage of the Cherokee Nation. Further proceedings in the matter of said application were had at Muskogee, Indian Territory, October 4, 1902, October 9, 1902 and January 4, 1907.

THE EVIDENCE IN THIS CASE SHOWS: That the applicant herein, Thomas Howie, was married in accordance with Cherokee law April 3, 1871 and also on November 10, 1872 to his wife Mary Howie, nee Trott, who was at the time of said marriage a recognized citizen by blood of the Cherokee Nation, who is identified on the Cherokee Authenticated Tribal roll of 1880, Cooweescoowee District, number 1335 as a native Cherokee, and whose name appears upon the approved partial roll of citizens by blood of the Cherokee Nation, opposite number 8917. It is further shown that since said marriage said Thomas Howie and Mary Howie have resided together as husband and wife, and have continuously lived in the Cherokee Nation. Said applicant is identified on

## Cherokee Intermarried White 1906
## Volume III

the Cherokee Authenticated Tribal Roll of 1880 as "Thomas Howey" and the Cherokee Census Roll of 1896 as an intermarried citizen of the Cherokee Nation.

IT IS THEREFORE ORDERED AND ADJUDGED: That in accordance with the decision of the Supreme Court of the United States dated November 5, 1906, in the case of Daniel Red Bird, et al. vs. the United States, numbers 125, 126, 127, 128, the said applicant Thomas Howie is entitled, under the provisions of Section 21, of the Act of Congress approved June 28, 1898 (30th. Stats. 495), to enrollment as a citizen by intermarriage of the Cherokee Nation, and his application for enrollment as such is accordingly granted.

Tams Bixby
Commissioner.

Dated at Muskogee, Indian Territory,
this    JAN 21 1907

◇◇◇◇◇

Cherokee 3666

Muskogee, Indian Territory, January 21, 1907.

W. W. Hastings,
Attorney for the Cherokee Nation,
Muskogee, Indian Territory.

Dear Sir:

There is enclosed herewith copy of the decision of the Commissioner to the Five Civilized Tribes, dated January 21, 1907, granting the application for the enrollment of Thomas Howie as a citizen by intermarriage of the Cherokee Nation.

Respectfully,

Enc I-40                              Commissioner.

RPI

◇◇◇◇◇

## Cherokee Intermarried White 1906
## Volume III

Cherokee 3666    W.W. HASTINGS, ATTORNEY.    OFFICE OF    H.M. VANCE, SECRETARY.

### Attorney for the Cherokee Nation,
MUSKOGEE, I. T.    January 21, 1907.

The Commissioner to the Five Civilized Tribes,
    Muskogee, Indian Territory.

Sir:

    Receipt is acknowledged of the testimony and of your decision enrolling Thomas Howie as a citizen by intermarriage of the Cherokee Nation. Time for protesting said decision is waived and I consent that said person may be placed upon the schedule immediately.

                  Respectfully,
                  W. W. Hastings
                  Attorney for the Cherokee Nation.

◇◇◇◇◇

Cherokee 3666

                  Muskogee, Indian Territory, January 24, 1907.

Thomas Howie,
    Vinita, Indian Territory.

Dear Sir:

    There is enclosed herewith a copy of the decision of the Commissioner to the Five Civilized Tribes, dated January 21, 1907, granting the application for your enrollment as a citizen by intermarriage of the Cherokee Nation.

    You will be advised when your name has been placed upon a schedule of citizens of the Cherokee Nation and approved by the Secretary of the Interior.

                  Respectfully,

Encl. H-1                               Commissioner.
JMH

# Cherokee Intermarried White 1906
## Volume III

Cher IW 84
Trans from Cher 3780  3-15-07

E.C.M.

## DEPARTMENT OF THE INTERIOR,

### COMMISSIONER TO THE FIVE CIVILIZED TRIBES.

In the matter of the application for the enrollment of

### ROBERT K. NIX

as a citizen by intermarriage of the Cherokee Nation.

### CHEROKEE 3780

### DEPARTMENT OF THE INTERIOR.
### COMMISSION TO THE FIVE CIVILIZED TRIBES.
### VINITA, I. T., SEPTEMBER 29th 1900.

IN THE MATTER OF THE APPLICATION OF Robert K. Nix, wife and children for enrollment as citizens of the Cherokee Nation, and he being sworn and examined by Commissioner, C. R. Breckinridge, testified as follows.

Q Give me your full name please?  A  Robert K. Nix.
Q How old are you?  A  Fifty five.
Q What is your Postoffice?  A  South West City, Missouri.
Q In what district do you live?  A  Delaware.
Q Who is it you want to have put on the roll; yourself?  A  My family.
Q Wife and children?  A  Yes sir.
Q Yourself, wife and children?  A  Yes sir.
Q How many children?  A  I do not know; I have to count them; I have a good many.
Q You apply for yourself, wife and five children?  A  Yes sir.
Q Are you a Cherokee by blood?  A  No sir.
Q White man?  A  Yes sir.
Q Is your wife a Cherokee by blood?  A  Yes sir.
Q What proportion of Cherokee blood do you claim for her?
A  About one sixteenth I think is what they claim.
Q Show me your marriage license and certificate?  A  I can not do it.
Q Why?  A  It was misplaced.

152

## Cherokee Intermarried White 1906
## Volume III

Q Are you on the roll of 1880? A Yes sir.
Q When were you married? A In 1869.
Q Have you lived in the Cherokee Nation ever since? A Yes sir.
Q Have you lived with your wife ever since? A Yes sir.
Q Gove me your wifes[sic] name, please? A Sabina Nix.
Q How old is she? A Forty nine.
Q What is the name of her father? A Isaac Nidiffer.
Q Dead or living? A Dead.
Q How long has he been dead? A I think he has been dead something like ten or twelve years; I can not say positively.
Q Give me her mother's name? A Lucy Nidiffer.
Q Dead or living? A Dead.
Q How long has she been dead? A About fifteen years I think.
Q Give ne now the names of the five children you apply for?
A James O.
Q How old is that child? A Eighteen/[sic]
Q The next child? A Frank E.
Q How old is he? A Sixteen.
Q Next child? A Maud.
Q How old is she? A Fifteen.
Q Next child? A William.
Q How old is he? A Thirteen.
Q Next child? A George.
Q How old is he? A Nine.
Q All living? A Yes sir.
   (1880 Roll, Page 292, #1870, Robert K. Nix, Delaware District)
   (1880 Roll, Page 292, #1871 Sabina Nix, Delaware District)
   (1896 Roll, Page 583, #391, Robert K. Nix, Delaware District)
   (1896 Roll, Page 511, #2253, Sabina E. Nix, Delaware District)
   (1896 Roll, Page 511, #2258, Fracis[sic] E. Nix, Delaware District)
   (1896 Roll, Page 511, #2257, James O. Nix, Delaware District)
   (1896 Roll, Page 511, #2260, William I. Nix, Delaware District)
   (1896 Roll, Page 511, #2261, George F. Nix, Delaware District)
Q Is there an "I" in Williams[sic] name? A Yes sir.
Q And an "F" in George's name? A Yes sir.
Q Had Maud an "E" in her name? A Yes sir.
Q Your wife has lived in the Cherokee Nation all her life, has she? A Yes sir.

    The applicant applies for the enrollment of himself, his wife and five children: His wife is identified on the rolls of 1880 and 1896, as a native Cherokee: She has lived in the Cherokee Nation all her life, and she will be listed now for enrollment as a Cherokee by blood.
    The applicant is identified on the rolls of 1880 and 1896, with his wife; they having lived together and in the Cherokee Nation since their marriage in 1869, and he will be listed now for enrollment as a Cherokee citizen by intermarriage.

## Cherokee Intermarried White 1906
## Volume III

His five children enumerated in the testimony are identified on the roll of 1896: They are minors, and are living now: They will be listed now for enrollment as Cherokees by blood.

---

The undersigned, being sworn, states that as stenographer to the Commission to the Five Civilized Tribes, he correctly recorded the testimony and proceedings in this case, and that the foregoing is a true and complete transcript of his stenographic notes thereof.

R R Cravens

Subscribed and sworn to before me this second day of September, 1900.

TB Needles
COMMISSIONER.

◇◇◇◇◇

Card #3780

### DEPARTMENT OF THE INTERIOR
### COMMISSION TO THE FIVE CIVILIZED TRIBES
### MUSKOGEE, I.T., OCTOBER 15TH, 1901.

In the matter of the application of Robert K. Nix for the enrollment of himself as a citizen by intermarriage, and for the enrollment of his wife, Sabina, and his children, James O., Frank E., Maude E., William S. and George F., as citizens by blood of the Cherokee Nation.

Robert K. Nix, being first duly sworn, under examination by the Commission, testified as follows:
Q What is your name? A Robert K. Nix.
Q How old are you? A 58
Q What is your postoffice? A Centralia at the present, when I enrolled it was Southwest City.
Q Centralia, Indian Territory? A Yes sir.
Q Are you a white man? A Yes sir.
Q Q[sic] Are you the same Robert K. Nix whose name appears upon the roll of 1880 as an intermarried white man? A Yes sir.
Q What is your wife's name? A Sabina L.
Q Sabina L.? A Yes sir.
Q Is she a Cherokee by blood? A Yes sir.
Q Was she your wife in 1880? A Yes sir.
Q She is the wife through whom you claim citizenship. A Yes sir.
Q Have you and your wife been living in the Cherokee Nation together since 1880? A Yes sir.
Q Never been separated? A No sir.

## Cherokee Intermarried White 1906
## Volume III

Q How many children have you by your wife, Sabina? A 10 children, one dead.
Q How many under age? A 4
Q 4 children living at home with you? A Yes sir.
Q Have you more than 4 under age? A No sir.
Q Which one is dead? A It is our first, dont[sic] suppose it has ever been put on the roll.
Q How long has it been dead? A 30 years.
Q All the children who have made application living? A Yes sir.
Q Been living in the Cherokee Nation all their lives. A Yes sir.

  Cora Moore, being first duly sworn, states that as stenographer to the Commission to the Five Civilized Tribes she reported in full the testimony and proceedings in this case and that the foregoing is a true and complete transcript of her stenographic notes thereof.

Cora Moore

Subscribed and sworn to before me this 24 day of October, 1902.

BC Jones   **NOTARY PUBLIC**

◇◇◇◇◇

Cherokee-3780.

### DEPARTMENT OF THE INTERIOR,
### COMMISSION TO THE FIVE CIVILIZED TRIBES.
Muskogee, Indian Territory. February 23, 1905.

--------------------

  In the matter of the application for the enrollment of Robert K. Nix as a citizen by intermarriage of the Cherokee Nation.

--------------------

Robert K. Nix, being first duly sworn, testified as follows:

Q. What is your name? A. Robert K. Nix.
Q. How old are you? A. 60.
Q. What is your post office address? A. Centralia.
Q. Are you a white man? A. Yes sir.
Q. You claim no right as a Cherokee by blood? A. No sir.
Q. How do you claim? A. By intermarriage.
Q. Through whom do you claim that right? A. My wife.
Q. What is her name? A. Savina[sic].
Q. What was her maiden name? A. Nidifer[sic].
Q. Was she your first wife? A. First and only one.
Q. Are you her first husband? A. Yes sir.

155

# Cherokee Intermarried White 1906
## Volume III

Q. When were you married? A. In the fall of '69.
Q. Since your marriage to her have you lived together as husband and wife? A. Yes sir.
Q. No separation, abandonment, or divorce? A. Nothing of the kind.
Q. Have you always lived in the Cherokee Nation since your marriage? A. Always.

WITNESS EXCUSED.

Eula Jeanes Branson, being first duly sworn, states that, as stenographer to the Commission to the Five Civilized Tribes, she reported the proceedings had in the above entitled cause on the 23rd. day of February, 1905, and that the above and foregoing is a full and complete transcript of her stenographic notes taken in said cause on said date.

Eula Jeanes Branson

Subscribed and sworn to before me this the 24th. day of February, 1905.

Myron White
Notary Public.

◇◇◇◇◇

Cherokee No. 3780.

DEPARTMENT OF THE INTERIOR,
COMMISSIONER TO THE FIVE CIVILIZED TRIBES.

Muskogee, Indian Territory. January 4, 1906.

In the matter of the application for the enrollment of Robert K. Nix as an intermarried citizen of the Cherokee Nation.

Robert K. Nix, being first duly sworn by Charles E. Webster, Notary Public, testified as follows:

BY THE COMMISSIONER:

Q What is your name? A Robert K. Nix.
Q What is your age, and postoffice address? A 62; Centralia.
Q You claim citizenship in the Cherokee Nation by intermarriage do you? A Yes, sir.
Q Through whom do you claim that right? A Through Sabina Nidiffer, my wife.
Q Is your wife living? A Yes, sir.
Q When were you and she married? A We were married November 18, 1869.
Q Where? A In Delaware District.
Q Were you married under a Cherokee license? A Yes, sir.
Q Who issued that license? A T. J. McGhee.

## Cherokee Intermarried White 1906
## Volume III

Q What was his office? A Clerk of the District.
Q Clerk of Delaware District? A Yes, sir.
Q Who performed the marriage ceremony? A A man by the name of Hastain.
Q Had either you or your wife been married prior to that time? A No, sir.
Q Was she a citizen of the Cherokee Nation when you married her? A Yes, sir.
Q Have you lived together continuously since that time? A Yes, sir
Q Where have you resided? A I resided in Delaware District from 1869 to 1900; in 1900; in 1900 I moved west into Cooweescoowee District.
Q Have you continued to live in Cooweescoowee District since your removal there in 1900? A Yes, sir.

An examination of the marriage records of Delaware District furnished this office by the Cherokee authorities fails to show any record of the marriage license alleged to have been issued to the applicant in the month of November, 1869.

Q Have you a certifiedte[sic] copy of your marriage record? A No, sir.
Q Did you ever have one? A Yes, sir.
Q What became of it? A Well, It got misplaced; there was a call for all those certificated just a while before the adopted men were enrolled by the Cherokees, I think when these certificates had to go before the Chief for his approval, and there was quite a stir in that direction, and I sent mine off to an attorney like several other did, and it was never returned. I called on him for it several times, but he said it was misplaced, and I never got it.
Q What procedure did you follow to obtain this license to marry in 1869? A The law, at the time I was married, required me to get six signers, six Cherokees to recommend me as a moral man, an honest man, or a man of good habits, for six months, and pay into the clerk's office $5.00. That is what the procedure was.
Q You complied with those provisions, did you? A Yes, sir.
Q Were there any witnesses present at your marriage? A Yes, sir, there was several.
Q Are they living at the present time? A Some of them are, a good many of them dead.
Q It if should be necessary could you produce those witnesses before this office?
A I could at considerable expense.

The said Sabina Nix, nee Nidiffer, is included in an approved partial roll of Cherokees by blood opposite No. 9137.

The applicant, Robert K. Nix, is identified on the authenticated Cherokee tribal roll of 1880, and Cherokee Census roll of 1896, Delaware District, opposite Nos. 1870 and 391, respectively, as an intermarried white.

### WITNESS EXCUSED.

F. Elma Lane, upon oath, states that as stenographer to the Commissioner to the Five Civilized Tribes, she reported the proceedings in the above entitled cause, and that the foregoing is a true and correct transcript of her stenographic notes therein.

## Cherokee Intermarried White 1906
## Volume III

F. Elma Lane

Subscribed and sworn to before me this 5th day of January, 1907.

Chas E Webster
Notary Public.

◇◇◇◇◇

C. F. B.                                                                   Cherokee 3780.

### DEPARTMENT OF THE INTERIOR,
### COMMISSION TO THE FIVE CIVILIZED TRIBES.
Muskogee, Indian Territory, January 7, 1907.

Supplemental proceedings in the Matter of the Application for the Enrollment of Robert K. Nix as a citizen by intermarriage of the Cherokee Nation.

APPEARANCES:    Sarah Mode for Applicant.

Cherokee Nation represented by H. M. Vance, in behalf of W. W. Hastings, Attorney.

Sarah Mode being first duly sworn by John E. Tidwell, Notary Public, testified as follows:

ON BEHALF OF COMMISSIONER.

Q What is your name?           A Sarah Mode.
Q What is your age?             A 52.
Q What is your post office address?
A Vinita.
Q Are you a citizen by blood of the Cherokee Nation?
A Yes sir.
Q Are you acquainted with a person in the Cherokee Nation by the name of Robert K. Nix?
A Yes sir.
Q Is he a married man?
A Yes sir.
Q What is his wife's name?
A Sabina Nix.
Q Robert K. Nix is not a Cherokee by blood?
A No sir.
Q Is his wife, Sabina Nix, a citizen by blood of the Cherokee Nation?
A Yes sir.

# Cherokee Intermarried White 1906
## Volume III

Q  You appear here to-day for the purpose of giving testimony relative to the right to enrollment of Robert K. Nix as a citizen by intermarriage of the Cherokee Nation?
A  Yes sir.
Q  How long have you known Robert K. Nix?
A  I can't say just how long.
Q  You knew him prior to his marriage to his wife, Sabina Nix?
A  Yes sir; sometime but I can't state just how long before.
Q  Did you know his wife before they were married?
A  Yes sir, she's my own sister.
Q  Was she a recognized citizen of the Cherokee Nation at the time she married her present husband?
A  Yes sir.
Q  Were you present at the Marriage ceremony?
A  Yes sir; I witnesses[sic] the marriage ceremony.
Q  Since their marriage, they have continuously lived together as husband and wife?
A  Yes sir.
Q  Is it your understanding that Robert K. Nix secured a license and married his wife in accordance with the law of the Cherokee Nation?
A  Yes sir.
Q  Did you see the license?
A  No sir; I don't remember seeing it but I remember of him getting the license.
Q  It is your understanding and belief that he secured the license and that they were married in accordance with the law of the Cherokee Nation?
A  Yes sir.
Q  He has been recognized by the people who have known him since his marriage as a citizen by intermarriage of the Cherokee Nation?
A  Yes sir.
Q  He has always enjoyed all the rights of that class of citizens?
A  Yes sir.

ON BEHALF OF CHEROKEE NATION.

Q  When were they married?
A  In '69 as well as I remember; in the fall.
Q  Have you any record that enables you to remember that it was in the fall of '69 or do you remember it just of your independent recollection?
A  I remember it by my own recollection; I kind of remember it by my age. I think I was about 14.
Q  They have lived together as husband and wife ever since they were married?
A  Yes sir; never had any trouble at all that I know of.
Q  What you know about them getting a license was merely hearsay on your part?
A  Yes sir; I don't remember of seeing the license; I was small.
Q  But it is your understanding that they had a license?
A  Yes sir.

# Cherokee Intermarried White 1906
# Volume III

Sam Nidiffer being first duly sworn by John E. Tidwell, Notary Public, testified as follows:

ON BEHALF OF COMMISSIONER.

Q What is your name?
A Sam Nidiffer.
Q What is your age?
A I was born in '47.
Q What is your post office address?
A Fairland.
Q Do you know a person in the Cherokee Nation by the name of Robert K. Nix?
A Yes sir.
Q Is he a married man?
A Yes sir.
Q What is his wife's name?
A Sabina Nix.
Q Did you know these parties before they were married?
A Yes sir.
Q Were you present when they were married?
A I was about the place; I can't say that I was in the house.
Q When were they married?
A In '69.
Q How do you fix that date?
A By one of my children born about that time.
Q Which one of your children?
A One that is dead now.
Q Is it our understanding that he secured a license and married his wife in accordance with the law of the Cherokee Nation?
A Yes sir; I went with him to help him secure his license; that is, the signers/[sic]
Q You aided him in securing signers to secure his license?
A Yes sir; I told him just what he would have to do and helped him get up his petition.
Q Did you secure the signers?
A We didn't just that day.
Q But he did afterwards?
A Yes sir.
Q Have you known these parties since they were married?
A Yes sir.
Q They have continuously lived together as husband and wife?
A Yes sir.
Q Up to and including the present time?
A Yes sir.
Q Has Robert K. Nix in your own personal knowledge always been recognized by the tribal authorities as a citizen by intermarriage of the Cherokee Nation?
A Yes sir.
Q He has always exercised all the rights and enjoyed all the privileges of that class of citizens?
A Yes sir.

# Cherokee Intermarried White 1906
## Volume III

Q Do you know who married these parties?
A No sir; I don't remember the man's name.
Q You didn't see them married but you were on the place?
A I can't say I saw them married but I was there and helped eat the dinner.
Q It is your understanding and you believe they were married at that time?
A Yes sir.

ON BEHALF OF CHEROKEE NATION.

Q When were you married?
A In '70 I guess.
Q The first time?                         A Yes sir.
Q Did you see Mr. Nix's petition for license after it had been signed?
A Not that I remember.
Q And you didn't see his license?
A Not that I remember.

    Thomas J. McGee being first duly sworn by John E. Tidwell, Notary Public, testified as follows:

ON BEHALF OF COMMISSIONER.

Q What is your name?                  A Thomas J. McGee.
Q What is your age?                   A 62; born in '44.
Q What is your post office address?
A Afton.
Q Are you a citizen by blood of the Cherokee Nation?
A Yes sir.
Q Do you know a person in the Cherokee Nation by the name of Robert K. Nix?
A Yes sir.
Q Is he a citizen by intermarriage of the Cherokee Nation?
A Yes sir; so recognized.
Q You appear here to-day for the purpose of giving testimony relative to his right to enrollment?
A Yes sir
Q What is the name of his wife?
A Sabina.
Q You knew them before their marriage?
A Yes sir.
Q When were they married?
A I issued him the license somewhere along in the year of 1869; just the exact date he was married, I can't state.
Q You are the man who issued him the license to marry his wife?
A Yes sir.
Q That license of course was issued in accordance with the law of the Cherokee Nation?
A Yes sir.

# Cherokee Intermarried White 1906
## Volume III

Q He had complied with all the terms of the law?
A Yes sir.
Q Do you know who married him?
A I couldn't be positive; the license was returned with the marriage certificate attached to the back of it, but I couldn't state positively.
Q You remember distinctly that this license was returned with this certificate of marriage attached to it?
A Yes sir, I do.

ON BEHALF OF CHEROKEE NATION.

Q How long were you clerk of Delaware District?
A Well, sir, I was first appointed clerk of Delaware District in the year 1867, on or about the third Monday in November, - and '68 and '69, then 70 and then '71, and then I was commissioned to District Judge of that District on until '75; then I retired five years and went in again in the year of '80 as clerk and served ten years, until '92.
Q During the different times that you were clerk, you issued a great many marriage licenses?
A Yes sir.
Q Have you any more reason for remembering when you issued a license to Robert K. Nix than to anyone else?
A Well, that was the second year after I was appointed Clerk and I had moved on a new place and he came to my house to get out his license; I remember that so well. I made a record of it of course and that will show when it was.
Q You know it was in '69.
A Yes sir.
Q You haven't refreshed your memory by the record?
A No sir; I have not.

---

The undersigned being first duly sworn states that as stenographer to the Commission to the Five Civilized Tribes, she correctly recorded the testimony taken in this case and that the foregoing is a full, true and correct transcript of her stenographic notes thereof.

Myrtle Hill

Subscribed and sworn to before me this the 8th day of January, 1907.

John E. Tidwell
Notary Public.

## Cherokee Intermarried White 1906
## Volume III

E C M  Cherokee 3780

DEPARTMENT OF THE INTERIOR,
COMMISSIONER TO THE FIVE CIVILIZED TRIBES.

In the matter of the application for the enrollment of Robert K. Nix as a citizen by intermarriage of the Cherokee Nation.

D E C I S I O N.

THE RECORDS OF THIS OFFICE SHOW: That at Vinita, Indian Territory, September 29, 1900, application was received by the Commission to the Five Civilized Tribes for the enrollment of Robert K. Nix as a citizen by intermarriage of the Cherokee Nation. Further proceedings in the matter of said application were had at Muskogee, Indian Territory, October 15, 1902, February 23, 1905, January 4, 1907 and January 7, 1907.

THE EVIDENCE IN THIS CASE SHOWS: That the applicant herein, Robert K. Nix, was married in accordance with Cherokee law November 18, 1869 to his wife Sabina Nix, nee Nadiffer[sic], who was at the time of said marriage a recognized citizen by blood of the Cherokee Nation, who is identified on the Cherokee Authenticated Tribal Roll of 1880, Delaware District, number 1871, as a native Cherokee, and whose name appears on the approved partial roll of citizens by blood of the Cherokee Nation, opposite number 9137. It is further shown that since said marriage the said Robert K. Nix and Sabina Nix have resided together as husband and wife and have continuously lived in the Cherokee Nation. Said applicant is identified on the Cherokee Authenticated Tribal Roll of 1880 and the Cherokee Census Roll of 1896.

IT IS THEREFORE ORDERED AND ADJUDGED: That in accordance with the decision of the Supreme Court of the United States dated November 5, 1906, in the case of Daniel Red Bird, et al. vs. the United State, numbers 125, 126, 127, 128, the applicant, Robert K. Nix is entitled under the provisions of Section 21, of the Act of Congress approved June 28, 1898 (30th. Stats. 495), to enrollment as a citizen by intermarriage of the Cherokee Nation.

Tams Bixby
Commissioner.

Dated at Muskogee, Indian Territory,
this    JAN 21 1907

## Cherokee Intermarried White 1906
## Volume III

Cherokee 3780

Muskogee, Indian Territory, January 21, 1907

W. W. Hastings,
    Attorney for the Cherokee Nation,
        Muskogee, Indian Territory.

Dear Sir:

    There is enclosed herewith copy of the decision of the Commissioner to the Five Civilized Tribes, dated January 21, 1907, granting the application for the enrollment of Robert K. Nix as a citizen by intermarriage of the Cherokee Nation.

        Respectfully,

                Commissioner.

Enc I-50
RPI

◇◇◇◇◇

Cherokee 3780

| W.W. HASTINGS. ATTORNEY. | OFFICE OF | H.M. VANCE. SECRETARY. |

**Attorney for the Cherokee Nation,**
    Muskogee, I. T.     January 21, 1907.

The Commissioner to the Five Civilized Tribes,
    Muskogee, Indian Territory.

Sir:

    Receipt is acknowledged of the testimony and of your decision enrolling Robert K. Nix as a citizen by intermarriage of the Cherokee Nation. Time for protesting said decision is waived and I consent that said person may be placed upon the schedule immediately.

        Respectfully,
             W. W. Hastings
            Attorney for the Cherokee Nation.

◇◇◇◇◇

# Cherokee Intermarried White 1906
## Volume III

Cherokee 3780

Muskogee, Indian Territory, January 24, 1907.

Robert K. Nix,
    Centralia, Indian Territory.

Dear Sir:

    There is enclosed herewith copy of the decision of the Commissioner to the Five Civilized Tribes, dated January 21, 1907, granting the application for your enrollment of as a citizen by intermarriage of the Cherokee Nation.

    You will be advised when your name has been placed upon a schedule of citizens of the Cherokee Nation and approved by the Secretary of the Interior.

                    Respectfully,

Enc I-106                                         Commissioner.

RPI

---

**Cher IW 85**
**Trans from Cher 3901  3-15-07**

                                                                                  C.E.W.

## DEPARTMENT OF THE INTERIOR,

## COMMISSIONER TO THE FIVE CIVILIZED TRIBES.

---

In the matter of the application for the enrollment of

### ENOCH S. SOUTHERLAND

as a citizen by intermarriage of the Cherokee Nation.

---

### CHEROKEE 3901

## Cherokee Intermarried White 1906
## Volume III

DEPARTMENT OF THE INTERIOR

COMMISSION TO THE FIVE CIVILIZED TRIBES.

Vinita, I.T. October 1st, 1900.

IN THE MATTER OF THE APPLICATION OF ENOCH S. SOUTHERLAND FOR THE ENROLLMENT OF HIMSELF AND WIFE AS CHEROKEE CITIZENS.

The said Enoch S. Southerland, being sworn and examined by Commissioner T. B. Needles, testified as follows:

Q What is your name? A Enoch S. Southerland.
Q What is your age? A Forty-nine.
Q What is your post office address? A Vinita.
Q What district do you live in? A Cooweescoowee.
Q Are you a recognized citizen of the Cherokee Nation? A Yes, sir.
Q By blood or intermarriage? A By intermarriage.
Q What is the name of your wife? A Arabella Scrimsher[sic].
Q When did you marry her? A In 1874.
Q What are the names of your children? A I ain't got any.
Q You just apply for yourself and wife? A Yes, sir.
Q Is your wife a Cherokee? A Yes, sir.
Q How long have you been in the Cherokee Nation? A Since October 1866.
Q You are living here now? A Yes, sir.
Q You never married before you married this woman? A No, sir.
Q You never married since? A No, sir.
1880 Roll, page 172, No. 2570, Enoch Southerland, Cooweescoowee District. Adopted white.
1880 Roll, page 172, No. 2571, Abigal Southerland, Cooweescoowee District. Native Cherokee.
1896 Roll, page 324, No. 937, Enoch Southerland, Cooweescoowee District.
1896 Roll, page 256, No. 4425, Arabella Southerland, Cooweescoowee District.

THE COMMISSIONER: The name of Enoch S. Southerland appears upon the roll of 1880 and the name of his wife Arabella appears upon said roll as Abigal. The name of Enoch Southerland appears upon the census roll of 1896, and also the name of his wife Arabella Southerland. They being duly identified according to the page and number of the roll as indicated in the testimony, and having made satisfacoty[sic] proof as to their residence, they will be duly listed for enrollment as Cherokee citizens, he by intermarriage, and she by blood.

---------o---------

The undersigned, being sworn, states that as stenographer to the Commission to the Five Civilized Tribes he correctly recorded the testimony and proceedings in this application for enrollment and that the foregoing is a correct and complete transcript of his stenographic notes thereof.

## Cherokee Intermarried White 1906
## Volume III

Wm S. Meeshean

Subscribed and sworn to before me this 18th day of October 1900.

CR Breckinridge
Commissioner.

◇◇◇◇◇

DEPARTMENT OF THE INTERIOR.<br>
Commission to the Five Civilized Tribes.<br>
Muskogee, Indian Territory, October 14th, 1902.

In the matter of the application of Enoch S. Southerland for the enrollment of himself as a citizen by intermarriage and his wife, Arebella[sic] Southerland, as a citizen by blood of the Cherokee Nation.

Supplemental to #3901.

ENOCH S. SOUTHERLAND, being duly sworn, testified as follows:<br>
Examination by the Commission.

Q. What is your name? A. Enoch S. Southerland.
Q. How old are you? A. 51.
Q. What is your post office? A. Vinita.
Q. You are a white man, are you? A. Yes, sir.
Q. You are on the roll of 1880 as an intermarried white man? A. Yes, sir.
Q. What is your wife's name? A. Arebella[sic].
Q. How old is your wife? A. 45.
Q. Was she your wife in 1880? A. Yes, sir.
Q. Have you and your wife been living together in the Cherokee Nation ever since 1880? A. Yes, sir.
Q. Never were separated? A. No, sir.
Q. Living together now? A. Yes, sir.
Q. Have you any children? A. No, sir.

IIIIIIIIIIIIIIIIIIIIIIIIII I I I

Jesse O. Carr, being first duly sworn, states that as stenographer to the Commission to the Five Civilized Tribes he reported the above entitled case and that the foregoing is a true and complete transcript of his stenographic notes thereof.

Jesse O. Carr

## Cherokee Intermarried White 1906
## Volume III

Subscribed and sworn to before me this 3rd day of January, 1903.

John O Rosson<br>Notary Public.

### DEPARTMENT OF THE INTERIOR
### COMMISSIONER TO THE FIVE CIVILIZED TRIBES
### MUSKOGEE, IND. TER.
### JAN. 4, 1907

### IN THE MATTER OF THE APPLICATION FOR THE ENROLLMENT AS A CITIZEN BY INTERMARRIAGE OF THE CHEROKEE NATION OF ENOCH S. SOUTHERLAND.

### CENSUS CARE NO. 3901.

ENOCH SYLVESTER SOUTHERLAND BEING FIRST DULY SWORN TESTIFIED AS FOLLOWS:

### EXAMINATION BY THE COMMISSIONER.

Q What is your name? A Enoch Sylvester Southerland, is the way I sign it in full.
Q How old are you? A Fifty six.
Q What is your post office address? A Woodland.
Q Do you claim to be a citizen of the Cherokee Nation by intermarriage? A Yes sir.
Q Thru whom do you claim to derive you intermarried rights?
A Arabella Schrimsher.
Q When were you married to your wife? A March 2, 1874.
Q Where? A Delaware District.
Q Were you married under a license? A Yes sir.
Q Is this the license? A A copy.
Q Were you ever married before you married your wife? A No sir.
Q Was she ever married before she married you? A No sir.
Q Have you lived together continuously as husband and wife in the Cherokee Nation since you married in 1874.[sic] A Yes sir
Q Are you living together at the present time? A Living together at the present time.

Applicant offer in evidence certified copy of the marriage license issued on March 2, 1874 which shows he was married on said date.

Applicant is identified on the 1880 Cherokee Roll opposite No. 2570; his wife thru whom he claims his right to enrollment is identified on said roll opposite No. 2571; she is also identified on the final roll of citizens by blood of the Cherokee Nation opposite No. 9397.

## Cherokee Intermarried White 1906
## Volume III

ooOoo

Clara Mitchell Wood being first duly sworn upon her oath states that as stenographer for the Commissioner to the Five Civilized Tribes she reported the above and foregoing proceedings and that this is a correct transcript of her stenographic notes thereof.

Clara Mitchell Wood

Subscribed and sworn to before me this 8th day of January 1907.

B.P. Rasmus<br>Notary Public.

◇◇◇◇◇

*(Below was originally a handwritten letter as given on the microfilm. The transcribed copy immediately followed and is given below and typed as given.)*

(COPY)

This is to certify that Enoch Sutherland A citizen of the U.S. was license to marry Miss Arabella Schrimsher A Citizen of the Cherokee Nation on March 2nd 1874 License Returned executed and hereby Recorded March 2nd 1874 On conformity with the Act Entitled an Act to provide for the licenity of Citizen of the U.S. to entermary with Citize of the Cherokee Nation, Approved Oct 15" 1855.

J. E. Harlin

Clerk Del Dist C.N.

This is to certify That the Above is a true and correct coppy of the Original

(SEAL)  J. R. Hastings
Clerk Del Dist.

The undersigned being first duly sworn states, that as stenographer to the Commissioner to the Five Civilized Tribes, he made the above and Foregoing copy of a copy of the original marriage record, and the same is a true and correct copy thereof.

Robert P. Ironside

Subscribed and sworn to before me this the 12 January 1907.

Chas E Webster<br>Notary Public

My commission expires_____

◇◇◇◇◇

## Cherokee Intermarried White 1906
## Volume III

C.F.B.

Cherokee 3901.

### DEPARTMENT OF THE INTERIOR,

### COMMISSIONER TO THE FIVE CIVILIZED TRIBES.

D E C I S I O N

THE RECORDS OF THIS OFFICE SHOW: That at Vinita, Indian Territory, October 1, 1900, application was received by the Commission to the Five Civilized Tribes for the enrollment of Enoch S. Southerland as a citizen by intermarriage of the Cherokee Nation. Further proceedings in the matter of said application were had at Muskogee, Indian Territory, October 14, 1902, and January 4, 1907.

THE EVIDENCE IN THIS CASE SHOWS: That the applicant herein, Enoch S. Southerland, a white man, was married in accordance with Cherokee law March 2, 1874, to his wife, Arabella Southerland, nee Scrimsher[sic], who was at the time of said marriage a recognized citizen by blood of the Cherokee Nation, who is identified on the Cherokee authenticated tribal roll of 1880, Cooweescoowee District, No. 2571, as a native Cherokee, and whose name appears on the approved partial roll of citizens by blood of the Cherokee Nation, opposite No. 9397. It is further shown that since said marriage the said Enoch S. and Arabella Southerland have resided together as husband and wife, and have continuously lived in the Cherokee Nation. Said applicant is duly identified on the Cherokee authenticated tribal roll of 1880, and the Cherokee census roll of 1896, as a citizen by adoption of the Cherokee Nation.

IT IS, THEREFORE, ORDERED AND ADJUDGED: That in accordance with the decision of the Supreme Court of the United States, dated November 5, 1906, in the cases of Daniel Red Bird et al. vs. the United States, Nos. 125, 126, 127 and 128, the said applicant, Enoch S. Southerland, is entitled, under the provisions of Section 21, of the Act of Congress approved June 28, 1898 (30 Stats., 495), to enrollment as a citizen by intermarriage of the Cherokee Nation, and his application for enrollment as such is accordingly granted.

Tams Bixby
Commissioner.

Dated at Muskogee, Indian Territory,
this JAN 21 1907

◇◇◇◇◇

# Cherokee Intermarried White 1906
## Volume III

Cherokee
3901

Muskogee, Indian Territory, January 23, 1907.

W. W. Hastings,
    Attorney for the Cherokee Nation,
        Muskogee, Indian Territory.

Dear Sir:

    There is enclosed herewith a copy of the decision of the Commissioner to the Five Civilized Tribes, dated January 21, 1907, granting the application for the enrollment of Enoch S. Southerland as a citizen by intermarriage of the Cherokee Nation.

        Respectfully,

E.R.C.                                                                    Commissioner.
Enc. E.C. 103

◇◇◇◇◇

Cherokee 3901

W.W. HASTINGS.      OFFICE OF      H.M. VANCE.
ATTORNEY.                                         SECRETARY.

**Attorney for the Cherokee Nation,**
MUSKOGEE, I.T.      January 23, 1907.

The Commissioner
    to The Five Civilized Tribes,
        Muskogee, Indian Territory.

Sir:

    Receipt is acknowledged of the testimony and of your decision enrolling Enoch S. Southerland as a citizen by intermarriage of the Cherokee Nation. Time for protesting said decision is waived and I consent that said person may be placed upon the schedule immediately.

        Respectfully,
        W. W. Hastings
        Attorney for Cherokee Nation.

◇◇◇◇◇

# Cherokee Intermarried White 1906
## Volume III

Cherokee
3901

Muskogee, Indian Territory, January 23, 1907.

Enoch S. Southerland,
    Vinita, Indian Territory.

Dear Sir:

    There is enclosed herewith a copy of the decision of the Commissioner to the Five Civilized Tribes, dated January 21, 1907, granting your application for enrollment as a citizen by intermarriage of the Cherokee Nation.

    You will be advised when your name has been placed upon a schedule of citizens of the Cherokee Nation and approved by the Secretary of the Interior.

    Respectfully,

E.R.C.                                                                                         Commissioner.
Enc. E.C. 104.

◇◇◇◇◇

CFB

REFER IN REPLY TO THE FOLLOWING:
Cherokee I.W. 85

**DEPARTMENT OF THE INTERIOR,**
**COMMISSIONER TO THE FIVE CIVILIZED TRIBES.**

Muskogee, Indian Territory, April 9, 1907.

Enoch S. Southerland,
    Woodland, Indian Territory.

Dear Sir:

    Your marriage license and certificate filed in the matter of the application for your enrollment as a citizen by intermarriage of the Cherokee Nation, is returned to you herewith, copies of the same being retained in the files of this office.

    Respectfully,
                                          Geo. D. Rodgers

Incl. P-4-10                             Acting Commissioner.
MMP

# Cherokee Intermarried White 1906
## Volume III

Cher IW 86
Trans from Cher 3955  3-15-07

F.R.

DEPARTMENT OF THE INTERIOR,
COMMISSIONER TO THE FIVE CIVILIZED TRIBES.

----------------------------

In the matter of the application for the enrollment of

HUFF D. COATS

as a citizen by intermarriage of the Cherokee Nation.

------------------

Cherokee 3955.

DEPARTMENT OF THE INTERIOR,
COMMISSION TO THE FIVE CIVILIZED TRIBES,
VINITA, I.T., OCTOBER 2, 1900.

  In the matter of the application of Huff D. Coats for enrollment of himself, wife and one child, said Coats being sworn by Commissioner Needles, testified as follows:

Q What is your name? A Huff D. Coats.
Q Your age? A 60.
Q Your postoffice? A Blue Jacket.
Q What district do you live in? A Cooweescoowee.
Q Are you a recognized citizen of the Cherokee Nation? A Yes.
Q By bllod[sic]? A My marriage.
Q Who do you want to enroll? A Myself, wife and one child.
Q What is your wife's name? A Louisa J. Craig when I married her.
Q When did you marry her? A In '69 in Missouri and here in '74.
Q What is the name of your child? A Annie L., 15 years old.
   On '96 roll, page 131, number 971.
Q Is Louisa J. your first wife? A Yes.
Q Are you her first husband? A Yes.
Q Have you been living together in the Cherokee Nation continuously since that time?
A Yes.
Q The child is living and living with you? A Yes.

## Cherokee Intermarried White 1906
## Volume III

Applicant on '80 roll, page 239, number 600, as H.D. Coats.
Applicant's wife on '80 roll, page 239, number 601.
Applicant on '96 roll, page 298, number 173.
Applicant's wife on '96 roll, page 131, number 970.
The name of Huff D. Coats appears upon the authenticated roll of '80 as well that of his wife, Louisa J., who is identified as a Cherokee citizen by blood. The name of the applicant and his wife also appear upon the census roll of '96, and the name of his child, Annie L. also appears upon the '96 census roll. His enrollment in '80 is H. D. Coats. Being duly identified and having made satisfactory proof as to his residence the said Huff D. Coats will be duly listed for enrollment as a Cherokee citizen by intermarriage, and his wife and child, Annie L., will be listed for enrollment as Cherokee citizens by blood.

The undersigned, being first duly sworn, states that as stenographers[sic] to the Commission to the Five Civilized Tribes, he correctly recorded the testimony and proceedings in this case, and that the foregoing is a true and complete transcript of his stenographic notes thereof.

B McDonald

Subscribed and sworn to before me this 2nd day of October, 1900.

TB Needles
Commissioner.

◇◇◇◇◇

R.

### DEPARTMENT OF THE INTERIOR.
Commission to the Five Civilized Tribes.
Muskogee, Indian Territory, October 8th, 1902.

In the matter of the application of Huff D. Coats for the enrollment of himself as a citizen by intermarriage of the Cherokee Nation and for the enrollment of his wife, Louisa J. Coats, and his daughter, Annie L. Coats, as citizens by blood of the Cherokee Nation.

Supplemental to #3955.

HUFF D. COATS, being duly sworn, testified as follows:--
Examination by the Commission.
Q. Your full name is Huff D. Coats? A. Yes, sir.
Q. What is your age A. 62.
Q. What is your post office? A. Bluejacket.
Q. You are a white man? A. Yes, sir.

## Cherokee Intermarried White 1906
## Volume III

Q. You are on the eighty roll as an intermarried white man? A. Yes, sir.
Q. What is the name of your wife? A. Louisa J.
Q. Is that the only wife you ever had? A. Yes, sir.
Q. You were married to her before 1880? A. Yes, sir.
Q. Have you and your wife been living together ever since 1880? A. Ever since.
Q. Never been separated? A. No, sir.
Q. Never lived outside of the Cherokee Nation? A. No, sir.
Q. Living together on the first of September, 1902, were you? A. Yes, sir.
Q. You have got one child? A. No, I have got four.
Q. One under age? A. One at home.
Q. That is all? A. Yes, sir.
Q. Is she living now? A. Yes, sir.
Q. And your wife is living[sic] A. Yes, sir.

IIIIIIIIIIIIIIIIIIIIIIIIII

Jesse O. Carr, being first duly sworn, states that as stenographer to the Commission to the Five Civilized Tribes he reported the above entitled case and that the foregoing is a true and complete transcript of his stenographic notes thereof.

Jesse O. Carr

Subscribed and sworn to before me this 26th day of November, 1902.

BC Jones
Notary Public.

◇◇◇◇◇

Cherokee No.
3955.

### DEPARTMENT OF THE INTERIOR,

### COMMISSIONER TO THE FIVE CIVILIZED TRIBES,

### MUSKOGEE, INDIAN TERRITORY, JANUARY 4, 1907.

IN THE MATTER of the application of Huff D. Coats for enrollment as a citizen by intermarriage of the Cherokee Nation.

HUFF D. COATS, being first duly sworn by Walter W. Chappell, Notary Public in the Western District of the Indian Territory, testified as follows:

# Cherokee Intermarried White 1906
# Volume III

## EXAMINATION

ON BEHALF OF THE COMMISSIONER:

Q What is your name, age and postoffice address?
A Huff D. Coats; my age is 66; postoffice is Blue Jacket, Indian Territory.
Q You claim to be a citizen by intermarriage of the Cherokee Nation, do you?
A Yes sir.
Q Through whom do you claim that right? A My wife, Louisa J. Craig, it was when I married her.
Q Is she living? A Yes sir.
Q What is her citizenship? A Cherokee.
Q By blood? A Yes sir.
Q Was she born and raised in the Cherokee Nation? A No sir, she was born in Missouri, and I married first in Missouri in 1869.
Q What was the citizenship of your wife when you married her in 1869? A She was an Indian, but was living in the States.
Q Was she a citizen of the state of Missouri? A Yes sir, she was born and raised there.
Q How long did you live in Missouri after your marriage to her? A Two years I believe.
Q Then where did you move to? A I moved to the Cherokee Nation. We come to the Cherokee Nation in April, 1872. Moved here in April, 1872.
Q Was your wife admitted to citizenship in the Cherokee Nation when you moved here?
A Yes sir, after we come here.
Q By what authority was she admitted? A By the Council; by the Citizenship Court, I think it was. You know the Council done away with these citizenship cases, and appointed a commission and called it the Citizenship court, to handle cases. I think that was what was done. She was on the roll from 1874 on up, - every one.
Q Do you know what court it was that admitted her?
A No sir, I don't know.
Q Have you a copy of the act or decree admitting your wife to citizenship in the Cherokee Nation? A No sir, I haven't.
Q After your removal to the Cherokee Nation, were you again married? A Yes sir.
Q In what year were you married the second time? A Married in April, 1875.
Q Where were you married? A Married on the Kansas line in the Delaware District.
Q Were you married under a Cherokee license? A Yes sir. (Hands examiner paper).
Q Were either you or your wife married prior to your marriage in 1869 in Missouri?
A No sir.
Q Have you and your wife lived together continuously since that time? A Yes sir.
Q Where have you lived since your removal to the Cherokee Nation in 1872? A In 1881 lived on the line of Kansas, and have lived north of Vinita ever since then.
Q On which side of the line were you living prior to 1881? Living on the south side.
Q Living in the Cherokee Nation? A Yes sir.

ON BEHALF OF THE COMMISSIONER:

## Cherokee Intermarried White 1906
## Volume III

On Page 14 of Book B, "Marriage Record 1875-Delaware District, C. N.", appears the following "I do hereby certify that a marriage license was granted H. D. Coats, a citizen of the United States to marry Eliza Jane Cregg, a citizen of the Cherokee Nation, on the first day of April, 1875. The license returned executed on the first day of April, 1875 and placed on record in conformity with the act regulating intermarriage of citizens of the United States with citizens of the C.N.
    (Signed) E. L. Harlin,
        Clerk, Delaware District."

  The applicant Huff D. Coats is identified on the authenticated Cherokee tribal roll of 1880, Delaware District and Cherokee Census roll of 1896, Coowees Coowee District, opposite Nos. 600 and 173 respectively, as an intermarried white.
  Louisa J. Coats (nee Craig) is identified on the approved partial roll of Cherokees by blood opposite No. 9559.

      (Witness dismissed).

I, S. T. Wright, stenographer to the Commissioner to the Five Civilized Tribes, on oath, state that I recorded the testimony and proceedings had in the above entitled cause on January 4, 1907, and that the above and foregoing is a true and correct transcript of my stenographic notes thereof taken on said date.
              S.T. Wright

Subscribed and sworn to before me this January 5th, 1907.

              Edward Merrick
              NOTARY PUBLIC.

## Cherokee Intermarried White 1906
## Volume III

F.R.  Cherokee 3955.

DEPARTMENT OF THE INTERIOR,

COMMISSIONER TO THE FIVE CIVILIZED TRIBES.

------------------------------

In the matter of the application for the enrollment of Huff D. Coats as a citizen by intermarriage of the Cherokee Nation.

D E C I S I O N .

THE RECORDS OF THIS OFFICE SHOW: That on October 2, 1900, application was received by the Commission to the Five Civilized Tribes for the enrollment of Huff D. Coats as a citizen by intermarriage of the Cherokee Nation. Further proceedings in the matter of said application were had at Muskogee, Indian Territory, October 8, 1902, and January 4, 1907.

THE EVIDENCE IN THIS CASE SHOWS: That the applicant herein, Huff D. Coats, a white man, was married in accordance with the Cherokee law April 1, 1875, to his wife, Louisa J. Coats, (nee Craig), who was at the time of said marriage a recognized citizen by blood of the Cherokee Nation, who is identified on the Cherokee authenticated tribal roll of 1880, Delaware District, No. 601, as a native Cherokee, and whose name is included in the approved partial roll of citizens by blood of the Cherokee Nation opposite No. 9559. It is further shown that from the time of said marriage the said Huff D. Coats and Louisa J. Coats resided together as husband and wife and lived continuously in the Cherokee Nation up to and including September 1, 1902. Said applicant is identified on the Cherokee authenticated tribal roll of 1880, and the Cherokee Census Roll of 1896 as an intermarried citizen of the Cherokee Nation.

IT IS, THEREFORE, ORDERED AND ADJUDGED: That in accordance with the decision of the Supreme Court of the United States, dated November 5, 1906, in the cases of Daniel Red Bird et al., vs. the United States, Nos. 125, 126, 127 and 128, the said applicant, Huff D. Coats is entitled, under the provisions of Section 21 of the Act of Congress approved June 28, 1898 (30 Stats., 495), to enrollment as a citizen by intermarriage of the Cherokee Nation, and his application for enrollment as such is accordingly granted.

Tams Bixby
Commissioner.

Dated at Muskogee, Indian Territory, this    JAN 23 1907

# Cherokee Intermarried White 1906
## Volume III

Cherokee
3955

Muskogee, Indian Territory, January 23, 1907.

W. W. Hastings,
    Attorney for the Cherokee Nation,
        Muskogee, Indian Territory.

Dear Sir:

    There is enclosed herewith a copy of the decision of the Commissioner to the Five Civilized Tribes, dated January 23, 1907, granting the application for the enrollment of Huff D. Coats as a citizen by intermarriage of the Cherokee Nation.

        Respectfully,

Encl. H-55                                 Commissioner.
JMH

◇◇◇◇◇

Cherokee 3955    W.W. HASTINGS,    OFFICE OF    H.M. VANCE.
                    ATTORNEY.                            SECRETARY.

**Attorney for the Cherokee Nation,**
        MUSKOGEE, I. T.    January 23, 1907.

The Commissioner to the Five Civilized Tribes,
    Muskogee, Indian Territory.

Sir:

    Receipt is acknowledged of the testimony and of your decision enrolling Huff D. Coats as a citizen by intermarriage of the Cherokee Nation. Time for protesting said decision is waived and I consent that said person may be placed upon the schedule immediately.

        Respectfully,
           W. W. Hastings
           Attorney for Cherokee Nation.

◇◇◇◇◇

Cherokee Intermarried White 1906
Volume III

Cherokee
3955

Muskogee, Indian Territory, January 23, 1907.

Huff D. Coats,
　Blue Jacket, Indian Territory.

Dear Sir:

　　There is enclosed herewith a copy of the decision of the Commissioner to the Five Civilized Tribes, dated January 23, 1907, granting your application for enrollment as a citizen by intermarriage of the Cherokee Nation.

　　You will be advised when your name has been placed upon a schedule of citizens of the Cherokee Nation and approved by the Secretary of the Interior.

　　　　　　　　　Respectfully,

E.R.C.　　　　　　　　　　　　　　　　　　Commissioner.
Enc. E.C. 80

---

**Cher IW 87**
**Trans from Cher 3972  3-15-07**

◇◇◇◇◇

F.R.

DEPARTMENT OF THE INTERIOR,

COMMISSIONER TO THE FIVE CIVILIZED TRIBES.

------------------------

In the matter of the application for the enrollment of

NAOMA A. SLOAN

as a citizen by intermarriage of the Cherokee Nation.

------------------------

CHEROKEE 3972.

## Cherokee Intermarried White 1906
## Volume III

DEPARTMENT OF THE INTERIOR,
COMMISSION TO THE FIVE CIVILIZED TRIBES,
VINITA, I.T., OCTOBER 2, 1900.

In the matter of the application of Edward E. Sloan for enrollment of himself, wife and children, as citizens of the Cherokee Nation, said Edward E. Sloan being sworn by Commissioner Needles, testified as follows:

Q What is your name? A Edward E. Sloan.
Q How old are you? A 49.
Q What is your postoffice address? A Big Cabin.
Q What district do you live in? A Delaware.
Q Are you a recognized citizen of the Cherokee Nation? A Yes, by blood.
Q What degree of blood? A About 1/8.
Q Who do you want to enroll? A Myself, wife and children.
Q What is your wife's name? A Naomi Ann.
Q Is she a citizen by blood? A No sir, adoption.
Q What was her name before you married her? A Coe.
Q What are the name of your children? A Mary D. 18 years old.
                On '96 roll, page 528, number 2707.
Q Next? A Minnie E. 16 years old.
                On '96 roll, page 528, number 2708.
Q Next? A Annie M. 13 years old.
                On '96 roll, page 528, number 2709, as Annie May.
Q Next? A Samuel J., 11 years old.
                On '96 roll, page 528, number 2710.
Q Next? A Eva L., 9 years old.
                On '96 roll, page 528, number 2711, as Eva Lenier.
Q Next? A James E., 6 years old.
                On '96 roll, page 528, number 2712, as James Ellis.
Q Next? A Nina P., 4 years old.
                On '96 roll, page 528, number 2713, as Nina Pearl.
Q Next? A Florence C., 1 year old.
Q Are these children all alive and living with you? A Yes.
Q How long have you lived in the Cherokee Nation? A All my life.
Q Had no other wife except Naomi? A No sir.
Q She was a United States citizen? A Yes.
Q You are a Cherokee or Shawnee? A Cherokee.
                Applicant on '80 roll, page 308, number 2229, as E. E. Sloan.
                Applicant's wife on '80 roll, page 308, number 2230, as N. M. Sloan.
                Applicant on '96 roll, page 528, number 2704.
                Applicant's wife on '96 roll, page 588, number 483, as Namora A., or Neomia Sloan.
Q These children are all alive and living with you? A Yes.

# Cherokee Intermarried White 1906
## Volume III

The name of Edward E. Sloan appears upon the authenticated roll of '80 as E. E. Sloan and upon the census roll of '96 as Edward E., and the name of his wife Naomi appears upon the '80 roll as N. M. Sloan and upon the '96 roll as Namora A., or Neomia Sloan; and the names of his children, Mary D., Minnie E., Annie M., Samuel J., Eva L., James E., and Nina P., appear upon the census roll of '96, and he presents satisfactory proof of birth as to Florence C., his youngest child, whose name does not appear upon said rolls. They all being duly identified according to page and number of the rolls, and making satisfactory proof of residence, the said Edward E. Sloan and his children will be duly listed for enrollment as Cherokee citizens by blood, and his wife, Naomi, as a Cherokee citizen by intermarriage.

The undersigned, being first duly sworn, states that as stenographer to the Commission to the Five Civilized Tribes, he correctly recorded the testimony and proceedings in this case, and that the foregoing is a true and complete transcript of his stenographic notes thereof.

B McDonald

Subscribed and sworn to before me this 2nd day of October, 1900.

TB Needles<br>Commissioner.

◇◇◇◇◇

Cherokee 3972.

Department of the Interior,<br>Commission to the Five Civilized Tribes,<br>Muskogee, I. T., October 15, 1902.

In the matter of the application of Edward E. Sloan for the enrollment of himself and children, Mary D. Minnie E., Annie M., Samuel J., Eva L., James E., Nina P. and Florence C. Sloan, as citizens by blood, and for the enrollment of his wife, Naoma A. Sloan, as a citizen by intermarriage of the Cherokee Nation; he being sworn and examined by the Commission, testified as follows:

Q What is your name? A Edward E. Sloan.
Q How old are you? A Fifty-one.
Q What is your postoffice? A Bigcabin.
Q Are you a Cherokee by blood? A Yes sir.
Q How long have you lived in the Cherokee Nation? A All my life.
Q What is your wife's name? A Naoma A.
Q How old is she? A She will be forty-eight December next I think.
Q Was she your wife in 1880? A Yes sir.
Q You were married prior to 1880? A I was married in 1874.
Q Have you and your wife been living together ever since 1880? A All the time since we were married.

## Cherokee Intermarried White 1906
## Volume III

Q Never been separated up to this time? A No sir.
Q How many children have you by your wife, Naoma? A Ten.
Q How many living? A All of them living.
Q The two oldest ones have enrolled themselves have they? A Yes sir.
Q You have eight living with you at home? A Yes sir.
Q None of your family died in the past two and a half years? A No sir.

---

The undersigned, being duly sworn, states that as stenographer to the Commission to the Five Civilized Tribes he correctly recorded the testimony and proceedings in this case, and that the foregoing is a true and correct transcript of his stenographic notes thereof.

E.G. Rothenberger

Subscribed and sworn to before me this 13th day of November, 1902.

BC Jones
Notary Public.

◇◇◇◇◇

DEPARTMENT OF THE INTERIOR
COMMISSIONER TO THE FIVE CIVILIZED TRIBES
MUSKOGEE, IND. TER.
JAN. 4, 1907.

IN THE MATTER OF THE APPLICATION FOR THE
ENROLLMENT OF NAOMI A. SLOAN AS A CITIZEN
BY INTERMARRIAGE OF THE CHEROKEE NATION.

CENSUS CARD NO. 3972.

B[sic]. E. SLOAN BEING FIRST DULY SWORN TESTIFIED AS FOLLOWS;

EXAMINATION BY THE COMMISSIONER:

Q What is your name? A B.E. Sloan.
Q How old are you? A Fifty six.
Q What is your post office address? A Big Cabin.
Q Are you a citizen by blood of the Cherokee Nation.[sic] A Yes sir.
Q Do you know Naomi A. Sloan? A yes sir.
Q What relation are you to Naomi A. Sloan.[sic] A She's my wife
Q When were you married to Naomi A. Sloan.[sic] A Married in 1874 in June in McDonald County Missouri.

## Cherokee Intermarried White 1906
## Volume III

Q How long did you live in Missouri after you married her in 1874.[sic]
A About six months.
Q Were you a citizen of the Cherokee Nation at that time.[sic] A Yes sir; born and raised her[sic].
Q Was you ever married before you married Naomi A. Sloan.[sic] A No sir.
Q Was she ever married before she married you? A No sir.
Q Have you lived together as husband and wife since you married in 1874 up to the present time? A Yes sir.
Q Have you got a license or certificate of your marriage to Naomi Sloan.[sic]
A No sir the certificate is registered at Pineville Missouri.

 Applicant is identified on the 1880 Cherokee Roll, Delaware District opposite No. 2230; her husband thru whom she claims her right to enrollment is identified on said roll, said district opposite No. 2229. He is also identified on the final roll of citizens by blood of the Cherokee Nation opposite No. 9605.

ooOoo

MARY C. McGEE BEING FIRST DULY SWORN TESTIFIED AS FOLLOWS;

EXAMINATION BY THE COMMISSIONER.

Q What is your name? A Macy C. McGee.
Q What is your age? A Fifty three.
Q What is your post office address? A Dodge.
Q Are you a citizen of the Cherokee Nation? A Yes sir.
Q Are you acquainted with Edward B[sic]. Sloan and Naomi A. Sloan.[sic] A Yes sir.
Q How long have you known them.[sic] A Well I've known them about twenty five years I guess; about that long.
Q Have they held themselves out in the community in which they lived as husband and wife ever since you have known them? A Yes sir.
Q You lived in the same community with them.[sic]
A I have; I don't right now tho.
Q Do you know when they were married? A No, sir.
Q Do you know where they were married? A No sir.

ooOoo

MARGARET FIELDS BEING FIRST DULY SWORN TESTIFIED AS FOLLOWS:

EXAMINATION BY THE COMMISSIONER:

Q What is your name? A Margaret Fields.
Q How old are you.[sic] A Soon be fifty nine years old.
Q What is your post office address.[sic] A Southwest City Missouri

## Cherokee Intermarried White 1906
## Volume III

Q Are you acquainted with Edward B[sic]. Sloan and Naomi A. Sloan.[sic]
A Yes sir.
Q How long have you known them? A I've known him ever since he was a little fellow, about five or six years old; I've known his wife ever since they married?
Q Do you know when they were married? A No sir.
Q How soon did you know them after they married? A O I dont[sic] know, some four or five or six years I guess.
Q You have lived in the same community in which they lived? A Yes sir.
Q They have always held themselves out as husband and wife in the community in which they lived. A Yes sir.

--O--

Clara Mitchell Wood being first duly sworn upon her oath states that as stenographer for the commissioner to the she reported the above and foregoing proceedings and that this is a correct transcript of her stenographic notes.

Clara Mitchell Wood

Subscribed and sworn to before me this 8th day of January 1907

B.P. Rasmus
Notary Public.

◇◇◇◇◇

F.R. Cherokee 3972.

### DEPARTMENT OF THE INTERIOR,
### COMMISSIONER TO THE FIVE CIVILIZED TRIBES.

---

In the matter of the application for the enrollment of Naoma A. Sloan as a citizen by intermarriage of the Cherokee Nation.

### D E C I S I O N .

THE RECORDS OF THIS OFFICE SHOW: That on October 2, 1900, application was received by the Commission to the Five Civilized Tribes for the enrollment of Naoma A. Sloan as a citizen by intermarriage of the Cherokee Nation. Further proceedings in the matter of said application were had at Muskogee, Indian Territory, October 15, 1902 and January 4, 1907.

THE EVIDENCE IN THIS CASE SHOWS: That the applicant herein, Naoma A. Sloan, a white woman, was lawfully married in June, 1874, to Edward E. Sloan, who was at the time of said marriage a recognized citizen by blood of the Cherokee Nation, who is

## Cherokee Intermarried White 1906
## Volume III

identified on the Cherokee authenticated tribal roll of 1880, Delaware District, No. 2229, as a native Cherokee, and whose name is included in the approved partial roll of citizens by blood of the Cherokee Nation opposite No. 9605. It is further shown that from the time of said marriage the said Edward E. Sloan and Naoma A. Sloan resided together as husband and wife and continuously lived in the Cherokee Nation up to and including September 1, 1902. The applicant is identified on the Cherokee authenticated tribal roll of 1880, and on the Cherokee census roll of 1896, as an intermarried citizen of the Cherokee Nation.

IT IS, THEREFORE, ORDERED AND ADJUDGED: That in accordance with the decision of the Supreme Court of the United States, dated November 5, 1906, in the cases of Daniel Red Bird et al., vs. the United States, Nos. 125, 126, 127 and 128, the said applicant Naoma A. Sloan is entitled, under the provisions of Section 21 of the Act of Congress approved June 28, 1898 (30 Stats., 495), to enrollment as a citizen by intermarriage of the Cherokee Nation, and her application for enrollment as such is accordingly granted.

            Tams Bixby
                Commissioner.

Dated at Muskogee, Indian Territory,
this    JAN 23 1907

◇◇◇◇◇

Cherokee 3972

            Muskogee, Indian Territory, January 23, 1907.

W. W. Hastings,
  Attorney for the Cherokee Nation,
    Muskogee, Indian Territory.

Dear Sir:

  There is enclosed herewith copy of the decision of the Commissioner to the Five Civilized Tribes, dated January 23, 1907, granting the application for the enrollment of Naoma A. Sloan as a citizen by intermarriage of the Cherokee Nation.

            Respectfully,

Enc I-78                 Commissioner.

RPI

◇◇◇◇◇

## Cherokee Intermarried White 1906
## Volume III

Cherokee 3972.

W.W. HASTINGS,
ATTORNEY.

OFFICE OF

H.M. VANCE,
SECRETARY.

### Attorney for the Cherokee Nation,

MUSKOGEE, I. T.    January 23, 1907.

The Commissioner to the Five Civilized Tribes,
    Muskogee, Indian Territory.

Sir:

    Receipt is acknowledged of the testimony and of your decision enrolling Naoma A. Sloan as a citizen by intermarriage of the Cherokee Nation. Time for protesting said decision is waived and I consent that said person may be placed upon the schedule immediately.

                  Respectfully,
                        W. W. Hastings
                        Attorney for the Cherokee Nation.

◇◇◇◇◇

Cherokee 3972

                    Muskogee, Indian Territory, January 23, 1907.

Naoma A. Sloan,
    Big Cabin, Indian Territory.

Dear Madam:

    There is enclosed herewith copy of the decision of the Commissioner to the Five Civilized Tribes, dated January 23, 1907, granting the application for your enrollment as a citizen by intermarriage of the Cherokee Nation.

    You will be advised when your name has been placed upon a schedule of citizens of the Cherokee Nation and approved by the Secretary of the Interior.

                    Respectfully,

Enc I-96                                           Commissioner.

RPI

---

**Cher IW 88**
**Trans from Cher 4018 3-16-07**

◇◇◇◇◇

# Cherokee Intermarried White 1906
# Volume III

DEPARTMENT OF THE INTERIOR,

COMMISSIONER TO THE FIVE CIVILIZED TRIBES.

---

In the matter of the application for the enrollment of

## JOHN PARKS

as a citizen by intermarriage of the Cherokee Nation.

### CHEROKEE 4018.

### DEPARTMENT OF THE INTERIOR.
### COMMISSION TO THE FIVE CIVILIZED TRIBES.
### VINITA, I.T., OCTOBER 3rd, 1900.

IN THE MATTER OF THE APPLICATION OF John Parks, wife and children for enrollment as citizens of the Cherokee Nation, and he being sworn and examined by Commissioner, T. B. Needles, testified as follows:

Q What is your name? A John Parks.
Q What is your age? A Forty six.
Q What is your Postoffice? A Vinita.
Q What district do you live in? A Delaware.
Q Are you a recognized citizen of the Cherokee Nation? A Yes sir.
Q By blood or intermarriage? A By blood.
Q For whom do you apply? A Myself, wife and children.
Q What is the name of your wife? A Margaret J. Praither[sic].
Q Have you any certificate of marriage? A Yes sir.
    The applicant presents a marriage license and certificate of marriage, certifying that he was married according to the laws of the Cherokee Nation to one, Nollie[sic] E. Prather, a Cherokee citizen, on the 20th day of September, 1871.
Q Is the Mollie E. Prather mentioned in the certificate the Margaret J. Parks, whom you now claim to be your wife? A Yes sir.
    (1896 Roll, Page 585, #438, John Parks, Delaware D'st)
    (1896 Roll, Page 517, #2417, Margaret J. Parks, Delaware D'st)
Q What are the names of your children under age and unmarried?
A John Parks.
Q Has he any middle name? A No sir.
Q How old is he? A Nineteen years old.
Q Next one? A Ora Ada Parks.
Q How old is she? A Fifteen.
Q Next one? A Owen B.

## Cherokee Intermarried White 1906
## Volume III

Q How old is he? A Nine.
Q Next A That is all
Q Are these children living and living with you now? A Yes sir.
Q How long have you lived in the Cherokee Nation? A Twenty eight years.
Q Have you been living with your wife continuously since you married her? A Yes sir.
Q Was she your first wife? A Yes sir.
Q Were you her first husband? A Yes sir.
   (1896 Roll, Page 517, #2421, John Parks, Delaware D'st)
   (1896 Roll, Page 517, #2422, Cora[sic] Ada Parks, Delaware D'st)
   (1896 Roll, Page 517, #2423, Owen Bell Parks, Delaware D'st)

   The names of John Parks, and his wife, Margaret J. Parks, appear upon the census roll of 1896: Applicant also presents a certificate of admission, certifying that his wife, Margaret J. Parks was admitted to citizenship on the 13th day of July, 1886, said certificate being signed by W. P. Boudinot, Executive Secretary of the Interior the Cherokee Nation under the great seal of the Cherokee Nation. He also presents satisfactory proof, by certificate issued from the Office of the Commission on Citizenship, June 27th, 1887, signed by W. M. Gullager, Assistant Executive Secretary, under the seal of the Nation, certifying that his wife, Margaret J. Parks was declared a citizen on the 19th day of December, 1870, said certificate being signed by J. T. Adair, Chairman, D. W. Lipe and H. C. Barnes, Commissioners, under the seal of the Cherokee Nation.
   The name of John Parks, being found upon the census roll of 1896, as well as the name of his wife, Margaret J., and he producing satisfactory proof of marriage to his wife, in the year 1871, her maiden name being Margaret Prather; and the names of his children, John, Cora[sic] Ada and Owen B. appearing upon the census roll of 1896; they all being duly identified and having made satisfactory proof both as to their citizenship and their residence, the said John Parks will be duly listed for enrollment as a Cherokee citizen by intermarriage, and his wife, Margaret J. Parks, and his children, John, Ora Ada and Owen B. as Cherokee citizens by blood.
   For more particular proof as to the citizenship of his wife, see the testimony in the case of his wife's mother, Caroline C. Prather, who was enrolled this day on Card #4014.

---

   The undersigned, being sworn, states that as stenographer to the Commission to the Five Civilized Tribes, he correctly recorded the testimony and proceedings in this case, and that the foregoing is a true and complete transcript of his stenographic notes thereof.

R R Cravens

Subscribed and sworn to before
me this 7th day of October, 1900.
                CR Breckinridge
                                          COMMISSIONER.

## Cherokee Intermarried White 1906
## Volume III

Cherokee 4018.

Department of the Interior,
Commission to the Five Civilized Tribes,
Muskogee, I. T., October 6, 1902.

In the matter of the application of John Parks for the enrollment of himself as a citizen by intermarriage, and for the enrollment of his wife, Margaret J., and children, John, Ora A., and Owen B. Parks, as citizens by blood of the Cherokee Nation; he being sworn and examined by the Commission, testified as follows:

Q What is your name? A John Parks.
Q What is your age at this time? A Forty-eight years old.
Q What is your postoffice? A Vinita.
Q Are you the same John Parks who made application to this Commission for enrollment as an intermarried citizen on October 31, 1900? A Yes sir.
Q What is your wife's name? A Margaret J.
Q Is she living at this time? A Yes sir.
Q Is she a citizen by blood? A Yes sir.
Q When were you and she married? A In '71, December 28 I believe.
Q Were you ever married prior to your marriage to your wife, Margaret? A No sir.
Q Was she ever married prior to her marriage to you? A No sir.
Q You her first husband and she is your first wife? A Yes sir.
Q Have you and your wife, Maragret[sic], lived together all the time since your marriage as husband and wife up until the present time? A We have.
Q Never been separated? A No sir.
Q Y never have been married to any other woman since your marriage to your wife, Margaret? A No sir.
Q You and she lived together as husband and wife on the first day of September, 1902? A Yes sir.
Q How long have you lived in the Cherokee Nation? A Ever since 1870.
Q All the time since 1870? A Yes sir.
Q How long has your wife, Margaret J., lived in the territory? A She has been here pretty near all her life.
Q Has she lived here in the territory ever since 1880 up until the present time? A Yes sir.
Q Are these children, John, Ora A. and Owen B., your children by your wife Margaret? A Yes sir.
Q Are they all living at this time? A They are.
Q And have the lived in the Cherokee Nation all their lives? A Yes, all their lives.

---------------------------------------

The undersigned, being duly sworn, states that as stenographer to the Commission to the Five Civilized Tribes he correctly recorded the testimony and proceedings in this

# Cherokee Intermarried White 1906
# Volume III

case, and that the foregoing is a true and correct transcript of his stenographic notes thereof.

E.G. Rothenberger

Subscribed and sworn to before me this 23rd day of October, 1902.

B C Jones
Notary Public.

◇◇◇◇◇

Cher
Supp'l to #4018

Department of the Interior,
Commission to the Five Civilized Tribes,
Vinita, I. T., April 8, 1903.

In the matter of the application of JOHN PARKS, for the enrollment of himself as a citizen by intermarriage, and his wife MARGARET J. PARKS, and his children, JOHN, ORA A. and OWEN B. PARKS, as citizens by blood, of the Cherokee Nation.

JOHN PARKS, being first duly sworn, and examined, testified as follows:

Examined by the Commission:

Q What is your name ? A John Parks.
Q How old are you ? A Forty nine.
Q What is your post office ? A Vinita.
Q You are a white man ? A Yes sir.
Q You are claiming citizenship by intermarriage are you ? A Yes sir.
Q What is the name of the wife through whom you claim citizenship ?
A Margaret J. Parks.
Q Is she your first wife ? A Yes sir.
Q Are you her first husband ? A Yes sir.
Q What was her name when you married her ? A Margaret J. Prather.
Q Has she ever been known as Mollie ? A Yes sir.
Q When were you married to her ? A The 28th of December, 1871.
Q How does it come that your name is not on the roll of 1880 ?
A Well our case was taken up; it was charged with fraud, and they failed to prove fraud.
Q That was the year 1880 ? A Yes sir.
Q Now you took out a Cherokee marriage license didn't you ? A Yes sir.
Q In what district ? A Delaware.
Q At the time you applied for enrollment you presented your original marriage license did you not ? A Yes sir

# Cherokee Intermarried White 1906
# Volume III

Q  Now what happened to this certificate, I see that it has been burned in several places, how did it get this way ?  A  I don't know nothing about that, we have had it on hand a good while; I can't account for how that has been done.
Q  Where was it kept ?  A  It was kept in the house among our papers.
Q  Did you ever have a fire in your house ?  A  Not that I recollect of
Q  Now is John Parks your name ?  A  Yes sir, I did use to sign it John K. Parks, and I quit that and I enrolled as John Parks.
Q  What does "K" stand for ?  A  Kreiger.
Q  Were you married under that name ?
A  I don't know, I believe I was.
Q  There appears to have been a middle initial in this marriage certificate here, but that is one of the places where it is burned. Do you know if you gave your name as John K. Parks at the time you were married ?  A  I don't know, I won't be positive.
Q  Now your wife is named in this marriage license as Mollie E.
A  Yes sir, that was a nick-name of hers.
Q  Now you say that it is Margaret J ?  A  That's her right name, but Mollie E., is what she went by.
Q  What does "J" stand for ?  A  Jane.
Q  What does "E" stand for ?  A  I don't know what it is.
Q  She has no "E" in her name ?  A  No sir.
Q  What was the name of that clerk that issued you that license ?
A  His name was S. S. Melton.
Q  Now who married you under this license ?  A  The white man that married us is named Hailey, but his name is not there, it was sent back and recorded by the clerk.
Q  And you and this wife Margaret have been living together in the Cherokee Nation ever since you were married, have you ?  A  Yes sir.
Q  You say you never married but once ?  A  Just the one time, that's all.
Q  And neither was she ?  A  Just the one time.
Q  How many children have you ?  A  Six.
Q  How many under age ?  A  Well there would be two, and then I have got one boy that I can't get up here to get his ticket and I can't enroll him, but he is twenty one. I don't know whether I can get him in.
Q  And there is Ora and Owen ?  A  Yes sir, Ora will be eighteen today, and John is twenty one, and I would be glad to file for him, for he's a funny boy, he's got to work but I don't know whether he will come in.
Q  On a closer examination of this license and the certificate attached to it, I find that the places in the paper which are burned the two places which are burned appear right between your first and last name in each instance, the hole burned in the paper occurs just between John and Parks, and then in the certificate of record there is another hole burned between the name John and Parks; now that seems somewhat singular Mr. Parks; you say you cannot account for that ?  A  No sir, I can't; I used to sign my name John K, but I quit that.
Q  You are certain that you are the same John Parks named in this Cherokee marriage license ?  A  Yes sir, I am the one.

## Cherokee Intermarried White 1906
## Volume III

Q Have you had this license in your possession ever since you were married ? A Why it has been in the house, yes sir; I don't think it has been away, we have had it among our papers.
Q Now this paper was apparently burned while it was straight open because the burns do not coincide with each other when the paper is folded up, so apparently it was not burned while the paper was folded up, it was burned while it was open. When did you first notice that ? A Why when I got it out my wife noticed that, and I did too, and we couldn't account for it how it burned
Q But you say you are the same John Parks ? A Yes sir, I am the same one.
Q And your wife Margaret J., is the identical one with the one named here as Mollie E. Prather ? A Yes sir.
Q You are sure of that ? A Yes sir.

------------------------

E. C. Bagwell, on oath states that, as stenographer to the Commission to the Five Civilized Tribes, he correctly recorded the testimony and proceedings had in the above entitled cause, and that the foregoing is an accurate transcript of his stenographic notes thereof.

E.C. Bagwell

Subscribed and sworn to before me this July 28, 1903.

Samuel Foreman<br>Notary Public.

◇◇◇◇◇

C.F.B.                                                        Cherokee 4018

DEPARTMENT OF THE INTERIOR,<br>COMMISSIONER TO THE FIVE CIVILIZED TRIBES.<br>MUSKOGEE, IND. TER. JANUARY 4, 1907.

In the matter of the application for the enrollment of
JOHN PARKS as a citizen by intermarriage of the
Cherokee Nation.

APPEARANCES:     APPLICANT appeared in person:

CHEROKEE NATION represented by H. M. Vance, on behalf of W. W. Hastings, Attorney.

JOHN PARKS being duly sworn by B.P. Rasmus, a Notary Public, testified as follows:

# Cherokee Intermarried White 1906
## Volume III

On Behalf of Commissioners:

Q. What is your name? A. John Parks
Q. What is your age? A. Fifty-four.
Q. What is your postoffice address? A. Vinita.
Q. Are you an applicant for enrollment as a citizen by intermarriage of the Cherokee Nation? A. Yes sir.
Q. You have no Cherokee blood? A. No sir, none that I know of.
Q. The only claim you make to enrollment as a citizen of the Cherokee Nation is by virtue of your marriage to a citizen of that Nation? A. Yes sir.
Q. What is the name of the citizen through whom you claim the right to enrollment as a citizen of the Cherokee Nation? A. Margaret J. Prather.
Q. Is she living or dead? A. She is living.
Q. Was she a recognized citizen of the Cherokee Nation when you married her? A. Yes sir.
Q. Where were you married? A. Near Mayesville[sic], Delaware District, Cherokee Nation.
Q. Did you secure a marriage license in accordance with the laws of the Cherokee Nation? A. Yes sir, I did.
Q. That license was issued in Delaware District, was it? A. Yes sir
Q. Who married you? A. A man by the name of Haley. Parson Haley.
Q. A. Judge of the Court, or a Minister? A. He was a minister of the Gospel.
Q. Were you ever married prior to your marriage to your wife Margaret J. Prather? A. No sir.
Q. Was she ever married before she married you? A. No sir.
Q. Since your marriage to her have you and she continuously resided together as husband and wife? A. Yes sir.
Q. And have lived continuously in the Cherokee Nation, have you? A. Yes sir.
Q. Why is it that your wife's name does not appear upon the Cherokee roll of 1880?
A. Well, I can explain that to you best by showing you some papers I have here?[sic] (Presents papers)
Q. Were you and your wife residing in the Cherokee Nation in 1880? A. Yes sir.
Q. Was your wife a member of the family of R. A. Prather?
Q. You say, and the papers you present here show that the family of R. A. Prather was admitted to citizenship in the Cherokee Nation in 1870? A. Yes sir.
Q. You were living in the Cherokee Nation in 1880? A. Yes sir
Q. Why were you and your wife not placed upon that roll, can you explain? A. Well, they had us charged with fraud but the case was not tried until 1886, I believe it was, The Council passed an Act to investigate all these cases, and when they investigated the matter they decided for us; that there was no fraud.
Q. In what District were you married? A. In Delaware.
Q. When were you married? A. December 28, 1871. My license is on file with your office.
Q. You say that your marriage license and certificate showing that you were married in accordance with the laws of the Cherokee Nation to your wife, Margaret J. Prather, is on file with this office? A. Yes sir. I believe you will find that the license is made

## Cherokee Intermarried White 1906
## Volume III

out to Mollie E. Prather; that is the nick-name she went by- call her Mollie yet- but her real name is Margaret J.

There is on file at this office a marriage license and certificate showing that on December 28, 1871, John Parks a citizen of the United States was licensed in accordance with the laws of the Cherokee Nation, to marry Mollie E. Prather, a Cherokee woman and that said parties were united in marriage on the 28th day of December, 1871.

The applicant, John Parks, is identified on the Cherokee Census Roll of 1896, Delaware District, No. 438. His wife Margaret J. Parks, is included in an approved partial roll of citizens by blood of the Cherokee Nation, opposite No. 9704

ROBERT W. TITTLE being first duly sworn by B. P. Rasmus, a Notary Public, testified as follows:

Q. What is your name? A. Robert W. Tittle.
Q. What is your age? A. My age is Fifty-seven.
Q. What is your postoffice address? A. Vinita.
Q. Do you know a man in the Cherokee Nation by the name of John Parks? A. I do, sir.
Q. He is an applicant for enrollment as a citizen by intermarriage of the Cherokee Nation? A. Yes sir.
Q. What is the name of his wife? A. Her name was Mollie Prather when he married her.
Q. When did he marry her? A. In the latter part of 1871.
Q. Did you know her prior to her marriage to him? A. Yes sir.
Q. Were they married in accordance with the laws of the Cherokee Nation?
A. Yes sir
Q. Did he secure a license under the Cherokee law? A. Yes sir.
Q. Where was it issued? A. In Delaware District; I went with him to the Clerk, and also went to Mayesville[sic] and got the preacher, myself and Jacob Hiser, and brought him out to old Mr. Prather's, house, and stood by and seen them married.

---

The undersigned being first duly sworn, states that as stenographer to the Commissioner to the Five Civilized Tribes she correctly recorded the testimony taken in this case and that the above and foregoing is a full, true and correct transcript of her stenographic notes thereof.

Lucy M Bowman

Subscribed and sworn to before me this 5th day of January, 1907.

John E. Tidwell
Notary Public.

## Cherokee Intermarried White 1906
## Volume III

*(The Marriage License below typed as given.)*

    this is to certify By That John Parks a Citizen of the U S A. was License to marry Molley E prather a Cherokee woman of Del Dis C.N. on the 28th of Dec 1871 Licens Returned duly Executed on the 28th day of Decembr 1871 it Being in accordance with the act passed by the National Council bearing Date Oct 15th 1855 in regard to white men marrying in the Cherokee Nation.

S. N. Melton<br>Clerke of Dis Court in Del D C.N.

    I hereby certify that the above is a true coppy from the record of this of regard to the marriage of John Parks this the 4th day of Sept 1879

(SEAL)
R. T. Casey<br>Clerk D. D. C. N.

---

    This is to certify that the undersigned, being first duly sworn, states that as stenographer to the Commissioner to the Five Civilized Tribes, she made the above and foregoing copy, and that the same is a full, true and correct copy of a copy of the original instrument now on file in this office.

Sarah Waters

Subscribed and sworn to before me this 17th day of January, 1907.

B.P. Rasmus<br>Notary Public.

◇◇◇◇◇

*(The Marriage License below typed as given.)*

This will certify by me by me that John % Parks a citizen of the United Stats was licens to marry Molly E. Praither a Cherokee woman of Del Des C.N. on the 28th., of December 1871 Licens return fully executed the 28th., day of Dec. 1871 being in accordance with the act passed by the National Council bearing date Oct. 15th. 1855 in regard to white men marrying in the Cherokee Nation.

## Cherokee Intermarried White 1906
## Volume III

Executive Department, Cheokee Nation
Tahlequah, Indian Territory.

I hereby certify that the above and foregoing is a true copy of the record now on file in this office, of which I am legal custodian.
(SEAL)  Given this the 13 th., day of xxx Nov. 1902.

J. T. Parks,
Executive Secretary.

---

This is to certify that the undersigned, being first duly sworn, states that as stenographer to the Commissioner to the Five Civilized Tribes, she made the above and foregoing copy, and that the same is a full, true and correct copy of a certified copy of record of marriage license now on file in this office.

Sarah Waters

Subscribed and sworn to before me this to before me this 17th day of January, 1907.

B.P. Rasmus
Notary Public.

◇◇◇◇◇

C.F.B.  Cherokee 4018

DEPARTMENT OF THE INTERIOR,

COMMISSIONER TO THE FIVE CIVILIZED TRIBES.

---

In the matter of the application for the enrollment of John Parks as a citizen by intermarriage of the Cherokee Nation.

### D E C I S I O N

THE RECORDS OF THIS OFFICE SHOW: That at Vinita, Indian Territory, October 3, 1900, application was received by the Commission to the Five Civilized Tribes, for the enrollment of John Parks, as a citizen by intermarriage of the Cherokee Nation. Further proceedings in the matter of said application were had at Muskogee, Indian Territory, October 6, 1902, at Vinita, Indian Territory, April 8, 1903, and at Muskogee, Indian Territory, January 4, 1907.

THE EVIDENCE IN THIS CASE SHOWS: That the applicant herein, John Parks, a white man, was married in accordance with Cherokee law December 28, 1871, to one

## Cherokee Intermarried White 1906
## Volume III

Margaret J. Prather, who was, at the time of said marriage, a recognized citizen by blood of the Cherokee Nation; that the said Margaret J. Prather was duly admitted to citizenship in the Cherokee Nation by the Adair Commission on citizenship December 9, 1870; that thereafter the decision of said Commission was questioned by the Cherokee authority, and a rehearing in said case was ordered by the National Council of the Cherokee Nation; that on July 13, 1886, the duly constituted authorities of the Cherokee Nation adjudged said Margaret J. Parks entitled to the right to citizenship in the Cherokee Nation. The said Margaret J. Parks, nee Prather, is identified on the approved partial roll of citizens by blood of the Cherokee Nation, opposite No. 9704. It is further shown that since said marriage, the said John and Margaret J. Parks have resided together as husband and wife and have continuously lived in the Cherokee Nation since their marriage December 28, 1871. Said applicant is identified on the Cherokee census roll of 1896 as an intermarried citizen of the Cherokee Nation.

IT IS, THEREFORE, ORDERED AND ADJUDGED: That in accordance with the decision of the Supreme Court of the United States, dated November 5, 1906, in the cases of Daniel Red Bird, et al., vs. the United States, Nos. 125, 126, 127 and 128, the said applicant, John Parks, is entitled, under the provisions of Section twenty-one of the Act of Congress approved June 28, 1898 (30 Stats. 495), to enrollment as a citizen by intermarriage of the Cherokee Nation, and his application for enrollment as such is accordingly granted.

Tams Bixby
Commissioner.

Dated at Muskogee, Indian Territory,
this     JAN 23 1907

◇◇◇◇◇

Cherokee 4018

Muskogee, Indian Territory, January 23, 1907.

W. W. Hastings,
    Attorney for the Cherokee Nation,
        Muskogee, Indian Territory.

Dear Sir:

    There is enclosed herewith copy of the decision of the Commissioner to the Five Civilized Tribes, dated January 23, 1907, granting the application for the enrollment of John Parks as a citizen by intermarriage of the Cherokee Nation.

Respectfully,

Enc I-72                                              Commissioner.

RPI

◇◇◇◇◇

## Cherokee Intermarried White 1906
## Volume III

Cherokee 4018.

W.W. HASTINGS, ATTORNEY.   OFFICE OF   H.M. VANCE, SECRETARY.

### Attorney for the Cherokee Nation,
MUSKOGEE, I. T.   January 23, 1907.

The Commissioner to the Five Civilized Tribes,
 Muskogee, Indian Territory.

Sir:

  Receipt is acknowledged of the testimony and of your decision enrolling John Parks as a citizen by intermarriage of the Cherokee Nation. Time for protesting said decision is waived and I consent that said person may be placed upon the schedule immediately.

          Respectfully,
           W. W. Hastings
           Attorney for the Cherokee Nation.

◇◇◇◇◇

Cherokee 4018

         Muskogee, Indian Territory, January 23, 1907.

John Parks,
  Vinita, Indian Territory.

Dear Sir:

  There is enclosed herewith copy of the decision of the Commissioner to the Five Civilized Tribes, dated January 23, 1907, granting the application for your enrollment as a citizen by intermarriage of the Cherokee Nation.

  You will be advised when your name has been placed upon a schedule of citizens of the Cherokee Nation and approved by the Secretary of the Interior.

          Respectfully,

Enc I-89                Commissioner.

RPI

◇◇◇◇◇

## Cherokee Intermarried White 1906
## Volume III

Cherokee I.W. 88

Muskogee, Indian Territory, April 9, 1907.

John Parks,
    Vinita, Indian Territory.

Dear Sir:

    Your marriage license and certificate filed in connection with your application for enrollment as a citizen by intermarriage of the Cherokee Nation, is returned to you herewith, copies of the same being retained in the files of this office.

        Respectfully,

Incl. P-4-9                             Acting Commissioner.
  MMP

---

**Cher IW 89**
**Trans from Cher 4076  3-16-07**

◇◇◇◇◇

F.R.

### DEPARTMENT OF THE INTERIOR,
### COMMISSIONER TO THE FIVE CIVILIZED TRIBES.

- - - - - - -

In the matter of the application for the enrollment of

### MARION HOLDERMAN

as a citizen by intermarriage of the Cherokee Nation.

- - - - - -

### CHEROKEE 4076.

◇◇◇◇◇

## Cherokee Intermarried White 1906
## Volume III

DEPARTMENT OF THE INTERIOR.
COMMISSION TO THE FIVE CIVILIZED TRIBES.
Vinita, I.T. October 3rd, 1900.

IN THE MATTER OF THE APPLICATION OF MARION HOLDERMAN FOR THE ENROLLMENT OF HIMSELF, HIS WIFE AND ONE CHILD, AS CHEROKEE CITIZENS.

The said Marion Holderman, being sworn and examined by Commissioner T. B. Needles, testified as follows:
Q What is your name? A Marion Holderman.
Q Any middle name? A No, sir.
Q What is your age? A Fifty-nine. I will be sixty this fall.
Q What is your post office address? A Chetopa, Kansas.
Q What district do you live in? A Cooweescoowee.
Q Are you a recognized citizen of the Cherokee Nation? What district do you live in? A Cooweescoowee.
Q Are you a recognized citizen of the Cherokee Nation? A Yes, sir.
Q By blood or intermarriage? A By marriage.
Q For whom do you apply? A For myself and wife and one child
Q What is the name of your wife? A Mary C.
Q What is her age? A Fifty-six.
Q Have you any certificate of marriage? A Yes, sir; I have, but I can't find it.
Q When were you married? A In 1870, that is according to the Cherokee law. We were married according to the State of Iowa law in 1866.
Q Well, you name is on the 1880 roll, then? A I suppose so.
Q What now what is the name of the child you apply for? A Pearl.
Q How old is Pearl? A She is seventeen.
Q Where do you reside? A In Cooweescoowee district, five miles southwest of Chetopa.
1880 Roll, page 113, No. 1313, Mary Holderman, Cooweescoowee District.
1896 Roll, page 176, No. 2216, Mary C. Holderman, Cooweescoowee District.
1896 Roll, page 176, No. 2219, Pearl Holderman, Cooweescoowee District.
[sic] You say you were married according to the Cherokee law in 1870? A Yes, sir.
Q Why is your name not on the roll of 1880? A I don't know. I wasn't here in 1880. My wife put in the name in 1880.

EXAMINATION BY MR. W. W. HASTINGS Representative of Cherokee Nation.
Q Who married you? A I was married at Fort Gibson by uncle Peter Wyley.
Q A minister of the gospel? A Yes, sir.
Q From whom did you get license? A Joel Mayes.
Q What office did he have at that time? A Clerk of the Cooweescoowee District.
Q In the year 1870? A Yes, sir.
Q Did you ever attempt to get a copy of the record? A Yes, sir; I had a copy once, but I don't know where it is. I sent it to the Dawes Commission a few years ago, and I don't know whether I have got it back or not. It seems to me like it was sent back, then then I

## Cherokee Intermarried White 1906
## Volume III

forgot to hunt it up this morning. I went before the Committee in 1896 at Tahlequah, Indian Territory and John Gunter was Chairman.
Q Are you and your wife living together now as husband and wife? A Yes, sir.
1896 Roll, page 309, No. 524, Marion Holderman Cooweescoowee District.

BY THE COMMISSIONER:
Q How long have you lived in the Cherokee Nation A Since 1866
Q Have you been living her[sic] continuously ever since? A Yes, sir
Q You don't know any reason why your name is not on the roll of 1880? A I understand there was no adopted citizens put on the roll of 1880 at the time.

THE COMMISSIONER: The name of Marion Holderman appears upon the census roll of 1896. The name of his [sic] Mary C., appears upon the authenticated roll of 1880 as a Cherokee citizen by blood. The name of his child Pearl appears upon the census roll of 1896?[sic] They being duly identified, and having made satisfactory proof as to their residence the said Mary C. Holderman and her child Pearl will be duly listed for enrollment as Cherokee citizens by blood.

The applicant, Marion Holderman, avers that he was married in the year 1870, according to the laws of the Cherokee Nation, but presents no proof of marriage. Upon satisfactory proof of his marriage being presented to this Commission, he will be duly listed for enrollment as a Cherokee citizen by intermarriage.

------o------

The undersigned, being sworn, states that as stenographer to the Commission to the Five Civilized Tribes he correctly recorded the testimony and proceedings in this application for enrollment, and that the foregoing is a correct and complete transcript of his stenographic notes thereof.

Wm S Meeshean

Subscribed and sworn to before me this 19th day of October A. D. 1900.

CR Breckinridge

Commissioner.

# Cherokee Intermarried White 1906
## Volume III

Cherokee 4076.

Department of the Interior,
Commission to the Five Civilized Tribes,
Muskogee, I. T., October 7, 1902.

In the matter of the application of Marion Holderman for the enrollment of himself as a citizen by intermarriage, and for the enrollment of his wife, Mary C., and child, Pearl Holderman, as citizens by blood of the Cherokee Nation.

Curtis E. Holderman, being sworn and examined by the Commission, testified as follows:

Q What is your name? A Curtis E. Holderman.
Q What is your age? A I am past thirty.
Q What is your postoffice? A Welch, Indian Territory.
Q Are you acquainted with Marion Holderman who is an applicant before this Commission for enrollment as an intermarried citizen? A Yes sir, he is my father.
Q What is his wife's name? A Mary C.
Q Is Mary C. a citizen by blood of the Cherokee Nation? A Yes sir.
Q When was your father married to Mary C. Holderman? A In '66 I believe.
Q Where were they married? A They were first married in Iowa and then remarried here. Their remarriage was on the old Delaware District Court records.
Q Have they lived together as husband and wife for the last twenty years? A With the exception of about twelve months.
Q Were they separated for twelve months? A Yes, I believe mother left home September 2, 1893.
Q Did they have a falling out and separated? A Yes, mother left home and came back the following summer, in about July I believe.
Q Well, they went to living together the same as ever? A They made up their difficulty and been living together as man and wife ever since.
Q Your father has never been married to any other woman since 1880? A No sir.
Q And they were living together as man and wife on the first day of September, 1902? A Yes sir.
Q Has your mother lived in the Cherokee Nation all the time since 1880?
A All her life.
Q Has your father lived in the Cherokee Nation all the time since 1880?
A Yes sir, since '66.
Q This daughter, Pearl, is she living? A Yes sir.
Q That is the daughter of Marion and Mary C.? A Yes sir.
Q Has Pearl lived in the Cherokee Nation all her life? A Yes sir, except the time she was away at school.

----------------------------

The undersigned, being duly sworn, states that as stenographer to the Commission to the Five Civilized Tribes he correctly recorded the testimony and proceedings in this

# Cherokee Intermarried White 1906
## Volume III

case, and that the foregoing is a true and correct transcript of his stenographic notes thereof.

         E.G. Rothenberger

Subscribed and sworn to before me this 1st day of November, 1902.

         BC Jones
         Notary Public.

C. F. B.                       Cherokee 4076.

## DEPARTMENT OF THE INTERIOR,
## COMMISSIONER TO THE FIVE CIVILIZED TRIBES.
## MUSKOGEE, I. T., JANUARY 2, 1907.

In the matter of the application for the enrollment of Marion Holderman as a citizen by intermarriage of the Cherokee Nation.

APPEARANCES:  Applicant appears in person.

        Cherokee Nation represented by H. M. Vance, on behalf of W. W. Hastings, Attorney.

MARION HOLDERMAN, being first duly sworn by B. P. Rasmus, notary public, testified as follows:-

ON BEHALF OF THE COMMISSIONER:

Q What is your name? A Marion Holderman.
Q What is your age? A 66 years.
Q What is your post office address? A Chetopah[sic], Kansas.
Q Are you an applicant for enrollment as a citizen by intermarriage of the Cherokee Nation? A Yes sir.
Q You have no Cherokee blood? A No sir.
Q Through whom do you claim the right to enrollment as a citizen by intermarriage of the Cherokee Nation? A Her name was Mary Elizabeth Covel.
Q Is she living or dead? A She is living.
Q When were you married to her? A We were married first on the 21st of June, 1866.
Q Where were you living at the time you were married? A We were then a school in Iowa.
Q Was she a recognized citizen of the Cherokee Nation at the time you married her? A Yes sir.
Q Were you ever married prior to your marriage to her? A No sir.
Q Was she ever married prior to her marriage to you? A No sir.

# Cherokee Intermarried White 1906
## Volume III

Q After your marriage in Iowa in 1866 did you and she remove to the Cherokee Nation? A Yes sir, during the same fall.
Q Were you remarried after coming to the Cherokee Nation? A Yes sir, to comply with the Cherokee law.
Q During what year were you remarried? A In 1870.
Q Did you secure a license in regular form? A Yes sir.
Q In what district were you living? A Cooweescoowee.
Q The license then was issued by the Clerk of Cooweescoowee District, was it? A Yes sir.
Q Have you a copy of the license? A No sir, I returned the license to the Clerk and never got it from the Clerk's office.
Q From the time of your removal to the Cherokee Nation with your wife in 1866, did you and she continuously live together as man and wife, and continuously reside in the Cherokee Nation, up until the present time? A Yes sir, with the exception of part of a year that she was away from home.

*(The remainder of this page is completely illegible.)*

◇◇◇◇◇

*(There are two pages for this applicant that are completely illegible.)*

◇◇◇◇◇

*(Illegible...)*

Muskogee, Indian Territory, January 23, 1907.

W. W. Hastings,
    Attorney for the Cherokee Nation,
        Muskogee, Indian Territory.

Dear Sir:

    There is enclosed herewith a copy of the decision of the Commissioner to the Five Civilized Tribes, dated January 23, 1907, granting the application for the enrollment of Marion Holderman as a citizen by intermarriage of the Cherokee Nation.

Respectfully,

Encl. H-66                                       Commissioner.
JMH

◇◇◇◇◇

## Cherokee Intermarried White 1906
## Volume III

Cherokee 4076  W.W.HASTINGS. ATTORNEY.  OFFICE OF  H.M. VANCE. SECRETARY.

**Attorney for the Cherokee Nation,**

MUSKOGEE, I. T.    January 23, 1907.

The Commissioner to the Five Civilized Tribes,
    Muskogee, Indian Territory.

Sir:

    Receipt is acknowledged of the testimony and of your decision enrolling Marion Holderman as a citizen by intermarriage of the Cherokee Nation. Time for protesting said decision is waived and I consent that said person may be placed upon the schedule immediately.

        Respectfully,
        W. W. Hastings
        Attorney for Cherokee Nation.

◇◇◇◇◇

Cherokee 4076

    Muskogee, Indian Territory, January 23, 1907.

Marion Holderman,
    Chetopa, Kansas.

Dear Sir:

    There is enclosed herewith a copy of the decision of the Commissioner to the Five Civilized Tribes, dated January 23, 1907, granting the application for your enrollment as a citizen by intermarriage of the Cherokee Nation.

    You will be advised when your name has been placed upon a schedule of citizens of the Cherokee Nation and approved by the Secretary of the Interior.

        Respectfully,

Encl. H-88          Commissioner.
JMH

---

**Cher IW 90**
**Trans from Cher 4206  3-16-07**

◇◇◇◇◇

## Cherokee Intermarried White 1906
## Volume III

F.R.

DEPARTMENT OF THE INTERIOR,
COMMISSIONER TO THE FIVE CIVILIZED TRIBES.

--------------------

In the matter of the application for the enrollment of

NELSON F. CARR

as a citizen by intermarriage of the Cherokee Nation.

--------------------

CHEROKEE 4206.

◇◇◇◇◇

Department of the Interior,
Commission to the Five Civilized Tribes,
Bartlesville, I. T. Oct. 8th 1900.

In the matter of the application of Nelson F. Carr for enrollment as citizens of the Cherokee Nation of himself his wife and two children Nelson F. Carr being duly sworn by Commissioner Breckinridge testified as follows-

Q. How old are you? A. 56.
Q. What is your post office? A. Bartlesville, I. T.
Q. Who is it that you want enrolled? A. Myself, my wife and two children.
Q. Are you a Cherokee by blood? A. No sir.
Q. White man? A. Yes sir.
Q. What is your wife? A. Cherokee.
Q. Let me see your marriage license./Have it not.
Q. Where is it[sic]
Q.[sic] I havent[sic] any.
Q. Are you on the roll of 1880? A. Yes sir.
Q. Have you lived in the Cherokee Nation ever since your marriage? A. Yes sir.
Q. Lived with your wife all that time? A. Yes sir.
Q. Is she living at this time? A. Yes sir.
Q. Give me the names of your wife? A. Sarah Ann Carr.
Q. How old is she? A. 51.
Q. What is the name of her father? A. Hilliard Rogers.
Q. Is he living or dead? A. Dead.
Q. Has he been dead as much as 20 years? A. Yes sir 30.

## Cherokee Intermarried White 1906
## Volume III

Q. What is the name of your wifes[sic] mother? A. Martha.
Q. Is she dead? A. Yes sir.
Q. Has she been dead as much as 20 years.[sic] A. Yes sir.
Q. Give me the names of your children? A. Josie May, age 15. Beulah M. age 8
Q. Are they both living now? A. Yes sir.

1880 Roll, page 82, No. 580, N. F. Carr, Cooweescoowee, adopted white.
1880,  "     "  82, "   581, S. A. Carr,           "         Native Chr.
1896,  "    " 300, "   266, Nelson F. Carr,       "         AD. What[sic].
1896   "    " 136 "  1120   Sarah A. Carr.        "         N. C.
1896   "    " 136 "  1123   Josie M. Carr,        "
1896   "    " 136 "  1124   Buela M. Carr         "

The applicant applies for the enrollment of himself his wife and 2 children His wife is identified on the 1880 and 1896 rolls as a native Cherokee, and he is identified on both of said rolls with his wife as an intermarried citizen, and they have been living together and in the Cherokee Nation ever since they were enrolled in 1880. His wife will be listed for enrollment as a Cherokee by blood and he will be listed for enrollment as an intermarried citizen of the Cherokee Nation; and their two children have been identified on the 1896 roll, and they are living at this time with their parents and will be listed for enrollment as Cherokees by blood.

Chas von Weise, being first duly sworn upon his oath states that as stenographer to the Commission to the Five Civilized Tribes he reported all proceedings in the above entitled cause on the 8th day of October, 1900, and that the above and foregoing is a full, true, and correct transcript of his stenographic notes taken in said proceedings on said date.

Chas von Weise

Subscribed and sworn to before me this the 8th of October, 1900.

C R Breckinridge

Commissioner.

◇◇◇◇◇

# Cherokee Intermarried White 1906
# Volume III

DEPARTMENT OF THE INTERIOR.
Commission to the Five Civilized Tribes.
Muskogee, Indian Territory, October 13th, 1902.

In the matter of the application of Nelson F. Carr for the enrollment of himself as citizen by intermarriage and for the enrollment of his wife, Sarah A. Carr, and his children, Josie M. and Beulah M. Carr, as citizens by blood of the Cherokee Nation.

Supplemental to #4206.

NELSON F. CARR, being duly sworn, testified as follows:
Examination by the Commission.
Q. What is your name? A. Nelson F. Carr.
Q. How old are you? A. 58 years old.
Q. What is your post office? A. Bartlesville.
Q. You are on the eighty roll, are you? A. Yes, sir.
Q. You are claiming as a citizen by intermarriage? A. Yes, sir.
Q. What is your wife's name? A. Sarah Ann Rogers.
Q. Was she your wife in 1880? A. I married her in '67.
Q. Have you lived in the Cherokee Nation ever since?
A. Yes, sir; lived on Caney ever since '67.
Q. How many children have you? A. Four.
Q. How many at home? A. Two
Q. Two living at home with you? A. Yes, sir.

I I I I I I I I I I I I I I I I I I I I I I I I I I I

Jesse O. Carr, being first duly sworn, states that as stenographer to the Commission to the Five Civilized Tribes he reported the above entitled case and that the foregoing is a true and complete transcript of his stenographic notes thereof.

Jesse O. Carr

Subscribed and sworn to before me this 20th day of December, 1902.

BC Jones
Notary Public.

◇◇◇◇◇

# Cherokee Intermarried White 1906
# Volume III

Cher
# 4206

Department of the Interior,
Commission to the Five Civilized Tribes,
Vinita, I. T., February 6, 1903.

In the matter of the application of NELSON F. CARR, for the enrollment of himself as a citizen by intermarriage, and his wife, SARAH A. CARR, and his children, JOSIE M. and BEULAH M. CARR, as citizens by blood, of the Cherokee Nation:

NELSON F. CARR, being first duly sworn, and examined, testified as follows:

Examined by the Commission:

Q Your name is Nelson F. Carr ? A Yes sir.
Q Where are you living now ? A I am living up on Caney, three miles north of Bartlesville.
Q Bartlesville is your post office ? A Yes sir.
Q You are a white man ? A Yes sir.
Q Are you on the 1880 roll ? A Yes sir.
Q You are claiming citizenship through your wife Sarah ? A Yes sir.
Q She was your wife in 1880 ? A She was in 1867, and has been ever since.
Q You and your wife have never been separated ? A No sir.
Q Still living together ? A Yes sir.

------------------------

E. C. Bagwell, on oath states, that as stenographer to the Commission to the Five Civilized Tribes, he correctly recorded the testimony and proceedings had in above entitled cause, and that the foregoing is an accurate transcript of his stenographic notes thereof.

E.C.Bagwell

Subscribed and sworn to before me this February 20, 1903.

Samuel Foreman
Notary Public.

## Cherokee Intermarried White 1906
## Volume III

DEPARTMENT OF THE INTERIOR
COMMISSIONER TO THE FIVE CIVILIZED TRIBES
MUSKOGEE, IND. TER.
JAN. 4, 1907.

IN THE MATTER OF THE APPLICATION FOR ENROLLMENT AS A CITIZEN BY INTERMARRIAGE OF THE CHEROKEE NATION OF NELSON F. CARR.

CENSUS CARE NO. 4206.

NELSON F. CARR BENG FIRST DULY SWORN TESTIFIED AS FOLLOWS:

EXAMINATION BY THE COMMISSIONER

Q What is your name.[sic]  A Nelson F. Carr.
Q How old are you.[sic]  A Sixty two years old.
Q What is your post office address?  A Bartlesville.
Q You claim to be a citizen by intermarriage of the Cherokee Nation.  A Yes sir.
Q Thru whom do you acquire your rights?  A Sarah Ann Rogers
A I was married the 25th day of August 1867. By a Kansas Methodist Preacher and married according to the Cherokee law on the 17th day of February 1868.
Q Was Sarah Ann Rogers a recognized citizen of the Cherokee Nation at the time you married her.[sic]  A Yes sir.
Q Where were you living when you married.[sic]  A Delaware District
Q Did she live at Delaware District at that time.[sic]  A Timber Hill Cherokee Nation.
Q You were both living in the Cherokee Nation at the time you married.[sic]
A No I lived at Oswega[sic] Kansas.
Q How soon did you move to the Cherokee Nation.[sic]  A Right away.
Q Have you lived continuously together as husband and wife in the Cherokee Nation since you married in 1868.[sic]  A Yes sir.
Q Living together at the present time.[sic]  A Yes sir.
Q Were you ever married before you married Sarah Ann Carr.[sic]  A No sir.
Q Was she ever married before she married you.[sic]  A No sir
Q Have you got a license issued to you by the Cherokee authorities.[sic]  A No sir I took it to have it recorded and I never did get it; here's a certified copy.

Applicant offers in evidence certificate by A.B. Cunningham dated December 11 A.D. 1905 which shows that the records of the Cherokee Nation show that applicant was licensed to marry S. A. Rogers female Cherokee on the 17th day of February 1868.

An examination of Book S. of the marriage record of Delaware District on page 9 shows that applicant received a license on the 17th day of February 1868; was married under the same on said date by E.J. McGee Clerk of the Delaware District.

## Cherokee Intermarried White 1906
## Volume III

Applicant is identified on the 1880 Cherokee Roll opposite No. 580; his wife thru whom he claims his right to enrollment is identified on said roll opposite No. 581; she is also identified on the final roll of citizens by blood of the Cherokee Nation opposite No. 10144.

Clara Mitchell Wood being first duly sworn upon her oath states that as stenographer for the Commissioner to the Five Civilized Tribes she reported the above and foregoing proceedings and that this is a correct transcript of her stenographic notes.

Clara Mitchell Wood

Subscribed and sworn to before me this 8th day of January 1907.

B.P. Rasmus<br>Notary Public.

◇◇◇◇◇

CERTIFIED COPY.

Executive Department,
Cherokee Nation,
Tahlequah, Indian Territory.

"This is to certify by me that N. F. Carr, a white man, was licensed to marry S. A. Rogers, a female Cherokee on the 17th day of Feb., 1868, and the license executed and returned Feb. 17th, 1868, being according to the Act passed by the National Council bearing date Oct. 15th, 1855, in regard to white men marrying in this nation."
T. H. McGhee, Clk. D.C.D.D.C.N

I, A. B. Cunningham, Executive Secretary of the Cherokee Nation, do hereby certify that the above and foregoing is a true and correct copy of the record of Marriage of N. F. Carr and S. A. Rogers, as taken from marriage record of Delaware District, Cherokee Nation, Book "S", page 9. Said marriage record being transferred to and made a part of the records of this Department and in my custody.

In testimony whereof, I hereunto set my hand and affix the seal of the Cherokee Nation, at Tahlequah, Indian Territory, this the 11th day of December A. D., 1905.

(Signed) A. B. Cunningham,<br>Executive Secretary Cherokee Nation

(SEAL)

---

## Cherokee Intermarried White 1906
## Volume III

I, Frances R. Lane, a stenographer to the Commissioner to the Five Civilized Tribes, do hereby certify that the above and forgoing is a true and complete copy of a marriage license issued to N. F. Carr to marry S. A. Rogers now on file with the records of this office in the matter of the application for the enrollment of Nelson F. Carr as a citizen by intermarriage of the Cherokee Nation.
Cherokee-4206.

Frances R Lane

Subscribed and sworn to before me this January 21, 1907.

Edward Merrick<br>Notary Public.

◇◇◇◇◇

F.R.                                                                                                                               Cherokee 4206.

DEPARTMENT OF THE INTERIOR,<br>COMMISSIONER TO THE FIVE CIVILIZED TRIBES.

----------------------

In the matter of the application for the enrollment of Nelson F. Carr as a citizen by intermarriage of the Cherokee Nation.

D E C I S I O N .

THE RECORDS OF THIS OFFICE SHOW: That on October 8, 1900, application was received by the Commission to the Five Civilized Tribes for the enrollment of Nelson F. Carr as a citizen by intermarriage of the Cherokee Nation. Further proceedings in the matter of said application were had at Muskogee, Indian Territory, October 13, 1902, at Vinita, Indian Territory, February 6, 1903, and at Muskogee, January 4, 1907.

THE EVIDENCE IN THIS CASE SHOWS: That the applicant herein, Nelson F. Carr, was married in accordance with the laws of the Cherokee Nation on February 17, 1868, to Sarah Ann Carr (nee Rogers), who was at the time of said marriage a recognized citizen by blood of the Cherokee Nation, who is identified on the Cherokee authenticated tribal roll of 1880, Cooweescoowee District, No. 581, as a native Cherokee, and whose name is included in the approved partial roll of citizens by blood of the Cherokee Nation opposite No. 10144. It is further shown that from the time of said marriage the said Nelson F. Carr and Sarah Ann Carr resided together as husband and wife and continuously lived in the Cherokee Nation up to and including September 1, 1902. The applicant is identified on the Cherokee authenticated tribal roll of 1880, and on the Cherokee census roll of 1896, as an intermarried citizen of the Cherokee Nation.

## Cherokee Intermarried White 1906
## Volume III

IT IS, THEREFORE, ORDERED AND ADJUDGED: That in accordance with the decision of the Supreme Court of the United States, dated November 5, 1906, in the cases of Daniel Red Bird et al., vs. the United States, Nos. 125, 126, 127 and 128, the said applicant, Nelson F. Carr, is entitled, under the provisions of Section 21 of the Act of Congress approved June 28, 1898 (30 Stats., 495), to enrollment as a citizen by intermarriage of the Cherokee Nation, and his application for enrollment as such is accordingly granted.

Tams Bixby
Commissioner.

Dated at Muskogee, Indian Territory,
this   JAN 23 1907

◇◇◇◇◇

Cherokee 4206

Muskogee, Indian Territory, January 23, 1907.

W. W. Hastings,
    Attorney for the Cherokee Nation,
        Muskogee, Indian Territory.

Dear Sir:

There is enclosed herewith copy of the decision of the Commissioner to the Five Civilized Tribes, dated January 23, 1907, granting the application for the enrollment of Nelson F. Carr as a citizen by intermarriage of the Cherokee Nation.

Respectfully,

Commissioner.

Enc I-68

RPI

◇◇◇◇◇

# Cherokee Intermarried White 1906
## Volume III

Cherokee 4206.

| W.W. HASTINGS. ATTORNEY. | OFFICE OF | H.M. VANCE. SECRETARY. |
|---|---|---|

**Attorney for the Cherokee Nation,**

Muskogee, I. T.   January 23, 1907.

The Commissioner to the Five Civilized Tribes,
    Muskogee, Indian Territory.

Sir:

    Receipt is acknowledged of the testimony and of your decision enrolling Nelson F. Carr as a citizen by intermarriage of the Cherokee Nation. Time for protesting said decision is waived and I consent that said person may be placed upon the schedule immediately.

                  Respectfully,
                  W. W. Hastings
                  Attorney for the Cherokee Nation.

◇◇◇◇◇

Cherokee
4206

                  Muskogee, Indian Territory, January 23, 1907.

Nelson F. Carr,
    Bartlesville, Indian Territory.

Dear Sir:

    There is enclosed herewith a copy of the decision of the Commissioner to the Five Civilized Tribes, dated January 23, 1907, granting your application for enrollment as a citizen by intermarriage of the Cherokee Nation.

    You will be advised when your name has been placed upon a schedule of citizens of the Cherokee Nation and approved by the Secretary of the Interior.

                  Respectfully,

E.R.C.                                                   Commissioner.
Enc. E.C. 101

## Cherokee Intermarried White 1906
## Volume III

**Cher IW 91**
**Trans from Cher 4238  3-16-07**

E.C.M.

## DEPARTMENT OF THE INTERIOR,

### COMMISSIONER TO THE FIVE CIVILIZED TRIBES.

---

In the matter of the application for the enrollment of

### PETER SMITH

as a citizen by intermarriage of the Cherokee Nation.

### CHEROKEE 4238.

### DEPARTMENT OF THE INTERIOR.

### COMMISSION TO THE FIVE CIVILIZED TRIBES.

Bartlesville I. T. October 9, 1900.

IN THE MATTER OF THE APPLICATION OF MAHALA SMITH FOR THE ENROLLMENT OF HERSELF, HER HUSBAND AND CHILDREN AS CHEROKEE CITIZENS.

The said Mahala Smith, being sworn by Commissioner C. R. Breckinridge, was examined by the Commission and testified as follows:

Q What is your name? A Hahala[sic] Smith.
Q How old are you? A Fifty-two.
Q What is your post office? A Coffeyville, Kansas.
Q What district do you live in? A Cooweescoowee.
Q Do you make your residence there? A Yes, sir.
Q How long have you lived there? A About five years, it will be this coming January.
Q Where did you live pryor[sic] to that time? A Dow below at Braggs.
Q Have you ever lived outside of the Cherokee Nation within the past three years? A No, sir.
Q For whom do you apply? A Me and my children.
Q How many children have you? A I have got eight.
Q Do you claim citizenship as a Cherokee by blood? A Yes, sir; bred and born here.

## Cherokee Intermarried White 1906
## Volume III

Q Is your husband living? A Yes, sir.
Q Do you make application for your husband? A Yes, sir; or he can apply for himself.
Q What is your husband's name? A Peter Smith.
Q How old is your husband? A Sixty-seven this coming November.
Q Is he a Cherokee by blood or a white man? A He is a German.
Q How long has he lived in the Cherokee Nation? A Well, he will have to answer that himself. He was married before me and him was married.

PETER SMITH, BEING SWORN AND EXAMINED, testified as follows:
Q What is your name? A Peter Smith.
Q How long have your lived in the Cherokee Nation?
A Since 1869, I was married in 1870.
Q You were married to your present wife in 1870? A To my first wife.
Q What was her name? A Miss Mary Hope.
Q Was she a Cherokee by blood? A Yes, sir.
Q Have you any evidence of your marriage to your present wife? A No, because the Judge told me I didn't need no more license because I was on the roll as a citizen.
Q Have you lived outside of the Territory within the last three years? A No, sir.
Q Does your name appear upon the authenticated roll of 1880[sic] A Yes, sir.
Q Were you also enrolled in 1896? A Yes, sir.

(Examination of Mrs. Smith continued)
Q What is the name of your oldest child for whom you desire to make application?
A Theodore.
Q How old is Theodore? A He is twenty-five.
Q He will have to apply for himself. Have you any children under twenty-one years of age for whom you wish to make application? A Yes, sir; I have four.
Q Give me the name of your oldest child who is living at home with you and unmarried.
A Theodore Smith.
Q He is over twenty-one. I want the ones under twenty-one years of age. A William.
Q How old is William? A He will be seventeen this coming December.
Q What is the next child's name? A James Smith.
Q How old is James? A He is fifteen.
Q What is the next child's name? A Elizabeth.
Q How old is Elizabeth? A She is thirteen years old.
Q What is the next child's name? A Catherine.
Q How old is Catherine? A Eleven years old.
Q Are these children all living at home with you at the present time? A No, sir; William is living with my daughter at the present time, but the others are with me.

(Examination of Mr. Smith, continued)
Q What is your father's name, Mr. Smith? A Meadow Smith.
Q What is your mother's name? A Mattie Ann.

(Examination of Mrs. Smith continues.
Q What is your father's name? A James Grigsby.

# Cherokee Intermarried White 1906
## Volume III

Q Is he living? A No, sir.
Q Cherokee by blood? A No, sir.
Q What is your mother's name? A Ruthie Grigsby.
Q Is she living? A No, sir.
Q Is she a Cherokee by blood? A Yes, sir; a half breed.

1880 Roll, page 582, No. 1732, Peter Smith, Illinois District. Adopted White.
1880 Roll, page 582, No. 1733, Mahala Smith, Illinois District. Native Cherokee.
1896 Roll, page 324, No. 965, Peter Smith, Cooweescoowee District.
1896 Roll, page 259, No. 4536, Mahala Smith, Cooweescoowee District.
1896 Roll, page 259, No. 4541, William Smith, Cooweescoowee District.
1896 Roll, page 259, No. 4542, James Smith, Cooweescoowee District.
1896 Roll, page 259, No. 4543, Elizabeth Smith, Cooweescoowee District.
1896 Roll, page 259, No. 4544, Catherine Smith, Cooweescoowee District.
Q When were you married to your first wife? A On the 15th day of January 1870.
Q Is she living or dead? A She is dead.
Q Did you live with her all the time until her death? A I did, sir.
Q When were you married to your present wife? A I was married, I believe in 1873, on the 11th day of July, I believe it was.
Q You have lived with your wife ever since that time, have you? A Yes, sir.

The applicant applies for the enrollment of herself, her husband and four children. She is identified on the rolls of 1880 and 1896 as a native Cherokee; she has lived in the Cherokee Nation all her life and will be listed now for enrollment by this Commission as a Cherokee by blood.

The applicant's husband, Peter Smith, who appears with her in the application, is identified with his wife on the rolls of 1880 and 1896. He avers that he married her in the year 1873, and that he has lived with her in the Cherokee Nation since that time. he will be listed now for enrollment as a Cherokee by intermarriage.

Their four children, William, James, Elizabeth and Catherine are all identified upon the roll of 1896; they are living at this time, and they also will be listed now for enrollment as Cherokees by blood.

------o------

The undersigned, being sworn, sates[sic] that as stenographer to the Commission to the Five Civilized Tribes he correctly recorded the testimony and other proceedings in this application for enrollment and that the foregoing is a correct and complete transcript of his stenographic notes thereof.

Wm S. Meeshean

Subscribed and sworn to before me this 9th day of October A. D. 1900.

C R Breckinridge

Commissioner.

## Cherokee Intermarried White 1906
## Volume III

Cherokee 4238.

Department of the Interior,
Commission to the Five Civilized Tribes,
Muskogee, I. T., October 14, 1902.

In the matter of the application of Peter Smith for the enrollment of himself as a citizen by intermarriage, and for the enrollment of his wife, Mahala, and children, William, James, Elizabeth and Catherine Smith, as citizens by blood of the Cherokee Nation: he being sworn and examined by the Commission, testified as follows:

Q What is your name? A Peter Smith.
Q How old are you? A Nearly seventy.
Q What is your postoffice? A Wann.
Q It used to be Coffeyville? A Yes, northeast of Coffeyville.
Q You are a white man are you? A Yes sir.
Q You are on the 1880 roll as an intermarried white? A Yes sir.
Q What is your wife's name? A Mahala Smith.
Q Was she your wife in 1880? A Yes sir.
Q Have you and your wife, Mahala, been living in the Cherokee Nation since 1880? A Yes sir.
Q Living together? A Yes sir.
Q Never been separated? A Never.
Q Never made your home outside of the Cherokee Nation? A No sir.
Q How many children have you? A Eight.
Q How many living at home? A At home, there is seven at home with me and one lives along the side of me.
Q How many of them under age? A There is four I think.
Q Those four are living with you? A Yes sir.

---

The undersigned, being duly sworn, states that as stenographer to the Commission to the Five Civilized Tribes he correctly recorded the testimony and proceedings in this case, and that the foregoing is a true and correct transcript of his stenographic notes thereof.

E.G. Rothenberger

Subscribed and sworn to before me this 7th day of November, 1902.

BC Jones
Notary Public.

## Cherokee Intermarried White 1906
## Volume III

Cherokee 4238

DEPARTMENT OF THE INTERIOR
COMMISSIONER TO THE FIVE CIVILIZED TRIBES
MUSKOGEE, INDIAN TERRITORY
January 3, 1907

In the matter of the application of Peter Smith for enrollment as a citizen by intermarriage of the Cherokee Nation

The applicant being first duly sworn by Walter W. Chappell a Notary Public for the Western District, testified as follows

Q What is your name? A Peter Smith.
Q What is your postoffice address? A Wann
Q Is that in the Cherokee Nation? A Yes sir
Q What is your age? A I am 74 since the 12th day of November
Q You claim to be a citizen of the Cherokee Nation by intermarriage? A Yes sir.
Q Through whom do you claim that right? A By my wife Mahalia[sic] Smith.
Q What was her maiden name? A Grigsby.
Q Is she living? A Yes sir.
Q Now you claim rights to citizenship by virtue of your marriage to Mahala Grigsby?
A Why, not altogether, I was married twice.
Q Who was your first wife? A Mrs Mary Holt
Q Is she living? A No sir, she died two years after we were married.
Q When did she die? A She died in 11872. I married her in 1870
Q What was her citizenship? A She was a Cherokee
Q Cherokee by blood? A Yes sir.
Q Was she born and raised in the Cherokee Nation? A Yes sir. Lived there all her life
Q When were you and she married? A The 15th day of January, 1870
Q Where were you married? A At Choteau, Cherokee Nation
Q In what district is that? A Cooesscoowee[sic] District
Q Were you married under Cherokee license? A Yes sir.
Q In what district did you secure that license? A Illinois district, Fort Gibson
Q Have you a certified copy of your marriage license? A I have not.
Q Did you and your first wife live together continuously until her death in 1872?
A Yes sir.
Q Had either one of you been married prior to that in 1870?
A Yes sir, she had been. She was a widow.
Q Had her husband died prior to your marriage.[sic] A Yes, her husband was killed during the war.
Q Did you have any children? A No sir.
Q After her death you married again did you? A Yes sir.
Q When did you marry the second time? A In Illinois District, Garfield Court House.
Q When was that? A That was on the 11th day of July, 1873 as near as I can recollect
Q Your second wife is still living is she? A Yes sir.

## Cherokee Intermarried White 1906
## Volume III

Q What is her citizenship? A Cherokee
Q Cherokee by blood? A Yes sir, by blood
Q Were you married the second time under Cherokee license? A The judge told me that I didn't need any license for a woman. That he would marry me the same as any other Cherokee citizen.
Q Have you and your second wife lived together continuously since your marriage?
A Yes sir
Q During that time you have lived all the time in the Cherokee Nation? A Yes sir.

The said Mahala Smith, nee Grigsby is identified on the approved partial roll of Cherokees by blood opposite No. 10207

The applicant Peter Smith is identified on the authenticated Cherokee tribal roll of 1880, Illinois District and Cherokee Census Roll of 1896 Cooesscoowee[sic] District opposite numbers 1732 and 965 respectively as an intermarried white.

On Page 170 Book A, Record of Marriage certificates, Illinois District Cherokee Nation appears the following:

"1870    Issued License of Marriage to Peter Smith to
January 9    marry Mrs Mary Holt"
Smith
Holt

Q Who performed the marriage ceremony over under this license? A A Baptist preacher, Mr. Cochran
Q You remember the date of the marriage? A Yes sir, on the 15th day of January, I was married, in the evening, 1870

Witness excused

Gertrude Hanna being first duly sworn, states on oath that as stenographer to the Commissioner to the Five Civilized Tribes she reported the proceedings in the above numbered case and that the above and foregoing is a true and correct transcript of her stenographic notes taken therein on January 3, 1907.

Gertrude Hanna

Subscribed and sworn to before me this 4th day of January, 1907.

Walter W. Chappell
Notary Public.

◇◇◇◇◇

## Cherokee Intermarried White 1906
## Volume III

E.C.M.

Cherokee 4238.

DEPARTMENT OF THE INTERIOR,

COMMISSIONER TO THE FIVE CIVILIZED TRIBES.

---

In the matter of the application for the enrollment of PETER SMITH as a citizen by intermarriage of the Cherokee Nation.

## D E C I S I O N

THE RECORDS OF THIS OFFICE SHOW: That at Bartlesville, Indian Territory, October 9, 1900, Mahala Smith appeared before the Commission to the Five Civilized Tribes, and made application for the enrollment of herself et al. as citizens by blood, and for the enrollment of her husband, Peter Smith, as a citizen by intermarriage of the Cherokee Nation. The application for the enrollment of the said Mahala Smith et al. as citizens by blood of the Cherokee Nation has been heretofore disposed of and their rights to enrollment will not be considered in this decision. Further proceedings in the matter of said application were had at Muskogee, Indian Territory, October 14, 1902, and January 3, 1907.

THE EVIDENCE IN THIS CASE SHOWS: That the applicant herein, Peter Smith, a white man, was married in accordance with Cherokee law in the year 1870 to his wife, Mary Smith, nee Holt, deceased, who was at the time of said marriage a recognized citizen by blood of the Cherokee Nation, and who died in the year 1872; that from the time of said marriage until the death of said Mary Smith, the said Peter Smith and Mary Smith resided together as husband and wife, and continuously lived in the Cherokee Nation; that on July 11, 1873, Peter Smith was married to his present wife, Mahala Smith, nee Grigsby, who was at the time of said marriage a recognized citizen by blood of the Cherokee Nation, and whose name appears on the approved partial roll of citizens by blood of the Cherokee Nation, opposite No. 10207; that since said marriage the said Peter Smith and Mahala Smith have resided together as husband and wife, and have continuously lived in the Cherokee Nation. Said Peter Smith is identified on the Cherokee authenticated tribal roll of 1880, and the Cherokee census roll of 1896, as an intermarried citizen of the Cherokee Nation.

IT IS, THEREFORE, ORDERED AND ADJUDGED: That in accordance with the decision of the Supreme Court of the United States, dated November 5, 1906, in the case of Daniel Red Bird et al. vs. the United States, under the provisions of Section 21, of the Act of Congress approved June 28, 1898 (30 Stats., 495), Peter Smith is entitled to enrollment as a citizen by intermarriage of the Cherokee Nation, and his application for enrollment as such is accordingly granted.

# Cherokee Intermarried White 1906
# Volume III

Tams Bixby<br>Commissioner.

Dated at Muskogee, Indian Territory,
this    JAN 21 1907

◇◇◇◇◇

Cherokee 4238

Muskogee, Indian Territory, January 21, 1907.

W. W. Hastings,
    Attorney for the Cherokee Nation,
        Muskogee, Indian Territory.

Dear Sir:

    There is enclosed herewith copy of the decision of the Commissioner to the Five Civilized Tribes, dated January 21, 1907, granting the application for the enrollment of Peter Smith as a citizen by intermarriage of the Cherokee Nation.

Respectfully,

Enc I-45

RPI                                                            Commissioner.

◇◇◇◇◇

Cherokee 4238

| W.W. HASTINGS. ATTORNEY. | OFFICE OF | H.M. VANCE. SECRETARY. |
|---|---|---|

**Attorney for the Cherokee Nation,**

MUSKOGEE, I. T.     January 21, 1907.

The Commissioner to the Five Civilized Tribes,
    Muskogee, Indian Territory.

Sir:

    Receipt is acknowledged of the testimony and of your decision enrolling Peter Smith as a citizen by intermarriage of the Cherokee Nation. Time for protesting said decision is waived and I consent that said person may be placed upon the schedule immediately.

Respectfully,<br>W. W. Hastings<br>Attorney for the Cherokee Nation.

◇◇◇◇◇

# Cherokee Intermarried White 1906
## Volume III

Cherokee 4238

Muskogee, Indian Territory, January 24, 1907.

Peter Smith,
    Wann, Indian Territory.

Dear Sir:

    There is enclosed herewith a copy of the decision of the Commissioner to the Five Civilized Tribes, dated January 21, 1907, granting your application for enrollment as a citizen by intermarriage of the Cherokee Nation.

    You will be advised when your name has been placed upon a schedule of citizens of the Cherokee Nation and approved by the Secretary of the Interior.

                      Respectfully,

Encl. H-4                 Commissioner.
JMH

---

**Cher IW 92**
**Trans from Cher 4493 3-16-07**

                                              E.C.M.

DEPARTMENT OF THE INTERIOR,

COMMISSIONER TO THE FIVE CIVILIZED TRIBES.

In the matter of the application for the enrollment of

CHARLOTTE COKER

As a citizen by intermarriage of the Cherokee Nation.

CHEROKEE NO. 4493

# Cherokee Intermarried White 1906
# Volume III

Department of the Interior,
Commission to the Five Civilized Tribes,
Nowata, I.T., October 16, 1900.

In the matter of the application of Lewis C. Coker for the enrollment of himself and children as Cherokees by blood and his wife as a Cherokee by intermarriage; being sworn and examined by Commissioner Needles, he testified as follows:

Q What is your name? A Lewis C. Coker.
Q What is your age? A 50 years old.
Q What is your post office address? A Nowata.
Q What district do you live in? A Cooweescoowee.
Q Are you a recognized citizen of the Cherokee Nation? A Yes, sir.
Q By blood? A Yes, sir.
Q What degree of blood do you claim? A 1/16.
Q Cherokee? A Yes, sir.
Q For whom do you apply for enrollment? A Myself, wife and children.
Q What is the name of your wife? A Charlotte.
Q She is a citizen by blood? A No, sir, by adoption.
Q What was her name before you married her? A Her name was Estes.
Q When did you marry her? A In 1872.
Q What are the names of your children? A Calvin F. is the first I wish to enroll, 19 years old.
Q The next child? A Arthur L., 16 years old.
Q The next one? A May L., 13 years old.
Q The next one? A Benjamin F., 10 years old.
Q The next one? A Kittie, 5 years old.
Q The next one? A Cynthia E., about a year and a half old.
Q Have you any proof of birth? A Yes, sir.
(On 1880 roll, page 81, No. 556, Lewis Coker, Cooweescoowee district.)
Charlotte Coker on 1880 roll, page 81, No. ($557) Cooweescoowee district #557 Lewis C. Coker on 1896 roll, page 131, No. 950, Lewis Coker, Cooweescoowee district. Charlotte Coker on 1896 roll, page 299, No. 223, Cooweescoowee district. Calvin F. Coker on 1896 roll, page 131, No. 951, Cooweescoowee district. Arthur L. Coker on 1896 roll, page 131, No. 952, Arthur Lee Coker, Cooweescoowee district. May L. Coker on 1896 roll, page 131, No. 953, Cooweescoowee district. Benjamin F. Coker on 1896 roll, page 131, No. 954, Bnejiman[sic] F. Coker, Cooweescoowee district. Kittie Coker on 1896 roll, page 131, No. 955, Kitty Coker, Cooweescoowee district.)
Q Are these children all alive and living with you at this time? A Yes, sir.
Q How long have you lived in the Cherokee Nation? A Since 1873.
Q Your wife also? A Yes, sir.
Q You living with your wife at this time? A Yes, sir.
Q She your first wife? A Yes, sir.
Q You her first husband? A Yes, sir.
    The name of Lewis C. Coker is found upon the authenticated roll of 1880 as Lewis Coker and upon the census roll of 1896 as Lewis Coker. The name of his wife, Charlotte,

## Cherokee Intermarried White 1906
## Volume III

is found upon the authenticated roll of 1880 as well as the census roll of 1896. The names of his children, Calvin F., Arthur L., Mary L., Benjamin F., and Kittie, are found upon the census roll of 1896, and he presents satisfactory proof of birth as to his youngest child, Cynthia E., whose name does not appear upon the census roll of 1896, having been born after the same was compiled, and they all being duly identified according to the page and number of the roll as indicated in the testimony, and having made satisfactory proof as to their residence, said Lewis C. Coker and his said children as enumerated in the testimony will be duly listed for enrollment as Cherokees by blood, and his wife, Charlotte, as a Cherokee citizen by intermarriage.

Bruce C. Jones, being duly sworn, says that as stenographer to the Commission to the Five Civilized Tribes he correctly recorded the proceedings and testimony in the above case, and the foregoing is a true and complete transcript of his stenographic notes thereof.

Bruce C Jones

Sworn to and subscribed before me this the 17th of October, 1900.

TB Needles<br>Commissioner.

◇◇◇◇◇

Cherokee 4493.

Department of the Interior,<br>Commission to the Five Civilized Tribes,<br>Muskogee, I. T., October 7, 1902.

In the matter of the application of Lewis C. Coker for the enrollment of himself and children, Calvin F., Arthur L., Mary L., Benjamin F., Kittie and Cynthia E. Coker, as citizens by blood, and for the enrollment of his wife, Charlotte Coker, as a citizen by intermarriage of the Cherokee Nation; he being sworn and examined by the Commission, testified as follows:

Q What is your name? A Lewis C. Coker.
Q What is your age at this time? A Fifty-two years.
Q What is your postoffice? A Nowata.
Q Are you a citizen by blood? A Yes sir.
Q What is your wife's name? A Charlotte.
Q Is she an applicant before the Commission for enrollment as an intermarried citizen? A Yes sir.
Q What is her age at this time A Forty-five years old.
Q When were you married to your wife, Charlotte? A '72.
Q Were you ever married prior to your marriage to this wife? A No sir.
Q Was she ever married prior to her marriage to you? A No sir.
Q She you first wife and you her first husband? A Yes sir.

## Cherokee Intermarried White 1906
## Volume III

Q Have you and she lived together all the time since your marriage up to the present time as husband and wife? A Yes sir.
Q Never been separated? A No sir, never been separated.
Q She has never married any other man? A No sir.
Q You lived together as husband and wife up to the first day of September, 1902? A Yes sir.
Q Have you and your wife lived together as husband and wife all the time since 1880 in the Cherokee Nation to the present time? A Yes sir.
Q Never lived out of the Cherokee Nation since 1880? A No sir.
Q These children, Calvin F., Arthur L., Mary L., Benjamin F., Kitty and Cynthia A., all your children by your wife, Charlotte? A Yes sir.
Q Are these children living at this time? A Yes sir.
Q Have these children all lived in the Cherokee Nation from the time of their birth to the present time? A Yes sir, all their lives.

-------------------------------

The undersigned, being duly sworn, states that as stenographer to the Commission to the Five Civilized Tribes he correctly recorded the testimony and proceedings in this case, and that the foregoing is a true and complete transcript of his stenographic notes thereof.

E.G. Rothenberger

Subscribed and sworn to before me this 29th day of October, 1902.

BC Jones<br>Notary Public.

◇◇◇◇◇

C.F.B.

Cherokee 4493.

## DEPARTMENT OF THE INTERIOR,
## COMMISSIONER TO THE FIVE CIVILIZED TRIBES.
### Muskigee[sic], I. T., January 4, 1907.

In the matter of the application for the enrollment of CHARLOTTE COKER as a citizen by intermarriage of the Cherokee Nation.

Lewis C. Coker being first duly sworn by B. P. Rasmus, a Notary Public for the Western District, Indian Territory, testified as follows:

By the Commissioner:
Q What is your name? A Lewis C. Coker.
Q Your age? A 56 years.

# Cherokee Intermarried White 1906
## Volume III

Q Your postoffice address? A Nowata, I. T.
Q Are you a citizen by blood of the Cherokee Nation? A Yes.
Q Are you married? A Yes sir.
Q What is your wife's name? A Charlotte Coker.
Q Is she a citizen of the Cherokee Nation? A By marriage.
Q She is not a Cherokee by blood? A No sir.
Q She claims her right to enrollment as a citizen of the Cherokee Nation solely by virtue of her marriage to you? A Yes sir
Q Is she living at this time? A Yes sir.
Q When were you married to your wife Charlotte Coker? A 1872.
Q Were you a recognized citizen of the Cherokee Nation at the time you married her? A Yes sir.
Q And living in the Cherokee country? A Not when I married her' we was living in Arkansas.
Q How soon after your marriage did you move to the Cherokee nation[sic]?
A Moved here the next year.
Q On coming to the Cherokee nation[sic] were you recognized as a citizen without having gone before the authorities? A I had been here before I married her.
Q But were you recognized as a citizen of the Cherokee Nation after your return without any re-admission? A Yes sir.
Q Since you came to the Cherokee nation[sic] shortly after you were married, have you continued to reside in the Cherokee Nation up to the present time? A Yes sir.
Q You and your wife have continuously lived together as husband and wife since your marriage, have you? A Yes sir.
Q Who married you? A A man by the name of Sutton.
Q Married by a minister? A Yes sir.
Q In the state of Arkansas? A Yes sir.
Q Were you ever married before you married your wife Charlotte Coker? A No sir.
Q Was she ever married prior to her marriage to you? A No sir.

> The applicant, Charlotte Coker, is identified on the Cherokee authenticated tribal roll of 1880, Cooweescoowee District, opposite No. 557.
> The name of her husband through whom she claims her right, is included in an approved partial list of citizens by blood of the Cherokee Nation opposite No. 10769.

Q Have you any evidence of a documentary character showing your marriage? A The records in the county where we was married got burned. I wrote to the clerk and have his letter here. I wrote to the clerk for a copy of it a month or two ago and here is what he says (Presenting letter)
Q This letter shows that the court house in which your marriage certificate was on file was burned in August, 1898? A Yes sir.
Q You have no copy of it? A No sir.
Q Are there any witness[sic] present here today who saw you married? A There was witness[sic] present, none of them here.

## Cherokee Intermarried White 1906
## Volume III

On behalf of the Cherokee Nation:

Q  How long did you live in Marion County, Arkansas?  A  I lived there until I was a little past 18 years, when I came to this country. I came here in January, 1869.
Q  Then since January, 1869, have you lived in Marion County, Kansas?  A  No, I was there just a little while.
Q  How long?  A  Well, possibly a year.
Q  Did you recognize the rights -- did you exercise the rights of a citizen in the state of Arkansas?  A  I never did. They compelled me to work the roads, but if a man was there three months they would make him do tha[sic].
Q  Did you vote there?  A  No sir.
Q  You was not old enough to vote?  A  No sir.
Q  Have you lived in Arkansas more than one year since you were married?  A  No, not over a year.
Q  You say you never applied to the Cherokee authorities to be readmitted when you came back there?  A  No sir.
Q  Have you any relatives living in Arkansas?  A  Yes sir.
Q  You have lived continuously in the Cherokee nation[sic] ever since your marriage with the exception of one year?  A  Yes sir, I came there in 1873 and have lived there continuously ever since.

------

Frances R. Lane upon oath states that as stenographer to the Commissioner to the Five Civilized Tribes she reported the testimony in the above entitled cause and that the foregoing is an accurate transcript of her stenographic notes thereof.

Frances R Lane

Subscribed and sworn to before me this 5th day of January, 1907.

Edward Merrick<br>Notary Public.

## Cherokee Intermarried White 1906
## Volume III

F.R.                                                                              Cherokee 4493.

DEPARTMENT OF THE INTERIOR,
COMMISSIONER TO THE FIVE CIVILIZED TRIBES.
Muskogee, I. T. January 17, 1907.

In the matter of the application for the enrollment of Charlotte Coker as a citizen by intermarriage of the Cherokee Nation.

Charlotte Coker being first duly sworn by Frances R. Lane, a Notary Public for the Western District, Indian Territory, testified as follows:

Cherokee Nation represented by W. W. Hastings.

By the Commissioner:
Q What is your name? A Charlotte Coker.
Q What is your age? A Fifty years.
Q What is your postoffice address? A Nowata, I. T.
Q You are an applicant for enrollment as a citizen by intermarriage of the Cherokee Nation? A Yes sir.
Q You are a white woman, not possessed of Indian blood? A Yes sir.
Q You claim your right to enrollment as an intermarried citizen by virtue of your marriage to a citizen of the Cherokee Nation? A Yes sir.
Q What is the name of the citizen through whom you claim? A Lewis Coker.
Q When were you married to Lewis Coker? A In 1872.
Q Where were you married to him? A In Marion county, Arkansas.
Q Who performed the marriage ceremony? A Mr. Sudden, a minister.
Q Was that marriage under a license of the state of Ark.?
A We didn't have to have any license then.
Q Did the minister give you any certificate showing your marriage? A No sir.
Q After your marriage in 1872 how long was it until you moved to the Cherokee nation[sic]? A In 1873.
Q At the time of your marriage to Lewis Coker was he a recognized citizen by blood of the Cherokee Nation? A Yes sir.
Q At the time of your marriage to him was the Cherokee Nation his home? A Yes sir.
Q Had you been married previous to your marriage to Lewis Coker? A Yes sir.
Q Had you been married previous to your marriage to Lewis Coker? A Yes sir.[sic]
Q How many times? A Just one time; never had been married but once.
Q You had never been married before you married Lewis Coker? A No sir, I never had been married before I married him.
Q Had Lewis Coker ever been married nefore[sic] he married you? A No sir.
Q Lewis Coker is living at this time? A Yes sir.
Q Since your marriage to Lewis Coker in 1872, have you lived together as husband and wife? A Yes sir.
Q And since 1873 you have lived continuously in the Cherokee Nation?
A Yes, been right here.

## Cherokee Intermarried White 1906
## Volume III

Q  Your husband, Lewis Coker, is his full name Lewis C. Coker?  A  Yes sir.
Q  Had you lived in Arkansas up to the time of your marriage?  A  Yes sir.

By Mr. Hastings:
Q  How long had you known your husband before you married him?  A  About three or four months.
Q  Did he live there when you married him?  A  No, he was just back there on a visit.
Q  His home was here in the Indian Territory?  A  Yes sir.

Witness excused.

------

Lewis C. Coker, being first duly sworn by Frances R. Lane, a Notary Public for the Western District, Indian Territory, testified as follows:

By the Commissioner:
Q  What is your name?  A  Lewis C. Coker.
Q  What is your age?  A  Fifty-six.
Q  You are a married man are you?  A  Yes sir.
Q  What is the name of your wife?  A  Charlotte Coker.
Q  When were you married to her?  A  In 1872.
Q  Have you any documentary evidence of that marriage?  A  No, I have not.
Q  Have you made any effort to procure any documentary evidence?  A  Yes, I have to show that the records of the county where it was, burned since that time. That is about all I can get.
Q  Have you a witness here today to testify to the authenticity of these records?  A  No, I have a witness to testify as to the yar[sic] we were married in.

> Applicant offfer[sic] in evidence letter dated Yellville, Arkansas, November 30, 1906, signed J. W. Smith, Clerk of Marion County, Arkansas. In said letter it is stated that the records of Marion county were destroyed by fire in August, 1878.
> This letter is accepted and filed with the records of this case.
> Mr. Hastings, representative for the Cherokee Nation, states that he has no objection to the above letter being accepted and filed as evidence in this case.

Q  This letter you have presented here is a reply you received from Mr. Smith that you wanted a copy of the marriage certificate which was filed there?  A  Yes, that is what I wrote to him for.
Q  You say you have a witness here was[sic] was present at your marriage?  A  No, he was not present. He knows of the marriage though. My wife's brother.
Q  What is his name?  A  Ben Ester.

Witness excused.

----

## Cherokee Intermarried White 1906
## Volume III

      Ben Estes being first duly sworn by Frances R. Lane, a Notary Public for the Western District of Indian Territory, testified as follows:

By the Commissioner.
Q What is your name? A Ben Estes.
Q Your age? A Forty-six.
Q What is your postoffice address? A Nowata, Ind. Ter.
Q Do you know Lewis C. Coker? A Yes sir.
Q He is a married man, is he? A Yes sir.
Q Do you know his wife, Charlotte Coker? A Yes sir.
Q Are you a relation of hers? A Brother.
Q Do you know when Lewis C. Coker and Charlotte Coker were married?
A Well, I can't say when they were married. I know when they went to get married. I was not at the wedding.
Q When did they go to get married? A They went along in 1872 as well as I remember.
Q Where did they go to get married? A To a man by the name of Sutton or Sudden.
Q Where was this? A Marion County, Arkansas.
Q Where were you living at that time? A We were living right there in Marion county.
Q How far did this man Sudden live from your house? A Lived about three miles.
Q Your sister, Charlotte Coker, was living in the same house with you? A No, we was living about half a mile apart She lived with my grandmother and I lived with one of [sic] uncles.
Q Of your own knowledge you don't know that the marriage ceremony was performed by Sudden? A No, only what this man Sudden told me himself. He told me about marring them. I Was not at the wedding; that is all I know about it.
Q It was your understanding from Mr. Sudden, the preacher, that Lewis C. Coker and his wife, Charlotte Coker, were lawfully married at that time. A Yes sir.
Q You have every reason to believe that they were lawfully married at that time?
A Yes sir.

Examination by Mr. Hastings;
Q They lived together and held themselves out as husband and wife since that time?
A Yes, I have been with them since about 1885, and they have lived together as man and wife ever since to my knowledge, and before they came here.

-------

Frances R. Lane upon oath states that as stenographer to the Commissioner to the Five Civilized Tribes she reported the testimony in the above entitled cause and that the foregoing is an accurate transcript of her stenographic notes thereof.

                                                         Frances R. Lane

Subscribed and sworn to before me this January 18, 1907.

                                                    Edward Merrick
                                                    Notary Public.

## Cherokee Intermarried White 1906
## Volume III

◇◇◇◇◇

E C M                                                                                                    Cherokee 4493.

### DEPARTMENT OF THE INTERIOR,

### COMMISSIONER TO THE FIVE CIVILIZED TRIBES.

---

In the matter of the application for the enrollment of CHARLOTTE COKER as a citizen by intermarriage of the Cherokee Nation.

### D E C I S I O N

THE RECORDS OF THIS OFFICE SHOW: That on October 16th, 1900 application was received by the Commission to the Five Civilized Tribes for the enrollment of Charlotte Coker as a citizen by intermarriage of the Cherokee Nation. Further proceedings in the matter of said application were had at Muskogee, Indian Territory, October 7th, 1902 and January 4th, 1907.

THE EVIDENCE IN THIS CASE SHOWS: That the applicant herein, Charlotte Coker, a white woman, married in 1872 one Lewis C. Coker, who was at the time of said marriage a recognized citizen by blood of the Cherokee Nation, who is identified on the Cherokee authenticated tribal roll of 1880, Cooweescoowee District No. 556 as a native Cherokee, and whose name appears upon the approved partial roll of citizens by blood of the Cherokee Nation opposite No. 10769. It is further shown that from the time of said marriage the said Lewis C. Coker and Charlotte Coker resided together as husband and wife and continuously lived in the Cherokee Nation up to and including September 1st, 1902. Said applicant is identified on the Cherokee authenticated tribal roll of 1880 and the Cherokee census roll of 1896 as an intermarried citizen of the Cherokee Nation.

IT IS, THEREFORE, ORDERED AND ADJUDGED: That in accordance with the decision of the Supreme Court of the United States, dated November 5, 1906 in the cases of Daniel Red Bird et al. vs. the United States, Nos. 125, 126, 127 and 128, the said applicant, Charlotte Coker is entitled, under the provisions of Section Twenty-one of the Act of Congress approved June 28, 1898 (30 Stats. 495), to enrollment as a citizen by intermarriage of the Cherokee Nation, and her application for enrollment as such is accordingly granted.

                                                    Tams Bixby
                                                              Commissioner.

Dated at Muskogee, Indian Territory,
this     JAN 23 1907

◇◇◇◇◇

## Cherokee Intermarried White 1906
## Volume III

Cherokee 4493

Muskogee, Indian Territory, January 23, 1907.

W. W. Hastings,
    Attorney for the Cherokee Nation,
        Muskogee, Indian Territory.

Dear Sir:

    There is enclosed herewith copy of the decision of the Commissioner to the Five Civilized Tribes, dated January 23, 1907, granting the application for the enrollment of Charlotte Coker as a citizen by intermarriage of the Cherokee Nation.

        Respectfully,

Enc I-61                                       Commissioner.

RPI

◇◇◇◇◇

Cherokee 4493

W.W. HASTINGS.     OFFICE OF     H.M. VANCE.
ATTORNEY.                                   SECRETARY.

### Attorney for the Cherokee Nation,
MUSKOGEE, I. T.     January 23, 1907.

The Commissioner to the Five Civilized Tribes,
    Muskogee, Indian Territory.

Sir:

    Receipt is acknowledged of the testimony and of your decision enrolling Charlotte Coker as a citizen by intermarriage of the Cherokee Nation. Time for protesting said decision is waived and I consent that said person may be placed upon the schedule immediately.

        Respectfully,
        W. W. Hastings
        Attorney for the Cherokee Nation.

◇◇◇◇◇

# Cherokee Intermarried White 1906
## Volume III

Cherokee 4493

Muskogee, Indian Territory, January 23, 1907.

Charlotte Coker,
    Nowata, Indian Territory.

Dear Madam:

    There is enclosed herewith a copy of the decision of the Commissioner to the Five Civilized Tribes, dated January 23, 1907, granting your application for enrollment as a citizen by intermarriage of the Cherokee Nation.

    You will be advised when your name has been placed upon a schedule of citizens of the Cherokee Nation and approved by the Secretary of the Interior.

Respectfully,

Enc I-81                                                            Commissioner.

RPI

---

**Cher IW 93**
**Trans from Cher 4578  3-16-07**

CFB

DEPARTMENT OF THE INTERIOR,

COMMISSIONER TO THE FIVE CIVILIZED TRIBES.

- - - - - -

In the matter of the application for the enrollment of

WILLIAM H. McANALLY

as a citizen by intermarriage of the Cherokee Nation.

- - - - - -

CHEROKEE 4578.

## Cherokee Intermarried White 1906
## Volume III

DEPARTMENT OF THE INTERIOR,
COMMISSION TO THE FIVE CIVILIZED TRIBES.
NOWATA, I.T., OCTOBER 18th, 1900.

IN THE MATTER OF THE APPLICATION OF William H. McAnally for the enrollment of himself, his wife and child as citizens of the Cherokee Nation, and he being sworn and examined by Commissioner, T. B. Needles, testified as follows:

Q What is your name? A William H. McAnally.
Q How old are you? A Fifty two.
Q What is your Postoffice? A Coffeyville.
Q What district do you live in? A Cooweescoowee.
Q Are you a recognized citizen of the Cherokee Nation? A Yes sir.
Q By intermarriage? A Yes sir.
Q What is the name of your wife? A Sallie McAnally.
Q When did you marry her? A In 1874.
Q She is a citizen by blood? A Yes sir.
Q For whom do you apply? A Myself, wife and one child.
Q What is the name of your child? A Ollie Tennessee.
Q How old is she? A She is nineteen years old.

    (1880 Roll, Page 554, #1156, Wm. McAnally, Illinois District)
    (1880 Roll, Page 554, #1157, Sallie McAnally, Illinois District)
    (1896 Roll, Page 315, #671, W. H. McAnnally[sic], Coo. District)
    (1896 Roll, page 206, #3033, Sallie McAnnelly[sic], Coo. District)
    (1896 Roll, page 206, #3036, Tennie or Tennessee McAnnelly, Cooweescoowee District)

Q How long have you lived in the Cherokee Nation? A Ever since 1870
Q Are you living here now? A Yes sir.
Q Is your daughter also living in the Cherokee Nation? A Yes sir.

By Mr. Cale Starr, Cherokee Represenative[sic]:
Q When were you living in Wagoner? A About ten years.
Q Since 1880? A Yes sir.

By the Commission:
    The name of William H. McAnnally[sic] appears upon the authenticated roll of 1880, as an intermarried white: His name also appears upon the census roll of 1896. The name of his wife, Sallie appears upon the authenticated roll of 1880, as well as the census roll of 1896; and the name of their child, Ollie Tennessee appears *(illegible...)*. They all being duly identified, according to the page and number of the rolls, and having made satisfactory proof as to residence, the said William H. McAnally will be duly listed for enrollment as a Cherokee citizen by intermarriage, and his wife, Sallie McAnally, and child, Ollie Tennessee McAnally as Cherokee citizens by blood.

## Cherokee Intermarried White 1906
## Volume III

---

The undersigned, being sworn, states that as stenographer to the Commission to the Five Civilized Tribes, he correctly recorded the testimony and proceedings in this case, and that the foregoing is a true and complete transcript of his stenographic notes thereof.

Subscribed and sworn to before
me this 19th day of October, 1900.

R R Cravens

CR Breckinridge

COMMISSIONER.

◇◇◇◇◇

Cherokee 4578.

DEPARTMENT OF THE INTERIOR,
COMMISSION TO THE FIVE CIVILIZED TRIBES.
Muskogee, I. T., October 30, 1902.

In the matter of the application of William H. McAnally for the enrollment of himself as a citizen by intermarriage, and for the enrollment of his wife, Sallie McAnally, his daughter, Ollie T. Barker, and his grandchild, William E. Barker, as citizens by blood, of the Cherokee Nation.

SUPPLEMENTAL PROCEEDINGS.

WILLIAM H. McANALLY, being sworn, testified as follows:

By the Commission,

Q What is your name? A William H. McAnally.
Q What is your postoffice address? A Coffeyville.
Q How old are you Mr. McAnally? A Fifty-four years old.
Q Are you an applicant for enrollment as an intermarried citizen of the Cherokee Nation? A Yes, sir.
Q What is your wife's name? A Sallie.
Q Is she a recognized citizen of the Cherokee Nation by blood? A Yes, sir.
Q When were you married to your wife, Sallie? A '74.
Q 1874? You're on the '80 roll with her? A Yes, sir, I think so.
Q Have you and your wife, Sallie, lived together since '80 up to the present time?
A Yes, sir, since '84.
Q Since '80. A Yes, sir, yes, sir.
Q Never have separated and you and she were living together on the first day of September, 1902? A Yes, sir.
Q Have you lived in the Cherokee Nation all the time since 1880 up until the present time? A No, sir.
Q Where have you lived part of the time? A Creek Nation.

# Cherokee Intermarried White 1906
## Volume III

Q  Have you lived in the Indian Territory all the time since 1880 up until the present time?  A  Yes, sir.
Q  You never have lived out of the Territory?  A  No, sir.
Q  Has your wife lived in the Territory all the time since 1880 up to the present time?  A  Yes, sir.
Q  How far do you live from Coffeyville?  A  Twelve or thirteen miles.
Q  You don't live in the town of Coffeyville?  A  I live about thirteen miles from Coffeyville.
Q  Never have lived in Coffeyville?  A  That's my trading place, though it is not my nearest postoffice.  I go there trading.
Q  This child, Ollie T., your daughter?  A  Yes, sir.
Q  Ollie T. is now married?  A  Yes, sir.  Married a man by the name of Barker and has one child.
Q  And William E. Barker is your grandchild?  A  Yes sir.
Q  Is Ollie T. and your grandchild, William E., both living now?  A  Yes, sir.
Q  That child has lived all its life in the Indian Territory, has it?  A  Yes, sir.

    Retta Chick, being first duly sworn, states that, as stenographer to the Commission to the Five Civilized Tribes, she recorded the testimony and proceedings in the matter of the foregoing application, and that the above is a true and complete transcript of her stenographic notes thereof.

                                                                       Retta Chick

Subscribed and sworn to before me this 10th day of December, 1902.

                                                   PG Reuter
                                                 Notary Public.

◇◇◇◇◇

                                                        Cherokee 4578.

## DEPARTMENT OF THE INTERIOR,
## COMMISSIONER TO THE FIVE CIVILIZED TRIBES.
### Muskogee, I. T., January 3, 1907.

    In the matter of the application for the enrollment of William H. McAnally as a citizen by intermarriage of the Cherokee Nation.

    William H. McAnally, being first duly sworn by Frances R. Lane, a Notary Public for the Western District, testified as follows:

By the Commissioner:
Q  What is your name?  A  William H McAnally.
Q  How old are you?  A  Fifty-nine years
Q  What is your postoffice address?  A  Catoosa, I. T.
Q  You claim to be an intermarried citizen of the Cherokee Nation?  A  Yes sir.

## Cherokee Intermarried White 1906
## Volume III

Q  Through whom do you claim to derive your right as such? A  Sallie McAnally.
Q  When were you married to Sallie McAnally? A  In 1874.
Q  What time of the year? A  17th of August.
Q  Were you married under Cherokee law? A  Yes sir.
Q  Got a Cherokee license? A  I got twelve signers and took them to Amos Thornton the District Judge of Illinois District, and was married there at his house. He wrote out the papers and said the ceremony, and I paid him for it.
Q  Have you got that license and certificate? A  No, it is in the clerk's office--- he said that the papers were moved here; I went there yesterday.. Colonel Haris[sic] said that the papers was moved here.
Q  Were you ever married prior to your marriage to Sallie McAnally? A  No sir.
Q  Was she ever married prior to her marriage to you? A  No sir.
Q  What was her maiden name? A  Hensley.
Q  Was she a citizen of the Cherokee nation at the time you married her in 1874?
A  Yes sir.

> Applicant is identified on the 1880 Cherokee roll opposite No. 1156. His wife through whom he claims right to enrollment is identified on said roll opposite No. 1157, and is also identified on the final roll of citizens by blood of the Cherokee nation[sic] opposite No. 10996.

Q  Have you and your wife lived together continuously as husband and wife since your marriage in 1874 up to the present time, in the Cherokee Nation? A  Yes sir.

> The original Cherokee marriage record for Illinois District, Book A., in the possession of this office, shows that on August 17, 1874, a license was issued by the clerk of said district to W. H. McAnally and Miss Sallie Hensley, a citizen of the Cherokee Nation.
> 
> The record also shows that said parties were united in matrimony on the same date by Amos Thornton, Judges[sic] of said District.

Witness excused.

------

Frances R. Lane, upon oath, states that as stenographer to the Commissioner to the Five Civilized Tribes she reported the testimony in the above entitled cause and that the above and foregoing is an accurate transcript of her stenographic notes thereof.

Frances R Lane

Subscribed and sworn to before me this January 4, 1907.

Edward Merrick<br>Notary Public.

◇◇◇◇◇

## Cherokee Intermarried White 1906
## Volume III

C.F.B.

Cherokee 4578

### DEPARTMENT OF THE INTERIOR,

### COMMISSIONER TO THE FIVE CIVILIZED TRIBES.

---

In the matter of the application for the enrollment of William H. McAnally as a citizen by intermarriage of the Cherokee Nation.

### D E C I S I O N

THE RECORDS OF THIS OFFICE SHOW: That on October 18, 1900, application was received by the Commission to the Five Civilized Tribes, for the enrollment of William H. McAnally as a citizen by intermarriage of the Cherokee Nation. Further proceedings in the matter of said application were had at Muskogee, Indian Territory, October 30, 1902, and January 3, 1907.

THE EVIDENCE IN THIS CASE SHOWS: That the applicant herein, William H. McAnally, a white man, was married in accordance with Cherokee law August 17, 1874, to his wife, Sallie McAnally, who was at the time of said marriage, a recognized citizen by blood of the Cherokee Nation, who is identified on the Cherokee authenticated tribal roll of 1880, Illinois District, No. 1157, as a native Cherokee, and whose name appears opposite No. 10996 upon the approved partial roll of citizens by blood of the Cherokee Nation. It is further shown that since said marriage the said William H. and Sallie McAnally have resided together as husband and wife and have continuously lived in the Cherokee Nation. Said applicant is identified on the Cherokee authenticated tribal roll of 1880, and the Cherokee census roll of 1896.

IT IS, THEREFORE, ORDERED AND ADJUDGED: That in accordance with the decision of the Supreme Court of the United States, dated November 5, 1906, in the cases of Daniel Red Bird, et al., vs. the United States, Nos. 125, 126, 127 and 128, the said applicant, William H. McAnally is entitled, under the provisions of Section twenty-one of the Act of Congress approved June 28, 1898 (30 Stat. 495), to enrollment as a citizen by intermarriage of the Cherokee Nation, and his application for enrollment as such is accordingly granted.

Tams Bixby
Commissioner.

Dated at Muskogee, Indian Territory,
this    JAN 23 1907

## Cherokee Intermarried White 1906
## Volume III

Cherokee
4578

Muskogee, Indian Territory, January 23, 1907.

W. W. Hastings,
    Attorney for the Cherokee Nation,
        Muskogee, Indian Territory.

Dear Sir:

    There is enclosed herewith copy of the decision of the Commissioner to the Five Civilized Tribes, dated January 23, 1907, granting the application for the enrollment of William H. McAnally as a citizen by intermarriage of the Cherokee Nation.

        Respectfully,

Enc I-27.                                                       Commissioner.

RPI

◇◇◇◇◇

Cherokee 4578.

W.W. HASTINGS.    OFFICE OF    H.M. VANCE.
ATTORNEY.                                     SECRETARY.

**Attorney for the Cherokee Nation,**
MUSKOGEE, I. T.    January 23, 1907.

The Commissioner to the Five Civilized Tribes,
    Muskogee, Indian Territory.

Sir:

    Receipt is acknowledged of the testimony and of your decision enrolling William H. McAnally as a citizen by intermarriage of the Cherokee Nation. Time for protesting said decision is waived and I consent that said person may be placed upon the schedule immediately.

        Respectfully,
                W. W. Hastings
                Attorney for the Cherokee Nation.

◇◇◇◇◇

# Cherokee Intermarried White 1906
## Volume III

Cherokee 4578

Muskogee, Indian Territory, January 23, 1907.

William H. McAnally,
　　Catoosa, Indian Territory.

Dear Sir:

　　There is enclosed herewith a copy of the decision of the Commissioner to the Five Civilized Tribes, dated January 23, 1907, granting the application for your enrollment as a citizen by intermarriage of the Cherokee Nation.

　　You will be advised when your name has been placed upon a schedule of citizens of the Cherokee Nation and approved by the Secretary of the Interior.

　　　　　　　　　Respectfully,

Encl. H-102
JMH
　　　　　　　　　　　　　　　　Commissioner.

---

**Cher IW 94**
**Trans from Cher 4659  3-16-07**

◇◇◇◇◇

E.C.M.

## DEPARTMENT OF THE INTERIOR,

### COMMISSIONER TO THE FIVE CIVILIZED TRIBES.

In the matter of the application for the enrollment of

**BETTIE A. MITCHELL**

As a citizen by intermarriage of the Cherokee Nation.

CHEROKEE NO. 4659.

◇◇◇◇◇

## Cherokee Intermarried White 1906
## Volume III

DEPARTMENT OF THE INTERIOR,
COMMISSION TO THE FIVE CIVILIZED TRIBES,
CLAREMORE, I.T., OCTOBER 22d, 1900.

In the matter of the application of William D. Mitchell for the enrollment of himself and wife as citizens of the Cherokee Nation; said Mitchell being sworn by Commissioner T. B. Needles, testified as follows:

Q What is your name? A William D. Mitchell.
Q What is your age? A 46.
Q What is your postoffice address? A Collinsville, I.T.
Q What district do you live in? A Cooweescooowee[sic].
Q Are you a recognized citizen of the Cherokee Nation? A Yes, sir.
Q By blood or intermarriage? A By blood.
Q Who do you want to enroll? A Myself and wife.
Q What is your wife's name? A Betty A.
Q Is she a citizen? A No, sir.
Q What is her age? A 45.
Q When did you marry her? A 17th of March, 1875.
    1880 enrollment; page 453, #1127, Wm. Mitchell, Going Snake.
    1880 enrollment; page 453, #1128, Eliza Mitchell, Going Snake.
    1896 enrollment, page 213, #3224, Wm. Mitchell, Cooweescoowee.
    1896 enrollment; page 315, #659, Elizabeth A. Mitchell,    "
Q Have you lived with you regularly? A Yes, sir.
Q Have you lived with her continuously since you married her? A Yes, sir.
Q How long have you lived in the Cherokee Nation? A I was raised here.

Com'r Needles:--The name of William D. Mitchell appears upon the authenticated roll of 1880 as well as the census roll of 1896. He avers that he was married to his wife, Betty, in the year 1875, she being a white person, and the name of his wife, Betty, is found upon the authenticated roll of 1880 as Eliza, and upon the census roll of 1896 as Elizabeth A. She being duly identified as well as himself, and having made satisfactory proof as to their residence said William D Mitchell will be duly listed for enrollment as a Cherokee citizen by blood, and his wife, Betty, as a Cherokee citizen by intermarriage.

---oooOOOooo---

J. O. Rosson, being first duly sworn, states that as stenographer to the Commission to the Five Civilized Tribes, he correctly recorded the testimony and proceedings in this case, and that the foregoing is a true and complete transcript of his stenographic notes thereof.

J O Rosson

## Cherokee Intermarried White 1906
## Volume III

Subscribed and sworn to before me this 22d day of October, 1900.

               TB Needles
               Commissioner.

◇◇◇◇◇

Cher-4659.

### DEPARTMENT OF THE INTERIOR.
### Commission to the Five Civilized Tribes,
### Muskogee, I.T., October 21, 1902.

In the matter of the application of William D. Mitchell for enrollment as a citizen by blood of the Cherokee nation, and for the enrollment of his wife, Bettie A. Mitchell as a Cherokee by intermarriage.

William D. Mitchell, called as a witness, being first duly sworn, and examined by the Commission, testified as follows:

Q What is your name? A William D. Mitchell.
Q How old are you? A I my 49th year.
Q What is your postoffice address? A Oolagah, I. T.
Q Are you a Cherokee by blood? A Yes sir.
Q What is your wife's name? A Bettie A.
Q Is she a white woman? A Yes sir.
Q Was she your wife in 1880? Yes sir.
Q Were you and your wife living together in the Cherokee nation[sic] in '80? A Yes sir.
Q You have never been separated have you? A No sir.
Q And are living together now? A Yes sir.
Q You have made your home in the Cherokee nation[sic] ever since 1880? A Yes.
Q Never lived anywhere else? A No sir.

-----0-----

Frances R. Lane upon oath states that as stenographer to the Commission to the Five Civilized Tribes she correctly recorded the testimony taken in the above entitled cause, and that the foregoing is an accurate transcript of her stenographic notes thereof.

               Frances R Lane

Subscribed and sworn to before me this 28th day of October, 1902.

               BC Jones
               Notary Public.

# Cherokee Intermarried White 1906
# Volume III

DEPARTMENT OF THE INTERIOR
COMMISSIONER TO THE FIVE CIVILIZED TRIBES
MUSKOGEE, IND. TER.
JAN. 4, 1907

IN THE MATTER OF THE APPLICATION FOR THE
ENROLLMENT OF BETTIE A. MITCHELL AS A CITIZEN
BY INTERMARRIAGE OF THE CHEROKEE NATION.

CENSUS CARD NO. 4659.

BETTIE A. MITCHELL BEING FIRST DULY SWORN TESTIFIED AS FOLLOWS

EXAMINATION BY THE COMMISSIONER:

Q What is your name? A Bettie A. Mitchell.
Q How old are you.[sic] A Fifty years old.
Q What is your post office address.[sic] A Collinsville.
Q Do you claim to be a citizen by intermarriage of the Cherokee Nation.[sic]
A Yes sir.
Q Thru whom do you claim your intermarried rights.
A William D. Mitchell.
Q William D. Mitchell. A Yes sir.
Q When were you married to William D. Mitchell. A March 7 1875.
Q Where were you living when you married Mr Mitchell
A He was living in Delaware District.
Q Where were you living. A My Paw was living in Delaware District
Q You were living in the Cherokee Nation Delaware District
A Yes sir
Q Was you ever married before you married Mr Mitchell
A No sir
Q Was he ever married before he married you. A No sir
Q Have you lived together continuously as husband and wife in the Cherokee Nation since you married in 1875. A Yes sir.
Q Living together at the present time. A Yes sir.

The applicant is identified on the 1880 Cherokee Roll Goingsnake District opposite No. 1128; her husband thru whom she claims intermarried rights is identified on said roll of said District opposite No. 1127; he is also identified on the final roll citizens by blood of the Cherokee Nation opposite No. 26648.

Q Did you get a certificate or anything showing your marriage
A I dont[sic] think I got any.
Q Who married you. A A preacher by the name of McGraw.
Q Is he living? A Yes sir.

# Cherokee Intermarried White 1906
# Volume III

Q He didn't give you any certificate of marriage?
A No sir.

WILLIAM D MITCHELL BEING FIRST DULY SWORN TESTIFIED AS FOLLOWS:

EXAMINATION BY THE COMMISSIONER:

Q What is your name[sic] A William D. Mitchell.
Q How old are you? A About fifty two years old.
Q What is your post office address.[sic] A Collinsville now.
Q What relation are you to Bettie A. Mitchell.[sic] A Husband.
Q When were you and Bettie A. Mitchell married.[sic]
A Seventh day of March 1875.
Q Where were you married. A Delaware District; I lived in Delaware District at the time.
Q Were you ever married before you married Bettie A Mitchell
A No sir
Q Was she ever married before she married you. A No sir.
Q Have you lived together continuously as husband and wife since you married.
A Yes sir.
Q Who married you. A McGraw.
Q Did he give you a certificate? A No sir.
Q Are there any witnesses here today who know of your marriage in 1875 to Bettie Mitchell. A No sir, I haven't, not here.

ooOoo

JOHN H. McCARTY BEING FIRST DULY SWORN TESTIFIED AS FOLLOWS:

EXAMINATION BY THE COMMISSIONER:

Q What is your name.[sic] A John M. McCarty.
Q How old are you? A About fifty four, fifty three or four, born in forty two.
Q What is your post office address. A Foyil
Q Do you know William D. Mitchell and Bettie A. Mitchell
A Yes sir
Q Do you know when they were married.
A No sir I dont[sic].
Q How long have you known them. A I've known Mr Mitchell about thirty years.
Q How long have you known his wife.
Q The last seven years I reckon.
Q Have they held themselves out as husband and wife ever since you have known them.
A Yes sir.

ooOoo

# Cherokee Intermarried White 1906
# Volume III

REESE HILDERBRAND BEING FIRST DULY SWORN TESTIFIED AS FOLLOWS:

EXAMINATION BY THE COMMISSIONER

Q What is your name.[sic] A Reese Hilderbrand.
Q How old are you. A About fifty six.
Q What is your post office address. A Webbers Falls.
Q Are you a citizen of the Cherokee Nation. A Yes sir.
Q Do you know William D. Mitchell. A Yes sir.
Q Do you know Bettie A. Mitchell. A No sir.
Q How long have you know[sic] William D. Mitchell.
A I knew him when we was boys together.
Q You dont[sic] know anything about his marriage to Bettie A. Mitchell. A No sir

Clara Mitchell Wood being first duly sworn upon her oath states that as stenographer for the Commissioner to the Five Civilized Tribes she reported the above and foregoing proceedings and that this is a correct transcript of her stenographic notes thereof stenographic notes.

Clara Mitchell Wood

Subscribed and sworn to before me this 8th day of January 1907

B.P. Rasmus<br>Notary Public.

◇◇◇◇◇

C. F. B.                                                               Cherokee 4659.

DEPARTMENT OF THE INTERIOR,<br>COMMISSION TO THE FIVE CIVILIZED TRIBES.<br>Muskogee, Indian Territory, January 9, 1907.

Supplemental Proceedings in the Matter of the Application for the Enrollment of Bettie A. Mitchell as a citizen by intermarriage of the Cherokee Nation.

Georgia A. Mitchell being first duly sworn by B. P. Rasmus, Notary Public, testified as follows:

Q What is your name? A Georgia A. Mitchell.
Q What is your age? A 46 years old.
Q What is your post office address?
A Oolagah.
Q Do you know a person in the Cherokee Nation by the name of Bettie A. Mitchell?
A Yes sir.
Q How long have you known Bettie A. Mitchell?
A I have known her all her life.

## Cherokee Intermarried White 1906
## Volume III

Q She is a white woman?
A Yes sir.
Q What is her husband's name?
A William D. Mitchell.
Q Is he a Cherokee by blood?
A Yes sir.
Q Do you know when William D. Mitchell was married to Bettie A. Mitchell?
A Yes sir.
Q What year?
A March 7, 1875.
Q Where were they married?
A Delaware District.
Q By whom were they married?
A Preacher McCraw.
Q Were you present when they were married?
A Yes sir.
Q Did you know both parties prior to their marriage?
A Yes sir.
Q Was William D. Mitchell a recognized citizen of the Cherokee Nation at the time they married?
A Yes sir.
Q They have since continuously lived together as husband and wife?
A Yes sir.

Franklin P. Mitchell being first duly sworn by B. P. Rasmus, testified as follows:

Q What is your name?
A Franklin P. Mitchell.
Q Are you related to William D. Mitchell?
A Yes sir.
Q How?
A Brother.
Q He is a Cherokee by blood?
A Yes sir.
Q His wife, Bettie A. Mitchell, is a white woman?
A Yes sir.
Q Did you know Bettie A. Mitchell prior to her marriage to your brother, William D. Mitchell?
A Yes sir.
Q Where were they married?
A Delaware District, Cherokee Nation.
Q Were you present at the marriage ceremony?
A Yes sir.
Q By whom were they married?
A Parson McCraw.
Q Your brother was a recognized citizen of the Cherokee Nation at the time of the marriage?
A Yes sir.
Q What was the date of their marriage?
A March 7, 1875.

## Cherokee Intermarried White 1906
## Volume III

The undersigned being first duly sworn states that as stenographer to the Commission to the Five Civilized Tribes, she recorded the testimony taken in this case and that the foregoing is a full, true and correct transcript of her stenographic notes thereof.

Myrtle Hill

Subscribed and sworn to before me this the 14th day of January, 1907.

John E. Tidwell
Notary Public.

◇◇◇◇◇

E C M                                                                                               Cherokee 4659.

### DEPARTMENT OF THE INTERIOR,

### COMMISSIONER TO THE FIVE CIVILIZED TRIBES.

In the matter of the application for the enrollment of BETTIE A. MITCHELL as a citizen by intermarriage of the Cherokee Nation.

### _D_E_C_I_S_I_O_N_

THE RECORDS OF THIS OFFICE SHOW: That ON October 22nd, 1900 application was received by the Commission to the Five Civilized Tribes for the enrollment of Bettie A. Mitchell as a citizen by intermarriage of the Cherokee Nation. Further proceedings in the matter of said application were had at Muskogee, Indian Territory, October 21st, 1902 and January 4th, 1907.

THE EVIDENCE IN THIS CASE SHOWS: That the applicant herein, Bettie A. Mitchell, a white woman, was married on March 7th, 1875 to one William D. Mitchell, who was at the time of said marriage a recognized citizen by blood of the Cherokee Nation, who is identified on the Cherokee authenticated tribal roll of 1880, Going Snake District No. 1127 as a native Cherokee and whose name appears upon the approved partial roll of citizens by blood of the Cherokee Nation. It is further shown that from the time of said marriage the said William D. Mitchell and Bettie A. Mitchell resided together as husband and wife and continuously lived in the Cherokee Nation up to and including September 1st, 1902. Said applicant is identified upon the Cherokee authenticated tribal roll of 1880, and the Cherokee census roll of 1896 as an intermarried citizen of the Cherokee Nation.

IT IS, THEREFORE, ORDERED AND ADJUDGED: That in accordance with the decision of the Supreme Court of the United States, dated November 5, 1906 in the cases of Daniel Red Bird et al. vs. the United States Nos. 125, 126, 127 and 128, the said applicant, Bettie A. Mitchell is entitled, under the provisions of Section Twenty-one of the

## Cherokee Intermarried White 1906
## Volume III

Act of Congress approved June 28, 1898 (30 Stats. 495), to enrollment as a citizen by intermarriage of the Cherokee Nation and her application for enrollment as such is accordingly granted.

             Tams Bixby
                Commissioner.

Dated at Muskogee, Indian Territory,
this   JAN 23 1907

◇◇◇◇◇

Cherokee 4659

          Muskogee, Indian Territory, January 23, 1907.

W. W. Hastings,
    Attorney for the Cherokee Nation,
       Muskogee, Indian Territory.

Dear Sir:

    There is enclosed herewith copy of the decision of the Commissioner to the Five Civilized Tribes, dated January 23, 1907, granting the application for the enrollment of Bettie A. Mitchell as a citizen by intermarriage of the Cherokee Nation.

            Respectfully,

Enc I-64                 Commissioner.

RPI

◇◇◇◇◇

Cherokee 4659

W.W. HASTINGS.     OFFICE OF      H.M. VANCE.
ATTORNEY.                SECRETARY.

### Attorney for the Cherokee Nation,
       MUSKOGEE, I. T.    January 23, 1907.

The Commissioner to the Five Civilized Tribes,
   Muskogee, Indian Territory.

Sir:

    Receipt is acknowledged of the testimony and of your decision enrolling Bettie A. Mitchell as a citizen by intermarriage of the Cherokee Nation. Time for protesting said decision is waived and I consent that said person may be placed upon the schedule immediately.

            Respectfully,
              W. W. Hastings
              Attorney for the Cherokee Nation.

## Cherokee Intermarried White 1906
## Volume III

◇◇◇◇◇

Cherokee 4659

Muskogee, Indian Territory, January 23, 1907.

Bettie A. Mitchell,
    Collinsville, Indian Territory.

Dear Madam:

    There is enclosed herewith copy of the decision of the Commissioner to the Five Civilized Tribes, dated January 23, 1907, granting your application for enrollment as a citizen by intermarriage of the Cherokee Nation.

    You will be advised when your name has been placed upon a schedule of citizens of the Cherokee Nation and approved by the Secretary of the Interior.

                  Respectfully,

Enc I-84

                                                      Commissioner.

RPI

---

**Cher IW 95**
**Trans from Cher 4679  3-16-07**

◇◇◇◇◇

                                                      E.C.M.

DEPARTMENT OF THE INTERIOR,

COMMISSIONER TO THE FIVE CIVILIZED TRIBES.

In the matter of the application for the enrollment of

JOHN H. McCARTY

As a citizen by intermarriage of the Cherokee Nation.

CHEROKEE NO. 4679.

◇◇◇◇◇

## Cherokee Intermarried White 1906
## Volume III

Department of the Interior,
Commission to the Five Civilized Tribes,
Claremore, I. T. October, 22d, 19oo[sic].

In the matter of the enrollment of John H. McCarty, for the enrollment of himself and children as Cherokee Citizens. He being sworn testified before the Commission as follows:

Q What is your name? A. John H. McCarty.
Q What is your age? A. 57.
Q What is your post office address? A. Foyl[sic], I. T.
Q What district do you live in? A. Cooweescoowee.
Q Are you a recognized citizen of the Cherokee Nation? A. Yes sir.
Q Who is it that you want to have enrolled? A. Myself and children.
Q Have you a wife? A. She is dead.
Q Do you apply for your self as a Cherokee by blood or intermarriage?
A Intermarriage.
Q What is the name of your wife? A. Francis Phillis.
Q When were you married to her? A. September, 1872.
Q Was she a Cherokee by blood? A. Yes sir.
Q What are the names of your children? A. Liddie F. age 17; Ruben C, age 15 and Moses age 11, John age 10 and Nancy age 7.
1880 roll, page 451, No 1073, John McCarter, Goingsnake, Adpt, White.

| 1896 | 315 | 661 John H. McCarty, Cooweescoowee. |
| 1896 | 205 | 2979 Lidia F. McCarty, " |
| 1896 | 205 | 2980 Rheubin McCarty, " |
| 1896 | 205 | 2981 Mose McCarty " |
| 1896 | 205 | 2982 John McCarty " |
| 1896 | 205 | 2983 Nancy McCarty " |

Q How long have you lived in the Cherokee Nation? A Came here in '70
Q Have you been living here ever since? A. Yes sir.
Q These children alive and living with you now? A. Yes sir.
The name of John H. McCarty appears on the authenticater[sic] roll of 1880 and the census roll of 1896 as an intermarried white. The names of his children Lidia, Ruben, Moses, John and Nancy appear on the census roll of 1896. They are all duly identified according to the page and number of the roll and have made satisfactory proof of their residence, consequentally[sic] they will now be listed for enrollment as Cherokees by blood.

Chas. von Weise being sworn states that as stenographer to the Commission to the firve[sic] Civilized tribes[sic] he reported in full all the proceedings in the above cause and that the foregoing is a full, true and correct transcript of his stenographic notes of said proceedings.

Chas von Weise

# Cherokee Intermarried White 1906
## Volume III

Subscribed and sworn to before me this the 23rd day of October, 1900.

TB Needles<br>Commissioner.

◇◇◇◇◇

DEPARTMENT OF THE INTERIOR.
Commission to the Five Civilized Tribes.
Muskogee, Indian Territory, October 9th, 1902.

In the matter of the application of John H. McCarty for the enrollment of himself as a citizen by intermarriage of the Cherokee Nation and for the enrollment of his children, Lydia F., Reuben C., Moses, John and Nancy McCarty, as citizens by blood of the Cherokee Nation.

Supplemental to #4679.

JOHN H. McCARTY, being duly sworn, testified as follows:
Examination by the Commission.

Q. Your full name is John H. McCarty? A. Yes, sir.
Q. How old are you? A. About 58.
Q. What is your post office address? A. Foyel[sic].
Q. You are on the eighty roll as an intermarried white citizen, are you? A. Yes, sir.
Q. What was the name of your wife at that time? A. Phillips.
Q. What as her first name? A. Frances.
Q. That wife is dead, is she? A. Yes, sir.
Q. When did she die? A. She has been dead 7 years last April.
Q. Did you live with her in the Cherokee Nation from 1880 up until the time of her death? A. Yes, sir.
Q. You have married since? A. No, sir.
Q. You haven't married since your wife's death? A. No, sir.
Q. You were married just once? A. Just once.
Q. How many children have you? A. Eight.
Q. How many living at home with you? A. There is three at home.
Q. How many did you make application for? A. Five, I think it was.
Q. Are they all living? A. Yes, sir.
Q. Three of them are now living with you? A. No, sir.
Q. You have never made your home outside of the Cherokee Nation since 1880? A. No, sir.

++++++++++++++++++++++++++++++++++++

## Cherokee Intermarried White 1906
## Volume III

Jesse O. Carr, being first duly sworn, states that as stenographer to the Commission to the Five Civilized Tribes he reported the above entitled case and that the foregoing is a true and complete transcript of his stenographic notes thereof.

Jesse O. Carr

Subscribed and sworn to before me this 10<sup>th</sup> day of December, 1902.

PG Reuter<br>Notary Public.

◇◇◇◇◇

### DEPARTMENT OF THE INTERIOR
### COMMISSIONER TO THE FIVE CIVILIZED TRIBES
### MUSKOGEE, IND. TER.
### JAN. 4, 1907

IN THE MATTER OF THE APPLICATION OF JOHN h. McCARTY FOR ENROLLMENT AS A CITIZEN BY INTERMARRIAGE OF THE CHEROKEE NATION.

CENSUS CARD NO. 4679.

JOHN HUGH McCARTY BEING FIRST DULY SWORN TESTIFIED AS FOLLOWS:

EXAMINATION BY THE COMMISSIONER:

Q What is your name.[sic]  A  John Hugh McCarty.
Q How old are you.[sic]  A  Born in forty two.
Q What is your post office address?  A  Foyil.
Q Do you claim to be a citizen by intermarriage of the Cherokee Nation.[sic]
A Yes sir.
Q Thru whom do you claim your intermarried rights.
A Frances Phillips.
Q Frances Phillips McCarty?  A  Yes sir[sic]
Q When were you married to Frances Phillips McCarty.
A The 15th day of September 1872.
Q Have you got a license.  A  I did have; they burned up in my house in '75.
Q You haven't had them since 1875.  No.
Q Were you ever married before you married Frances McCarty?
A No sir.
Q Was she ever married before she married you.  A  No sir.
Q Is Frances McCarty living at this time.  A  No sir.
Q When did she die.  A  Died the 11th day of April '94; 11th day of April.

## Cherokee Intermarried White 1906
## Volume III

Q 11th day of April 1894. A Yes sir.
Q Was you ever married before you married Frances McCarty?
A No sir.
Q Where were you married? A Married in Goingsnake District
Q Did you live together continuously as husband and wife from the date of your marriage in 1872 up to and including the date of the death of your wife in 1894.
A Yes sir.
Q Were you living together at that time? A Yes sir.
Q Have you married again since your wife died in 1894.
A No sir.
Q Still live in the Cherokee Nation. A Yes sir.
Q Was your wife a citizen of the Cherokee Nation at the time you married her.
A Yes sir.
Q Was she born in the Cherokee Nation? A Yes sir, never was out of it I dont[sic] reckon in her life.
Q Her parents were recognized citizens by blood of the Cherokee Nation were they.
A Yes sir.

The applicant is identified on the 1880 Cherokee Roll of Goingsnake District opposite No. 1073.

Q It will be necessary for you to show by two witnesses that you were married under a license issued by the Cherokee authorities before anything further can be done in the matter of your application for enrollment.

ooOoo

Clara Mitchell Wood being first duly sworn upon her oath states that as stenographer for the Commissioner to the Five Civilized Tribes she reported the above and foregoing proceedings and that this is a correct transcript of her stenographic notes.

Clara Mitchell Wood

Subscribed and sworn to before me this 8th day of January 1907.

*(No Signature Given)*
Notary Public.

## Cherokee Intermarried White 1906
## Volume III

DEPARTMENT OF THE INTERIOR
COMMISSIONER TO THE FIVE CIVILIZED TRIBES
MUSKOGEE, IND. TER.
JAN. 4, 1907

ADDITIONAL TESTIMONY IN THE MATTER OF THE APPLICATION OF JOHN H. McCARTY FOR ENROLL MENT AS A CITIZEN BY INTERMARRIAGE OF THE CHEROKEE NATION.

CENSUS CARD NO. 4679.

E.E. SLOAN BEING FIRST DULY SWORN TESTIFIED AS FOLLOWS:

EXAMINATION BY THE COMMISSIONER:

Q What is your name.[sic]  A E.E. Sloan
Q How old are you.  A Fifty six.
Q What is your post office address.  A Big Cabin.
Q Are you acquainted with John H. McCarty.
A Yes sir
Q Do you know his wife Frances McCarty.  A Yes sir
Q Do you know when they were married.  A I know just about the time they was married but I cant[sic] tell just exactly.
Q Were you present at the wedding.  A Yes I was right there and seen them married.
Q Do you know whether John H. McCarty was married under a Cherokee license or not.
A I dont[sic] know anything about that; he was married in the Cherokee Nation by a Cherokee officer, that is a judge.
Q What was his name.  A Crittendon.
Q You didn't see the license.  A No I never seen the license
Q Has he been recognized as a citizen of the Cherokee Nation ever since his marriage to Frances McCarty
A Ever since he married as far as I know.
Q Would you know it if he had not been recognized as a citizen
A He was recognized at that time but whether he married out since or not I dont[sic] know.
Q Do you know whether Frances McCarty was a citizen at the time of her marriage.
A Yes sir.
Q She was so recognized at that time.  A Yes she was an Indian girl; Mrs Phillips' daughter.

ooOoo

Clara Mitchell Wood being first duly sworn upon her oath states that as stenographer for the Commissioner to the Five Civilized Tribes she reported the above and foregoing proceedings and that this is a correct transcript of her stenographic notes.

# Cherokee Intermarried White 1906
## Volume III

Clara Mitchell Wood

Subscribed and sworn to before me this 8th day of January 1907

*(No Signature Given)*
Notary Public.

◇◇◇◇◇

C.F.B.                                                                                              Cherokee 4679.

## DEPARTMENT OF THE INTERIOR,
## COMMISSIONER TO THE FIVE CIVILIZED TRIBES.
## MUSKOGEE, I. T., JANUARY 7, 1907.

SUPPLEMENTAL PROCEEDINGS in the matter of the application for the enrollment of JOHN H. MCCARTY as a citizen by intermarriage of the Cherokee Nation.

APPEARANCES:   Applicant appears in person
W. W. Hastings, Attorney for Cherokee Nation.
George Crittendon appears on behalf of applicant.

GEORGE CRITTENDON, being first duly sworn by John E. Tidwell, Notary Public, testified as follows:

ON BEHALF OF THE COMMISSIONER:

Q What is your name? A George Crittendon.
Q What is your age? A 62.
Q What is your post office address? A Westville.
Q You are a citizen by blood of the Cherokee Nation, are you? A Yes sir.
Q You desire to give testimony, do you, in the matter of the application for the enrollment of John H. McCarty as a citizen by intermarriage of the Cherokee Nation? A Yes sir.
Q How long have you known John H. McCarty? A Well, it has been over 30 years.
Q He is a white man, is he? A Yes sir.
Q Did you know him before his marriage? A Yes sir.
Q What is the name of his wife? A Frances Phillips.
Q She was a recognized citizen by blood of the Cherokee Nation at the time of their marriage, was she? A Yes sir.
Q And resided in the Cherokee Country? A Yes sir; born and raised there, near Westville.
Q Were you present at their marriage? A No sir.

# Cherokee Intermarried White 1906
## Volume III

Q Do you remember atout[sic] the time they were married? A I just remember it in this way: my father was District Judge at that time, and I heard them talk about McCarty and Miss Phillips getting married.
Q You remember, then, that your father married him? A Yes sir.
Q And that has been your understanding, has it? A Yes sir.
Q It has always been your understanding that your father married him in accordance with Cherokee law, has it? A Well, that is the way my father married them; I would judge that my father would not do anything that was not right.
Q Do you know of your own personal knowledge that John H. McCarty has exercised all the rights and enjoyed all the privileges of a citizen by intermarriage of the Cherokee Nation? A While he stayed there he always provided for his family; he lived close to me; he moved out west.
Q. He and his wife resided together continuously as husband and wife, did they? A Yes sir, up until the time they left; I dont[sic] know how it was after that.
Q Where did they move to? A Out west somewhere. They started to go to my sister's place, but it was rented by some other parties.
Q You have always known John H. McCarty as a citizen by intermarriage of the Cherokee Nation.[sic] A Yes sir.
Q And you have every reason to believe that he was married in accordance with Cherokee law? A Yes sir

------------------------

The undersigned, being first duly sworn, states that as stenographer to the Commissioner to the Five Civilized Tribes, she correctly recorded the above and foregoing testimony; and that the same is a full, true and correct transcript of her stenographic notes thereof.

Sarah Waters

Subscribed and sworn to before me this 9th day of January, 1907.

John E. Tidwell
Notary Public.

## Cherokee Intermarried White 1906
## Volume III

E. C. M.                                                                                                                         Cherokee 4679.

### DEPARTMENT OF THE INTERIOR,
### COMMISSIONER TO THE FIVE CIVILIZED TRIBES.

In the matter of the application for the enrollment of John H. McCarty as a citizen by intermarriage of the Cherokee Nation.

### D E C I S I O N.

THE RECORDS OF THIS OFFICE SHOW: That on October 22, 1900, application was received by the Commission to the Five Civilized Tribes for the enrollment of John H. McCarty as a citizen by intermarriage of the Cherokee Nation. Further proceedings in the matter of said application were had at Muskogee, Indian Territory, October 9, 1902, and January 4, 1907, and January 7, 1907.

THE EVIDENCE IN THIS CASE SHOWS: That the applicant herein, John H. McCarty, a white man, was married in accordance with Cherokee law September 15, 1872, to his wife, Francis McCarty, deceased, nee Phillips, who was at the time of said marriage a recognized citizen by blood of the Cherokee Nation, who is identified on the Cherokee authenticated tribal roll of 1880, Going Snake District, as "Francis McCarter", No. 1074, as a native Cherokee. It is further shown that from the time of said marriage until the death of said Francis McCarty, which occurred on April 11, 1894, the said John H. McCarty and Francis McCarty resided together as husband and wife and continuously lived in the Cherokee Nation; that after the death of said Francis McCarty the said John H. McCarty remained unmarried and continuously lived in the Cherokee Nation up to and including September 1, 1902. Said applicant is identified on the Cherokee authenticated tribal roll of 1880 as "John McCarter" and the Cherokee census roll of 1896 as John McCarty as an intermarried citizen of the Cherokee Nation.

IT IS, THEREFORE, ORDERED AND ADJUDGED: That in accordance with the decision of the Supreme Court of the United States, dated November 5, 1906, in the cases of Daniel Red Bird et al. vs. the United States, Nos. 125, 126, 127 and 128, the said applicant, John H. McCarty, is entitled, under the provisions of Section 21 of the Act of Congress approved June 28, 1898 (30 Stats., 495), to enrollment as a citizen by intermarriage of the Cherokee Nation, and his application for enrollment as such is accordingly granted.

                                                          Tams Bixby
                                                                                    Commissioner.

Dated at Muskogee, Indian Territory,
this     JAN 23 1907

## Cherokee Intermarried White 1906
## Volume III

Cherokee 4679

Muskogee, Indian Territory, January 23, 1907.

W. W. Hastings,
    Attorney for the Cherokee Nation,
        Muskogee, Indian Territory.

Dear Sir:

    There is enclosed herewith a copy of the decision of the Commissioner to the Five Civilized Tribes, dated January 23, 1907, granting the application for the enrollment of John H. McCarty as a citizen by intermarriage of the Cherokee Nation.

        Respectfully,

Encl. H-67                                                   Commissioner.
JMH

◇◇◇◇◇

Cherokee 4679

W.W. HASTINGS.         OFFICE OF         H.M. VANCE.
ATTORNEY.                                           SECRETARY.

**Attorney for the Cherokee Nation,**
MUSKOGEE, I. T.     January 23, 1907.

The Commissioner to the Five Civilized Tribes,
    Muskogee, Indian Territory.

Sir:

    Receipt is acknowledged of the testimony and of your decision enrolling John H. McCarty as a citizen by intermarriage of the Cherokee Nation. Time for protesting said decision is waived and I consent that said person may be placed upon the schedule immediately.

        Respectfully,
        W. W. Hastings
        Attorney for Cherokee Nation.

◇◇◇◇◇

# Cherokee Intermarried White 1906
# Volume III

Cherokee
4679

Muskogee, Indian Territory, January 23, 1907.

John H. McCarty,
   Foyil, Indian Territory.

Dear Sir:

    There is enclosed herewith a copy of the decision of the Commissioner to the Five Civilized Tribes, dated January 23, 1907, granting your application for enrollment as a citizen by intermarriage of the Cherokee Nation.

    You will be advised when your name has been placed upon a schedule of citizens of the Cherokee Nation and approved by the Secretary of the Interior.

                Respectfully,

E.R.C.                                                Commissioner.
Enc. E.C. 88

---

**Cher IW 96**
**Trans from Cher 4764  3-16-07**

◇◇◇◇◇

                                                              E.C.M.

## DEPARTMENT OF THE INTERIOR,

## COMMISSIONER TO THE FIVE CIVILIZED TRIBES.

In the matter of the application for the enrollment of

### ELIZABETH E. COKER

As a citizen by intermarriage of the Cherokee Nation.

CHEROKEE NO. 4764.

◇◇◇◇◇

## Cherokee Intermarried White 1906
## Volume III

Separate application for ELIZABETH E. COKER.

Department of the Interior
Commissioner to the Five Civilized tribes[sic],
Claremore, I. T. October, 23rd, 19oo[sic].

In the matter of the application of Josephine A. Fults for the enrollment of her mother Elizabeth E. Coker. Josephine A Fults being sworn testified before the Commission as follows.

Q What is your name? A. Josephine A. Fults
Q How old are you? [sic] 24.
Q What is your post office? A. Chouteau.
Q What district do you live in? A. Cooweescoowee.
Q Who is it that you want to have enrolled? A. My mother.
Q What is her name? A. Elizabeth E. Coker.
Q Does she live in your family? A. Yes sir.
Q What is her age? A. 60.
Q Why does she not come here and make her own application? A. It is difficult and inconvenient for her to come by herself and we cannot both leave at the same time. It is a long drive across the country and to go by rail it is very inconvenient.
Q Is she white? A. Yes sir.
Q How long has she lived in the Cherokee Nation? A. I dont know, ever since before my birth.
Q For mote[sic] than 24 years? A. Ye sir.
Q When did your father die? A. I dont[sic] really know. Some 15 years ago.
Q What was his name? A. Dempsey F. Coker.
Q Is your mother a Cherokee by blood? A. No sir she is a white woman
Q Your father was a Cherokee by blood was he? A. Yes sir.
Q Has your mother ever married since his death? A. No sir.
1880 roll, page 87, No. 693, E. E. Coker, Cooweescoowee, Adpt. white
1880        87        692, D. F. Coker,        "        N. C.
1896        299      213 Elizabeth Coker,      "
Q Did your father and mother live together from their marriage until your fathers[sic] death? A. Yes sir.

The applicant applies for the enrollment of her mother who is unable to apply for herself and who is living in the family of applicant. She is identified on the 1880 and 1896 rolls as an adopted Cherokee. Her Cherokee husband with whom she is identified on the 1880 roll died some 15 years ago. She has never married since his death. She lived with him from the time of their marriage until his death, has lived in the Cherokee Nation more than 24 years and she will be lised[sic] now for enrollment as a Cherokee by adoption.

Chas. con Weise being sworn states that as stenographer to the Commission to the Five Civilized Tribes he reported in full all the proceedings in the above entitled cause and

# Cherokee Intermarried White 1906
## Volume III

that the foregoing is a full true and correct transcript of his stenographic notes in said proceedings.

Chas von Weise

Subscribed and sworn to before me this the 24th of October, 19oo[sic].

MD Green<br>
~~Commissioner~~.<br>
Notary Public

◇◇◇◇◇

*(The testimony below does not belong with the current applicant.)*

R
Cher
   D 2953

Department of the Interior,<br>
Commission to the Five Civilized Tribes,<br>
Muskogee, I. T., June 30, 1902.

In the matter of the application of JAMES BULLETT, ET AL., for enrollment as citizens of the Cherokee Nation:

EMMET STARR, being duly sworn and examined by the Commission, testified as follows:

Q What is your name? A Emmet Starr.
Q What is your age? A Thirty one years.
Q What is your post office address? A Claremore, I. T.
Q Are you a citizen by blood of the Cherokee Nation? A Yes sir, I am.
Q For whom do you desire to make application for enrollment?
A For the following named persons on the 1896 Cherokee roll, their families and descendants:

    Martin Gertrude #1255 Illinois District.
    Edmond Martin #1256 Illinois District.
    Tandy W. Martin #1258 Illinois District.

Q Are there any other persons for whom you desire to make application for enrollment?
A I desire to apply for the following named persons on the 1880 Cherokee roll, their families and their descendants:

*(No names listed.)*

--------------------------

## Cherokee Intermarried White 1906
## Volume III

E. C. Bagwell, on oath states that as stenographer to the Commission to the Five Civilized Tribes, he correctly recorded the testimony and proceedings had in the above entitled cause, and that the foregoing is an accurate transcript of his stenographic notes thereof.

E.C. Bagwell

Subscribed and sworn to before me this December 9, 1902.

BC Jones<br>Notary Public.

◇◇◇◇◇

*(The testimony below does not belong with the current applicant.)*

R
Cher
    D 2997

Department of the Interior,<br>Commission to the Five Civilized Tribes,<br>Muskogee, I. T., June 30, 1902.

In the matter of the application of JAMES BULLETT, ET AL., for enrollment as citizens of the Cherokee Nation:

EMMET STARR, being duly sworn and examined by the Commission, testified as follows:

Q What is your name? A Emmet Starr.
Q What is your age? A Thirty one years.
Q What is your post office address? A Claremore, I. T.
Q Are you a citizen by blood of the Cherokee Nation? A Yes sir, I am.
Q For whom do you desire to make application for enrollment?
A For the following named persons on the 1896 Cherokee roll, their families and descendants:

    Ellen N. Martin #138 Illinois District;
    Gertrude Martin #1255 Illinois District;
    Edmond Martin #1256 Illinois District.
    Tandy W. Martin #1258 Illinois District.

Q Are there any other persons for whom you desire to make application for enrollment?
A I desire to apply for the following named persons on the 1880 Cherokee roll, their families and their descendants:

*(No names listed.)*

# Cherokee Intermarried White 1906
## Volume III

---

E. C. Bagwell, on oath states that as stenographer to the Commission to the Five Civilized Tribes, he correctly recorded the testimony and proceedings had in the above entitled cause, and that the foregoing is an accurate transcript of his stenographic notes thereof.

E.C. Bagwell

Subscribed and sworn to before me this December 9, 1902.

BC Jones<br>Notary Public.

◇◇◇◇◇

Cherokee 4764.

Department of the Interior,<br>Commission to the Five Civilized Tribes,<br>Muskogee, I. T., October 7, 1902.

In the matter of the application of Elizabeth E. Coker for the enrollment of herself as a citizen by intermarriage of the Cherokee Nation: she being sworn and examined by the Commission, testified as follows:

Q What is your name? A Elizabeth E. Coker.
Q What is your age at this time? A I will be sixty-four next month.
Q What is your postoffice? A Claremore.
Q Are you the same Elizabeth E. Coker who made application to this Commission for enrollment as an intermarried citizen on October 23, 1900? A Yes sir.
Q What is your husband's name? A Dempsey Coker.
Q Is he living or dead? A He has been dead over twenty years.
Q Was he a Cherokee by blood? A Yes sir.
Q When were you and your husband, Dempsey Coker, married? A Well, it has been about thirty-five years ago.
Q Where were you married, here in the Cherokee Nation? A No sir, we were married in the states, but we were readmitted.
Q Did you live with your husband, Dempsey Coker, as his wife from the time you were married until the time of his death? A Yes sir.
Q You and he never were separated during his lifetime? A No sir.
Q He was your first husband? A Yes sir.
Q Were you his first wife? A No, I was his second wife.
Q He was married before? A Yes sir.
Q Was that wife living or dead when you and he married? A She was dead.
Q After his death have you married since his death? A No sir.
Q You are still a widow and was single on the first day of September, 1902? A Yes sir.
Q Have you lived all the time in the Cherokee Nation since 1880 up to the present time? A Yes sir.
Q Never lived out of the nation since then? A No sir.

265

## Cherokee Intermarried White 1906
## Volume III

-----------------

The undersigned, being duly sworn, states that as stenographer to the Commission to the Five Civilized Tribes he correctly recorded the testimony and proceedings in this case, and that the foregoing is a true and complete transcript of his stenographic notes thereof.

E.G. Rothenberger

Subscribed and sworn to before me this 31st day of October, 1902.

BC Jones<br>Notary Public.

◇◇◇◇◇

C. F. B.   Cherokee 4764.

### DEPARTMENT OF THE INTERIOR,
### COMMISSION TO THE FIVE CIVILIZED TRIBES.
Muskogee, Indian Territory, January 7, 1907.

In the Matter of the Application for the Enrollment of Elizabeth E. Coker as a citizen by intermarriage of the Cherokee Nation.

Applicant appears in person.

APPEARANCES:

Cherokee Nation represented by
W. W. Hastings, Attorney.

Elizabeth Coker being first duly sworn by John E. Tidwell, Notary Public, testified as follows:

ON BEHALF OF COMMISSIONER.

Q What is your name?
A Elizabeth E. Coker.
Q What is your age?
A 70 last November.
Q What is your post office address?
A Claremore.
Q Did you formerly live at Choteau?
A I lived there six years with my daughter.
Q When did you leave there?
A Four years ago.
Q You are an applicant for enrollment as a citizen by intermarriage of the Cherokee Nation?
A Yes sir.
Q You have no Cherokee blood?
A No sir.

## Cherokee Intermarried White 1906
## Volume III

Q  Your only claim to the right to enrollment as a citizen by the Cherokee Nation is by virtue of your marriage to a citizen by blood of the Nation?
A  Yes sir.
Q  What is the name of the citizen through whom you claim that right?
A  Dempsie[sic] Coker.
Q  Was he a recognized citizen of the Cherokee Nation at the time you married him?
A  Yes sir; but we were in the States when we were married.
Q  Where were you married?
A  Out in Arkansas.
Q  In what year were you married.[sic]
A  I can't remember dates" this paper will show.
Q  This paper shows that you were married in 1867. Do you believe that is the date of your marriage?
A  Yes sir; I think it is.
Q  You say this marriage was solemnized in Arkansas?
A  Yes sir.
Q  How long did you live in Arkansas after your marriage to dempsie Coker?
A  We lived there one year.
Q  Was he your first husband?
A  Yes sir.
Q  You were not his first wife?
A  No sir.
Q  Was his former wife living or dead at the time you married him?
A  She was dead. They had lived here and they went out there in Arkansas and she died there; and then we married and came here.
Q  On your coming to the Cherokee Nation, was your husband recognized as a citizen of the Cherokee Nation or did he have to go before the authorities and be re-admitted?
A  He was re-admitted at Tahlequah not long after we came here.
Q  Almost immediately after your coming to the Cherokee Nation?
A  Yes sir; we came in February and he was re-admitted soon after that.
Q  From the date of your marriage to Dempsie Coker until the time of his death, did you continuously live together as husband and wife?
A  Yes sir.
Q  Have you resided in the Cherokee Nation from that time to the present time?
A  Yes sir.
Q  When did he die?
A  He has been dead 25 years next March.

The applicant, Elizabeth E. Coker is identified on the Cherokee authenticated tribal roll of 1880 at No. 693.

Q  Was your husband living in 1880?
A  Yes sir, I think he was. He was counsellor[sic] in November and I went with him to Tahlequah in November and he came home and died the next March.
Q  In what year was it he died?
A  It was 25 years ago; about 1882.

## Cherokee Intermarried White 1906
## Volume III

ON BEHALF OF CHEROKEE NATION.

Q How long did you live in Arkansas after you were married?
A We married in May, and the next February year we left there.
Q Then you came to the Cherokee Nation in February of '69?
A Yes, that's right.
Q Then how long after you moved to the Cherokee Nation was it until your husband was re-admitted to citizenship?
A Well, right away; inside of a month; I don't remember just when.

ON BEHALF OF COMMISSIONER.

Q Have you any marriage certificate showing your marriage to your husband Dempsey Coker?
A No, only one witness; my step-son.
Q Has he ever testified before the commissioner?
A I don't know. He has come here time and again. He lives at Nowata. His name is Lewis Coker.

---

The undersigned being first duly sworn, states that as stenographer to the Commission to the Five Civilized Tribes, she recorded the testimony taken in this case and that the foregoing is a full, true and correct copy of her stenographic notes thereof.

Myrtle Hill

Subscribed and sworn to before me this the 8th day of January, 1907.

John E. Tidwell
Notary Public.

◇◇◇◇◇

Koo,wee,skoo,wee Continued

Native Cherokees whose rights are Doubtful.

"14 Dempsy Coker & family) Decided in favor of Defendant & Children
March 30, 1871."

---

This is to certify that the ahdersigned[sic], being first duly sworn, states that as stenographer to the Commissioner to the Five Civilized Tribes, she made the above and foregoing copy, and that the same is a full, true and correct copy of record found on page 8, of "Docket of Doubtful Cases for Cherokee Citizenship tried in 1871."

# Cherokee Intermarried White 1906
## Volume III

Sarah Waters

Subscribed and sworn to before me this 16th day of January, 1907.

Chas E Webster<br>Notary Public.

◇◇◇◇◇

| | |
|---|---|
| Department of The Interior, | ) |
| | ) |
| Commissioner To Five Civilized Tribes. | ) |

The Hon. Tams Bixby,

    Commissioner.

In the Matter of the enrollment of Elizabeth Coker, Louis Coker of Nowata Indian Territory, of lawful age being sworn upon his oath states that he is a step-son of the applicant Elizabeth Coker, being a son by a former marriage of Dempsey Coker deceased, that he was present at the marriage of his Father and Elizabeth Sigmon, (Now Elizabeth Coker) that said marriage occurred in the month of May 1867, that the said Elizabeth Coker, and his Father Dempsey Coker continued to live together as man, and wife from, and after said marriage until the death of the said Dempsey Coker which occurred in March 1882.

Affiant further states that the said Elizabeth Coker has never re-married since the death of the said Dempsey Coker, Affiant says that he is 56 years of age and that his Post Office address is Nowata Indian Territory.

Lewis Coker

United States of America,
Indian Territory Northern
    District.

    Subscribed, and sworn to before me this 29<sup>th</sup> day of December 1906.

Ella *(Illegible)*<br>Notary Public.

My Commission expires, Nov-1-1910

◇◇◇◇◇

## Cherokee Intermarried White 1906
## Volume III

E.C.M.

Cherokee 4764.

DEPARTMENT OF THE INTERIOR,

COMMISSIONER TO THE FIVE CIVILIZED TRIBES.

In the matter of the application for the enrollment of ELIZABETH E. COKER as a citizen by intermarriage of the Cherokee Nation.

_D_E_C_I_S_I_O_N_ _

THE RECORDS OF THIS OFFICE SHOW: That on October 23rd, 1900, application was received by the Commission to the Five Civilized Tribes for the enrollment of Elizabeth E. Coker as a citizen by intermarriage of the Cherokee Nation. Further proceedings in the matter of said application were had at Muskogee, Indian Territory, October 7th, 1902 and January 7th, 1907.

THE EVIDENCE IN THIS CASE SHOWS: That the applicant herein, Elizabeth E. Coker, a white woman, was married in the State of Arkansas in May, 1867 to Dempsey Coker, deceased; that shortly after said marriage they removed to the Cherokee Nation where the said Dempsey Coker was admitted to citizenship as a citizen by blood of the Cherokee Nation by an Act of the "Daniels Court", dated March 30th, 1871; that said Dempsey Coker is identified on the Cherokee authenticated tribal roll of 1880, Cooweescoowee District No. 692 as a native Cherokee marked "Dead". It is further shown that from the time of said marriage the said Dempsey Coker and Elizabeth E. Coker resided together as husband and wife and continuously lived in the Cherokee Nation from the time of their removal there until the death of said Dempsey Coker, which occurred about 1882; that from the time of the death of said Dempsey Coker the said Elizabeth E. Coker remained unmarried and continuously lived in the Cherokee Nation up to and including September 1st, 1902. Said applicant is identified on the Cherokee authenticated tribal roll of 1880 and the Cherokee census roll of 1896 as an intermarried citizen of the Cherokee Nation.

IT IS, THEREFORE, ORDERED AND ADJUDGED: That in accordance with the decision of the Supreme Court of the United States, dated November 5, 1906, in the cases of Daniel Red Bird et al. vs. the United States, Nos. 125, 126 the said applicant, Elizabeth E. Coker is entitled, under the provisions of Section Twenty-one of the Act of Congress approved June 28th, 1898 (30 Stats. 495), to enrollment as a citizen by intermarriage of the Cherokee Nation, and her application for enrollment as such is accordingly granted.

Tams Bixby
Commissioner.

Dated at Muskogee, Indian Territory,
this    JAN 21 1907

## Cherokee Intermarried White 1906
## Volume III

| COUNTY COURT. | PROBATE COURT. | CHANCERY COURT. | CIRCUIT COURT. |
|---|---|---|---|
| First Monday in January, April, July and October. | First Monday in February, May, August and November. | Fourth Monday in April and October. | Sixth Monday after the First Monday in January and July of each year. |

OFFICE OF ..

**J. W. SMITH, Clerk**

Of the Circuit, Chancery, County and Probate Courts and Recorder of Marion County.

YELLVILLE, ARKANSAS, Nov 30$^{th}$ 190 6

Mr. Lewis Coker

Nowata, Ind. Ter

Dear Sir: The Records of Marion County was destroyed by fire in August 1878. Therefore I can not give you the information you wish.

Yours truly

J Q Smith Clerk.

◇◇◇◇◇

Muskogee, Indian Territory, December 15, 1906

Elizabeth Coker,
    Claremore, Indian Territory.

Dear Madam:

Replying to your letter of December 11, 1906, in reference to your right to enrollment as a citizen by intermarriage of the Cherokee Nation, and in which you state you were married prior to 1875, you are advised that the United States Supreme Court in its decision of November 5, 1906, held that white persons who intermarried according to Cherokee law with Cherokee citizens prior to November 1, 1875, are entitled to enrollment as citizens by intermarriage of the Cherokee Nation.

If you claim to be entitled to enrollment under the Court's decision you will be permitted to appear before the Commissioner at Muskogee, Indian Territory at any time within the near future, and submit such testimony as you desire, relative to your marriage to your Cherokee husband, by reason of your marriage to whom you claim the right to enrollment as a citizen by intermarriage of the Cherokee Nation, and as to the date of your marriage.

The Act of Congress approved April 26, 1906 provides that the Secretary of the Interior shall have no jurisdiction to approve the enrollment of any person as a citizen of

# Cherokee Intermarried White 1906
## Volume III

the Cherokee Nation, after March 4, 1907, and the matter of your enrollment should, therefore, receive your immediate attention.

Respectfully,

L M B                                         Commissioner

◇◇◇◇◇

Cherokee
4764

Muskogee, Indian Territory, January 21, 1907.

W. W. Hastings,
    Attorney for the Cherokee Nation,
        Muskogee, Indian Territory.

Dear Sir:

    There is enclosed herewith a copy of the decision of the Commissioner to the Five Civilized Tribes, dated January 21, 1907, granting the application of Elizabeth E. Coker as a citizen by intermarriage of the Cherokee Nation.

Respectfully,

Encl. H-1                                         Commissioner.
JMH

◇◇◇◇◇

Cherokee 1764

| W.W. HASTINGS, ATTORNEY. | OFFICE OF | H.M. VANCE, SECRETARY. |
|---|---|---|

**Attorney for the Cherokee Nation,**
Muskogee, I. T.    January 21, 1907.

The Commissioner to the Five Civilized Tribes,
    Muskogee, Indian Territory.

Sir:

    Receipt is acknowledged of the testimony and of your decision enrolling Elizabeth E. Coker as a citizen by intermarriage of the Cherokee Nation. Time for protesting said decision is waived and I consent that said person may be placed upon the schedule immediately.

Respectfully,
W. W. Hastings
Attorney for the Cherokee Nation.

# Cherokee Intermarried White 1906
# Volume III

Cherokee 4764

Muskogee, Indian Territory, January 24, 1907.

Elizabeth E. Coker,
    Choteau, Indian Territory.

Dear Madam:

    There is enclosed herewith a copy of the decision of the Commissioner to the Five Civilized Tribes, dated January 21, 1907, granting the application for your enrollment as a citizen by intermarriage of the Cherokee Nation.

    You will be advised when your name has been placed upon a schedule of citizens of the Cherokee Nation and approved by the Secretary of the Interior.

                      Respectfully,

Encl. H-8                                                           Commissioner.
JMH

---

**Cher IW 97**
**Trans from Cher 4774  3-16-07**

                                                                                        E.C.M.

## DEPARTMENT OF THE INTERIOR,

### COMMISSIONER TO THE FIVE CIVILIZED TRIBES.

In the matter of the application for the enrollment of

                JOHN W. HOLLAND

As a citizen by intermarriage of the Cherokee Nation.

                CHEROKEE NO. 4774.

## Cherokee Intermarried White 1906
## Volume III

DEPARTMENT OF THE INTERIOR.
COMMISSION TO THE FIVE CIVILIZED TRIBES.
CLAREMORE, I.T., OCTOBER 23rd, 1900.

IN THE MATTER OF THE APPLICATION OF John W. Holland for the enrollment of himself, his wife and child as citizens of the Cherokee Nation, and he being sworn and examined by Commissioner, C. R. Breckinridge, testified as follows:

Q What is your full name? A John W. Holland.
Q How old are you? A Sixty five.
Q What is your Postoffice? A Foyil.
Q In what district do you live; Cooweescoowee? A Yes sir.
Q Who is it you want to have put on the rolls: Yourself and family?
A Myself, wife and one child.
Q Are you a Cherokee by blood? A No sir.
Q White man? A Yes sir.
Q What is your wife; Cherokee? A Yes sir.
Q How long have you lived in the Cherokee Nation? A I came here in 1871.
Q Are you on the roll of 1880? A I think so.
Q Were you married to your present wife before 1880? A Yes sir. I have been married twice to the same woman: I was married back in Georgia, and when I came to the Cherokee Nation in 1871 I was re-married to the same woman.
Q You have lived here ever since you came in 1871? A Yes sir.
Q Now give me the name of your wife? A Mary Elviry[sic] Holland.
Q How old is she? A Sixty four.
Q You and your wife have lived together since 1871, here in the Cherokee Nation?
A Yes sir.
Q Now give me the name of your child? A William H. Holland.
Q How old is that child? A Eighteen.
Q He is living, is he, at this time? A Yes sir.
(1880 Roll, Page 370, #578, J. W. Holland, Flint District)
(1880 Roll, Page 370, #579, M. E. Halland[sic], Flint District)
(1896 Roll, Page 713, #45, John W. Holland, Flint District)
(1896 Roll, Page 672, #893, Mary E. Holland, Flint District)
(1896 Roll, Page 672, #894, William H. Holland, Flint District)

The applicant applies for the enrollment of himself, his wife and one child: He is identified on the rolls of 1880 and 1896, as an adopted white: He has continued to live in the Cherokee Nation with his Cherokee wife since 1871; and he will be listed now for enrollment as a Cherokee by intermarriage.

His wife is identified on the rolls of 1880 and 1896, as a native Cherokee: She has lived in the Cherokee Nation since 1871, and she will be listed for enrollment as a Cherokee by blood.

The child, William H. Holland is identified on the roll of 1896: He is living now, and will be listed for enrollment as a Cherokee by blood.

# Cherokee Intermarried White 1906
## Volume III

------------------------------

The undersigned, being sworn, states that as stenographer to the Commission to the Five Civilized Tribes, he correctly recorded the testimony and proceedings in this case, and that the foregoing is a true and complete transcript of his stenographic notes thereof.

R R Cravens

Subscribed and sworn to before
me this 23rd day of October, 1900.

C R Breckinridge
COMMISSIONER.

◇◇◇◇◇

Card #4774

## DEPARTMENT OF THE INTERIOR
## COMMISSION TO THE FIVE CIVILIZED TRIBES
## MUSKOGEE, I.T., OCTOBER 15TH, 1902.

In the matter of the application of John W. Holland for the enrollment of himself as an intermarried citizen, and for the enrollment of his wife, Mary E., and child, William H., as citizens by blood of the Cherokee Nation.

John W. Holland, being first duly sworn, under examination by the Commission, testified as follows:

Q What is your name? A John W. Holland.
Q How old are you? A What did you say?
Q How old are you? A If I live to see the 19th of October will be 67.
Q 67? A Yes sir.
Q What is your postoffice? A Foyil.
Q You are a white man are you? A Yes sir.
Q Is your name on the roll of 1880 as an adopted citizen? A I think so
Q What is your wife's name? A Mary E.
Q Have you and your wife lived together in the Cherokee Nation ever since 1880? A Yes sir.
Q Never been separated? A No sir.
Q Living together yet? A Yes sir.
Q She is the wife through whom you claim your citizenship? A Yes sir.
Q How many children have you by your wife, Mary? A I have one child under age.
Q One child under age? A Yes.
Q Son, William H.? A Yes.
Q Living at home with you? A He is at Tahlequah at school.
Q Your wife is living isnt[sic] she? A Yes sir.

## Cherokee Intermarried White 1906
## Volume III

Cora Moore, being duly sworn first, states that as stenographer to the Commission to the Five Civilized Tribes she reported in full the testimony and proceedings in this case and that the foregoing is a true and complete transcript of his stenographic notes thereof.

Cora Moore

Subscribed and sworn to before me this 24 day of October, 1902.

BC Jones
NOTARY PUBLIC

◇◇◇◇◇

No. 4774

DEPARTMENT OF THE INTERIOR
COMMISSIONER TO THE FIVE CIVILIZED TRIBES
Muskogee, Indian Territory
January 4, 1907

In the matter of the application of John W. Holland for enrollment as a citizen of the Cherokee Nation by intermarriage.

The applicant being first duly sworn, testified as follows

Q What is your name? A Holland
Q Full name please? A John W. Holland
Q How old are you? A I am 71
Q What is your Postoffice address? A Foyil
Q Do you claim to be a citizen by intermarriage of the Cherokee Nation? A Yes sir
Q Through whom do you claim your intermarried right?
A Through Mary Elvira Ward
Q When were you married to Mary Elvira Ward.[sic]
A I was married to her twice. I was married back east and then when we come to the Territory in '71 I was married sometime during that year.
Q Did you get a license.[sic] A I got a license from Warren Adair. I lived in Flint District.
Q Have you got that license? A No sir--we didn't get any license they said there was no necessity for that. He would just put it on the record.
Q What time of the year were you married? A I don't remember.
Q Winter or Summer? A Either in the Spring or Fall--ut[sic] was tolerably warm weather

Book B Marriage Records for Flint District, on page 118 shows that a license was granted the applicant herein to marry Mary E. Hollen[sic] ("formerly Mrs. Mary E. Ward" on July 18 1871 by James W. Adair Clerk of Flint District, Cherokee

## Cherokee Intermarried White 1906
## Volume III

Nation and that the applicant and his wife were married on said date under said license by T.B. Ruble an ordained minister of the gospel.

Q Were you ever married to any one prior to your marriage to Mary E. Ward? A No sir.
Q Was she ever married prior to her marriage with you? A No sir.
Q Have you lived together continuously as husband and wife since your marriage in 1871 in the Flint District? A Yes sir

The applicant is identified on the 1880 Cherokee roll opposite No. 578. His wife through whom he claims right to enrollment is identified on said roll opposite No. 579. She is also identified on the final roll of citizens by blood of the Cherokee Nation opposite No. 11433.

Witness excused

Gertrude Hanna, being duly sworn, states that she as stenographer to the Commissioner to the Five Civilized Tribes reported the proceedings had in the above numbered case and that the above and foregoing is a true and correct transcript of her stenographic notes taken therein.

Gertrude Hanna

Subscribed and sworn to before me this 5 day of January, 1907

Chas E Webster
Notary Public

E.C.M.                                                          Cherokee 4774.

DEPARTMENT OF THE INTERIOR,

COMMISSIONER TO THE FIVE CIVILIZED TRIBES.

In the matter of the application for the enrollment of JOHN W. HOLLAND as a citizen by intermarriage of the Cherokee Nation.

_D_E_C_I_S_I_O_N_

THE RECORDS OF THIS OFFICE SHOW: That on October 23rd, 1900, application was received by the Commission to the Five Civilized Tribes for the enrollment of John W. Holland as a citizen by intermarriage of the Cherokee Nation. Further proceedings in the matter of said application were had at Muskogee, Indian Territory, October 15th, 1902 and January 4th, 1907.

## Cherokee Intermarried White 1906
## Volume III

THE EVIDENCE IN THIS CASE SHOWS: That the applicant herein, John W. Holland. a white man, was married in accordance with Cherokee law on July 18th, 1871 to his wife, Mary E. Holland, nee Ward, who was at the time of said marriage a recognized citizen by blood of the Cherokee Nation, who was identified on the Cherokee authenticated tribal roll of 1880, Flint District No. 579 as an adopted Cherokee and whose name is included in the approved partial roll of citizens by blood of the Cherokee Nation opposite No. 11433. It is further shown that from the time of said marriage the said John W. Holland and Mary E. Holland resided together as husband and wife and continuously lived in the Cherokee Nation up to and including September 1st, 1902. Said applicant is identified on the Cherokee authenticated tribal roll of 1880 and the Cherokee census roll of 1896 as an intermarried citizen of the Cherokee Nation.

IT IS, THEREFORE, ORDERED AND ADJUDGED: That in accordance with the decision of the Supreme Court of the United States, dated November 5, 1906, in the cases of Daniel Red Bird et al. vs. the United States, Nos. 125, 126, 127 and 128, the said applicant, John W. Holland is entitled, under the provisions of Section Twenty-one of the Act of Congress approved June 28th, 1898 (30 Stats., 495), to enrollment as a citizen by intermarriage of the Cherokee Nation, and his application for enrollment as such is accordingly granted.

Tams Bixby<br>Commissioner.

Dated at Muskogee, Indian Territory,
this    JAN 21 1907

◇◇◇◇◇

Cherokee 4774

Muskogee, Indian Territory, January 21, 1907.

W. W. Hastings,
    Attorney for the Cherokee Nation,
        Muskogee, Indian Territory.

Dear Sir:

    There is enclosed herewith copy of the decision of the Commissioner to the Five Civilized Tribes, dated January 21, 1907, granting the application for the enrollment of John W. Holland as a citizen by intermarriage of the Cherokee Nation.

Respectfully,

Enc I-26                                             Commissioner.

RPI

# Cherokee Intermarried White 1906
## Volume III

Cherokee 4774    W.W. HASTINGS. ATTORNEY.    OFFICE OF    H.M. VANCE. SECRETARY.

**Attorney for the Cherokee Nation,**

MUSKOGEE, I. T.    January 21, 1907.

The Commissioner to the Five Civilized Tribes,
     Muskogee, Indian Territory.

Sir:

     Receipt is acknowledged of the testimony and of your decision enrolling John W. Holland as a citizen by intermarriage of the Cherokee Nation. Time for protesting said decision is waived and I consent that said person may be placed upon the schedule immediately.

                           Respectfully,
                           W. W. Hastings
                           Attorney for the Cherokee Nation.

◇◇◇◇◇

Cherokee 4774

                           Muskogee, Indian Territory, January 23, 1907.

John W. Holland,
     Foyil, Indian Territory.

Dear Sir:

     There is enclosed herewith copy of the decision of the Commissioner to the Five Civilized Tribes, dated January 21, 1907, granting the application for your enrollment as a citizen by intermarriage of the Cherokee Nation.

     You will be advised when your name has been placed upon a schedule of citizens of the Cherokee Nation and approved by the Secretary of the Interior.

                           Respectfully,

Enc I-92                                            Commissioner.

RPI

---

**Cher IW 98**
**Trans from Cher 4897 3-16-07**

◇◇◇◇◇

## Cherokee Intermarried White 1906
## Volume III

C.E.W.

### DEPARTMENT OF THE INTERIOR,

### COMMISSIONER TO THE FIVE CIVILIZED TRIBES.

---

In the matter of the application for the enrollment of

JOSEPH A. DENBO

as a citizen by intermarriage of the Cherokee Nation.

---

CHEROKEE 4897

◇◇◇◇◇

Department of the Interior,
Commission to the Five Civilized Tribes,
Claremore, I.T., October 24, 1900.

In the matter of the application of Letitia Denbo for the enrollment of herself, husband and children as Cherokee citizens; being sworn and examined by Commissioner Breckinridge she testified as follows:

Q What is your full name? A Letitia Denbo.
Q How old are you? A 57
Q What is your post-office? A Catoosa.
Q Do you live in Cooweescoowee District? A Yes sir.
Q Who is it you want to have put on the roll? A Myself and family, I have three minor children.
Q And husband? A Yes sir.
Q You want to apply then for yourself, husband and three minor children? A Well, if it is necessary for me to put my husband down I can put him down; I didn't know but he would have to apply for himself, he is a white man. We were married in 1871.
Com'r You can apply for him if you like.
Q Are you a Cherokee by blood? A Yes sir.
Q Is your husband a Cherokee by blood? A No sir, he is a white man.
Q How long have you lived in the Cherokee Nation? A 57 years.
Q All your life? A All but during the time of the War.
Q Give me the name of your father? A Leroy Keys.
Q Is he dead or alive? A Dead.
Q Give me the name of your mother? A Jane.
Q Is she dead? A Yes sir.
Q When were you married? A 1871.

# Cherokee Intermarried White 1906
## Volume III

Q  Have you been married more than once? A  Yes sir, twice.
Q  Was your first marriage in 1871? A  No sir. My first marriage was in 1860.
Q  To whom were you married in 1871? A  Joseph A. Denbo.
Q  He is the husband you are living with now? A  Ye sir.
Q  Your first marriage was to whom? A  Mitchell Harlin.
Q  Is he dead or alive? A  Dead.
Q  Did he die before you married Joseph Denbo? A  Yes sir.
Q  When did he die? A  Died in 1862.
Q  Now the full name of your present husband is Joseph A. Denbo? A  Yes sir.
Q  How old is he? A  56
Q  Was he ever married except to you? A  Yes sir.
Q  Was his former wife dead when he married you? A  No, he was divorced.
Q  But he is on the roll of 1880, isn't he? A  Yes sir.
Q  Now give me the names of your three minor children? A  Robert Leroy Denbo.
Q  How old is that child? A  20
Q  Give me the name of the next child? A  Oce Denbo.
Q  No middle name? A  No sir.
Q  How old is he? A  18
Q  Give me the name of the next child? A  Belle Cleveland.
Q  How old is she? A  15
Q  Are these children all living now? A  Yes sir.
1880 roll page 245 #756 Lettia Denboe[sic] Delaware Dist; native Cherokee;
1880 roll page 245 #755 Joseph Denboe Delaware Dist, adopted white;
1896 roll page 150 #1525 Lettia Denbo Cooweescoowee Dist;
1896 roll page 302 #317 Joseph Denbo         "
1896 roll page 150 #1526 Robert L. Denbo      "
1896 roll page 150 #1527 Osie Denbo           "
1896 roll page 150 #1528 Belle Denbo          "
Q  Your husband has been living with you ever since you and he were married?
A  Yes sir.

Com'r Breckinridge: The applicant applies for the enrollment of herself, her husband and three children; she is identified on the rolls of 1880 and 1896 as a native Cherokee; she has lived in the Cherokee Nation all her life, and she will be listed for enrollment as a Cherokee by blood;

Her husband is identified with her on the roll of 1880 and 1896; he has lived with her ever since his enrollment in 1880, and he will be listed for enrollment as a Cherokee by intermarriage;

The three children named in the testimony are identified with their parents on the roll of 1896; they are all minors, are living at this time and will be listed for enrollment as Cherokees by blood

M.D. Green, being first duly sworn, states that as stenographer to the Commission to the Five Civilized Tribes he correctly recorded the testimony and proceedings in this case and that the foregoing is a true and complete transcript of his stenographic notes thereof.

# Cherokee Intermarried White 1906
# Volume III

MD Green

Subscribed and sworn to before me this 25th day of October 1900.

CR Breckinridge

Commissioner.

◇◇◇◇◇

DEPARTMENT OF THE INTERIOR.
Commission to the Five Civilized Tribes.
Muskogee, Indian Territory, October 9th, 1902

In the matter of the application of Joseph A. Denbo for the enrollment of himself as a citizen by intermarriage of the Cherokee Nation and for the enrollment of his wife, Letitia V. Denbo; his children, Robert L. and Oce Denbo and Belle C. Daugherty, and his grand daughter, Lou T. Daugherty, as citizens by blood of the Cherokee Nation.

Supplemental to #4897.

JOSEPH A. DENBO, being duly sworn, testified as follows:--
Examination by the Commission.

Q. State your full name? A. Joseph A. Denbo.
Q. How old are you? A. 58.
Q. What is your post office? A. Catoosa.
Q. You are a white man, are you? A. Yes, sir.
Q. Claiming as an intermarried citizen? A. Yes, sir.
Q. What is the name of the wife through whom you claim citizenship?
A. Letitia V. Denbo.
Q. How did you enroll her? A. Letitia V.
Q. How do you want her enrolled? A. Letitia V.
Q. Is she a Cherokee by blood? A. Yes, sir.
Q. You have been living in the Cherokee Nation ever since 1880[sic]? A. Yes, sir.
Q. When did you marry her? A. 15th day of December, 1871.
Q. Have you and your wife been living together in the Cherokee Nation ever since 1880?
A. Yes, sir.
Q. Never been separated? A. No, sir.
Q. You were living together on the first day of last September[sic] A. Yes, sir.
Q. How many children have you? A. Six.
Q. How many living at home with you? A. None.
Q. None? No. All married off.
Q. Who is Lou T. Daugherty? A. That is my youngest daughter.
Q. That is your grand daughter? A. Yes, that is my grandchild.
Q. That is a child of Belle? A. Yes, sir.

## Cherokee Intermarried White 1906
## Volume III

Q. Belle and her child are living in the Cherokee Nation? A. Yes, sir.
Q. You say Robert L. is married? A. Yes, sir.
Q. And Oce is married? A. Yes, sir; he is married too.
Q. They are living in the Cherokee Nation? A. Yes, sir.

---

Jesse O. Carr, being first duly sworn, states that as stenographer to the Commission to the Five Civilized Tribes he reported the above entitled case and that the foregoing is a true and complete transcript of his stenographic notes thereof.

Jesse O. Carr

Subscribed and sworn to before me this 8<sup>th</sup> day of December, 1902.

BC Jones<br>Notary Public.

◇◇◇◇◇

### DEPARTMENT OF THE INTERIOR
### COMMISSIONER TO THE FIVE CIVILIZED TRIBES
### MUSKOGEE, IND. TER.
### JAN. 4 1907

### IN THE MATTER OF THE APPLICATION FOR THE ENROLLMENT AS A CITIZEN BY INTERMARRIAGE OF THE CHEROKEE NATION OF JOSEPH A. DENBO.

CENSUS CARE NO. 4897.

JOSEPH A. DENBO BEING FIRST DULY SWORN TESTIFIED AS FOLLOWS:

EXAMINATION BY THE COMMISSIONER:

Q What is your name.[sic] A Joseph A. Denbo.
Q How old are you.[sic] A Sixty two.
Q What is your post office address. A Catoosa.
Q Do you claim to be a citizen of the Cherokee Nation by intermarriage. A Yes sir.
Q Thru whom do you claim your intermarried rights[sic] A My wife
Q What is her name. A Letitia B[sic]. Denbo.
Q When was[sic] you married to Letitia B. Denbo. A 15th of December 1871.
Q Were you ever married before you married Letitia B. Denbo. A Yes
Q To whom. A I married in Indianna[sic] before I ever come to this country.
Q What was your first wife's name. A Irena Smith.
Q Was she a citizen or non citizen. A Non citizen.

## Cherokee Intermarried White 1906
## Volume III

Q Was she living or dead. A At the time I married this woman I was divorced; she's living yet I reckon.
Q Have you got a copy of your divorce. A No sir.

It will be necessary that you supply this office with evidence of your divorce from your former wife.

Q Was your present wife ever married before you married her A Yes sir.
Q What was her husband's name. A A man named Harlin
Q Was he living or dead at the time you married her[sic] A He was dead.
Q She had no living husband at the time you married her. A No sir.
Q Where were you married to your present wife. A Fort Gibson.
Q Cherokee Nation. A Cherokee Nation.
Q Married under the Cherokee laws. A Yes sir.
Q Have you got your license. A No sir
Q Where is your license[sic]
A I never did receive my licnense[sic]; Albert Barnes was clerk at Ft. Gibson; I got my license; took the signers there and the judge married us and he told me to call at the clerk's office and get my marriage certificate and I never did do it.
Q Is Letitia B[sic]. Denbo living at this time. A No sir.
Q Did you live with Letitia Denbo continuously from the date of your marriage in 1871 up until the time of her death last April. A Yes sir.
Q Living in the Cherokee Nation. A Yes sir.
Q Were you ever separated during your married life. A No sir

Applicant is identified on the 1880 Cherokee Roll Delaware District opposite No. 755; his wife thru whom he claims his right to enrollment is identified on said roll in said district opposite No. 756; she is also identified on the final roll of citizens by blood of the Cherokee Nation opposite No. 11688.

Q What district, do you know, were you married in.
A Fort Gibson; Illinois District.

Book "A" of the marriage register of Illinois District page twentyfive shows that marriage license was issued to Joseph A. Denbon[sic] to marry Leutisia[sic] Keys by Albert Barns[sic] Clerk of the Illinois District of the Cherokee Nation on hte[sic] 13th day of December 1871 and that said parties were married on December 14 1871 by Tim N. Walker, judge.

Q Are you the Joseph A. Denbon referred to in the certificate shown on page 25 of the book I have just read. A Yes sir.
Q You received your license from Albert Barns. A Yes sir
Q And were married by Judge Tim Walker. A Yes sir

ooOoo

# Cherokee Intermarried White 1906
## Volume III

Clara Mitchell Wood being first duly sworn upon her oath states that as stenographer for the Commissioner to the Five Civilized Tribes she reported the above and foregoing proceedings and that this is a correct transcript of her stenographic notes.

Clara Mitchell Wood

Subscribed and sworn to before me this 8th day of January 1907.

B.P. Rasmus
Notary Public.

◇◇◇◇◇

COPY

UNITED STATES OF AMERICA )
   INDIAN TERRITORY        ) SS
NORTHERN JUDICIAL DISTRICT )

George W. Tyner, being by me first duly sworn, deposes and says that he was present on the 15th day of December 1871 and witnessed the marriage of Joseph A. Denbo, and Letitia Harlin, (nee Keys) said marriage was solemnized by Judge Tim Walker.

(Singed[sic]) George W. Tyner

Subscribed and sworn to before me this to before me this 3rd. day of Jan'y 1907.

(Singed) Allen Holt
(SEAL)                           Notary Public.
My commission expires April 25th. 1909.

The undersigned being first duly sworn states that as stenographer to the Commissioner to the Five Civilized Tribes she made the above copy and that the same is a true and correct copy of the original affidavit of George W. Tyner.

Lola W. Champlin

Subscribed and sworn to before me this 17 day of January 1907.

Chas E Webster
Notary public.

◇◇◇◇◇

## Cherokee Intermarried White 1906
## Volume III

*(The below typed as given.)*

4897

COPY

STATE OF INDIANA, Crawford, County, ss:

| | |
|---|---|
| Ireinia Denbo, ) | |
| ) | Crawford-- Circuit Court, |
| Divorce ) | |
| ) | May, 1870. Term, 10 189--- |
| Joseph A. Denbo ) | |

BE IT REMEMBERED, That on the 24, day of May 1870 the same being the 2nd. judicial day of the May, 1870 Term, 189---, of the Crawford, Circuit Court, begun, held and continued at the Court House in Leavenworth, commencing on Monday, the 23,rd. day of May 1870, before the Honorable David T. Laird, Judge of said Court, the following proceedings were had in the above entitled cause, towit;

Now come the parties herein by their Attorneys and the defendant files his answer and cross complaimt and the plaintiff fils her reply in the denial of the cross complaint and this cause coming on for trial on motion is submitted to the court without a jury and the proffs and allegatoions of the parties be heard and the court being sufficiently advised in the premises for the plaintiff and against the defendant in his cross complaint and the plaimtiff is entitled to a divorce and on notion the court further finds that said plaintiff is entitled to the care and custody of the child the issue of the marriage of said parties and allmony in the sum of $100.

And on motion it is thereupon ordered adjudged and decreed by the court that the bonds of matrimony subsisting between said parties be fully completely finially and forever dissolved and annulled it is on motion further ordered and adjudged by the court that said plaintiff have custody controll and guardianship of the children Charles H. Denbo mentioned in the complaint herein free from any interference of the defendant,

It is further ordered and adjudged by the court that said plaintiff recover of said defendant as and for her reasonable alimony the sum of One hundred Dollars, and the costs of this suit.

David T. Laird, Judge.

# Cherokee Intermarried White 1906
## Volume III

STATE OF INDIANA, Crawford County, ss:

I, William L. Gregory, Clerk of the Circuit Court of the County of Crawford, in the State of Indiana, do hereby certify that the foregoing is a true and complete copy of the proceedings and judgment of said Court in the above entitled cause, on the day and year first aforesaid, as appears on the records in my office, of which records I am the legal custodian.

IN TESTIMONY WHEREOF, I hereunto subscribe my name and hereto affix the seal of said Circuit Court, at my office in English, the 8th. day of January 1907.

Signed. William L. Gregory.

(SEAL) Clerk of the Circuit Court

The undersigned being first duly sworn states that as stenographer to the Commissioner to the Five Civilized Tribes, she made the above and foregoing copy and that the same is a true and correct copy of the original divorce now on file in this office.

Lola M Champlin

Subscribed and sworn to before me this 17 day of January 1907.

Chas E Webster<br>notary public.

C.E.W. Cherokee 4897.

## DEPARTMENT OF THE INTERIOR,

## COMMISSIONER TO THE FIVE CIVILIZED TRIBES.

------------------------

In the matter of the application for the enrollment of Joseph A. Denbo, as a citizen by intermarriage of the Cherokee Nation.

## D E C I S I O N

THE RECORDS OF THIS OFFICE SHOW: That at Claremore, Indian Territory, October 24, 1900, application was received by the Commission to the Five Civilized Tribes for the enrollment of Joseph A. Denbo, as a citizen by intermarriage of the Cherokee Nation. Further proceedings in the matter of said application were had at Muskogee, Indian Territory, October 9, 1902, and January 4, 1907.

## Cherokee Intermarried White 1906
## Volume III

THE EVIDENCE IN THIS CASE SHOWS: That the applicant herein, Joseph A. Denbo, a white man, married in accordance with Cherokee law December 14, 1871 to one Letitia V. Denbo, nee Keys, who was at the time of said marriage a recognized citizen by blood of the Cherokee Nation, and who is identified on the Cherokee authenticated tribal roll of 1880, Delaware District, page 245, number 756, as a native Cherokee; that after said marriage the said Joseph A. Denbo and Letitia V. Denbo resided together as husband and wife and have continuously lived in the Cherokee Nation until the death of the said Letitia V. Denbo, which occurred in April 1906. Said Joseph A. Denbo is identified on the Cherokee authenticated tribal roll of 1880, and the Cherokee census roll of 1896 as an intermarried citizen of the Cherokee Nation.

IT IS, THEREFORE, ORDERED AND ADJUDGED: That in accordance with the decision of the Supreme Court of the United States, dated November 5, 1906, in the cases of Daniel Red Bird, et al., vs. the United States, Nos. 125, 126, 127 and 128, the said applicant Joseph A. Denbo is entitled, under the provision of Section 21 of the Act of Congress approved June 28, 1898, (30 Stat., 495), to enrollment, as a citizen by intermarriage of the Cherokee Nation, and his application for enrollment as such is accordingly granted.

Tams Bixby
Commissioner.

Dated at Muskogee, Indian Territory,
this      JAN 21 1907

◇◇◇◇◇

Cherokee 4897

Muskogee, Indian Territory, January 21, 1907.

W. W. Hastings,
    Attorney for the Cherokee Nation,
        Muskogee, Indian Territory.

Dear Sir:

There is enclosed herewith copy of the decision of the Commissioner to the Five Civilized Tribes, dated January 21, 1907, granting the application for the enrollment of Joseph A. Denbo as a citizen by intermarriage of the Cherokee Nation.

Respectfully,

Enc I-46

Commissioner.

RPI

◇◇◇◇◇

## Cherokee Intermarried White 1906
## Volume III

Cherokee 4897

W.W. HASTINGS.
ATTORNEY.

OFFICE OF

H.M. VANCE.
SECRETARY.

**Attorney for the Cherokee Nation,**

MUSKOGEE, I. T.   January 21, 1907.

The Commissioner to the Five Civilized Tribes,
    Muskogee, Indian Territory.

Sir:

    Receipt is acknowledged of the testimony and of your decision enrolling Joseph A. Denbo as a citizen by intermarriage of the Cherokee Nation. Time for protesting said decision is waived and I consent that said person may be placed upon the schedule immediately.

                      Respectfully,
                            W. W. Hastings
                            Attorney for the Cherokee Nation.

◇◇◇◇◇

Cherokee 4897

                      Muskogee, Indian Territory, January 24, 1907.

Joseph A. Denbo,
    Catoosa, Indian Territory.

Dear Sir:

    There is enclosed herewith copy of the decision of the Commissioner to the Five Civilized Tribes, dated January 21, 1907, granting the application for your enrollment as a citizen by intermarriage of the Cherokee Nation.

    You will be advised when your name has been placed upon a schedule of citizens of the Cherokee Nation and approved by the Secretary of the Interior.

                      Respectfully,

Enc I-97                                                       Commissioner.

RPI

---

**Cher IW 99**
**Trans from Cher 4992 3-16-07**

◇◇◇◇◇

# Cherokee Intermarried White 1906
## Volume III

E.C.M.

## DEPARTMENT OF THE INTERIOR,

## COMMISSIONER TO THE FIVE CIVILIZED TRIBES.

---

In the matter of the application for the enrollment of

### JOSEPH ROLLENS

As a citizen by intermarriage of the Cherokee Nation.

---

CHEROKEE NO. 4992.

◇◇◇◇◇

Department of the Interior.
Commission to the Five Civilized Tribes.
Claremore, I. T., October 27, 1900.

Q Give me your full name? A Joseph Rollens.
Q How old are you? A 49.
Q What is your postoffice? A Claremore.
Q Do you live in Cooweescoowee district? A Yes sir.
Q Do you want to enroll yourself and family? A Yes sir.
Q Have you a wife? A Yes sir.
Q How many children have you? A Not any.
Q Just you and your wife? A Yes sir.
Q Are you a Cherokee by blood? A No sir.
Q Your wife's a Cherokee? A Yes sir.
Q Let me see your marriage license and certificate. A Haven't got it.
Q Give me your wife's name? A Elmina.
Q How old is she? A She's 49.
Q She's on the roll of '80, is she? A Yes sir.
Q She's a Cherokee by blood? A Yes sir.
Q Has she lived here all her life? A All her life.
Q Give me the name of her father. A Larkin Beavertt[sic].
Q He's dead is he? A Yes sir.
Q Give me her mother's name? A Charlotte.
Q Is she alive? A She's living.
Q Have you lived in the Cherokee Nation with your wife ever since your enrollment in 1880? A Yes sir.

1880 roll: page 167, #2471, Joe Roland[sic], Cooweescoowee.
1880 roll: page 167, #2472, Elmina Roland, Cooweescoowee.

## Cherokee Intermarried White 1906
## Volume III

1896 roll: page 321, #832, Joseph Rolland, Cooweescoowee.
1896 roll: page 238, #3917, Elmina Rolland, Cooweescoowee.
Commissioner Breckinridge-
    The applicant applies for the enrollment of himself and his wife: he is identified with his wife on the rolls of 1880 and 1896 and he has continued to live with her and in the Cherokee Nation ever since his enrollment in 1880, and he will be listed now for enrollment as a Cherokee by intermarriage. His wife is identified on the rolls of 1880 and 1896 as a native Cherokee; she has lived in the Cherokee Nation all her life, and she will be listed for enrollment as a Cherokee by blood.

    E. G. Rothenberger, being duly sworn, states that as stenographer to the Commission to the Five Civilized Tribes, he reported in full all proceedings in the above case, and that the foregoing is a true and complete translation of his stenographic notes in said case.

                                      E.G. Rothenberger

Subscribed and sworn to before me this 17th day of October, 1900.

                                                      MD Green
                                                      Notary Public.

◇◇◇◇◇

### DEPARTMENT OF THE INTERIOR.
### Commission to the Five Civilized Tribes.
### Muskogee, Indian Territory, October 7th, 1902.

    In the matter of the application of Joseph Rollens for the enrollment of himself as a citizen by intermarriage of the Cherokee Nation and for the enrollment of his wife, Elmina Rollens, as a citizen by blood of the Cherokee Nation.

Supplemental to #4992.

JOSEPH ROLLENS, being duly sworn, testified as follows:
Examination by the Commission.
Q. What is your name? A. Joseph Rollens.
Q. How old are you? A. 49.
Q. 49 years old now, are you. You gave your age 49 two years ago.
A. I am 50.
Q. What is your post office? A. Claremore.
Q. You are a white man? A. Yes, sir.
Q. You are the same Joseph Rollens who made application to this Commission on October 27th, 19oo[sic], to be enrolled as a citizen of the Cherokee Nation by intermarriage? A. Yes, sir.

## Cherokee Intermarried White 1906
## Volume III

Q. What is the name of your wife? A. Elmina Beavers.
Q. That is her maiden name? A. Yes, sir.
Q. She is your first wife? A. Yes, sir.
Q. Is she a Cherokee by blood? A. Yes, sir.
Q. When did you marry her? A. In '73.
Q. Have you and your wife been living in the Cherokee Nation ever since 1880? A. Yes, sir.
Q. Never been separated? A. No, sir.
Q. Never made your home elsewhere? A. No, sir.
Q. Your wife has never been married before? A. No, sir.

I I I I I I I I I I I I I I I I I I I I I I I I I I I

Jesse O. Carr, being first duly sworn, states that as stenographer to the Commission to the Five Civilized Tribes he reported the above entitled case and that the foregoing is a true and complete transcript of his stenographic notes thereof.

Jesse O. Carr

Subscribed and sworn to before me this 22nd day of November, 1902.

BC Jones
Notary Public.

◇◇◇◇◇

Cherokee 4992.

### DEPARTMENT OF THE INTERIOR,
### COMMISSION TO THE FIVE CIVILIZED TRIBES.
Muskogee, Indian Territory, January 4, 1907.

In the Matter of the Application for the Enrollment of James Rollens as a citizen by intermarriage of the Cherokee Nation.

APPEARANCES:
Elmina Rollens appears for Applicant.
Cherokee Nation represented by H. M. Vance, in behalf of W. W. Hastings, Attorney.

Elmina Rollens being first duly sworn by B. P. Rasmus, Notary Public, testified as follows:

ON BEHALF OF COMMISSIONER.

Q What is your name?   A Elmina Rollens.
Q What is your age?    A 54.

# Cherokee Intermarried White 1906
# Volume III

Q What is your post office address?
A Claremore, Indian Territory.
Q Are you a citizen by blood of the Cherokee Nation?
A Yes sir.
Q Are you married?
A No sir.
Q Have you ever been married?
A Yes sir. My husband is dead.
Q What was the name of your husband?
A James Rollens.
Q When did he die?
A 18th of last December year ago.
Q He died then in December, 1905?
A Yes sir.
Q Was he an applicant for enrollment as a citizen by intermarriage of the Cherokee Nation? A Yes sir.
Q He had no Cherokee blood?
A No sir.
Q His only claim to the right to enrollment as a citizen of the Cherokee Nation is by virtue of his marriage to you?
A Yes sir.
Q When were you and he married?
A 15th of April, 1873.
Q Were you a recognized citizen of the Cherokee Nation at the time he married you?
A Yes sir.
Q Were you living in the Cherokee Nation?
A Yes sir.
Q Were you ever married before you married him?
A No sir.
Q Was he ever married before he married you?
A No sir.
Q From the time of your marriage to your husband, James Rollens, in 1873, did you and he continuously live together as husband and wife and reside in the Cherokee Nation until the time of his death?
A Yes sir.

The applicant, James Rollens, is identified on the Cherokee Authenticated Tribal Roll of 1880 Cooweescoowee District, 2471. The name of his wife, Elmina Rollens, is included in the approved partial roll of citizens by blood of the Cherokee Nation, opposite No. 11931.

Q At the time you and your husband were married, did he secure a marriage license?
A Yes sir.
Q In what district were you living when you were married?
A Talequah[sic].
Q Who married you?
A A preacher by the name of George Swimmer.

## Cherokee Intermarried White 1906
## Volume III

Q Is he living at this time?
A No sir.
Q You haven't a copy of the marriage license that was issued for you?
A No sir.
Q Was it ever in your possession?
A No sir.
Q Are there any persons who were witnesses to your marriage?
A No sir.
Q Are there any persons living who saw your marriage?
A I don't know of any.
Q You were married you say in 1873?
A Yes sir.
Q In accordance with the terms of a license issued in Talequah[sic] District, authorizing the marriage of James Rollens and Elmina Beavert[sic]?
A Yes sir.
Q Was this license returned to the Clerk of the District?
A Yes sir.
Q And you have every reason to believe that it was recorded there?
A Yes sir.

The applicant, James Rollens, is identified on Cherokee Authenticated Tribal Roll of 1880, Cooweescoowee District, 2471. The name of his wife, Elmina Rollens, is included in the approved partial roll of citizens by blood of the Cherokee Nation opposite number 11931.

---

Subscribed and sworn to before me this the 5th day of January, 1907.

John E. Tidwell
Notary Public.

◇◇◇◇◇

"No. 40:- License granted Jo Roland to marry Mina Beavert Apl 14th, 1873"

Ceremony by George Swinmer[sic], M.G."

---

This is to certify that the undersigned, being first duly sworn, states that, as stenographer to the Commissioner to the Five Civilized Tribes, she made the above and foregoing copy, and that same is a full, true and complete copy of record of Marriage License No. 40, found in "Marriage Records from 1870 - 1892 Tahlequah Dist.", now on file in this office.

Sarah Waters

## Cherokee Intermarried White 1906
## Volume III

Subscribed and sworn to before me this 18th day of January, 1907.

John E. Tidwell
Notary Public.

◇◇◇◇◇

E C M                                                                                           Cherokee 4992.

### DEPARTMENT OF THE INTERIOR,

### COMMISSIONER TO THE FIVE CIVILIZED TRIBES.

In the matter of the application for the enrollment of JOSEPH ROLLENS as a citizen by intermarriage of the Cherokee Nation.

### D E C I S I O N

THE RECORDS OF THIS OFFICE SHOW: That on October 27th, 1902[sic] application was received by the Commission to the Five Civilized Tribes for the enrollment of Joseph Rollens as a citizen by intermarriage of the Cherokee Nation. Further proceedings in the matter of said application were had at Muskogee, Indian Territory, October 7th, 1902 and January 4th, 1907.

THE EVIDENCE IN THIS CASE SHOWS: That the applicant herein, Joseph Rollens, a white man, was married in accordance with Cherokee law April 15th, 1873 to his wife, Elmina Rollens, nee Beverett[sic], who was at the time of said marriage a recognized citizen by blood of the Cherokee Nation; who is identified on the Cherokee authenticated tribal Roll of 1880, Cooweescoowee District No. 2472 as a native Cherokee, and whose name is included in the approved partial roll of citizens by blood of the Cherokee Nation opposite No. 11931. It is further shown that from the time of said marriage the said Joseph Rollens and Elmina Rollens resided together as husband and wife and continuously lived in the Cherokee Nation up to and including September 1st, 1902. Said applicant is identified on the Cherokee authenticated tribal roll of 1880 and the Cherokee census roll of 1896 as an intermarried citizen of the Cherokee Nation.

IT IS, THEREFORE, ORDERED AND ADJUDGED: That in accordance with the decision of the Supreme Court of the United States, dated November 5, 1906, in the cases of Daniel Red Bird et al. vs. the United States Nos. 125, 126, 127 and 128, the said applicant, Joseph Rollens is entitled, under the provisions of Section Twenty-one of the Act of Congress approved June 28th, 1898 (30 Stats. 495), to enrollment as a citizen by intermarriage of the Cherokee Nation, and his application for enrollment as such is accordingly granted.

## Cherokee Intermarried White 1906
## Volume III

Tams Bixby
Commissioner.

Dated at Muskogee, Indian Territory,
this    JAN 23 1907

◇◇◇◇◇

Cherokee 4992

Muskogee, Indian Territory, January 23, 1907.

W. W. Hastings,
    Attorney for the Cherokee Nation,
        Muskogee, Indian Territory.

Dear Sir:

    There is enclosed herewith copy of the decision of the Commissioner to the Five Civilized Tribes, dated January 23, 1907, granting the application for the enrollment of Joseph Rollens as a citizen by intermarriage of the Cherokee Nation.

                Respectfully,

Enc I-65                                         Commissioner.

RPI

◇◇◇◇◇

Cherokee 4992

W.W. HASTINGS.      OFFICE OF      H.M. VANCE.
ATTORNEY.                                               SECRETARY.

### Attorney for the Cherokee Nation,
MUSKOGEE, I. T.           January 23, 1907.

The Commissioner to the Five Civilized Tribes,
    Muskogee, Indian Territory.

Sir:

    Receipt is acknowledged of the testimony and of your decision enrolling Joseph Rollen as a citizen by intermarriage of the Cherokee Nation. Time for protesting said decision is waived and I consent that said person may be placed upon the schedule immediately.

                Respectfully,
                    W. W. Hastings
                    Attorney for the Cherokee Nation.

## Cherokee Intermarried White 1906
## Volume III

Cherokee 4659

Muskogee, Indian Territory, January 23, 1907.

Joseph Rollens,
    Collinsville, Indian Territory.

Dear Sir:

    There is enclosed herewith copy of the decision of the Commissioner to the Five Civilized Tribes, dated January 23, 1907, granting your application for enrollment as a citizen by intermarriage of the Cherokee Nation.

    You will be advised when your name has been placed upon a schedule of citizens of the Cherokee Nation and approved by the Secretary of the Interior.

        Respectfully,

Enc I-83                               Commissioner.

RPI

---

**Cher IW 100**
**Trans from Cher 5023 3-16-07**

DEPARTMENT OF THE INTERIOR.
COMMISSION TO THE FIVE CIVILIZED TRIBES.
CLAREMORE, I. T., OCTOBER 27th, 1900.

IN THE MATTER OF THE APPLICATION OF William Fry for the enrollment of himself and children as citizens of the Cherokee Nation, and he being sworn and examined by Commissioner, C. R. Breckinridge, testified as follows:

Q What is your full name? A William Fry.
Q How old are you? A Sixty six /[sic]
Q What is your Postoffice? A Claremore.
Q In what district do you live; Cooweescoowee? A Yes sir.
Q Who is it you want to have put on the rolls; yourself and family?
A Yes sir /[sic]
Q Have you a wife? A No sir.
Q How many children have you? A Seven.

297

## Cherokee Intermarried White 1906
## Volume III

Q Are you a Cherokee by blood? A No sir; white man.
Q Let me see your marriage license and certificate? A I have not got it; it is on the records.
Q Were you married before 1880? A Yes sir.
Q You are on the roll of 1880, are you? A Yes sir /[sic]
Q When were you married to your Cherokee wife? A I was married twice; in the Choctaw Nation during the war; and married according to Cherokee law back in 1866, if I am not mistaken.
Q You claim under the marriage of 1866? A Yes sir.
Q Give me he name of the woman you married? A Lettie Chambers.
Q That was her name before she married you? A Yes sir.
Q Is she dead? A Yes sir.
Q When did she die? A Seventeen years ago.
Q Did you live with her until she died? A Yes sir.
Q Have you lived in the Cherokee Nation ever since 1880? A Yes sir.
Q Have you married since your wife died? A No sir.
Q Give me the names of your children under twenty one years of age? A I have only one under age; that is Amelia.
Q How old is that child? A She is seventeen?[sic]
Q Is she living now? A Yes sir.
    (1880 Roll, Page 105, #1155, Wm. Frye, Cooweescoowee D'st)
    (1880 Roll, Page 105, #1156, Lettie Frye, Cooweescoowee D'st)
    (1896 Roll, Page 304, #359. William Frye, Coo. D'st)
    1896 Roll, Page 157, #1738, Amelia Frye, Coo. D'st)
By the applicant: "I have one other under twenty one years of age.
Q What is the child's name? A Annie Frye.
Q How old is she? A Nineteen.
Q Have you any other unmarried daughter that is under twenty one years of age? A No sir.
Q Is your daughter, Annie living? A Yes sir.
    (1896 Roll, Page 157, #1737, Annie Frye, Coo. D'st)

    The applicant applies for the enrollment of himself and two children: He is identified on the rolls of 1880 and 1896, as an adopted white: He lived with his Cherokee wife in the Cherokee Nation since his marriage to her in accordance with Cherokee law until she died some seventeen years ago: He has continued to live in the Cherokee Nation since that time, and has not remarried: He will be listed now for enrollment as a Cherokee by intermarriage.
    His two daughters, Amelia and Annie are identified on the roll of 1896: They are minors; are living now, and they will be listed for enrollment as Cherokees by blood.

---

    The undersigned, being sworn, states that as stenographer to the Commission to the Five Civilized Tribes, he correctly recorded the testimony and proceedings in this case, and that the foregoing is a true and complete transcript of his stenographic notes thereof.

# Cherokee Intermarried White 1906
# Volume III

R R Cravens

Subscribed and sworn to before
me this 29th day of October, 1900.

C R Breckinridge
COMMISSIONER.

◇◇◇◇◇

R.

## DEPARTMENT OF THE INTERIOR.
Commission to the Five Civilized Tribes.
Muskogee, Indian Territory, September 29th, 1902.

In the matter of the application of William Fry[sic] for the enrollment of himself as an intermarried citizen of the Cherokee Nation and for the enrollment of his children Amelia and Annie Fry as citizens by blood of the Cherokee Nation.

Supplemental to #5023.

Appearances:
Applicant appears in person.
Cherokee Nation by J. C. Starr.

WILLIAM FRY, being duly sworn, testified as follows: --
Examination by the Commission.

Q. What is your name? A. William Fry.
Q. What is your age at this time? A. 68.
Q. What is your post office? A. Claremore.
Q. Are you the same William Fry that applied to this Commission for enrollment as an intermarried citizen on October 27th, 1900?
A. Yes, sir.
Q. Is your wife living? A. No, sir.
Q. What was your wifes[sic] name? A. Lettie Chamber.
Q. Lettie Chambers before you were married? A. Yes, sir.
Q. Was she a Cherokee citizen? A. Yes, sir.
Q. When were you and she married? A. Well, I was married twice. I was married once during the war in the Choctaw Nation and married under the Cherokee laws the next year after the war.
Q. You were first married under the United States laws? A. No, Choctaw. There was no Cherokee laws in force.

## Cherokee Intermarried White 1906
## Volume III

Q. That was during the war? A. That was during the war. Then after peace we married under the Cherokee law.
Q. Were you ever married prior to your marriage to your wife Lettie?
A. No, sir.
Q. Was she ever married to any man besides you? A. No, sir.
Q. You are her first husband? A. Yes, sir.
Q. She is your first wife? A. Yes, sir.
Q. When did she die? A. Well, I don't recollect. It has been 19 years, however.
Q. Did you and she live together from the time of your marriage up to the time of her death? A. Yes, sir.
Q. Never separated? A. No, sir.
Q. Have you married again since her death? A. No, sir.
Q. Still single? A. Yes, sir.
Q. You were still single on the first day of September, 1902? A. Yes, sir.
Q. Never have been married except to this woman? A. No, sir.
Q. These children, Amelia and Annie Fry[sic], are your children by this wife?
A. Yes, sir.
Q. Are these two children both living at this time?
A. Yes, sir.
Q. How long have you lived in the Cherokee Nation? A. Ever since 1858.
Q. Except what time you were out during the war? A. Except what time I was out during the war. I was with the same people but I want's in the Cherokee Nation.
Q. Have you lived here ever since the war? A. Yes, sir.
Q. Made your home no where else? A. No, sir.

Jesse O. Carr, being first duly sworn, states that as stenographer to the Commission to the Five Civilized Tribes he reported the above entitled case and that the foregoing is a true and correct transcript of his stenographic notes thereof.

Jesse O. Carr

Subscribed and sworn to before me this 3rd day of October, 1902.

BC Jones<br>Notary Public.

◇◇◇◇◇

## Cherokee Intermarried White 1906
## Volume III

Cherokee No. 5023

DEPARTMENT OF THE INTERIOR
COMMISSIONER TO THE FIVE CIVILIZED TRIBES
Muskogee, Indian Territory
January 4, 1907

In the matter of the application of William Fry for enrollment as a citizen by intermarriage of the Cherokee Nation.

The applicant being duly sworn, testified as follows:

Q What is your name? A William Fry.
Q How old are you Mr. Fry? A 72.
Q What is your postoffice address? A Claremore
Q You claim to be a citizen by intermarriage of the Cherokee Nation?
A Yes sir.
Q Through whom do you claim your intermarried rights?
A By marrying Lettie Chambers.
Q When were you married to Lettie Chambers?
A I was married according to the laws in '67.
Q 1867? A Yes sir.
Q Where did you get your license, In what district? A I was married in Cooweescoowee district. They didn't require a license then like they did later. I was married by Judge Hicks

> Page 2 of Book A, Cooweescoowee Registry of Marriages contains the following entry:
>
> ": : : : :  24, issued lisence[sic] of marriage to Wm Frye citizen of the U.S. to marry Letty Chambers of Cooweescoowee District"

Q Were you ever married before you married Lettie Chambers?
A No sir.
Q Was she ever married before she married you? A No sir.
Q Is she living or dead? A She's dead
Q When did she die? A I don't recollect the date, but I think its[sic] been over twenty years.
Q Were you married in the Cherokee Nation? A Yes sir.
Q Married according to the Cherokee Law? A Yes sir.
Q Did you live with Lettie Chambers continuously after your marriage to her up to the time of her death? A Yes sir
Q Did you ever marry any more after she died? A No sir
Q Was Lettie Chambers a recognized citizen of the Cherokee Nation at the time of your marriage to her? A Yes sir.

## Cherokee Intermarried White 1906
## Volume III

Q Were you always recognized as a citizen of the Cherokee Nation after your marriage to Lettie Chambers? A Yes sir
Q Did you vote in the Cherokee elections? A Yes sir
Q Did you hold property in the Cherokee Nation as a citizen? A Yes sir.

The applicant is identified on the 1880 Cherokee Roll, opposite No. 1155.

Witness excused.

Ada C. Foreman being called as a witness for the applicant and being first duly sworn, testified as follows:

Q What is your name? A Ada C. Foreman.
Q Your age? [sic] 53
Q What is your postoffice address? A Claremore
Q Are you a citizen of the Cherokee Nation? A Yes sir
Q Are you acquainted with William Fry? A Yes sir
Q Did you know his wife Lettie Fry during her life time? A Yes sir.
Q Do you know when they were married? A They were married before I came to the Territory, but the lived in the same neighborhood I lived in ---
Q How long have you know them? A Ever since 1874
Q Did they always hold themselves to be husband and wife in that neighborhood up to the time of the death of Lettie Fry? A Yes sir
Q Was Lettie Fry recognized as a citizen by blood of the Cherokee Nation? A Yes sir, her father was one of the leading men of that district.
Q Was William Fry always recognized as a citizen by adoption of the Cherokee Nation after his marriage to Lettie Fry? A Yes sir

Witness excused

Gertrude Hanna, being duly sworn, on her oath states that as stenographer to the Commissioner to the Five Civilized Tribes she reported the proceedings had in the above numbered case on January 4, 1907 and that the above and foregoing is a true and correct transcript of her stenographic notes taken therein.

Gertrude Hanna

Subscribed and sworn to before me this 5 day of January, 1907.

Chas E Webster
Notary Public.

◇◇◇◇◇

## Cherokee Intermarried White 1906
## Volume III

(COPY)

Cherokee 4754 & 5023.

### MARRIAGE LICENSE.

United States of America, )
    Indian Territory,    ) ss.                       No. 40/
Northern District.     )

TO ANY PERSON AUTHORIZE BY LAW TO SOLEMNIZE MARRIAGE--GREETING:
    You are hereby commanded to solemnize the rite and publish the banns of matrimony between Mr. Charley Langley of Claremore, in the Indian Territory, aged 25 years, and Miss Anna Fry, of Claremore, in the Indian Territory, aged 22 years, according to law, and do you officially sign and return this license to the parties therein named. Witness my hand and official seal at Claremore, Indian Territory, this 29 day of November, A. D. 1902.

                                                Chas. A. Davidson,
                                            Clerk of the U. S. Court.
By R. C. Hunter, Deputy.

### CERTIFICATE OF MARRIAGE.

United States of America, )
    Indian Territory,    ) ss.
Northern District.     )

    I, Al Foster, A minister of the Gospel, do hereby certify, that on the 30 day of November, A. D. 1902, did duly and according to law as commanded in the foregoing license, solemnize the rite and publish the banns of matrimony between the parties therein named. Witness my hand this 1 day of December, A. D. 1902.
My credentials are recorded in the office of the Clerk of the United States Court, Indian Territory, Northern District, Book B, Page 18.

                                                Al Foster,
                                          A Minister of the Gospel.

### CERTIFICATE OF RECORD.

United States of America, )
    Indian Territory,    ) ss.
Northern District.     )

    I, Charles A. Davidson, Clerk of the United States Court in the Northern District, Indian Territory, do hereby certify that the instrument hereto attached was filed for record in my office the 7 day of Jany 1903 and duly recorded in Book A, Marriage Record, Page 263.
Witness my hand and seal of said Court at Vinita, in said Territory this 7 day of Jany, A.D. 1903.

                                              Chas. A. Davidson, Clerk.

## Cherokee Intermarried White 1906
## Volume III

Department of the Interior,
COMMISSION TO THE FIVE CIVILIZED TRIBES.
Cherokee Land Office,
Tahlequah, I. T., September 24, 1903.

I, the undersigned, Clerk in Charge Cherokee Land Office, and custodian of the records of said office, being first duly sworn, state that the above and foregoing is a true and correct copy of the original now on file in the said Cherokee Land Office.

W J Cook

Subscribed and sworn to before me this 24th day of September, 1903.

JO Rosson
Notary Public.

GRS

◇◇◇◇◇

E.C.M.                                                                                   Cherokee 5023.

DEPARTMENT OF THE INTERIOR,

COMMISSIONER TO THE FIVE CIVILIZED TRIBES.

In the matter of the application for the enrollment of WILLIAM FRY as a citizen by intermarriage of the Cherokee Nation.

_D_E_C_I_S_I_O_N_

THE RECORDS OF THIS OFFICE SHOW: That on October 27th, 1900, application was received by the Commission to the Five Civilized Tribes for the enrollment of William Fry as a citizen by intermarriage of the Cherokee Nation. Further proceedings in the matter of said application were had at Muskogee, Indian Territory, September 29th, 1902 and January 4th, 1907.

THE EVIDENCE IN THIS CASE SHOWS: That the applicant herein, William Fry, a white man, was married in accordance with Cherokee law in 1867 to his wife, Letty Fry, nee Chambers, since deceased, who was at the time of said marriage a recognized citizen by blood of the Cherokee Nation, who was identified on the Cherokee authenticated tribal roll of 1880, Cooweescoowee District No. 1156, as a native Cherokee, marked "Dead". It is further shown that from the time of said marriage until the death of said Letty Fry, which occurred about the year 1887, the said William Fry and Letty Fry resided together as husband and wife and continuously lived in the Cherokee Nation; that since the death of said Letty Fry the said William Fry has remained unmarried and continuously lived in the Cherokee Nation up to and including September

## Cherokee Intermarried White 1906
## Volume III

1st, 1902. Said applicant is identified on the Cherokee authenticated tribal roll of 1880 and the Cherokee census roll of 1896 as an intermarried citizen of the Cherokee Nation.

IT IS, THEREFORE, ORDERED AND ADJUDGED: That in accordance with the decision of the Supreme Court of the United States, dated November 5, 1906, in the cases of Daniel Red Bird et al. vs. the United States, Nos. 125, 126, 127 and 128, the said applicant, William Fry, is entitled, under the provisions of Section Twenty-one of the Act of Congress approved June 28th, 1898 (30 Stats. 495), to enrollment as a citizen by intermarriage of the Cherokee Nation, and his application for enrollment as such is accordingly granted.

Tams Bixby
Commissioner.

Dated at Muskogee, Indian Territory,
this      JAN 21 1907

◇◇◇◇◇

Cherokee 5023

Muskogee, Indian Territory, January 21, 1907.

W. W. Hastings,
  Attorney for the Cherokee Nation,
    Muskogee, Indian Territory.

Dear Sir:

There is enclosed herewith copy of the decision of the Commissioner to the Five Civilized Tribes, dated January 21, 1907, granting the application for the enrollment of William Fry as a citizen by intermarriage of the Cherokee Nation.

Respectfully,

Enc I-38.                                                          Commissioner.

RPI

◇◇◇◇◇

# Cherokee Intermarried White 1906
## Volume III

Cherokee 5023

W.W. HASTINGS.
ATTORNEY.

OFFICE OF

H.M. VANCE.
SECRETARY.

**Attorney for the Cherokee Nation,**

Muskogee, I. T.      January 21, 1907.

The Commissioner to the Five Civilized Tribes,
Muskogee, Indian Territory.

Sir:

Receipt is acknowledged of the testimony and of your decision enrolling William Fry as a citizen by intermarriage of the Cherokee Nation. Time for protesting said decision is waived and I consent that said person may be placed upon the schedule immediately.

Respectfully,
W. W. Hastings
Attorney for the Cherokee Nation.

◇◇◇◇◇

Cherokee 5023

Muskogee, Indian Territory, January 24, 1907.

William Fry,
Claremore, Indian Territory.

Dear Sir:

There is enclosed herewith a copy of the decision of the Commissioner to the Five Civilized Tribes, dated January 21, 1907, granting your application for enrollment as a citizen by intermarriage of the Cherokee Nation.

You will be advised when your name has been placed upon a schedule of citizens of the Cherokee Nation and approved by the Secretary of the Interior.

Respectfully,

Encl. H-2
JMH

Commissioner.

---

**Cher IW 101**

◇◇◇◇◇

## Cherokee Intermarried White 1906
## Volume III

E.C.M.

### DEPARTMENT OF THE INTERIOR,

### COMMISSIONER TO THE FIVE CIVILIZED TRIBES.

In the matter of the application for the enrollment of

### ADA C. FOREMAN

As a citizen by intermarriage of the Cherokee Nation.

### CHEROKEE NO. 5256.

Department of the Interior,
Commission to the Five Civilized tribes[sic],
Claremore, I. T. November, 9th 1900

In the matter of the application of Ada C. Foreman for the enrollment of herself and children as Cherokee citizens. She being sworn testified before the Commission as follows:

Q What is your name? A. Ada C. Foreman.
Q What is your age? A. 47.
Q What is your post office address? A. Claremore.
Q What district do you live in? A. Cooweescoowee.
Q Are you a recognized Cherokee citizen by blood? A. No sir by adoption.
Q Who do you want to have enrolled? A. Myself and children.
Q Are you married? A. My husband is dead.
Q What was his name? A. Stephen T. Foreman.
Q Was he a Cherokee by blood? A. Yes sir.
Q Have you a certificate of marriage? A. Yes sir.
Q What are the names of your children? A. Laura A. Q How old? A. 19
Q What is the next one? A. Ermina V. Q How old? A. 17.
Q What is the next one? A. Taylor W. Q How old? A. 12.
Q What is the next one? A. Perry A. Q How old? A. 10.
Q Are these children all alive and living with you at this time? A. Yes sir.
Q How long since the death of your husband? A. 10 years.
Q Have you ever married since his death? A. No sir.
Q Are you living in the Cherokee Nation now? A. Yes sir.
Q Lived here since his death all the time? A. Yes sir.
1880 roll, page 104, No. 1128, Ada C. Foreman  Cooweescoowee.
1896        304        354   Ada C. Foreman               "

## Cherokee Intermarried White 1906
## Volume III

| 1896 | 158 | 1711 Ada L. Foreman | " |
|---|---|---|---|
| 1896 | 158 | 1712 Vic M. Foreman | " |
| 1896 | 158 | 1713 Taylor W. Foreman | " |
| 1896 | 158 | 1714 Perry A. Foreman | " |

The name of Ada C. Foreman appears on the authenticated 1880 roll as an intermarried white, and also on the census roll of 1896. The names of her children, Laura A., Ermina V., Taylor W. and Perry A. Foreman also appear on the census roll of 1896. They all being fully identified and having made satisfactory proof as to their residence consequently the said Ada C. Foreman will be listed for enrollment as a Cherokee citizen by intermarriage and the said children as enumerated in the testimony will be listed for enrollment as Cherokees by blood.

O%O%O%O%O%O%O%O%O%

Chas. von Weise being sworn states that as stenographer to the Commission to the Five Civilized Tribes he reported in full all the proceedings in the above entitled cause and the foregoing is a full, true and correct transcript of his stenographic notes in said proceedings.

Chas von Weise

Subscribed and sworn to before me this the 10th day of November, 1900.

TB Needles<br>Commissioner.

◇◇◇◇◇

DEPARTMENT OF THE INTERIOR.
Commission to the Five Civilized Tribes.
Muskogee, Indian Territory, October 7th, 1902.

———————

In the matter of the application of Ada C. Foreman for the enrollment of herself as a citizen by intermarriage of the Cherokee Nation and for the enrollment of her children, Laura A., Ermina V., Taylor W. and Perry A. Foreman, as citizens by blood of the Cherokee Nation.

———————

Supplemental to #5256.

———————

Applicant appears in person.
Cherokee Nation by J. C. Starr.

———————

## Cherokee Intermarried White 1906
## Volume III

ADA C. FOREMAN, being duly sworn, testified as follows:
Examination by the Commission.

Q. State you[sic] full name? A. Ada C. Foreman.
Q. How old are you? A. 49.
Q. What is your post office? A. Claremore.
Q. You are a white woman, are you? A. Yes, sir.
Q. Claiming as a citizen of the Cherokee Nation by intermarriage?
A. Yes, sir.
Q. What is the name of the hsband[sic] through whom you claim?
Q[sic]. Taylor Foreman.
Q. Is he living? A. No, sir.
Q. When did he die? A. He died the first day of January, 1891.
Q. He was a Cherokee by blood, was he? A. Yes, sir.
Q. When were you married to him? A. I was married in 1874.
Q. And lived with him in the Cherokee Nation from that time up until his death, did you?
A. Yes, sir.
Q. Have you ever married since the death of your husband?
A. No, sir.
Q. Have you lived in the Cherokee Nation ever since the death of your husband?
A. Yes, sir.
Q. How many children have you? A. I have six living, two dead.
Q. You have six living? A. Yes, sir.
Q. Two of them over age? A. Two over age.
Q. You have four living with you? A. Yes, sir.
Q. Have they lived in the Cherokee Nation all their lives?
A. Yes, sir. We have lived right on the same place ever since we were married.

By Mr. Starr:
Q. This man Foreman is your first husband? A. Yes, sir.
Q. Are you his first wife? A. Yes, sir.

++++++++++++++++++++++++++++++++++++++++++++

Jesse O. Carr, being first duly sworn, states that as stenographer to the Commission to the Five Civilized Tribes he reported the above entitled case and that the foregoing is a true and complete transcript of his stenographic notes thereof.

Jesse O. Carr

Subscribed and sworn to before me this 13<sup>th</sup> day of November, 1902.

BC Jones<br>Notary Public.

## Cherokee Intermarried White 1906
## Volume III

Cherokee
No. 5256

DEPARTMENT OF THE INTERIOR
COMMISSIONER TO THE FIVE CIVILIZED TRIBES
MUSKOGEE, INDIAN TERRITORY
January 4, 1907

In the matter of the application for the enrollment of Ada C. Foreman as a citizen by intermarriage of the Cherokee Nation.

The applicant being first duly sworn, testified as follows:

Q What is your name? A Ada C. Foreman
Q How old are you? A 53.
Q What is your postoffice address? A Claremore
Q Do you claim to be a citizen by intermarriage of the Cherokee Nation? A Yes sir.
Q Through whom do you claim your rights? A Stephen Taylor Foreman
Q Is he living now? A No sir
Q When did he die? A He died sixteen years ago the first day of this month.
Q When did you marry Stephen T. Foreman?
A The 28th day of April, 1874.
Q Where? A Cane Hill, Arkansas.
Q Were you ever married before you married Stephen T. Foreman?
A No sir.
Q Was he ever married before he married you? A No sir.
Q How long did you live in Arkansas after your marriage.[sic]
A We came right back, didn't stay there at all
Q Was your husband a recognized citizen of the Cherokee Nation at the time you married him? A Yes, he was raised here, at Park Hill --never lived anywhere else.
Q Have you ever married since the death of your husband, Stephen T. Foreman?
A No sir.
Q You have lived continuously in the Cherokee Nation since your marriage?
A Yes sir.

The applicant is identified o the 1880 Cherokee roll, Cooweescoowee District, opposite No. 1128

Witness excused


George W. Eaton being called as a witness for the applicant and being duly sworn, testified as follows:

Q What is your name? A George W. Easton
Q How old are you? A 61.
Q What is your postoffice address? A Claremore.

# Cherokee Intermarried White 1906
# Volume III

Q Are you a citizen of the Cherokee Nation? A Yes sir.
Q By blood or adoption? A By adoption.
Q Are you acquainted with Ada C. Foreman? A Yes sir.
Q Did you know her husband Stephen T. Foreman? A Yes sir
Q Do you know when they were married? A Well no, I was not present, but if you will allow me to tell you what I know--they lived together from '74 until his death as man and wife. I don't recollect what year Mr. Foreman died, its[sic] been a good while ago.
Q Was Ada C. Foreman always recognized as a citizen by adoption of the Cherokee Nation after her marriage to Stephen T. Foreman? A Yes sir.

Witness excused

William L. Trott being called as a witness for the applicant, and being first duly sworn, testified as follows:

Q What is your name? A William A. Trott
Q How old are you? A 62.
Q Your postoffice address? A Vinita.
Q Are you acquainted with Ada C. Foreman? A Yes sir.
Q Did you know Stephen T. Foreman in his life time? A Yes sir.
Q Do you know when they were married? A I do not.
Q How long have you known them? A I think I have known then[sic] about must be thirty years, 27 or 30.
Q Did they always hold themselves out as husband and wife in the community in which they lived? A Yes sir.
Q Lived together as husband and wife up to the death of Stephen T. Foreman? A Yes sir.
Q Was Ada C. Foreman always recognized as a citizen by adoption of the Cherokee Nation after her marriage to Stephen T. Foreman? A Yes sir.

Witness excused.

-----

Gertrude Hanna, stenographer to the Commissioner to the Five Civilized Tribes on her oath states that she reported the proceedings had in the above numbered case on January 4, 1907, and that the above and foregoing is true and correct transcript of her stenographic notes therein.

Gertrude Hanna

Subscribed and sworn to before me this to 5 day of January, 1907

Chas E Webster<br>Notary Public.

## Cherokee Intermarried White 1906
## Volume III

E.C.M.

Cherokee 5256.

### DEPARTMENT OF THE INTERIOR,

### COMMISSIONER TO THE FIVE CIVILIZED TRIBES.

---

In the matter of the application for the enrollment of ADA C. FOREMAN as a citizen by intermarriage of the Cherokee Nation.

### _D_E_C_I_S_I_O_N_

THE RECORDS OF THIS OFFICE SHOW: That on November 9th, 1900, application was received by the Commission to the Five Civilized Tribes for the enrollment of Ada C. Foreman as a citizen by intermarriage of the Cherokee Nation. Further proceedings in the matter of said application were had at Muskogee, Indian Territory, October 7th, 1902 and January 4th, 1907.

THE EVIDENCE IN THIS CASE SHOWS: That the applicant herein, Ada C. Foreman, a white woman, was married in the year 1874 to one Taylor Foreman, since deceased, who was at the time of said marriage a recognized citizen by blood of the Cherokee Nation, who is identified on the Cherokee authenticated tribal roll of 1880, Cooweescoowee District No. 1127 as a native Cherokee; that from the time of said marriage until the death of said Taylor Foreman, which occurred on January ist[sic], 1891, the said Taylor Foreman and Ada C. Foreman resided together a husband and wife and continuously lived in the Cherokee Nation; that since the death of said Taylor Foreman said Ada C. Foreman has remained unmarried and continuously lived in the Cherokee Nation up to and including September 1st, 1902. Said applicant is identified on the Cherokee authenticated tribal roll of 1880 and the Cherokee census roll of 1896, as an intermarried citizen of the Cherokee Nation.

IT IS, THEREFORE, ORDERED AND ADJUDGED: That in accordance with the decision of the Supreme Court of the United States, dated November 5, 1906, in the cases of Daniel Red Bird et al. vs. the United States Nos. 125, 126, 127 and 128, the said applicant, Ada C. Foreman, is entitled, under the provisions of Section Twenty-one of the Act of Congress approved June 28th, 1898 (30 Stats., 495), to enrollment as a citizen by intermarriage of the Cherokee Nation, and her application for enrollment as such is accordingly granted.

Tams Bixby
Commissioner.

Dated at Muskogee, Indian Territory,
this    JAN 21 1907

◇◇◇◇◇

# Cherokee Intermarried White 1906
## Volume III

Cherokee
525

Muskogee, Indian Territory, January 21, 1907.

W. W. Hastings,
    Attorney for the Cherokee Nation,
        Muskogee, Indian Territory.

Dear Sir:

    There is enclosed herewith copy of the Decision of the Commissioner to the Five Civilized Tribes, dated January 21, 1907, granting the application for the enrollment of Ada C. Foreman as a citizen by intermarriage of the Cherokee Nation.

        Respectfully,

Enc I-25                                 Commissioner.

RPI

◇◇◇◇◇

Cherokee 5256

W.W. HASTINGS.     OFFICE OF     H.M. VANCE.
ATTORNEY.                              SECRETARY.

**Attorney for the Cherokee Nation,**

MUSKOGEE, I. T.      January 21, 1907.

The Commissioner to the Five Civilized Tribes,
    Muskogee, Indian Territory.

Sir:

    Receipt is acknowledged of the testimony and of your decision enrolling Ada C. Foreman as a citizen by intermarriage of the Cherokee Nation. Time for protesting said decision is waived and I consent that said person may be placed upon the schedule immediately.

        Respectfully,
           W. W. Hastings
           Attorney for the Cherokee Nation.

◇◇◇◇◇

# Cherokee Intermarried White 1906
## Volume III

Cherokee 5256

Muskogee, Indian Territory, January 24, 1907.

Ada C. Foreman,
Claremore, Indian Territory.

Dear Madam:

There is enclosed herewith copy of the decision of the Commissioner to the Five Civilized Tribes, dated January 21, 1907, granting the application for your enrollment as a citizen by intermarriage of the Cherokee Nation.

You will be advised when your name has been placed upon a schedule of citizens of the Cherokee Nation and approved by the Secretary of the Interior.

Respectfully,

Enc I-101

Commissioner.

RPI

---

**Cher IW 102**

◇◇◇◇◇

F.R.

### DEPARTMENT OF THE INTERIOR,
### COMMISSIONER TO THE FIVE CIVILIZED TRIBES.

In the matter of the application for the enrollment of

MARION W. COUCH

as a citizen by intermarriage of the Cherokee Nation.

---

CHEROKEE 5397.

◇◇◇◇◇

## Cherokee Intermarried White 1906
## Volume III

Department of the Interior.
Commission to the Five Civilized Tribes.
Chelsea, I. T., November 15, 1900.

In the matter of the application of Marion W. Couch for the enrollment of himself and five children as Cherokee citizens; he being sworn and examined by Commissioner C. R. Breckinridge, testified as follows:

Q Give me your full name. A Marion W. Couch.
Q How old are you? A 58 years old.
Q What is your postoffice? A Chelsea.
Q Do you live in Cooweescoowee district? A Yes, herein Chelsea.
Q Do you want to enroll yourself and family? A Yes sir.
Q Have you a wife? A No sir, she's dead.
Q How many children? A Five.
Q Are you a Cherokee by blood? A NoB[sic] sir.
Q Let me see your marriage license and certificate.
Q Were you married before 1880? A Yes sir.
Q When were you married? A Jan. 22, 1870.
Q What was your wife's name when you married her? A Mary Wright.
Q When did she die? A She died in May, 1876.
Q Did you live with her from the time you married her until she died? A Yes sir.
Q Have you married since she died? A Yes sir; my last wife's name was Victoria Riley.
Q Is she dead? A Yes sir.
Q When did you marry her? A I married her in '77.
Q When did she die? A She died in July 1897.
Q Did you live with her until she died? A Yes sir.
Q Have you lived ever since she died in the Cherokee Nation? A Yes sir.
Q Have you married since she died? A No sir.
Q Was she ever married except to you? A No sir.
Q How old was your wife Victoria when she died? A 41 years old I believe.
Q What was her father's name? A Samuel Riley.
Q He dead? A Yes sir, he died before I married her.
Q Give me her mother's name. A Sallie.
Q Is she dead? A Yes sir.
Q How long since she died? A She died in '78, I guess.
Q Give me the names of your children please? A Clara C.
Q How old is that child? A 16 years old.
Q Next child? A Cherokee R.
Q How old is that child? A 14 years old.
Q Next child? A Marion W., Jr.
Q When was he born? A in '88, 12 years old.
Q Next child? A James C., born in '90; 10 years old.
Charles E., Born in '96; four years old.
Q Are these children all living now? A Yes sir.
1880 roll; page 79, #495, M. W. Couch, Cooweescoowee.

315

## Cherokee Intermarried White 1906
## Volume III

1880 roll; page 79, #496, Vic. Couch, Cooweescoowee.
1896 roll; page 388, #268 1/2 Marion W. Couch, "
1896 roll; page 135, #1092, Clara C. Couch,
1896 roll; page 135, #1093, Cherokee R. Couch,
1896 roll; page 135, #1094, Marion W. Couch, Jr.,
1896 roll; page 135, #1095, James C. Couch,
1896 roll; page 135, #1097, Charles E. Couch,
1896 roll; page 135, #1090, Victoria E. Couch,

Commissioner Breckinridge-
    The applicant applies for the enrollment of himself and five children. He is married to his second wife who is now dead. Both his first and second wives were Cherokees by blood. He is identified with his second wife on the rolls of 1880 and 1896; he has lived in the Cherokee Nation ever since his enrollment in 1880; he has not remarried since the death of his second wife, and he will now be listed for enrollment as a Cherokee by intermarriage.
The five children named in the testimony are all identified with their parents on the roll of 1896; they are minors, and are living now, and they will be listed for enrollment as Cherokees by blood.

E.G. Rothenberger, being duly sworn, states that as stenographer to the Commission to the Five Civilized Tribes, he reported in full all proceedings in the above case, and that the foregoing is a true and complete transcript of his stenographic notes in said case.

                                                                  E.G. Rothenberger

Subscribed and sworn to before me this 15th day of November, 1900.

                                                                  TB Needles
                                                                             Commissioner.

# Cherokee Intermarried White 1906
# Volume III

R.

DEPARTMENT OF THE INTERIOR.
Commission to the Five Civilized Tribes.
Muskogee, Indian Territory, October 1st, 1902.

In the matter of the application of Marion W. Couch for the enrollment of himself as a citizen by intermarriage of the Cherokee Nation and for the enrollment of his children Clara C., Cherokee R., Marion W. Jr., James C. and Charles E. Couch as citizens by blood of the Cherokee Nation.

Supplemental to #5397.

Appearances:
Applicant appears in person.
Cherokee Nation by J. C. Starr.

MARION W. COUCH, being duly sworn, testified as follows:
Examination by the Commission.

Q. What is your name? A. Marion W. Couch.
Q. What is your age? A. 60.
Q. What is your post office? A. Chelsea.
Q. Are you the same Marion W. Couch for whom application was made to this Commission for enrollment as an intermarried citizen on November 15th, 19oo[sic]?
A. Yes, sir.
Q. What is your wife's name? A. Victoria E.
Q. Is she living or dead? A. Dead.
Q. When did she die? A. 1897.
Q. When were you and Victoria E. Married? A. 7th of May, 1877; if I am not mistaken.
Q. Were you ever married prior to your marriage to her? A. Yes, sir.
Q. How many times before you were married to her? A. Once.
Q. Was that wife living or dead at the time you married her? A. She was dead.
Q. Had Victoria E. ever been married prior to her marriage to you? A. No, sir.
Q. She is your second wife and you are her first husband? A. Yes, sir.
Q. Did you and Victoria E. live together continuously from the time of your marriage up to the time of her death? A. Yes, sir.
Q. Have you ever been married to any other woman since your marriage to Victoria E.? A. No, sir.
Q. Still single on the first of September, 1902? A. Yes, sir.
Q. Are these children, Clara C., Cherokee R., Marion W. Jr., James C. and Charles E., your children by your wife Victoria E.? A. Yes, sir.
Q. Are they living at this time? A. Yes, sir.

## Cherokee Intermarried White 1906
## Volume III

Q. Always lived in the Cherokee Nation? A. Yes, sir.
Q. How long have you lived here? A. Since 1868.
Q. Never lived any where else? A. No, sir.
Q. How long did your wife lived[sic] in the Cherokee Nation? A. Born and raised here.
Q. Has she lived there all her life? A. All the time unless she went south during the war. She might have went south during the war.

Jesse O. Carr, being first duly sworn, states that as stenographer to the Commission to the Five Civilized Tribes he reported the above entitled case and that the foregoing is a true and complete transcript of his stenographic notes thereof.

Jesse O. Carr

Subscribed and sworn to before me this 20th day of October, 1902.

BC Jones<br>Notary Public.

◇◇◇◇◇

Cherokee) 5397.

DEPARTMENT OF THE INTERIOR,<br>COMMISSIONER TO THE FIVE CIVILIZED TRIBES.<br>Muskogee, Indian Territory, January 4, 1907.

-------------------------------

In the matter of making proof of the marriage of Marion W. Couch to his Cherokee wife, prior to November 1, 1875.

-------------------------------

Marion W. Couch, being sworn by W. W. Chappell, a Notary Public, testified as follows.

COMMISSIONER:

Q. What is your name? A. Marion W. Couch.
Q. Your age? A. 64.
Q. Your post office address? A. Chelsea.
Q. Do you claim citizenship in the Cherokee by intermarriage? A. I do.
Q. Through whom do you claim such citizenship? A. Mary E. Wright.
Q. Is she living? A. No.
Q. What was her citizenship? A. Cherokee by blood.
Q. When were you married to her? A. I was first married to her in '63 in Texas.
Q. Were you married under a license issued by the State of Texas? A. Yes sir.

# Cherokee Intermarried White 1906
# Volume III

Q. Have you a copy of that marriage license with you? A. No sir.
Q. Can you get a copy of that license? A. No sir.
Q. Why can't you? A. I guess I could.
Q. When did you remove to the Cherokee Nation? A. In '68.
Q. Were you married again according to the laws of the Cherokee Nation? A. Yes sir.
Q. When? A. In '69 I think.
Q. Where were you married in '69. A. In Cooweescoowee District.
Q. By whom were you married? A. His name was Cochram[sic].
Q. What was he? A. A full blood Cherokee.
Q. Was he a preacher? A. Yes sir.
Q. This marriage in the Cherokee Nation -- was that under a license of the Cherokee Nation? A. Yes sir.
Q. Have you a copy of that Cherokee License with you? A. I filed it herewith the Dawes Commission last December, through Col. Bell.

(Commissioner -- The applicant offers in evidence an instrument which shows that he was married under a Cherokee license on January 22, 1870, to Mary Wright, same being filed herewith, and made a part of the record in this case.)

Q. When did you wife die? A. In '76.
Q. Did you live with her from '69 until '76 in the Cherokee Nation? A. Yes sir.
Q. Have you married since her death? A. Yes sir.
Q. Who did you marry? A. Another Cherokee woman.
Q. What was her name? A. Victoria E. Riley.
Q. When did you marry her? A. In '77.
Q. Where? A. On the Verdigris River.
Q. What is her citizenship? A. Cherokee by blood.
Q. Is she living now? A. No.
Q. When did she die? A. In '96.
Q. Was Victoria E. Riley identified upon the rolls of the Cherokee Nation? A. Yes sir.
Q. Did you live with Victoria E. Riley in the Cherokee Nation? A. Yes sir, up on the Verdigris River.
Q. This marriage to Victoria E. Riley -- was that under a license of the Cherokee Nation? A. No we were married by a preacher.
Q. Have you any documentary evidence of this second marriage? A. No.
Q. Didn't the preacher give you a certificate showing your marriage? A. I think so -- I think he gave it to my wife.
Q. What became of those papers? A. I think they were burned.
Q. When? A. In '92 or '93.
Q. Were they filed for record? A. No.
Q. Is there anyone present who was present at your marriage in '&&[sic]? A. Not that I know of.
Q. Is there anyone living that you know of that was present at that marriage? A. Not that I know of.
Q. Is any one living that was present at the marriage of yourself and your first wife, in the Cherokee Nation, that you know of? [sic] No sir, not that I know of.

## Cherokee Intermarried White 1906
## Volume III

Witness excused.

(Commissioner --Applicant is identified upon the 1880 Roll, opposite No. 495; also upon the 1896 Census Roll opposite No. 268-1/2.)

---

Eula Jeanes Branson, being sworn, states that she correctly reported the proceedings had in the above and foregoing on the 4th. day of January, 1907.

Eula Jeanes Branson

Subscribed and sworn to before me, this the 4th. day of January, 1907.

Edward Merrick<br>Notary Public.

◇◇◇◇◇

CERTIFIED COPY.

Saline District
Cherokee Nation

    Know ye all men by these presents that marriage license are hereby granted to Mc[sic] W. Couch, a white man and citizen of the United States, to marry Mrs. Mary Wright, a Cherokee woman and citizen of the aforesaid nation, the said Couch having complied with the requirements of the law in such cases, and any of the judges of the several courts of this Nation or any Regular Ordained Minister of the Gospel having the care of souls, are hereby authorized to perform the marriage ceremony and return the same, with a certificate of service.

    Given from under my hand on the 19th dayof Dec., A. D., 1869.

(Signed) J. L. Springston,<br>District Court, Saline Dist., C. N.

---

    I hereby certify that I have married M. W. Couch to Mary Wright, this January 22d, 1870.

(Signed) George Cochran.

---

    I hereby certify that the above is a true and correct copy of the original now on file in this office this the 5th day of August A. D., 1897.

## Cherokee Intermarried White 1906
## Volume III

(SEAL)

(Signed) J. M. Ross,
Clk. S.D.C.N.

Endorsed:
Copy.
Marriage License
M. W. Couch
&
Mrs. Mary Wright.
-----------------------

    I, Frances R. Lane, a stenographer to the Commissioner to the Five Civilized Tribes, do hereby certify that the above and foregoing is a true and complete copy of a certified copy of a marriage license and certificate issued to Mc. W. Couch and Mrs. Mary Wright, now on file with the records of the Commission to the Five Civilized Tribes in the matter of the application for the enrollment of Marion W. Couch as a citizen by intermarriage of the Cherokee Nation, Cherokee--5397.

Frances R Lane

Subscribed and sworn to before me this January 15, 1907

Edward Merrick
Notary Public.

◇◇◇◇◇

F.R.                                                                                                                Cherokee 5397

### DEPARTMENT OF THE INTERIOR,

### COMMISSIONER TO THE FIVE CIVILIZED TRIBES.

    In the matter of the application for the enrollment of Marion W. Couch as a citizen by intermarriage of the Cherokee Nation.

### D E C I S I O N

    THE RECORDS OF THIS OFFICE SHOW: That at Chelsea, Indian Territory, November 15, 1900, application was received by the Commission to the Five Civilized Tribes, for the enrollment of Marion W. Couch as a citizen by intermarriage of the Cherokee Nation. Further proceedings in the matter of said application were had at Muskogee, Indian Territory, October 1, 1902, and January 4, 1907.
    THE EVIDENCE IN THIS CASE SHOWS: That the applicant herein, Marion W. Couch, a white man, was married in accordance with Cherokee law, January 22, 1870, to his wife, Mary Couch, formerly Wright, who was, that the time of said marriage, a

## Cherokee Intermarried White 1906
## Volume III

recognized citizen by blood of the Cherokee Nation; that the said Marion W. Couch and Mary Couch resided together as husband and wife from the date of their marriage until the death of said Mary Couch, which occurred in 1876; that subsequent to the death of said Mary Couch, in 1877, said Marion W. Couch married one Victoria E. Riley, who was at the time of said marriage, a recognized citizen by blood of the Cherokee Nation, and who is identified upon the Cherokee authenticated tribal roll of 1880, Cooweescoowee District, No. 496, as a native Cherokee; that the said Marion W. Couch and Victoria E. Couch resided together as husband and wife from the date of their marriage in 1877, until the death of Victoria E. Couch in 1896; that since the death of the said Victoria E. Couch, said Marion W. Couch has remained unmarried, and that he has resided continuously in the Cherokee Nation since 1870. Said applicant is identified on the Cherokee authenticated tribal roll of 1880, and the Cherokee census roll of 1896, as an intermarried citizen of the Cherokee Nation.

IT IS, THEREFORE, ORDERED AND ADJUDGED: That in accordance with the decision of the Supreme Court of the United States, dated November 5, 1906, in the cases of Daniel Red Bird et al., vs. the United States, Nos. 125, 126, 127 and 128, the said applicant, Marion W. Couch is entitled, under the provisions of Section twenty-one of the Act of Congress approved June 28, 1898 (30 Stats. 495), to enrollment as a citizen by intermarriage of the Cherokee Nation, and his application for enrollment as such is accordingly granted.

            Tams Bixby
                 Commissioner.

Dated at Muskogee, Indian Territory,
this  JAN 23 1907

◇◇◇◇◇

Cherokee 5397

          Muskogee, Indian Territory, January 23, 1907

W. W. Hastings,
  Attorney for the Cherokee Nation,
    Muskogee, Indian Territory.

Dear Sir:

  There is enclosed herewith a copy of the decision of the Commissioner to the Five Civilized Tribes, dated January 23, 1907, granting the application for the enrollment of Marion W. Couch as a citizen by intermarriage of the Cherokee Nation.

            Respectfully,

Encl. H-68                 Commissioner.
 JMH

◇◇◇◇◇

*(The above letter given again.)*

◇◇◇◇◇

## Cherokee Intermarried White 1906
## Volume III

Cherokee 5397    W.W. HASTINGS, ATTORNEY.    OFFICE OF    H.M. VANCE, SECRETARY.

**Attorney for the Cherokee Nation,**

MUSKOGEE, I. T.    January 23, 1907.

The Commissioner to the Five Civilized Tribes,
    Muskogee, Indian Territory.

Sir:

    Receipt is acknowledged of the testimony and of your decision enrolling Marion W. Couch as a citizen by intermarriage of the Cherokee Nation. Time for protesting said decision is waived and I consent that said person may be placed upon the schedule immediately.

                        Respectfully,
                        W. W. Hastings
                        Attorney for Cherokee Nation.

◇◇◇◇◇

Cherokee
5397

                        Muskogee, Indian Territory, January 23, 1907.

Marion W. Couch,
    Chelsea, Indian Territory.

Dear Sir:

    There is enclosed herewith a copy of the decision of the Commissioner to the Five Civilized Tribes, dated January 23, 1907, granting your application for enrollment as a citizen by intermarriage of the Cherokee Nation.

    You will be advised when your name has been placed upon a schedule of citizens of the Cherokee Nation and approved by the Secretary of the Interior.

                        Respectfully,

E.R.C.                                           Commissioner.
Enc. E.C. 89.

◇◇◇◇◇

                    Cherokee 5397
                    1 I W Granted
                    OK CFB

# Index

ADAIR
  Ann .................................................. 11
  J T ................................................. 189
  James W ........................................ 276
  John T ............................................. 16
  John Thompson .............................. 15
  Margaret M .................. 14,15,16,17,18
  Margaret Martha ............................. 15
  W P ............................................. 15,16
ALLISON
  John R ......................................... 15,16
  John Rufus ....................................... 15
BAGWELL, E C ....... 90,193,210,264,265
BALENTIME, Hamilton .................... 147
BALLARD, Eliza ................. 129,130,131
BARKER
  Ollie T ..................................... 237,238
  William E ................................ 237,238
BARNES, H C .................................... 189
BARNETT, Jesse ................................. 44
BARNS, Albert ................................... 284
BATISE, Mary A .................................. 51
BEAN, Thompson .............................. 119
BEAVERS, Elmina ............................. 292
BEAVERT
  Elmina ............................................ 294
  Mina ............................................... 294
BEAVERTT
  Charlotte ........................................ 290
  Larkin ............................................. 290
BELL, Col .......................................... 319
BEVERETT, Elmina .......................... 295
BIXBY, Tams .......... 8,18,34,48,57,67,76,
86,96,105,112,124,132,141,150,163,170,
178,186,198,214,223,233,240,250,259,
269,270,278,288,296,305,312,322
BOUDINOT, W P ............................. 189
BOWMAN, Lucy M ................ 56,102,195
BRANSON, Eula Jeanes .......... 43,85,120,
156,320
BRECKENRIDGE, Commissioner ...... 88
BRECKINRIDGE
  C R .......... 12,61,70,81,89,99,108,116,
    136,144,152,167,189,202,208,216,218
    ,237,274,275,282,297,299,315
  Commissioner ................... 280,291,316
  Com'r ...................... 70,71,136,144,281

BRINK, William E .............................. 51
BROWN, William ............................. 145
BUFFINGTON, George ..................... 103
BULLETT, James ........................ 263,264
BUTLER
  Bill .................................................. 84
  Eloway ............................................. 83
  Judge ............................................... 84
CAMPBELL, Annie E ....................... 122
CARR
  Beulah M ....................... 208,209,210
  Buela M ........................................ 208
  Jesse O .......... 4,13,73,82,110,128,137,
    167,175,209,254,283,292,300,309,318
  Josie M ......................... 208,209,210
  Josie May ...................................... 208
  N F ................................ 208,212,213
  Nelson F ........... 207,208,209,210,211,
    213,214,215
  S A ................................................ 208
  Sarah A ......................... 208,209,210
  Sarah Ann ...................... 207,211,213
CASEY, R T ...................................... 196
CHAMBERS
  Lettie ....................... 298,299,301,302
  Letty .............................................. 301
CHAMPLIN
  Lola M ....................... 30,31,32,75,287
  Lola W .......................................... 285
CHANDLER
  Ann E ............................... 115,116,124
  Anna Eliza .................. 43,117,118,119
  Annie E .......................................... 121
  B G ......................................... 115,121
  Burges G ............ 114,115,116,117,119,
    120,121,122,124,125,126
  David ........................................ 115,116
  Mr B G .................................... 122,123
  Nannie L .................................. 115,116
  Vann S ..................................... 115,116
  Vann Stewart ................................. 115
CHANLER ........................................ 115
CHAPPELL
  W W ............ 42,43,83,84,117,119,318
  Walter W ........... 24,25,40,41,44,46,62,
    73,175,220,221
CHAPPELLE, Walter W ..................... 45

# Index

CHICK, Retta .................... 14,100,238
COATS
   Annie L .............................. 173,174
   H D ...................................... 174,177
   Huff D ........ 173,174,175,176,177,178, 179,180
   Louisa J ............. 173,174,175,177,178
COBERLY, Georgia ........................ 131
COCHRAM .................................... 319
COCHRAN, Mr ............................. 221
COE, Naomi Ann ........................... 181
COKER
   Arthur L .......................... 225,226,227
   Arthur Lee ................................. 225
   Benjamin F ..................... 225,226,227
   Bnejiman F ................................ 225
   Calvin F ........................... 225,226,227
   Charlotte ........... 224,225,226,227,228, 230,231,232,233,234,235
   Cynthia A ................................... 227
   Cynthia E ............................... 225,226
   D F ............................................ 262
   Dempsey ................... 265,268,269,270
   Dempsey F ................................. 262
   Dempsie ..................................... 267
   Dempsy ...................................... 268
   E E ............................................ 262
   Elizabeth ................... 262,266,269,271
   Elizabeth D ................................ 267
   Elizabeth E .............. 261,262,265,266, 270,272,273
   Kittie ..................................... 225,226
   Kitty ..................................... 225,227
   Lewis .......... 225,230,231,268,269,271
   Lewis C ....... 225,226,227,231,232,233
   Louis ......................................... 269
   Mary L ................................ 226,227
   May L ....................................... 225
COOK, W J .................................... 304
COUCH
   Charles E ........................ 315,316,317
   Cherokee R ..................... 315,316,317
   Clara C ............................ 315,316,317
   James C .......................... 315,316,317
   M W ............................... 315,320,321
   Marion W ......... 314,315,316,317,318, 321,322,323
   Marion W, Jr ..................... 315,316,317
   Mary ...................................... 321,322
   Mc W ................................... 320,321
   Vic ............................................. 316
   Victoria E ......................... 316,317,322
COVEL, Mary Elizabeth ................... 204
CRAIG, Louisa J ............. 173,176,177,178
CRAVENS, R R .......... 22,38,52,154,189, 237,275,299
CREGG, Eliza Jane ........................... 177
CRITTENDEN, Mr .......................... 256
CRITTENDON, George .................... 257
CUNNINGHAM
   A B ...................................... 211,212
   Dr ............................................... 74
   J T ............................................. 75
DAUGHERTY
   Belle .......................................... 282
   Belle C ....................................... 282
   Lou T ........................................ 282
DAVIDSON
   Charles A .................................... 303
   Chas A ....................................... 303
DAVIS, Preston S ............................... 95
DENBO
   Belle .......................................... 281
   Belle C ....................................... 282
   Belle Cleveland ............................ 281
   Charles H .................................... 286
   Ireinia ........................................ 286
   Joseph ....................................... 281
   Joseph A ............ 280,281,282,283,285, 286,287,289
   Letitia .................................. 280,284
   Letitia B .............................. 283,284
   Letitia V .............................. 282,288
   Lettia ........................................ 281
   Oce ..................................... 281,282,283
   Osie .......................................... 281
   Robert L ............................. 281,282,283
   Robert Leroy .............................. 281
DENBOE
   Joseph ....................................... 281
   Lettia ........................................ 281
DENBON, Joseph A ......................... 284
DICKSON, Mr ................................. 73
DUCKWORTH

# Index

Lafayette ........................................ 118
Lewis L .................................... 42,119
Mr ...................................................... 41
DUNCAN
   Amanda C .................................... 140
   Amanda Cherokee ................... 135,138
   Cherokee ........................................ 139
   Siney .............................................. 136
   W A ......................................... 110,111
   Watt ............................................... 110
   Y C G ............................................ 136
EATON, George W .......................... 310
ELLIOTT, Judge ............................... 102
ENGLAND
   Benjamin .................................. 81,82
   Benjamin C .................. 81,82,83,84,85
   Benjamin Cornelius .................... 80,81
   Bnej ................................................. 81
   Bnejamin C ..................................... 81
   Bnejamin Cornelius ........................ 81
   Jensey C .......................................... 81
   Jincy J ................. 80,81,83,84,85,86,87
   Jincy Jane .................................. 81,82
   Joseph ............................................. 80
   Sabra ............................................... 80
ESTES
   Ben ......................................... 231,232
   Charlotte ....................................... 225
FARTHING, Reverend ........................ 63
FIELDS, Margaret ............................. 184
FOREMAN
   Ada C .......... 302,307,308,309,310,311,
   312,313,314
   Ada L ............................................ 308
   Ermina V ................................. 307,308
   Laura A ................................... 307,308
   Perry A .................................... 307,308
   Samuel ............................... 54,193,210
   Stephen T ......................... 307,310,311
   Stephen Taylor ............................. 310
   Taylor ...................................... 309,312
   Taylor W ................................. 307,308
   Vic M ............................................ 308
FOSTER
   Al .................................................. 303
   F J .................................................. 94
FOX, Joe ............................................. 84

FRAZIER, Mary Trout ...................... 144
FRY
   Amelia .................................... 299,300
   Anna ............................................. 303
   Annie ...................................... 299,300
   Lettie ...................................... 300,302
   Letty ............................................. 304
   William ............. 297,299,301,302,304,
   305,306
FRYE
   Amelia .......................................... 298
   Annie ............................................ 298
   Lettie ............................................ 298
   William ......................................... 298
   Wm ......................................... 298,301
FULTS, Josephine A ......................... 262
GIBSON, J H ........................................ 46
GLENN
   Ann ............................................ 21,22
   Annie .............................................. 21
   Nancy A ................................ 22,25,33
   Nancy Ann ....................... 21,22,23,25
   S C .................................................. 21
   Samuel ................................... 21,22,27
   Samuel C ...... 21,22,23,24,25,26,27,28,
   29,30,32,33,34,35,36
GREEN, M D ........... 99,108,136,263,281,
282,291
GREGORY, William L ..................... 287
GRIGSBY
   James ............................................ 217
   Mahala .................................... 221,222
   Malala ........................................... 220
   Ruthie ........................................... 218
GULLAGER, W M ........................... 189
GUNTER
   Ann E ........................................... 122
   Anna Eliza .................................... 117
   John .............................................. 202
GUNTHER
   Anna E ..................................... 121,123
   Annie E ......................................... 121
HAILEY, Mr ...................................... 192
HALEY, Parson ................................. 194
HALLAND, M E ............................... 274
HANNA, Gertrude .. 149,221,277,302,311
HARIS, Colonel ................................. 239

## Index

HARLAN
  James E ............................................. 29
  Mr ...................................................... 27
HARLIN
  E L ................................................... 177
  J E .................................................... 169
  James ............................................... 25
  James E ............................... 25,30,31,32
  Letitia ..................................... 284,285
  Mitchell ......................................... 281
  Nancy A .................................... 31,32
HARRISON
  D W ................................................ 108
  D Wilson ........................................ 111
  David W ............. 107,108,109,110,112,
  113,114
  David Wilson ................................ 108
  M A ................................................. 109
  Mary A ............... 108,109,110,111,112
  Mary F ........................................... 108
HARRY, Harry ...................................... 94
HASTAIN, Mr. ..................................... 157
HASTINGS
  Bill .................................................... 63
  J R .................................................. 169
  Mr ........................................ 7,231,232
  W W ........... 3,5,6,9,10,15,19,20,35,36,
  49,58,59,64,68,69,78,79,86,87,96,97,
  110,105,106,113,124,125,133,138,141
  ,142,150,151,158,164,171,179,186,
  187,193,198,199,204,205,206,214,215
  ,223,230,234,241,250,257,260,266,
  272,278,279,288,289,292,296,305,306
  ,313,322,323
HAWK, A G ........................................ 103
HENSLEY, Sallie ............................... 239
HILDERBRAND, Reese .................... 247
HILL, Myrtle ............. 66,139,162,249,268
HISER, Jacob .................................... 6,7
HOGAN
  Graham .............................. 11,12,13,14
  John ................................................. 12
  John C .. 11,12,13,14,15,16,17,18,19,20
  Mabel ................................... 12,13,14
  Mable ............................................... 12
  Margaret .......................................... 12
  Margaret M ............. 11,12,13,14,17,18

  Margrette N ..................................... 12
  Mayble ............................................. 11
HOLDERMAN
  Curtis E .......................................... 203
  Marion .. 200,201,202,203,204,205,206
  Mary C .............................. 201,202,203
  Pearl .................................. 201,202,203
HOLLAND
  J C, MD ............................................ 31
  J W .................................................. 274
  John W .............. 273,274,275,276,277,
  278,279
  Mary ............................................... 275
  Mary E ..................................... 274,278
  Mary Elviry ................................... 274
  William H .................................274,275
HOLLEN, Mary ................................. 276
HOLT
  Allen .............................................. 285
  Mary ........................................ 220,221,222
HOPE, Mary ...................................... 217
HORN
  Cynthia .......................................... 102
  Cynthia J ....................................... 101
  Sinethey ........................................ 103
  Synthia ........................................... 103
HOWEIE, Thomas ............................ 144
HOWEL, William H ......................... 130
HOWELL
  Eliza ......................... 126,127,128,131
  William ................................... 93,126
  William H .......... 126,127,128,129,131,
  132,133,134
HOWEY
  Mary ............................................. 144
  Thomas ................................... 144,150
HOWIE
  Mary .................. 144,145,146,148,149
  Thomas ............. 143,144,145,146,147,
  148,149,151
  Thos ............................................... 147
HUNTON, W H .................................. 121
HURST, Harry .............................. 94,95
HUTCHINSON, Wm ...................... 24,40
IRONSIDE, Robert P ....................... 169
JONES
  B C .......... 3,13,14,55,62,73,82,90,110,

328

## Index

117,128,146,155,175,183,191,204,209
,219,227,244,264,265,266,276,283,
292,300,309,318
    Bruce C ...................................81,89,226
KETCHUM
    James ........................................102,103
    Preacher ............................................ 129
KEYS
    Jane.................................................... 280
    Leroy .................................................. 280
    Letitia ................................................. 285
    Letitia V .............................................. 288
    Leutisia ............................................... 284
LAIRD, David T .................................... 286
LANDRUM
    David .................................................. 103
    John .................................................... 103
LANE
    F Elma .....................................92,157,158
    Frances R ..........17,46,47,122,213,229,
    230,231,232,238,239,244,321
LANGLEY, Charley........................... 303
LESSLEY, Geo H ............................7,111
LIPE, D W ............................................. 189
MALLORY, Mary Tabor ................... 140
MARTIN
    Edmond ......................................263,264
    Ellen N............................................... 264
    Gertrude.....................................263,264
    Tandy W ....................................263,264
MAXWELL, Mabel F .......................... 53
MAYES
    J B ...................................................... 147
    Joel ..................................................... 201
    S H ....................................................... 13
MCANALLY
    Ollie Tennessee ............................... 236
    Sallie........................... 236,237,239,240
    W H .................................................... 239
    William H ..........235,236,237,238,240,
    241,242
    Wm ..................................................... 236
MCANNALLY
    Ollie Tennessee ............................... 236
    Sallie.................................................. 236
    W H .................................................... 236
    William H ......................................... 236

MCANNELLY
    Sallie.................................................. 236
    Tennessee ......................................... 236
    Tennie................................................ 236
MCCARTER, John............................. 252
MCCARTER, Francis ....................... 259
MCCARTY, John H .....................251,252
MCCARTY
    Frances ............................254,255,256
    Frances Phillips .............................. 254
    Francis............................................... 259
    John ............................................252,253
    John H ........246,252,253,254,256,257,
    258,259,260,261
    John Hugh........................................ 254
    John M.............................................. 246
    Liddie F ............................................ 252
    Lidia .................................................. 252
    Lidia F .............................................. 252
    Lydia F ............................................. 253
    Mose.................................................. 252
    Moses ..........................................252,253
    Nancy ..........................................252,253
    Reuben C ......................................... 253
    Rheubin ............................................ 252
    Ruben ................................................ 252
    Ruben C ............................................ 252
MCCRAIRY
    Alzira................................................... 89
    Gemima .............................................. 88
    Joannah............................................... 88
MCCRARY, Jemima............................ 92
MCCRARY
    Alzema ............................................... 88
    Elzemar.......................................88,89,90
    Jamima .......................................88,90,91
    Jemima ..........88,89,90,92,93,95,96,97
    Mary E ...........................................94,95
    N B ........................88,89,91,92,93,96
    Sterling ...........................................89,90
    Sterling P .......................................... 89
    Stirling P............................................ 88
MCCULLOCH, Mr .......................91,96
MCDONALD
    B .....................................61,116,174,182
    Mary A .............................................. 112
    Mary Ann ......................................... 111

# Index

MCGEE
  Jeff .................................................. 26
  Judge ............................................... 26
MCGEE
  Dave ................................................ 83
  David A ............................................ 84
  E J .................................................. 211
  Jeff .................................................. 74
  Mary C ........................................... 184
MCGEHEE, T J .................................... 129
MCGHEE
  David A ............................................ 27
  Jeff .................................................. 56
  T H ................................................ 212
  T J ................... 102,103,104,130,156
  Thomas J .................................. 28,161
MCGRAW
  Mr .............................................. 245,246
  Preacher ....................................... 248
MEESHEAN
  William S ........................................... 2
  Wm S ............................... 167,202,218
MELTON
  S N ................................................ 196
  S S ................................................ 192
MERRICK, Edward ........ 17,43,47,85,94, 120,121,122,130,177,213,229,232,239, 320,321
MILLER, Martha A ............................. 91
MITCHELL
  Bettie ....................................... 246,250
  Bettie A ...... 242,244,245,246,247,248, 249,251
  Betty ............................................. 243
  Eliza .............................................. 243
  Elizabeth ...................................... 243
  Elizabeth A .................................. 243
  Franklin P ..................................... 248
  Georgia A ..................................... 247
  Nora Belle ...................................... 77
  Thaddeus ....................................... 77
  William D ......... 243,244,245,246,247, 248,249
  Wm .............................................. 243
MODE
  Elizabeth ........................................ 74
  Frances M ................................... 72,73

  Francis M ........................................ 71
  George F ......................................... 71
  George M ........................................ 71
  Georgia ........................................ 72,73
  Henry D ................................... 71,72,73
  Isaac ........................................ 70,74,75
  Isaac M ................. 70,72,73,76,78,79
  Maud M ................................... 71,72,73
  Sarah ....................... 71,72,74,76,158
  Sarah Elizabeth ............................ 74
  Viola ........................................ 71,72,73
  William E ................................ 71,72,73
MODENIDIFFER, Sarah ................... 75
MOORE, Cora .............................. 155,276
MOSELEY, Mr .................................... 63
NADIFFER, Sabina .......................... 163
NEEDLED, T B ................................. 308
NEEDLES
  Commissioer ................................. 98
  Commissioner ............. 80,173,181,225
  Com'r ......................... 99,108,127,243
  T B ............ 2,11,21,22,37,38,51,52,72, 126,127,145,154,174,182,188,201,226 ,236,243,244,253,316
NEIDIFFER
  Sarah ............................................. 74
  Sarah Elizabeth ............................ 74
NIDIFER, Savina ............................. 155
NIDIFFER
  Isaac ........................................ 71,153
  Lucy ........................................ 71,153
  Sabina ..................................... 156,157
  Sam .............................................. 160
  Sarah ............................................. 70
NIX
  Fracis E ........................................ 153
  Frank E .................................... 153,154
  George ......................................... 153
  George F .................................. 153,154
  James O ................................... 153,154
  Maud ............................................ 153
  Maude E ...................................... 154
  Robert K ..... 152,153,154,155,156,157, 158,159,160,161,162,163,164,165
  Sabina ............... 153,154,155,157,158, 159,163
  Sabina E ....................................... 153

## Index

Sabina L .................................. 154
Savina ....................................... 155
William ..................................... 153
William J .................................. 153
William S .................................. 154
PACE, Mattie M ...................... 104
PARKS
   Cora Ada ................................ 189
   J T ........................................... 197
   John ............ 188,189,190,191,192,193, 194,195,196,197,198,199,200
   John K .................................... 192
   John Kreiger ........................... 192
   Maragret ................................. 190
   Margaret ................................. 190
   Margaret J .... 188,189,190,191,193,195
   Margaret Jane ........................ 192
   Mollie E .................................. 192
   Ora .......................................... 192
   Ora A ................................. 190,191
   Ora Ada ............................. 188,189
   Owen ...................................... 192
   Owen B .................... 188,189,190,191
   Owen Bell ............................... 189
PHILLIPS
   Frances ..................... 253,254,257
   Francis .................................... 259
   Miss ........................................ 258
   Mrs ......................................... 256
PHILLIS, Francis ....................... 252
POWEL
   Anna E .................................... 123
   Anne ....................................... 122
POWELL
   Ann E ...................................... 121
   Anna E .................................... 121
   Annie E ................................... 121
   Dr ........................................ 41,45
   John .............................. 118,120,121
PRAITHER
   Margaret J .............................. 188
   Molly E ................................... 196
PRATHER
   Caroline C .............................. 189
   Margaret ................................. 189
   Margaret J ................. 194,195,198
   Molley E ................................. 196

Mollie ....................................... 195
Mollie E ....................... 188,193,195
Nollie E ................................... 188
R A ........................................... 194
RASMUS, B P ............ 5,6,15,16,26,27,42, 55,56,64,75,92,101,110,129,169,185,193, 195,196,197,204,212,227,247,248,285, 292
RAYMOND, Alfred C ........................ 92
RED BIRD, Daniel ... 8,18,33,47,57,67,76, 86,96,105,112,124,131,141,150,163,170, 178,186,198,214,222,233,240,249,259, 270,278,288,295,305,312,322
REDFERRY
   (Parson) ..................................... 7
   Parson ....................................... 5
REMSEN, T S .................... 30,31,32
REUTER, P G ............... 101,137,238,254
RICHARDS, Rev John A .................. 147
RILEY
   Sallie ....................................... 315
   Samuel .................................... 315
   Victoria ................................... 315
   Victoria E ........................ 319,322
ROBERTSON
   B F ............................................ 95
   Hattie .................................. 89,90
   Mr B F ...................................... 94
RODGERS, Geo D ...................... 172
ROGERS
   Elizabeth .................................. 51
   Hilliard .................................... 207
   Martha .................................... 208
   Nancy .................................. 51,52
   Nancy E ............ 50,51,52,53,54,55,56, 57,58,59
   Nancy Elizabeth ..................... 51,52
   Robert R .................................. 51
   Rolie E .................................. 51,52
   Rollie E .............................. 51,53,54
   S A ............................. 211,212,213
   Sarah Ann ................. 209,211,213
   Thomas ............................... 51,52
   Thomas T ............ 51,52,53,54,55,56,57
   William E ..................... 51,52,53,54
   Zilpha ....................................... 51
   Zilpha E .............................. 52,53,54

# Index

ROGGERS, Luise................... 103
ROLAND
   Elmina ........................................ 290
   Jo ................................................ 294
   Joe ............................................... 290
ROLLAND
   Elmina ........................................ 291
   Joseph ........................................ 291
ROLLENS
   Elmina ......... 290,291,292,293,294,295
   James ....................... 292,293,294
   Joseph ................ 290,291,295,296,297
ROSS, J M .................................... 321
ROSSON
   J O ............ 12,72,127,144,145,243,304
   John O .............................. 5,24,40,168
ROTHENBERGER, E G ....... 3,54,62,117, 145,146,183,191,204,219,227,266,291, 316
RUBLE, T B .................................... 277
SCHRIMSHER, Arabella ............. 168,169
SCOTT
   Alice N ............................................. 1
   Amanda C ........... 136,137,139,140,141
   Amanda Cherokee ........................ 136
   Charles D .............................. 136,137
   Charles Duncan ............................ 135
   Cherokee........................................ 136
   George W .............................. 136,137
   George Washington ...................... 135
   J T ........................................... 139,140
   James W ............................... 136,137
   James William ............................... 135
   John ................................................ 136
   John T ......... 135,136,137,138,139,140, 141,142,143
   Martha ............................................... 2
   William J ........................................... 1
SCRIMSHER, Arabella ................ 166,170
SHARP, Mr ..................................... 118
SIGMON, Elizabeth ......................... 269
SLOAN
   Annie M ................................. 181,182
   B E .................................................. 183
   E E .............................. 181,182,256
   Edward ........................................... 181
   Edward B ............................... 184,185

Edward E ................... 181,182,185,186
Eva L .................................... 181,182
Florence C ............................. 181,182
James E ................................. 181,182
Mary D .................................. 181,182
Minnie E ............................... 181,182
N M ........................................ 181,182
Namora A ............................. 181,182
Naoma ............................................ 183
Naoma A ............ 180,182,185,186,187
Naomi .................................... 181,182
Naomi A ......................... 183,184,185
Naomi Ann ................................... 181
Neomia .................................. 181,182
Nina P .................................... 181,182
Samuel J ............................... 181,182
SMITH
   Catherine .......................... 217,218,219
   Elizabeth ........................... 217,218,219
   Hahala ........................................... 216
   Irena .............................................. 283
   J W ....................................... 231,271
   James .............................. 217,218,219
   John D ............................................ 41
   Mahala ............... 216,218,219,221,222
   Mahalia .......................................... 220
   Mattie Ann .................................... 217
   Meadow ........................................ 217
   Mrs ................................................ 217
   Peter ............ 216,217,218,219,220,221, 222,223,224
   Theodore ....................................... 217
   William .......................... 217,218,219
SOUTHERLAND
   Abigal ........................................... 166
   Arabella ................................. 166,170
   Arebella ........................................ 167
   Enoch ............................................ 166
   Enoch S ............ 165,166,167,168,170, 171,172
   Enoch Sylvester ........................... 168
SPAUGH
   W J ................................................ 123
   Wesley J ................................. 121,123
SPRINGSTON, J L ......................... 320
STARR
   Cale ............................................... 236

# Index

Emmet .................................................. 264
Emmet .................................................. 263
J C ........ 13,72,82,109,127,299,308,317
Mr ........................................................ 309
STEDEFAN, Malinda ......................... 38
STILL, George .................................... 45
STRANGE, Mary R ............................ 93
STUBBLEFIELD, Demie T ........... 93,130
STUDEFAN
   Buck ................................................ 38
   Malinda ........................................... 38
STURDEVANT
   Buck ................................................ 38
   Martin B .............................. 44,45,46
   Martin Butler ............................ 37,38
   Matilda ........................ 37,38,44,45,46
   Matilsa ............................................ 46
   Richard ........................................... 38
   Tilda ................................................ 38
STURDIVANT
   Buck ................................................ 42
   Martin B .......................... 40,41,43,47
   Martin Butler ................................. 39
   Matilda ............. 37,39,40,41,42,43,47,
   48,49,50
   Richard ........................................... 39
SUDDEN, Mr ............................... 230,232
SUTHERLAND, Enoch ..................... 169
SUTTON
   Anna ................................................ 32
   Annie ............................................... 29
   John ................................................. 21
   Mary A ............................................ 21
   Mr ............................................ 228,232
   Nancy A ............................ 22,25,30,33
   Nancy Ann ..................................... 24
SWIMMER, George ..................... 293,294
TAYLOR
   Bertie ................................. 98,99,100
   Circy ................................................ 99
   Cynthia .......................................... 100
   Cynthia J ........................ 98,99,102,104
   Gertie ................................ 98,99,100
   Herbert ........................................... 99
   Hubert ..................................... 99,100
   Jamima W ...................................... 99
   Jemima W ................................. 99,100

R R .............................................. 102,103
Robert L ........................................ 99,100
Robert Lee ......................................... 98
Robert R ............... 98,99,100,101,104,
105,106,107
Surse ............................................ 98,99,100
THOMAS, Nicholas ......................... 103
THORNTON
   Amos ............................................ 239
   John .............................................. 122
   Mr ................................................. 118
   W G .......................................... 123,140
   W G, Jr ......................................... 139
TIDWELL
   John E ......... 7,28,29,64,65,66,102,123,
   138,139,158,160,161,162,195,249,258
   ,294,295
   John R ........................................... 257
TIGER, Mary ............................. 147,148
TITTLE, Robert W ..................... 148,195
TROTT
   Louisa J ....................................... 148
   Mary ............................................. 147
   William L ............................... 147,311
TYNER, George W ........................... 285
VANCE, H M ......... 138,158,193,204,292
VON WEISE, Chas ............. 208,252,262,
263,308
WALKER
   Tim ......................................... 284,285
   Tim N ........................................... 284
WARD
   Alice ................................................. 6
   Alice N ................... 1,2,3,4,5,7,8,9,10
   Eliza .......................................... 60,66
   Eliza F ............. 60,61,62,63,64,65,66,
   67,68,69
   Ethelyne ......................................... 61
   Etheylnne ....................................... 61
   Ethlynne .................................... 61,62
   G D ................................................. 61
   George ........................................ 65,66
   George D ........................ 60,61,62,67
   George Deshields ........................... 63
   James ............................................... 1
   Joe .................................................. 84
   Joe L ................................................ 3

# Index

Joseph L.................. 1,2,4,5,6,7,8
Katherine J...................... 64
Louisa M ........................... 1
Martha L ........................2,4,5
Mary E............................276,277,278
Mary Elvira...................... 276
W Mae ..........................2,4,5
W W ............................64,65
Willie Mae........................ 2
WATERS, Sarah..........28,29,123,196,197, 258,269,294
WEBSTER
    Charles E ...................... 156
    Chas E ...........30,31,33,75,92,104,111, 131,140,149,158,169,269,277,285,287,302,311
WELCH, Cobb ..................... 84
WHITE, Myron ................... 156
WOOD, Clara Mitchell......... 169,185,212, 247,255,256,257,285
WRIGHT
    Mary ..................315,319,320,321
    Mary E............................ 318
    Mr .................................. 120
    S T .....................26,42,64,75,177
WYLEY, Peter ................... 201

www.ingramcontent.com/pod-product-compliance
Lightning Source LLC
Chambersburg PA
CBHW020243030426
42336CB00010B/597